Second Edition

Contested Federalism

Certainty and Ambiguity in the Canadian Federation

Douglas Brown • Herman Bakvis • Gerald Baier

OXFORD
UNIVERSITY PRESS

OXFORD
UNIVERSITY PRESS

Oxford University Press is a department of the University of Oxford.
It furthers the University's objective of excellence in research, scholarship,
and education by publishing worldwide. Oxford is a registered trade mark of
Oxford University Press in the UK and in certain other countries.

Published in Canada by
Oxford University Press
8 Sampson Mews, Suite 204,
Don Mills, Ontario M3C 0H5 Canada

www.oupcanada.com

Library and Archives Canada Cataloguing in Publication

Title: Contested federalism: certainty and ambiguity in the Canadian federation /
Douglas Brown, Herman Bakvis, and Gerald Baier.
Names: Bakvis, Herman, 1948- author. | Brown, Douglas M. (Douglas Mitchell),
1954- author. | Baier, Gerald, 1971- author.
Description: Second edition. | Revision of: Bakvis, Herman, 1948-. Contested federalism. |
Includes bibliographical references and index.
Identifiers: Canadiana (print) 20189066741 | Canadiana (ebook) 2019006174X |
ISBN 9780195445909 (softcover) | ISBN 9780199034697 (loose-leaf) |
ISBN 9780199000807 (EPUB)
Subjects: LCSH: Federal government—Canada—Textbooks. |
LCSH: Canada—Politics and government—Textbooks. |
CSH: Federal-provincial relations—Canada—Textbooks. | LCGFT: Textbooks.
Classification: LCC JL27 B34 2019 | DDC 320.471—dc23

Cover image: © Arthimedes/Shutterstock.com
Cover design: Sherill Chapman
Interior design: Sherill Chapman

MIX
Paper from
responsible sources
FSC® C008955

Printed and bound in the United States of America

1 2 3 4 — 22 21 20 19

Contents

4 ❖ **Judicial Review and Dispute Resolution   67**

Week 5

5 ❖ **Executive Federalism: Back to the Future?   87**

Weeks 6 & 7

6 ❖ **Fiscal Relations: Basic Principles and Current Issues   116**

Week 8

11 ❖ Indigenous Peoples and Federalism   236

Week
14

12 ❖ Quebec and the Future of Canadian Federalism   251

Conclusion   Ambivalent Federalism   271

Tables and Figures

Tables

Figures

Preface to the Second Edition

In recent years many fine studies have examined federalism and the constitution, the courts, democracy, and various aspects of social and economic policy. But until our first edition of *Contested Federalism*, there had been no recent work offering a comprehensive overview of the Canadian federation or a critical examination of its component parts. It had been two decades since the publication of classics such as *The Federal Condition in Canada* by Donald Smiley and *Unfilled Union* by Garth Stevenson, two books that scrutinized the main issues at play in the Canadian federation in the early 1980s. But, of course, so much has happened in the federation since then—perhaps too much, too quickly, to tempt a brave soul to record it, let alone make sense of it all.

Our aim in the second edition is to continue to fulfill this role by providing an examination of the main institutions and processes of the Canadian federation as well as the major policy areas that are the subject of the debates, negotiations, and decisions reached within the different federal–provincial–territorial arenas. Our ambit is not only well-established themes, such as judicial review and dispute resolution, executive federalism, and the economic union, but also newer ones, such as the environmental union and the role of local and Indigenous governments in the federation.

In assessing the state of Canadian federalism we highlight what we consider some of the major debates in the federation concerning, among other things, the interdependencies between the roles and responsibilities of the different orders of government, the gap between the formal rules and institutions of the federation and the expectations citizens have of it, and the unique role played by Quebec and Indigenous peoples. In doing so, we focus on a theme we feel cuts across a number of these issues, namely the inherent tension between the need for a degree of flexibility and ambiguity, on the one hand, and the certainty of fixed rules, on the other. Cloaking important intergovernmental agreements in ambiguity, as we argue, has long played a beneficial role in keeping the federation intact. But it has its drawbacks, particularly when Ottawa ends up relying on unilateral action in the face of an ambiguous or failed consensus, thereby effectively centralizing decision-making within the federation. We have no easy solutions for resolving this conundrum; but drawing attention to it, we argue, provides insight both into the way the different and competing orders of government interact with each other and the consequences of those interactions.

The authors have undertaken a number of important changes to the text in this second edition, much of it upon the advice of other scholars and teachers in the field. To begin with, we cut down or pruned certain topics as unnecessary to a book on federalism and intergovernmental relations, thus dropping a chapter on more general policy process in Canadian governance. Also, we now have only one chapter rather than two on the topics of executive federalism and fiscal relations. Finally, we have added a wholly new chapter on Quebec and the federation, placed just before the Conclusion. This placement is deliberate, in that a full understanding of Quebec's role in federalism comes only after understanding the key elements of the entire federal system, but teachers and students are free to skip ahead to this chapter if they wish to cover this content earlier.

The most significant revisions made in this second edition from the first remain the updating of virtually every major policy field and set of developments, to reflect the challenges, ideas, and political outcomes that have changed since 2008 when research on the first edition was completed. Ten years later we are now able to cover the entirety of the Conservative federal government under Stephen Harper, and the first three years of the Liberal government under Justin Trudeau.

In researching and writing both editions of this book we are indebted to several individuals and institutions. The Social Sciences and Humanities Research Council of Canada graciously provided financial support for the initial research used in the first edition under its Federalism and Federations Program. This support made possible the convening of a series of focus groups in Canada and Australia on a variety of federalism-related themes and topics ranging from the "federal spending power" to Senate reform. At that time, we relied on a number of excellent research assistants, including Devin Anderson, Karen Diepeveen, Penny Frearson, Carmel McCauley, and Shannon Wells. James Boxall, map curator and head of the Map and Geospatial Information Collection at Dalhousie University, kindly produced the map used in Chapter 3. At St Francis Xavier, we benefited from able research assistance provided by Marianne Gillis, Dr Allison Butler, and Michael MacIsaac. For the second edition, we relied on the able assistance of Izaak McMullin at St Francis Xavier and David Bakvis at the University of Victoria.

Early drafts of a number of the chapters in the first edition were initially used in an online course on intergovernmental relations developed by Herman Bakvis, delivered first at Dalhousie University and then at the University of Victoria. We are grateful to the students for feedback on the material. Subsequently, all three of us used further drafts of various chapters in our regular courses on federalism, Canadian politics, and intergovernmental relations at Dalhousie University, Queen's University, St Francis Xavier University, the University of British Columbia, and the University of Victoria. We are grateful to our students for allowing us to use them as sounding boards for our ideas and our approaches on the best way of tackling and discussing the complexities of federalism.

We are grateful to Oxford University Press Canada and its staff for their sustained support, in particular over a much longer than anticipated period to produce this second edition. Our thanks go to several persons at OUP, notably Mark Thomson, Meg Patterson, Steve Kotowych, Lauren Wing, and Elizabeth Ferguson.

We are deeply obliged to the numerous scholars who have contributed to the federalism literature. Like the Canadian federation itself, this book covers broad ground. Yet each chapter encompasses only the most prominent features of the topics and debates at hand. Deeper understanding can be reached only by exploring directly what the authors we note or cite had to say on the topic at hand. We urge you to conduct your own explorations. By far the largest numbers of citations are from English-language sources, which we feel is appropriate to our intended readership, including our students, but we have attempted to be sensitive to key sources available only in the French language. An excellent point of departure for a rich literature, mainly from Quebec, is Alain-G. Gagnon's edited collection *Le Fédéralisme canadien contemporain: Fondements, traditions, institutions* (2006)— also available in English as *Contemporary Canadian Federalism: Foundations, Traditions and Institutions* (2009).

While it is impossible to list the numerous people who have contributed to this literature, it would be remiss not to cite those most instrumental in shaping our views on Canadian federalism, some of whom are regrettably no longer alive. For all three of us, Richard Simeon was variously teacher, mentor, and colleague. The framework for studying Canadian intergovernmental relations he originally developed in his classic study, *Federal–Provincial Diplomacy*, still remains extraordinarily useful and its influence is evident in this book. Harvey Lazar, both when he was in government and in his capacity as director of the Institute of Intergovernmental Relations at Queen's, has always been supportive of our inquiries into Canadian federalism and social policy. He also kindly commented on some of the draft chapters in the first edition. Brian Galligan, Peter Meekison, Grace Skogstad, Ronald Watts, Alain-G. Gagnon, Jennifer Smith, Robert Young, Peter Aucoin, Michael Murphy, Kathy Brock, Keith Banting, Evert Lindquist, and Kathryn Harrison have been among those we have relied on for advice and support over the years in our academic endeavours, both separately and in connection with this project.

Finally, we owe gratitude to colleagues at our home universities of St Francis Xavier, the University of Victoria, and the University of British Columbia as we worked on this project. Last but not least, we are grateful to our families for support of the kind that only close family members can provide. They, in turn, are no doubt equally grateful that the second iteration of this project is now complete.

Antigonish, Vancouver, Victoria
17 July 2018

Introduction

> The distinguishing characteristic of federalism is the peculiar ambivalence
> of the ends men seek to make it serve. Quite literally an ambivalence: Fed-
> eralism is always an arrangement pointed in two contrary directions or
> aimed at securing two contrary ends. (Diamond, 1973: 129)

Martin Diamond's observation is as true today as it was nearly five decades ago.
The decision to form a federation often has less to do with a desire for union
between constituent units—former colonies of an imperial power, for example—
than with a distrust of complete union. The understandings reached between
the founding units regarding the powers that will be shared—held by a national
government—and the powers that they will retain are usually reflected in a federal constitutional "bargain." But this bargain itself can become a source of tension and is likely to be incomplete, with parts of it expressed in an equivocal
manner, leading to more ambivalence and contestation with the passage of time.
Constitutional documents pronounce on the respective responsibilities of the
orders of government, a matter of some dispute itself, but they rarely have much
to say about the institutions that will coordinate the activities and priorities of the
various governments, or how disputes between them will be resolved.

Closely allied to the concept of ambivalence is the idea of "ambiguity," a state of
uncertainty, haziness, or opacity, for example, when the rules are unclear or where
different, even competing understandings exist as to what rules are actually in play.
The term can also be applied to outcomes such as when it is said that negotiations
lead to an ambiguous decision or agreement. Ambiguity can be seen as the product
of ambivalence or vice versa. Ambivalence about a situation can lead to ambiguity,
if only as a strategy in order to avoid making firm decisions or to postpone a difficult
discussion. While the two concepts are closely related, ambivalence relates more
to feelings or emotions whereas ambiguity relates more to perception or cognition.
The literature, especially on Canadian federalism, often talks about ambivalence
and ambiguity being "institutionalized," embedded into the formal and informal
rules and norms of the federation (Smiley, 1981; Tuohy, 1992).

The Canadian federation is no exception in these respects. In this book we
examine the relations among Canada's governments—federal, provincial, territorial, local, and Indigenous[1]—along with the tensions, conflicts, and adaptations
they have given rise to. In so doing, we explore both the basic federal and intergovernmental structure—the constitutional and institutional framework—and what
we might term "federal governance." With respect to the latter, our discussions invariably revolve around the shifting relations between and among government and
non-government actors, their interests and policy objectives, the resources available to them, and the strategies they deploy in pursuit of their objectives. Both

the objectives and the strategies in many ways reflect a basic tension between the desire for autonomy and the desire to be part of a larger whole, between what Daniel Elazar (1996) has called "shared rule" and "self-rule." Thus federalism, particularly in its Canadian form, entails an ongoing contestation of interests, ideas, and identities. This contestation sometimes clarifies and sometimes obscures the issues at stake, if only because (as we will argue) ambiguity is often a precondition to their resolution. At the same time, we will also argue that in certain instances clarity and certainty are highly beneficial and at times even necessary in order to settle or forestall protracted conflict.

This ambivalent quality colours many of the debates specific to federations: debates over matters such as the appropriate balance between the national government and regional and local governments, the adjudication of intergovernmental disputes, and even whether federalism is still the appropriate form of governance for the nation in light of changing domestic needs and global conditions. Two other frequent topics of debate are the function of central institutions, such as courts and second chambers (e.g., the federal Senate), in managing issues affecting the federation as a whole and the role that federalism plays, or should play, in expanding or limiting democratic rights and freedoms. These themes are relevant to most federations.

Other themes are more specific (though not necessarily unique) to Canada as a federation characterized by distinct regional, cultural, and linguistic differences. Matters related to Quebec's constitutional status, or the possibility of Quebec's secession, appear regularly on the political agenda not only inside Quebec but also in Ottawa, where from 1993 to 2011 the Bloc Québécois represented the sovereignist vision, and in the federation as a whole, where federal and provincial leaders spend considerable energy trying to accommodate Quebec's unique demands. More homogeneous nations such as Australia and Germany do not experience the same kinds of tensions, and therefore their federal systems are subject to somewhat fewer and certainly less intense pressures for decentralization. For this reason, we will argue, Canada has been particularly inclined towards ambivalence and ambiguity in its intergovernmental institutions and practices.

Another distinctive feature of the Canadian federation is the reliance it places on "executive federalism." Much of the negotiating and compromise required to manage the federation takes place between the executives, elected and unelected, of the main orders of government (Smiley, 1987; Watts, 1999). Instead of more public accommodation through the open forums of legislatures and other democratic institutions, the executive network is relatively closed and elitist. It builds on the ways that Canada's parliamentary institutions encourage executive dominance by concentrating power in the hands of "first ministers" (premiers and prime minister) (Savoie, 1999, 2008; White, 2005; Aucoin, Bakvis, and Jarvis, 2013). Executive federalism contributes both to the Canadian version of the democratic deficit and to what some believe is an unusually high level of conflict between and among the federal and provincial/territorial governments by making the personalities of and "chemistry" between executives a variable in the accommodative capacity of the intergovernmental system.

All the above problems, questions, and conundrums come into play at some point or other in our examination of the underpinnings of Canadian federalism. Finally, though, we consider two factors, along with ambiguity, to be crucial. One is balance. This is not simply a matter of balancing unity and diversity, preserving the autonomy of two or more orders of government, and providing for some rough equality between the constituent units (provinces or states). These are all important, but we believe it is also crucial to find a balance between flexibility and certainty in the norms and rules involved in the governance of the Canadian federation. Federal institutions and processes must be flexible enough to adapt to a rapidly changing domestic and global environment; yet they must also be clear and firm enough to give citizens a sense of certainty. The other factor is the relevance of the basic federal framework to the social, economic, and political conditions in which citizens and political elites find themselves. Earlier writers on federalism (e.g., Wheare, 1963) emphasized that practically all federations have felt the need for a written constitution spelling out, at least in broad terms, the responsibilities and powers of the two (or more) constituent orders of government, the degree of autonomy each is to enjoy, and some basic mechanisms for resolving disputes between them. Even with provisions for judicial interpretation and formal amendment, however, virtually every federal constitution will fall out of sync with its times. Key constitutional provisions will become outdated; judicial rulings will be found misguided; and amending procedures, typically requiring super majorities, will prove too inflexible to permit essential changes (Smith, 2004; Watts, 2005).

In fact, attempts at constitutional change affecting the balance between the main orders of government are rare in modern federations, and they even more rarely succeed. The double failure of the Meech Lake (1990) and Charlottetown (1992) Accords to amend Canada's constitution illustrates the point. The inevitability that the constitution will become outdated makes it all the more crucial that a federation have a variety of ways—formal and informal—for its governments to reach political understandings and agreements. The need is perhaps especially acute in Canada's case, partly because the distribution of powers between federal and provincial governments in the original 1867 Constitution Act is both detailed and outdated; partly because of the horizontal imbalances between provinces in natural resources and other forms of wealth; and partly because of unresolved regional differences and the ambiguity of Quebec's position in Confederation.

Given the importance, in federations, of intergovernmental coordination, some attention should be paid in a federal constitution to establishing the basic institutional framework within which negotiations will take place—specifying the arena(s), for instance, and setting out rules for decision-making. But some constitutions do a better job than others in this respect. The German constitution provides for the direct representation of Länder (state governments) in the second chamber of the parliament, the Bundesrat. And the constitution of the European Union specifies that, to pass, decisions made by the Council of the EU require more than a simple majority but less than unanimity. In Canada, however, institutional arrangements for intergovernmental relations are almost non-existent.[2] In the twenty-first century, the absence not only of decision rules to resolve the inevitable intergovernmental disputes, but of formal provisions for interaction between governments, or between government and civil society, raises serious questions about the relevance of the institutional provisions in Canada's nineteenth-century constitution.

In fact, a number of critics, and not just in Canada, have called for major reform or even questioned the value of federalism itself. In 2008, for instance, when Australia's then new Labor government convened a "summit" on the country's future, a major theme was "the need to fix federalism to create a modern Australian federation" (Australia, 2008). More recently a different federal government in Australia has narrowed its reform focus to restoring state autonomy and reducing federal–state overlap (Australia, 2014). More than a century earlier, the English constitutional scholar A.V. Dicey—a true believer in the virtues of parliamentary government—was dismayed by the formalization and legal strictures that a federal constitution introduced. In his view, federal law was stiff and uncompromising; it forced governments into narrow roles and constrained the creativity necessary to address public problems (see Dicey, 1959 [1885]). The British political scientist Harold Laski (1939) believed that federal systems were too fragmented to stand up to the forces of capitalism and deal adequately with the damage wrought by the Great Depression. In the 1960s, in a frequently cited essay, the American William Riker questioned not so much the dysfunctional aspects of federalism as its very relevance; having posed the question "Does federalism make any difference in the way people are governed?" he supplied the answer himself: "Hardly any at all" (Riker, 1969: 145).

The Canadian political scientist Roger Gibbins took quite a different view in the late twentieth century. Unlike Laski or Riker, Gibbins sees relevance and value in federalism. However, he worried that Canadians no longer see federalism as an "anchor or point of reference" and that their political identities now "bear little relationship to formal federal structures" (Gibbins, 1999: 218). Likewise, Fafard, Rocher, and Côté (2010) have found that Canadians have only a weak sense of the federal culture, and that even provincial government officials have a poor sense of the logic of the federal system and, outside of Quebec, place federalism values behind other values like efficiency or the attainment of private goods. In short, provincial officials do not try necessarily to represent unique provincial interests so much as they pursue general bureaucratic interests, or just aim to "get a deal done." Richard Simeon (2006 [1972]), in his classic study of intergovernmental policy-making in Canada, *Federal–Provincial Diplomacy*, noted a significant disjunction between the constitution, which envisions federal and provincial areas of jurisdiction as entirely separate (the "watertight compartments" theory) and actual practice, in which the two orders of government, despite their formal autonomy, are often highly interdependent when it comes to policy-making and program delivery. This interdependence limits what governments can do on their own and means that they must be able to pool or share their autonomy or sovereignty—in other words, to collaborate. At the same time, we note that the Harper Conservative government, especially the majority government of 2011–15, actively pursued a more "classical federalism" model, calling for disentanglement between governments and less federal government involvement in areas under provincial jurisdiction, such as health care. It remains an open question as to how successful the Harper strategy was (and this issue is discussed fully in this book), but it does suggest that ever-increasing interdependence or federal involvement in provincial policy matters is not necessarily preordained.

Canadians generally are aware of the shared nature of power and decision-making in many policy fields, if only because they are routinely exposed to the wrangling, complaints, blame-shifting, and red tape that seem to come with any sharing of governmental responsibility. The provinces blame the federal government for what they say is the impoverished state of the health-care system; the federal government harangues provincial governments for failing to recognize the need for a single national securities regulator run by Ottawa in light of the national and global nature of stock markets and capital flows. Meanwhile, municipal governments plead for funds to improve the infrastructure and services deemed essential to the prosperity of their cities and regions, and ultimately the country. The squabbling that Canadians witness is just the public window into the intergovernmental negotiation that is a constant in a system of shared rule. Experienced observers may dismiss much of the squabbling as a matter of strategic posturing. Yet at times it can be legitimate to ask, as Gibbins (1999) does, how well contemporary federalism is meeting the needs of urban areas and citizens (including members of ethnic minorities).

Overall, though—as we argue throughout this book—the system works well. Agreements may sometimes be long in coming, or so clouded in ambiguity that citizens have no idea what has been accomplished on their behalf, but they get made and they make many important things possible. It would be poor social science to specify causes in the absence of more specific evidence. Yet it seems that Canada's above-average performance on a host of global indicators pertaining to educational achievement, health outcomes, economic well-being, and, not least, political stability has at least not been harmed by federalism; in some areas, perhaps, federalism has even contributed something to that performance. Our particular federal system has its flaws, but we believe some sort of federalism is essential to sustain the political unity that has been the foundation for much of what Canada and Canadians have achieved since 1867.

The institutions and processes of intergovernmental relations are generally pragmatic. Over the years there have been demands for greater formalization of those processes, largely to make them more transparent and increase the opportunities for public input (Skogstad, 2003). But the system has resisted those pressures, even when governments (the primary participants in the federal system) have been the advocates of formalization. As we examine the characteristics of the intergovernmental system in the chapters that follow, this tension between formality and flexibility will become more apparent. Elites in the intergovernmental system appear to prefer secrecy for its own sake. Yet it can be argued that a modicum of secrecy, coupled with ambiguity, is nonetheless necessary if elites are to reach agreement on ways to accommodate the tensions within a divided larger society.[3] In other words, despite the rancour and disputatiousness that sometimes seem the hallmarks of Canada's federal system, the Canadian model is by many important measures peaceful and stable, with governments working quietly behind the scenes on both major and minor issues.

In this book we focus mainly on the relations between the two orders of government formally recognized in Canada's constitution: federal and provincial/territorial. But these are not the only components of the intergovernmental system. Two other components, both of which are now seeking to expand their self-governing capacities, are municipal and Indigenous governments. Constitutionally, municipal and other local government is directly controlled by the provinces, which have the power to alter the roles and responsibilities of municipalities at will. Yet municipal governments do have some resources, as well as a certain amount of political and moral authority, that they can use to press their case for greater autonomy. And in the past 20 years, as amalgamation has created larger municipalities with increasingly significant infrastructure needs, provincial and federal governments alike have become interested in the possibility that municipalities might play a more active role in the intergovernmental system. Such a change would be in keeping with the trend towards what political economists have described as "glocalization": a double movement of power and influence away from the national level and towards both the local and the global—with external actors such as Washington or the World Trade Organization (WTO) increasingly playing a part in the framing of domestic policy decisions (Courchene, 1995; Hale, 2004).

Meanwhile, Canada's Indigenous peoples continue to seek recognition as full-fledged sovereign entities (Cairns, 2000) with their own place in the intergovernmental system. Some progress is being made, but the pace has been slow. The difficulty of achieving even urgently needed improvements in the management and delivery of basic public services for Indigenous people, on and off reserves, is an illustration of the challenges posed by a system of shared rule in areas where both federal and provincial governments have responsibilities. To work effectively, the system requires acceptance of the roles and responsibilities assigned by the constitution, but it also needs cooperation, trust, and collaboration among governmental partners. The failure, so far, to reach agreement on what those roles and responsibilities are has an effect on the intergovernmental system as a whole.

These developments outside the old federal–provincial relationship have led some analysts to focus on what has been called "multi-level governance" (Piattoni, 2010); we will discuss this concept in Chapter 1. Even so, most political activities and significant relationships in Canada continue to centre on the federal–provincial/territorial nexus. Issues involving other types of government or civil society entities—international, local, Indigenous—may have significant consequences for intergovernmental relations, but they are still best understood through the prism of federal–provincial relations. The two autonomous orders of government with constitutionally defined powers are the keys to the directions that major public policies take. And the political climate in which they share rights and responsibilities has a definite bearing on the kinds of outcomes the intergovernmental system produces.

In the chapters that follow we will examine the social, economic, and institutional bases of Canadian federalism, the role of the constitution and the courts, and the machinery, institutions, and processes of executive federalism, as well as four crucial policy areas: fiscal federalism, the social union, the economic union, and the environmental union. First, though, we will look at the concept of federalism itself and review some of the principal approaches that have been taken to the subject, with emphasis on the Canadian variants. This review is intended to familiarize readers with the basic assumptions that we make as authors about how federal systems work and are best understood. The perspectives sketched in this brief introduction will become clearer in the context of other efforts to understand the perennial tension in federalism between its demands for certainty and ambiguity.

Notes

1. In this chapter and elsewhere in this book the authors will generally use the term "Indigenous" rather than "Aboriginal" to refer to the original, continuing inhabitants of Canada. "Indigenous" is the term adopted by the international political movement to recognize the conditions, status, and rights of these populations worldwide, culminating in the United Nations Declaration on the Rights of Indigenous Peoples. The term "Indigenous" has been adopted by the Truth and Reconciliation Commission, as well as by the Canadian government and many other public entities in Canada and, in general, by the academic community.

The term "Aboriginal" will continue to be applied selectively to indicate a specific historic or institutional reference, such as "aboriginal peoples" in the Constitution Act, 1982.

2. There are two exceptions. One of the constitutional amending formulae, i.e., section 38, specifies the so-called 7/50 rule—seven provinces encompassing 50 per cent of the population—for certain areas (further enhanced through federal legislation in 1996 to accommodate Quebec and the West); and unanimity in other areas (Smith, 2002; Heard and Swartz, 1997). A similar rule applies for the Canada and Quebec Pension

Plan agreements (see discussion of the Canada/Quebec Pension Plan in Chapter 7).
3. On the importance of elite accommodation in divided societies, see Lijphart (1977, 1999). Lijphart and others note that elite accommodation generally involves acceptance of principles of non-majoritarian

decision-making so that typically minorities have a good chance to exercise a veto over matters of importance to them and dominant groupings in turn respect the idea that more than a simple majority is required for the passage of significant measures.

References

Aucoin, P., H. Bakvis, and M.D. Jarvis. 2013. "Constraining Executive Power in the Era of New Political Governance." In *Governing: Essays in Honour of Donald J. Savoie*, edited by J. Bickerton and B.G. Peters, 32–52. Montreal and Kingston: McGill-Queen's University Press.

Australia. 2008. *Australia 2020 Summit Report: Initial Summit Report*. Canberra: Department of Prime Minister and Cabinet.

———. 2014. *Reform of the Federation White Paper*. Canberra: Commonwealth of Australia. https://federation.dpmc.gov.au/.

Cairns, A.C. 2000. *Citizens Plus: Aboriginal Peoples and the Canadian State*. Vancouver: University of British Columbia Press.

Courchene, T.J. 1995. "Glocalization: The Regional/International Interface." *Canadian Journal of Regional Science* 18, no. 1: 1–20.

Diamond, M. 1973. "The Ends of Federalism." *Publius* 3, no. 2: 129–52.

Dicey, A.V. 1959 [1885]. *Introduction to the Study of the Law of the Constitution*, 10th edn, edited by E.C.S. Wade. London: Macmillan.

Elazar, D. 1996. *Federalism: An Overview*. Pretoria: Human Sciences Research Council.

Fafard, P., F. Rocher, and C. Côté. 2010. "The Presence (or Lack Thereof) of a Federal Culture in Canada: The Views of Canadians." *Regional and Federal Studies* 20, no. 1: 19–43.

Gibbins, R. 1999. "Taking Stock: Canadian Federalism and Its Constitutional Framework." In *How Ottawa Spends, 1999–2000*, edited by L. Pal, 197–220. Toronto: Oxford University Press.

Hale, G.H. 2004. "Canadian Federalism and the Challenge of North American Integration." *Canadian Public Administration* 47, no. 4: 497–524.

Heard, A., and T. Swartz. 1997. "The Regional Veto Formula and Its Effects on Canada's Constitutional Amendment Process." *Canadian Journal of Political Science* 30, no. 2: 339–56.

Laski, H.J. 1939. "The Obsolescence of Federalism." *New Republic*: 367–9.

Lijphart, A. 1977. *Democracy in Plural Societies: A Comparative Exploration*. New Haven, CT: Yale University Press.

———. 1999. *Patterns of Democracy: Government Forms and Performance in Thirty-Six Countries*. New Haven, CT: Yale University Press.

Piattoni, S. 2010. *The Theory of Multi-Level Governance*. Oxford: Oxford University Press.

Riker, W. 1969. "Six Books in Search of a Subject or Does Federalism Exist and Does It Matter?" *Comparative Politics* 2, no. 1: 135–46.

Savoie, D. 1999. *Governing from the Centre: The Concentration of Power in Canadian Politics*. Toronto: University of Toronto Press.

———. 2008. *Court Government and the Collapse of Accountability in Canada and the United Kingdom*. Toronto: University of Toronto Press.

Simeon, R. 2006 [1972]. *Federal–Provincial Diplomacy: The Making of Recent Policy in Canada*. Toronto: University of Toronto Press.

Skogstad, G. 2003. "Who Governs? Who Should Govern? Political Authority and Legitimacy in Canada in the Twenty-First Century." *Canadian Journal of Political Science* 36, no. 5: 955–73.

Smiley, D.V. 1981. "The Challenge of Canadian Ambivalence." *Queen's Quarterly* 88, no. 1: 1–12.

———. 1987. *The Federal Condition in Canada*. Toronto: McGraw-Hill Ryerson.

Smith, J. 2002. "Informal Constitutional Development: Change by Other Means." In *Canadian Federalism: Performance, Effectiveness, and Legitimacy*, edited by H. Bakvis and G. Skogstad, 40–58. Toronto: Oxford University Press.

———. 2004. *Federalism: Canadian Democratic Audit*. Vancouver: University of British Columbia Press.

Tuohy, C. 1992. *Policy and Politics in Canada: Institutionalized Ambivalence*. Philadelphia: Temple University Press.

Watts, R.L. 1999. *Comparing Federal Systems*, 2nd edn. Montreal and Kingston: McGill–Queen's University Press.

———. 2005. "Comparing Forms of Federal Partnerships." In *Theories of Federalism*, edited by D. Karmis and W. Norman. Houndsmills, UK: Palgrave Macmillan.

Wheare, K.C. 1963. *Federal Government*, 4th edn. London: Oxford University Press.

White, G. 2005. *Cabinets and First Ministers*. Vancouver: University of British Columbia Press.

Chapter 1

Understanding Federalism and
Intergovernmental Relations

Weeks 1 & 2

Learning Objectives

- To understand the basic objectives and political values of federalism as an idea.
- To evaluate the ideal institutional arrangements in federations and how and whether they are realized in practice in Canada and other federations.
- To appreciate the differences between federal institutions and federal society.
- To see how intergovernmental relations are a vital part of the political and policy-making process.

Federalism is something of a chicken-and-egg phenomenon. Do certain societal or geographical characteristics compel a country to adopt a federal system? Or does the adoption of a federal system allow different cultures and regions to flourish in a way that otherwise would not be possible? In other words, is federalism simply a response to societal differences? Or does federalism itself create more important differences, which then need dedicated intergovernmental institutions to accommodate them? Since one of our central concerns in this book is the structure of intergovernmental relations in Canada, it is worth investigating the origins of that diversity.

For many people, federalism may be defined in terms of the division of powers on the basis of territory or geography rather than function. By dividing authority between two or more orders of government[1] to provide representation for territorial, religious, linguistic, or ethnic differences in the decision-making structures of the state, federalism essentially creates conditions that may entrench differences over time. The reasons that lead a state to opt for federalism will have some bearing on how much or how little intergovernmental "relating" is required to promote stability and responsiveness.

This chapter surveys the origins of the federal idea or principle, along with the different schools of thought regarding diversity and societal differences in federal systems. Federal institutions are meant to channel diversity, sometimes to resolve conflicts and sometimes to allow for diversity to be reflected in the decisions made by the state at different levels. Federalism is indeed an "-ism": a set of beliefs about the correct way to organize political life. But it is a complicated one, which must simultaneously maintain unity among the diverse parts and allow those parts to flourish and express their differences in tangible policy choices. Federalism endorses the idea that for purposes of governance, different communities may need some degree of unity without being strictly unified—in other words, unity without uniformity. As an ideology it affirms the appropriateness of two or more governments exercising authority on behalf of a single community and its parts. Canadians may find it easier than others to grasp the idea that federalism is an ideological choice. This is especially clear in Quebec's relations with the rest of Canada. Quebecers who support the Canadian national government or strong(er) ties with the rest of Canada are routinely described as federalists, while those who do not support the federal union are commonly labelled separatists or sovereign-ists. Both camps are seen as endorsing a particular position loaded with normative ideas about the value of group rights and individual rights or about the need for self-governing at a more local level and ultimately about the very nature of the state and the kinds of collective goals that it might or might not wish to pursue.

Overall, federalism is no less normative an idea. The adoption of a federal system implies a society's preference for a degree of collective unity offset by genuine autonomy for individual regions, with a written constitution and the rule of law to keep the various elements in check. Canada's choice of a federal system indicates an ideological preference for some kind of balance between the concentration of power at the national level (as in a unitary system) and the dispersion of power to the provinces (as in a confederal alliance).

If this ideological dimension is sometimes forgotten, it is because the choice of federalism seems above all to imply that the society has decided to put a certain set of institutional commitments ahead of any commitment to specific ideas or values. As teachers we are all too aware that federalism in Canada is often seen as a set of dry, boring procedural rules and neutral institutions that the more exciting forces of collective life, such as politics and ideology, have to work *through* if cit-izens are to realize their social goals or policy preferences. In reality, however, the decision to adopt and maintain a federal system is anything but neutral. It reflects a commitment on the part of both the united subunits and the population, a com-mitment that needs perpetual reinforcement and affirmation—that is why consti-tutional discussions that question the very basis of federal unity can be so risky.

The consequence of choosing federalism is federation. The ideological choice of a federal model leads to certain kinds of observable institutions and rules. The institutions and rules characteristic of federated governments look fairly similar from one federation to the next, but they work differently in different contexts and may have quirks that undermine or exaggerate the intent of the system's designers. That said, federations do appear to have some universal traits that distinguish them from other forms of political organization. The minimum requirements are usually seen as including a written constitution with a division of legislative powers, a constitutional court to serve as umpire when disputes arise between governments, a mechanism for coordination between governments (intergovernmental relations), and representation of subunits in national institutions (Watts, 1999).

Once again, at the core of federalism is a commitment to organizing political life so as to recognize regional and societal diversity and preserve self-government at a local level. Federalism began as a response to the challenge of governing complicated societies and spaces, and so it remains. Where students of federalism differ is on the relative importance of institutions and societal differences in explaining how federations operate and evolve. This is a perennial question of political science: what matters more to outcomes, the demands and preferences of a political community, or the institutions through which those demands and preferences are channelled?

In this chapter we first survey the origins of the federal idea; we then discuss the differences between two basic perspectives, societal and institutional. A discussion of varying Canadian conceptions of the purpose and meaning of our federal system reinforces our point about the ideological character of federalism and reminds us of the contending viewpoints that continue to drive much of the activity in Canadian intergovernmental relations. Finally, we discuss the value of bringing a comparative perspective to the examination of intergovernmental relations and institutions, and why we think federalism is indeed an important variable in the kinds of political outcomes that the citizens of federal polities experience.

The Origins of Federalism

The idea of federalism is an ancient one; its roots can be traced to the medieval period or even earlier (Hueglin, 2003). In North America, the Iroquois nations had formed a confederacy before the first European settlers arrived, and a number of other Indigenous nations had established power-sharing arrangements (Ladner, 2003). Some of these models may have provided inspiration to the American colonists when they were looking for ways to establish a greater union. What we call federalism today, however, is of much more recent vintage. The plan for the first modern federation was laid out with the drafting of the American constitution in 1787. The advocates of that constitution, particularly the authors of *The Federalist Papers*, essentially co-opted the term "federal" for a system of government that had never been seen before, even by those with a nominal notion of federalism (Diamond, 1961). In the American constitution, legitimate governing authority was distributed between the federal (national) and state governments, but was not held by either: it remained independent of both orders of government, residing in the constitution and, ultimately, the people. Prior to the final ratification of this document in 1789, the 13 American states were linked together rather loosely under the Articles of Confederation, which was the first arrangement for governing the former British colonies after the Revolution.

Among the notable features of the early American confederation was the absence of an independent central government. In this respect it resembled many earlier federal-style arrangements such as the Dutch and Swiss confederacies. The partners to the compact shared some nominal sense of unity, but kept for themselves all governing authority and sovereignty. We now describe these federal arrangements as "confederal." Under such arrangements, the collective can do nothing without the unanimous agreement of its component parts. The pre-constitution American union had neither an executive nor a judicial branch; executive tasks were entrusted to committees struck by the Continental Congress. The 1787 US constitution rectified what were seen as major deficiencies, primary among them the absence of an independent federal government with meaningful powers. The creation of such an entity was not without controversy. Self-governing states had little interest in transferring significant power to a distant new national government that provided for, among other things, a directly elected legislature with representation based on population and separate executive and judiciary branches. The rhetorical victory of the Federalists was to claim for their invention, a system of compound sovereignty, the name "Federal." Their opponents, who wanted to maintain the dispersed power of the older arrangement, were reduced to the status of Anti-Federalists.

The American constitution has served as the prototype for modern federations. It challenged the idea that collective sovereignty could be realized only in a unitary form. Its invention made it possible for the people of a state to exercise local sovereignty in some matters and to be part of a greater sovereignty at the national level. The independence of the individual governments in such an arrangement was critical. It was the basis for the famous definition of the federal principle put forward by K.C. Wheare in his book *Federal Government*: "By the federal principle I mean the method of dividing powers so that the general and regional governments are each, within a sphere, coordinate and independent" (Wheare, 1963: 10). The key terms in this definition are "coordinate" and "independent." The former denotes a lack of hierarchy: the two orders of governments are of equal standing. The latter states that neither depends on the other: each is sovereign in its own sphere of jurisdiction.

In this federal context the life of the citizen is also bifurcated. Two orders of government overlap in the same citizen body, and each has a direct relationship with the people (Vernon, 1988). Thus in modern federations such as the United States, Canada, and Australia, citizens elect representatives to both the state/provincial and federal legislatures. Deriving government authority from a constitution whose authority in turn is grounded in popular sovereignty freed the national government from the dictates of its component parts. This was not the case with earlier confederal models; in 1775, for example, when the 13 colonial governments sent delegates to the Continental Congress, each state had exactly one vote. We describe such a system as confederal because, although it still has some features of union, the national or union level depends on the parts for its authority. Delegates to Congress under the Articles of Confederation were true delegates, chosen to faithfully transmit the views of the governments they represented. These delegates were selected by the governments—not directly elected by the people. Federalism before 1787 had meant some kind of union government, but one that was in effect created and controlled by the regional governments. The US constitution, in providing for the direct election of members of the House of Representatives, freed those representatives from the instructions of their state governments. The presidency draws its legitimacy from the people as well, but indirectly, through the state-based electoral college, which means that the candidate coming first in the popular vote is not necessarily the winner in the college (as happened in 2016 with Hillary Clinton, who won the popular vote but lost to Donald Trump in the electoral college). This gives the federal government something of a compound character. Once in office, however, neither the lower house of the national legislature nor the national executive owes any allegiance to subnational governments. Each order of government, therefore, enjoys an independent source of authority and legitimacy.

Its democratic character was not the only feature that made the American system so revolutionary. Few people in 1787 had any notion of government authority as anything other than unitary. Since the Treaties of Westphalia of 1648, European sovereignty had been considered indivisible, even to the point of suppressing previous federal experience (Hueglin, 1999). In the British parliamentary model to which most of the American colonists were accustomed, the final authority for making and approving laws rested with a single legislature or government.[2] This is still the case in France and other unitary systems today: regional or local governments may exist, but they lack the constitutionally protected independent authority, autonomy, and jurisdiction enjoyed by states and provinces in constitutionalized federal systems. Their status and privileges can be altered at will by the national legislature, and decisions rendered by lower-level governments can be nullified by the same legislature. The relationship between Canada's municipal and provincial governments is of this type. In recent years, provincial governments have exercised significant authority over municipalities—changing their responsibilities, for example, and forcing amalgamations. The federal government does not have any equivalent power over the provinces.

The autonomy and dispersion of power we've discussed in these three models—confederal, federal, and unitary—can be placed on a continuum, as in Figure 1.1. These are ideal types, and most systems of government combine elements of each. Federations nominally occupy the middle ground on this continuum, but they also represent a compound of unitary and confederal elements. For example, the second chambers of federations vary in form from mildly to

Figure 1.1 Degrees of Centralization in Federal and Confederal Forms

explicitly confederal. In the US, until the 17th Amendment in 1913, members of the national senate were selected by state legislatures rather than directly by the citizens of the states. In Germany, the second chamber of the national legislature, the Bundesrat, is populated by the premiers and senior members of state governments. In these cases, state governments have the capacity to impose direct checks on the power of the federal legislature. Other federations, including the present-day US, elect upper house members directly, and those representatives feel much less loyalty to state governments than they do to state citizens. Within their spheres of jurisdiction, governments can theoretically act as though they were quite unitary. But in practice, national institutions make it possible for regions or regional governments to have a say in what the federal government does. In this respect, while Canada has a second chamber based on regional representation—the Senate—its members are appointed directly by the federal government and thus lack the legitimacy accorded by either direct election or appointment by provincial governments. Canada stands in contrast to other federations in this respect, and many observers would argue that the Canadian federation is essentially incomplete because of it (King, 1982).

Given the need to balance elements of unitary and confederal decision-making (or centralizing and decentralizing forces, if you prefer), federations generally look to second chambers, although the form of the national executive (a regionally representative cabinet, for example) can also mitigate this tension. A baseline requirement for realizing the federal idea is a written constitution, which can divide power on a territorial basis to ensure the coordinate and independent status of two or more orders of government. To ensure the representation of regions or regional governments in central government decision-making, however, federations typically rely on a body whose members are either elected by the citizens of the various regions or appointed by the regional governments. But these two features do not necessarily provide an accurate or complete picture of how federations function.

It is important to note that the coordinate and independent status emphasized by Wheare is premised on what has been labelled in Canada the "watertight compartments" metaphor of federalism,[3] in which each government is seen as operating in its own separate sphere, never really overlapping or crossing paths with the other level. The metaphor of watertight compartments, drawn from marine architecture, assumes that such compartments will keep a ship afloat even with a hole in its hull. In applying this idea to Canadian federalism in the 1930s, the Judicial Committee of the Privy Council (JCPC) assumed the classic notion of independence and autonomy with no need for regular interaction between the different orders of government in a federation. For most of the twentieth century, however, experience suggested that this was an unrealistic assumption. In fact, it was discovered even earlier in the life of the American federation that extensive cooperation between federal and state governments was necessary for the new nation to develop its infrastructure, allowing the country to develop its full potential, whether it was with respect to education, canals, roads, or railways (Elazar, 1962). It also became evident that the distinct jurisdictional spheres or functions of the two orders of government were soon thoroughly intertwined—a development that led one writer to liken the American federation to a marble cake (Grodzins, 1966). Compared with the US, Canadians have often made greater efforts to maintain a strict division between provincial and national jurisdiction, but as shown in the chapters that follow, this effort has not always been successful.

Indeed, the federal government under the Harper Conservatives attempted as much of a strict division as possible, adopting what can be called the classical view of federalism. Historically, however, when governments started to be more active in such areas as taxation and health and social services the responsibilities of the two orders could not easily be separated. Thus, interdependence rather than independence is more commonly the hallmark of modern federalism. And this interdependence of government functions in turn requires considerable interaction between governments on a large variety of administrative and policy issues (Lindquist, 1999). Increasing interdependence does not necessarily mean that one order of government exercises control over the other, though this is one possible outcome. Certainly in Canada we have a high level of autonomy on the part of the constituent units (the federal and provincial governments) coupled with considerable interdependence (Simeon, 2006 [1972]). What this means in practice is that when a policy initiative needs to be moved forward, the two orders of government will usually need to cooperate; conversely, if one government or set of governments refuses to cooperate, the initiative could well be stymied. How governments negotiate, the strategies they use, the objectives they seek to attain in various policy areas, and the constraints under which they operate: these are what intergovernmental relations are largely about.

Institutional and Societal Views of Federalism

The two principal views of federalism differ in their responses to the question we asked at the outset of this chapter. Societal explanations maintain that the root cause of federation is difference, that intergovernmental institutions are created to recognize and accommodate differences, and that those institutions must adapt to meet changing patterns of diversity. From this perspective there would be little need for federalism at all if the differences were to disappear.

Institutional explanations, by contrast, focus on the impact that the particular intergovernmental institutions of a given federation have on the way it accommodates differences or even ensures that differences have the opportunity to flourish. Institutionalists want to know what kinds of institutions are in place and how they operate. In fact, as we shall see, the institutions themselves can contribute to diversity even in a relatively homogeneous population where most people are exposed to the same culture and media influences. Both perspectives acknowledge that federations are complex; where they differ is on the source of the energy that drives the federal system.

Societal accounts of federalism point to societal factors as the reasons for choosing federalism in the first place and see popular attitudes and cultural traits as the main sources of federalism's staying power. Societal influence is most evident in what have come to be called multinational or multi-ethnic federations, where there are clear differences in the languages people speak or the cultural practices they follow (Erk, 2007). But important societal differences can also be found in federations that appear more homogeneous. For William Livingston (1952, 1956), an early proponent of the society-first view, the distinguishing feature of federations was diversity—economic, cultural, linguistic, religious, climactic, with a geographic or territorial connection. This geographic element distinguishes federal societies from those in which differences may exist—and need governmental accommodation—but are not associated with particular regions. In short, federalism is necessary when you have differences plus geography. Without a geographic connection, what you have is simply a diverse society. The concentration of a particular language group in a particular territory, or vast differences in geography (and therefore in natural resources and economic conditions), will compel a society to organize itself on a territorial basis and allow for the expression and representation of those differences. It is no accident that federations do not fit well into the nation-state model and lack homogeneity in language and culture. It is also no accident that the world's largest states have opted for federalism to accommodate the enormous territorial distinctions within their borders.

For Livingston, the societal differences underlying federalism were the main variables determining how a federal system worked. Institutions—he called them "instrumentalities"—had to be responsive to societal differences. A federal system in which the instrumentalities were not responsive to societal diversity, in his view, risked serious trouble. Livingston was particularly interested in the mechanisms used by federations to make constitutional change, because the formal alteration of instrumentalities was evidence of the primacy of societal forces in shaping federalism. Livingston's approach was famously criticized by the Canadian political scientist Alan Cairns (1977) as overemphasizing the importance of organic, inherent differences within federations and underestimating the extent to which governments themselves promote diversity in the federal state. While there is no denying that territorially concentrated differences remain in Canada today, equally strong forces serve to unify Canadians—and yet federalism persists. For Cairns and others, provincial governments will always seek to justify their own existence, and if endowed with sufficient powers they will persevere long after their usefulness has passed.

Other scholars have been more inclined to approach federalism as a largely in-stitutional phenomenon. As we have seen, the introduction of federalism required considerable institutional invention. Little surprise, then, that people seeking to understand the impact of a federal system look at the influence of institutions as well as their capacity to accommodate diversity. A focus on institutions was also compatible with the dominant trends in political science in its early development as a discipline. Political science in Canada, and elsewhere, was initially concerned with explaining the minutiae of institutional arrangements and their operations (Smith, 2005). Federalism lends itself to such an analysis because the institutions of different federations vary in the weight they give to uniting and self-governing forces. However, there is some danger in too literal an institutional approach. Canadian scholars, for instance, initially attributed the early decentralization of Canadian federalism almost wholly to a province-favouring interpretation of the division of powers by the Judicial Committee of the Privy Council (JCPC). (The JCPC is the highest court of appeal in the United Kingdom and until 1949 was also the final court of appeal for Canada—see discussion in Chapter 4.) Those scholars were later scolded for not acknowledging the influence of Canada's geographic realities, which would inevitably be decentralizing, nor the increase in importance of the subject matters (such as health care and social welfare) that were originally assigned to the provinces at Confederation (Cairns, 1971). In other words, insti-tutional explanations of federalism have to take into account the context in which intergovernmental institutions operate. Decentralization was virtually inevitable in Canada, regardless of what any court might decide on the basis of the constitu-tion. The decentralizing preferences of the courts helped, but the direction of the country's development would almost certainly have been the same in any event.

Institutions created to serve federal systems are not neutral on the question of diversity. The Canadian experience has shown that federal institutions intended to cope with diversity can often reinforce differences between subnational com-munities. In some provinces the differences in geography, language, or culture are small, but because of the choices made early in their history, and because of the trajectories taken by particular governments, some differences in attitude and perspective became so entrenched that they are now cherished. Perhaps the best examples are the divergent directions taken by Alberta and Saskatchewan after they were carved out of the Northwest Territories in 1905. Alberta became home to some of the most ideologically conservative governments in Canadian history, while Saskatchewan elected the first socialist government in North America and served as the incubator for many of the earliest efforts to develop a welfare state in Canada, including universal medical care. It is true that the two provinces have had rather different settlement patterns, and that the oil industry has historically been much more important to Alberta's economy than Saskatchewan's. Nonetheless, a large part of the difference between them can be attributed to the institutional and policy choices made by governments early in the provinces' history. Yet they owe their existence as separate provinces largely to a decision to create two provinces where there might have been one, with a somewhat arbitrary line on the map to divide them. The ability of provincial executive branches to realize their policy goals—sometimes even when diffuse majorities oppose them—contributes to the strength of the provincial state vis-à-vis the provincial society. What the state wants and what society wants is not always the same thing. The parliamentary system gives the state the upper hand in the articulation of preferences. In a federal system this means that federal diversity reflects diversity in government positions as much as it does organic diversity among provincial societies. So even societal explanations of federalism have to account for the fact that the mere existence of federal institutions and subunit governments is likely to result in some degree of manufactured—as opposed to organic—diversity.

As will be evident throughout the book, we are inclined to give considerable explanatory power to institutions, however changeable they may be. Intergovernmental affairs work the way they do because actors in the system are endowed with certain powers by the institutional structure of parliamentary government in the federal and provincial orders and are constrained by the rules in the constitution and the practices and habits of previous governments.

The Institutions of Federalism

What are the primary institutions that a student of federalism, particularly Canadian federalism, looks at? We have already noted some aspects of the institutional framework, such as the distribution of powers and the nature of regional representation in central institutions, for example, a second legislative chamber or the federal executive. It is worth elaborating on why this framework is important and the variety of forms it may take.

First, virtually every federation has some kind of written constitution. One of the most important functions of that document is to spell out the distribution of powers. The mere existence of a written constitution speaks to the contractual nature of federalism. Maintaining autonomy seems to require fallback rules that cannot easily be changed to suit current circumstances. Within a written division of powers there are various ways of allocating responsibilities to the different orders of government. Canada is what has sometimes been called a jurisdictional federation. In such cases the constitution includes at least two lists, one defining the powers of the central government, the other the powers of the regional government. Thus in Canada education, local government, the operation of hospitals, and the licensing of physicians are all assigned to provincial jurisdiction, while currency, banking, and national defence are assigned to federal jurisdiction. Other federations enumerate the powers of only one order of government (usually a newly created central government), assuming that the remainder of the legislative sovereignty will continue to reside with the other order.

Some federations have an additional list of "concurrent powers": areas in which both orders of government have jurisdiction. In Canada agriculture is an example—although in this case the federal government was granted paramountcy, meaning that its laws will prevail in any conflict between federal and provincial laws in this field. Finally, there is a category of power known as "residual" that covers all matters not already assigned to either federal or provincial/state jurisdiction. This category has often been used to cover policy fields that could not be foreseen by the founders, such as advances in technology or (in Canada's case) the nation's assumption of full control over its foreign relations. The residual power can be allocated to one order or the other. In Australia and the US it was assigned to the state governments. In Canada, however, section 91 of the Constitution Act of 1867 assigned this undefined residual power to the federal government. Ironically, though the intention of founders such as John A. Macdonald was to ensure a strong central government (Waite, 1963), Canada became one of the world's more decentralized federations, especially in fiscal measures, while the US and especially Australia have evolved in the opposite direction, towards a more centralized model.

Allocating powers on the basis of policy fields, such as education or banking, is not the only way of designing a federal constitution. Another way is to allocate separate powers for the *design* and the *administration* of policy and programs. This model may be described as horizontal or administrative federalism. In the German federation, for example, law-making in most policy fields is the responsibility of the national government; the responsibility for administering policy, however, rests largely with the Länder (state) governments (Gunlicks, 2003). That means that within the various substantive policy areas there tends to be a division of labour rather than a division by subject area: the central government designs the general policy framework and the laws necessary to implement it, while the states implement and administer the laws written at the national level by running programs and interacting with citizens. It is worth stressing that in Germany the state governments are represented directly in the federal second chamber (the Bundesrat). In this body, state governments are in a position to shape the relevant legislation that will be administered by them.

In Canada there is only one area where horizontal federalism prevails: in the field of justice. Ottawa is responsible for the legal framework governing the justice system, largely encompassed in the federal Criminal Code. The provinces in turn have the primary responsibility for the administration of justice, such as policing and the management of the court system. Here it is worth noting that the provinces—unlike the German Länder—do not have any direct input in the formulation of laws in this policy area. They can put pressure on Ottawa to revise a law (e.g., to amend the Young Offenders Act to make it more punitive for particular crimes), but—unlike their German counterparts—they have no opportunity to block or veto such legislation. In the US, senators (two per state) are elected directly by the people rather than appointed by state governments. Nevertheless, they frequently act on behalf of their states' values and interests in the Senate, effectively giving state governments and state-based interests the opportunity to shape national legislation (this sort of activity is facilitated by the fact that party discipline in the US Congress as a whole is much weaker than in Canada). In Germany and the US alike, the representation of regional interests in central institutions—also known as *intra*state federalism, *intra* being Latin for "within"— reflects the confederal elements that we referred to earlier. Canada, by contrast, is largely lacking in formal opportunities for this kind of representation. Despite the bicameral structure of the federal Parliament, regional interests are much more likely to be conveyed to the centre by provincial governments, which make their representations directly to the federal government. Most intergovernmental interaction in Canada, therefore, takes place between governments rather than within central institutions. For this reason Canada is more accurately described as an *inter*state federation—*inter* meaning "between" (Smiley and Watts, 1985).

With respect to the distribution of powers, one additional set of powers is critical: the power to tax, raise revenue, and/or regulate and own revenue sources. Wheare, concerned as he was with the autonomy of governments in a federal system, pointed out that without adequate fiscal resources to meet its constitutional responsibilities, the legislative autonomy claimed by any one government is effectively meaningless. Furthermore, if a government is responsible for delivering policies but depends for the funding on another order of government that attaches conditions to those funds, then the implementing government can hardly be said to be fully in control of that field. In Australia the centralization of financial arrangements is one of the primary sources of the central government's relative strength when compared to Canada (Brown, 2002b). Revenues and responsibilities are regularly out of sync in federations, and Canada is certainly no exception. Because of this mismatch between revenue and responsibilities, much if not most of the intergovernmental activity that takes place in Canada concerns the financing of programs delivered by provincial governments—including those crucial to the well-being of most Canadians, such as health care, education, and social services.

There are some additional institutional features worth highlighting. If federations were to conform to Wheare's dictum, they would need to be ever vigilant about the boundaries between their constitutionally assigned responsibilities. Yet even when the component governments are inclined to be more relaxed about their interconnectedness and interdependence, there will still be occasions when their interests collide and they demand clarity from the constitution. For instance, even the kinds of programs and services that citizens in a democracy come to expect and demand can be a poor fit for a decades-old division of powers. To use a Canadian example, do labour market training programs fall under the heading of education (a provincial responsibility) or economic management (an area where the federal government can claim to have a role)? Many such disputes can be resolved through negotiation. But not all of them can. In the latter case it is not uncommon for the result to be a stalemate. Therefore, just as in civil disputes among citizens, courts have been given the mandate to adjudicate on disputes among governments. In short, every federation needs a constitutional court to adjudicate or arbitrate disputes over jurisdiction and interpretation of the federal compact.

The role played by this court—known in Canada and the US as the Supreme Court and in Australia as the High Court—is critical in two respects: in helping to maintain the overall relationship between the national and regional governments, and thus in the federation as a whole; and in serving as an arena in which disputes between governments can be resolved. The courts are not the only, or necessarily the most desirable, arena for settling disagreements, but they are in keeping with the spirit of federalism as a system that insists on preserving the rule of constitutional law and some baseline of autonomy for its component governments, even when they acknowledge that much of what they do requires cooperation or collaboration with one another.

The courts are not always neutral bystanders. One advantage of approaching federalism from the institutional angle is that it allows us to isolate some of the effects that individual institutions might have on the way a federation evolves. Certainly a constitutional court can alter the balance between the two orders of government by subtly, or not so subtly, reinterpreting jurisdictional powers. Another way in which the balance of powers can be redefined is through a constitutionally entrenched amending procedure—something that most, though not all, federations have (Canada did not acquire its formal amending procedure until 1982). The use of such constitutional amending procedures is relatively rare, in part because the threshold for successful change is so high. However, de facto changes have taken place as a result of judicial decisions. Still more change occurs at the level of informal rules, norms, and understandings agreed to by the two orders of government and shaped to a considerable degree by public opinion, usually as a consequence of negotiations and interactions between elected and unelected officials—in other words, as a product of intergovernmental relations. These kinds of informal rules and norms, which often have a kind of opaque quality, are conducive to resolving problems in the short to medium run so long as everyone understands the context. Yet the very informality proves to be deleterious if the actual practice of federalism falls seriously out of sync with the formal rules of the federation.

Finally, some features of Canada's parliamentary democracy are not part of the federal arrangement as such, but nonetheless have a powerful impact on the nature of federalism and the conduct of intergovernmental relations. British parliamentary systems, such as Canada's, fuse executive and legislative power in the hands of the prime minister and cabinet, who are both appointed by the Crown as executives but also are elected members of Parliament. So long as party discipline in the Parliament is maintained (and Canada has an especially strong tradition of strict party discipline) the elected executive is in a very strong position to pursue and pass a coherent legislative agenda. This institutional setting differs significantly from that of the United States with its separation of powers between the legislature and the executive. The US president does not sit in the legislature and is rarely in a position to push through a legislative agenda without challenge, even when both houses of Congress are under the control of the president's party. In Canada, however, the concentration of legislative and executive authority in the government not only makes for a more powerful executive in relation to the legislature but also leads to a marked executive dominance of intergovernmental relations. In federal–provincial relations the first ministers not only can speak for all of the government, including the legislature, but they can usually guarantee that any budgetary and/or legislative implementation required for an intergovernmental deal will be passed by the legislature.

In recent decades in Canada some analysts would argue that this concentration of power has become even more pronounced (Savoie, 1999; Simpson, 2001). With powerful central agencies and government departments organized on a hierarchical basis, the prime minister has available a wide variety of mechanisms to ensure that power remains concentrated within a relatively small circle of key advisers, ministers, and senior civil servants (Savoie, 1999). The same is true at the provincial level. Even minority governments do little to weaken the centralization of power in the prime ministership. The ability of powerful governments—federal and provincial alike—to concentrate their resources behind their first minister can result in dramatic and often personalized confrontations between governments.

Executive Federalism

Among the institutions of Canadian federalism, none has more influence on policy outcomes and the shape of intergovernmental relations than the fact of executive federalism. Executive dominance means that most of the interaction in Canada's federal system takes place between executives, whether at the political or the permanent bureaucratic level.[4] As Ronald Watts suggests, executive federalism captures "the predominant role of governmental executives (ministers and their officials) in intergovernmental relations in parliamentary federations where responsible first ministers and cabinet ministers tend to predominate within both levels of government" (Watts, 1999: 58). The fact that executive federalism is the norm reinforces the government-to-government nature of relations between the federal and provincial orders and makes it difficult to form regionally based legislative coalitions that cut across governmental jurisdictions.

Executive federalism works in two reasonably distinct ways. On an everyday basis, the bulk of intergovernmental interaction is carried out by "officials" on each side: permanent public servants. For example, federal Finance officials work with their provincial counterparts to implement federal transfers to the provinces; federal and provincial health bureaucrats cooperate on national surgery wait-time protocols; and educational administrators work to ensure that academic standards and university admissions policies are comparable across provinces. Without all these interactions at the functional level, joint or coordinated action is impossible. The complexity of policy delivery means that neither order of government can achieve its goals without cooperating to take advantage of the experience and opportunities offered by the other.

A more familiar form of executive federalism, perhaps, is the one that operates at the "summit" level. Federal and provincial or territorial cabinet ministers, as the political heads of their departments, can work together to establish policies and approaches that will be implemented by their officials. This is also a more conflict-driven form of executive federalism, however, as it serves as a forum for the expression of political differences. Since the people involved are more prominent, it also attracts more attention both from the media and from citizens who expect solutions to persistent intergovernmental coordination problems. At the peak of the hierarchy are interactions between first ministers. The federal prime minister and provincial premiers potentially have the power to set directions without the consent or even the knowledge of departments and ministers, and their interactions have the highest public profile. At this level, the personalities of the politicians involved become critical variables in negotiations. If a prime minister and a premier take a strong dislike to each other, this can affect a whole range of issues between the two governments.

From the viewpoint of effective intergovernmental governance, this system has advantages and disadvantages. The limited number of actors involved in executive federalism sometimes makes it easier to reach agreement. On the other hand, personality issues can become amplified and the system generally can encourage a competitive approach. In particular, there may be a tendency to link several diverse issues in a single, large package for debate and negotiation, making agreement more difficult to reach than is usually the case with the smaller, more manageable issues handled at lower levels. This is not to say that under executive federalism intergovernmental agreement is always difficult to achieve or that conflict is inevitable. In fact, Canada's stability—despite awesome challenges of geography, language, and regional economic disparities—suggests that the federal system might be doing something right. The elite accommodation that executive federalism allows is essentially good for stability; but it may not be good for the transparency of decision-making or accountability to the electorate (concerns that we will discuss in later chapters).

It might also be said that a certain amount of competition between governments can be healthy. Indeed, some theorists of federalism have cited competition between governments as one of the normative advantages of federation over unitary government (Breton, 1985). Much as a separation of powers within any given order of government results in a more responsive (if not efficient) system, competition between federal subunits can also make them more responsive to popular demands. In Canada's case, the distribution of legislative powers, which is so much more exclusive, and therefore less concurrent, provides significant incentives to both federal–provincial and interprovincial competition. But competition also has the potential to be detrimental to the public interest, especially if provinces get into what has been described as a "race to the bottom." If competition for jobs and investment leads provinces to lower taxes and regulatory hurdles, or to decrease the generosity of their social welfare standards to avoid becoming "welfare magnets," the result may be an overall deterioration in public goods and services. Although the extent of this problem in Canada is unclear, governments certainly point to competition as a reason for the unpopular choices they sometimes make (Harrison, 2006).

This inherent tendency within the Canadian system towards competition between governments, fuelled in part by the adversarial norms typical of Westminster systems, is at odds with some of the other important principles of federalism. Essentially, modern-day federalism often prefers consensus-based decision-making, since in a well-balanced federation neither order of government would be in a position to dominate the other and each would require some minimum of cooperation or tolerance from the other in order to deliver its programs effectively. This accommodative capacity of executive federalism is the practice of elites from opposing factions or communities in society reaching compromises in the face of dissent at the societal level.[5] In Canada these opposing communities are often, though not always, represented by provincial political elites, especially the heads of provincial governments. The role of Canadian political elites has been seen as crucial, both in the striking of the original Confederation package and in maintaining the stability of the federation over time (McRae, 1974). To preserve the overall stability of the system, leaders will often strike agreements on the quiet where the general public is not in a position to make a compromise.

Three prime examples of elite accommodation on contentious issues are the agreements reached regarding medicare and the Canada Pension Plan (CPP) in the 1960s and the Meech Lake Accord on the constitution in 1987. The two latter cases both represented efforts to create a unique space for Quebec within the federation, by allowing the creation of a separate Quebec Pension Plan and, in the proposed Meech Lake Accord, by giving constitutional recognition to Quebec's status as a distinct society within Canada.

But Meech Lake also illustrated the limitations of elite accommodation and executive federalism. The agreement reached by the federal prime minister and the 10 provincial premiers ultimately collapsed when two provincial legislatures failed to ratify the amendments within the required time frame, largely because of negative public sentiment outside Quebec and pressure from constituencies such as women and Indigenous peoples. While many opposed Meech Lake for substantive reasons—such as concern that it would compromise the operation of the Charter of Rights and Freedoms—most also disapproved of the exclusive and secretive process by which the Accord was negotiated. Since that time in particular, executive federalism has often come under challenge, especially from those who believe that the intergovernmental process should be not only more transparent but also open to a broader range of actors, including non-government actors such as public advocacy groups. The ongoing desire to increase the power of federal and provincial legislatures vis-à-vis the cabinet, and the prospect of subjecting intergovernmental agreements to legislative review, may also serve as constraints on executive federalism in the future.

These developments are generally seen as consistent with good democratic practice. But they may also undermine the more traditional forms of elite accommodation and the benefits they offer with respect to national unity. Elite accommodation depends in part on secrecy and lack of transparency, while executive federalism also benefits from a general lack of procedural and decision-making rules, which allows for compromise and a shrugging acceptance of difference that has helped Quebec attain a certain de facto recognition of its special status. The 2004 Health Care Accord, signed by the federal and provincial governments, included a codicil explicitly endorsing the idea of asymmetry in federal–provincial relations; this effectively allowed Quebec or other provinces to opt out of the general terms agreed to by the other provinces and make its own arrangements with the federal government. (We will return to this subject at several points in later chapters.) Regardless of whether intergovernmental relations constitute elite accommodation or are the product of broader consensus, a workable federalism requires the generation of trust ties, mutual respect and understanding, and a willingness to accept that decisions should be based on mutual consent (Dupré, 1988). In contrast is the court system which, like Parliament and the provincial legislatures, is based on adversarial norms and legal certainties. This arena, as we shall see, produces results that are not always predictable and are often quite unsatisfactory for all parties concerned. Whereas the norm in intergovernmental negotiation is compromise, court proceedings are often zero-sum games, producing winner-take-all results.

Competing Canadian Conceptions of Federalism

Related to the notion of accommodation we have just discussed, but perhaps more revealing of the ideological character of federalism, are the different conceptions of federalism held by Canadians. More specifically, there are different accounts of the compromise that created Confederation and the kind of accommodation that Canadian federalism is meant to represent. In this case, the differences centre on what federalism was meant to protect and promote, and what the Canadian federation should be in the long term.

According to one vision, Canadian federalism represents a compact between two nations. In the 1860s the majority of political forces in British North America supported unification of the colonies for military, economic, and political reasons. Many of the Fathers of Confederation would have preferred a more unitary form of government for the proposed union, but the differences in culture, governance traditions, and legal systems between Canada East and Canada West (the future Quebec and Ontario) were so pronounced as to require a federal form. In this compact, Quebec became the centre of French Canada (though it retained an influential anglophone minority), while the other partners in the compact together constituted English Canada. The "two-nations" interpretation of the Canadian compromise persisted as a kind of national myth through much of the twentieth century as Canada gradually gave fuller expression to its bilingual and bicultural character, going so far as to designate both French and English as official languages. For advocates of the two-nations theory, federalism in Canada must operate accordingly. The division of powers must be sensitive to issues around language, culture, and education, allowing the provinces, particularly Quebec, the flexibility necessary to protect and preserve local distinctiveness.

Perhaps more important, this vision assumes that Quebec is not a province like the others. Thus, according to its proponents, major national policies or constitutional changes require the agreement of both parties to the two-nations compact. When the 1981 constitutional settlement that established Canada's own amending formula and introduced the Charter of Rights was reached, without Quebec's agreement, Quebec argued that it could veto the proposed changes. The Supreme Court did not agree and thus the Constitution Act of 1982 went ahead. Nonetheless, major constitutional change without the consent of one of the partners to the federal compact remains unacceptable to Quebec elites. A two-nations theory of federalism is also more likely than other models to support a classical interpretation of federalism, at least when it comes to protecting a strict definition of Quebec autonomy.

The two-nations compact was meant to serve a functional purpose, with the constitution essentially serving as a contract between the dominant majority and the national minority provincially concentrated in Quebec. A territorially concentrated minority seeking the protection of a federal state is less likely than the national majority to tolerate blurred jurisdictional lines and efforts by the national level to interfere in the fields assigned to provincial governments. However, the two-nations compact theory is undermined by the notion that Quebec does not necessarily represent all the French-speaking people in Canada. For many advocates of a bilingual and bicultural Canada, the existence of French communities outside Quebec, and a significant anglophone minority (not to mention First Nations) inside Quebec weaken the Quebec claim to nationhood. Supporting such minority language communities has been a priority of Canada's federal government, particularly under Prime Minister Pierre Trudeau (1968–79, 1980–4), who sought to delegitimize Quebec's claim to speak for all of French Canada. Finally, and significantly, the two-nations theory does not reflect the presence of other national communities within Canada, most notably the constitutionally recognized "aboriginal peoples of Canada." Some have therefore adopted a broader vision of federal diversity that embraces at least three national identities (Taylor, 1991; Kymlicka, 1998; Gagnon, 2010).

An alternative version of the compact theory is that Canadian federalism is a compact not of nations but of provinces. In this view, Quebec was not the only province with an identity too distinctive to allow for a unitary form of government: the differences among the English-speaking provinces also warranted a federal system. The provincial-compact theory conceives of the provinces as equal partners in the Confederation compromise. Different provinces may have joined Confederation under different circumstances and to some degree on different terms, but they are still seen as the primary building blocks of the federal society. Advocates of this interpretation of the compact theory, for whom the constitution was created by the constituent units, naturally call for unanimity on constitutional change. Another hallmark of the provincial-compact view is hostility to some nationwide goals on the grounds that such goals ignore provincial differences and marginalize provincial cultures. For the provincial-compact theorists, the growth of the federal government and the substitution of national projects for provincial ones is the biggest threat to their conception of the federation. Opponents of the Charter of Rights and Freedoms argued that the pan-Canadian identity it promoted would ultimately make it difficult for provincial governments to express their distinctive identities through their policy choices. The provincial-compact theory is reinforced by the practice of executive federalism, which privileges the premiers above all other representatives of provincial societies.

The third vision of federalism in Canada rejects both "compact" views in favour of the realist proposition that the original act of union was simply that: a piece of legislation enacted by the British Parliament. The British North America (BNA) Act of 1867 (since 1982 known as the Constitution Act, 1867) clearly reflected the preferences of a strong coalition of pro-union forces in British North America, but it was not the product of an explicit treaty. The federal Parliament of Canada inherited Britain's job of maintaining unity, and now represents much more than the sum of the constituent parts. The dominance of the federal government was demonstrated in the 1982 patriation of the constitution without the consent of all the provinces and in the face of active opposition from Quebec. Of those who accept this vision, many acknowledge that the Confederation compromise was premised on the protection of local governance for a number of somewhat distinct political societies; but they believe that modern technology, communications, and globalization in general have made those communities less critical to good government and good outcomes and that the federal system should evolve accordingly. It is still a vision of federalism, but one with more centralized and standardized outcomes (as occurred in Australia, for example). What matters most to those in this camp is that Canada is a whole and continuing national (as in Canadian) project of integration and development.

Comparative Federalism and Multi-level Governance

We would be remiss if we were to end this chapter without noting another aspect of our approach to the topic of federalism both generally and in the remainder of this book. Increasingly, students of federalism tend to set their discussions of federalism, even within a single country, in a comparative context. We are likewise inclined. The discussion of Canadian intergovernmental relations in this book is informed by comparisons with the experience of other federations. For example, we know that the structure of parliamentary institutions at both the national and the provincial levels results in a form of intergovernmentalism that is shared by other parliamentary federations, i.e., what has been called "executive federalism." We also know that weaknesses in the present intergovernmental system might be addressed through institutional changes inspired by the practices of other federations. Examples are peppered throughout the chapters that follow. Not every feature of one federation will be suitable for another, but there are similarities in the problems that all federations are trying to address.

One by-product of this comparative research is an expansion of what now qualifies as federal. Few scholars today are as strict as K.C. Wheare was, a generation ago, about the kinds of arrangements that qualify as "federal." For example, Wheare refused even to recognize Canada as a federation on the grounds that Ottawa's control of the residual powers, along with the powers of reservation and disallowance (which theoretically allow it to overturn any provincial legislation), violated the federal principle. The fact that those powers had fallen into disuse (today they may be considered effectively dead) led Wheare to identify Canada as federal in practice if not in law—hence his term "quasi-federal." Today our notions of what makes a system federal are much more relaxed. New federal-type systems such as those in Spain, Belgium, and South Africa are helping to redefine the terms of federalism and federation, both of which are becoming more elastic. Another major experiment in formalized power-sharing and pooled sovereignty is the evolving European Union (EU). Having started out in 1951 as an international treaty among a few European countries with rudimentary common institutions, it has evolved into a powerful hybrid, somewhere between a confederal system and a federation. In the process the member states have achieved significant political and economic integration. Since the global financial crisis of 2008–9, even this degree of integration has been under strain because of the indebtedness of some weaker member states and, most recently, the move by Britain to leave the EU following its successful Brexit referendum in 2016. As well, the influx of migrants from Africa and elsewhere has contributed to the rise of populist quasi-authoritarian governments in member countries such as Poland and Hungary challenging the democratic principles underpinning the EU (Brunet-Jailly, Hurrelmann, and Verdun, 2018).

In any case, notions of what qualifies as federal have become less strict, and our terminology has changed. The label "federal" may still be reserved, much as it was by Wheare, for systems that faithfully preserve the autonomy of individual orders of government within a constitutionally allocated legislative sphere. But there are many systems in which both collective and local governance is significant, even if those collective and local governments do not enjoy federal-style autonomy. These are generally referred to as multi-level systems of governance. The term is meant to capture significant developments in local government as well as the increased relevance of transnational decision-making bodies, whether formal and deeply integrated entities such as the European Union or more dispersed but still influential organizations such as trade and tariff agreements, or the protocols that arise from United Nations conventions on climate change.

Multi-level governance may be defined as a situation in which power and authority are shared, sometimes in relationships established by constitutional law or treaty, sometimes in more informal working arrangements. In this shared governance, decision-making is effectively delegated, depending on the case, downwards to decentralized government agencies, upwards to supranational agencies, or outwards to private or other civil-society agents—or to all or to a combination of all the above! In all cases the scope and mechanisms of public policy extend beyond the central state. And in all cases policy outcomes are achieved that can no longer (or never could) be achieved by a single government on its own.[6] In the Canadian context, multi-level governance can be external in the sense that it includes either the continental region of North America or the global community into which the Canadian society and economy are becoming increasingly integrated. Or it can be domestic, including local governments, Indigenous governments, and civil-society actors of various kinds. In areas such as public health and the environment it can stretch from local to global. A second new development is encompassed by the word "governance" itself, which implies that governing is being done, but not necessarily by governments alone, and is often not structured by constitutional and legalized power-sharing, but rather by less formal, more limited forms of power-sharing.

Thus multi-level governance is important for two reasons. First, insofar as multi-level systems resemble federations, they may have some worth for institutional comparison. The institutions that systems like the European Union have developed to make and legitimate policies, and the arrangements they have put in place to cope with complexity and overlap in jurisdictions and policies, might all be useful for our investigation of how Canada currently pursues similar goals. Likewise, the experience of resolving disputes among partners to trade agreements can tell us much about the potential or the limitations of pacts that do not provide for collective autonomy. Second, multi-level governance is relevant to the following chapters because Canada, like almost every other state, is party to supranational agreements that have characteristics of multi-level governance. How federal systems interact with supranational decision-making bodies is particularly interesting because allocations of authority within the federation may limit the national government's ability to pursue policies at the international level, such as provincial jurisdiction over labour relations, which complicates negotiations with the International Labour Organization, while supranational agreements such as the World Trade Organization may restrict the autonomy of subunits even in areas of their exclusive constitutional jurisdiction. Moreover, Canada's diversity does not wholly respect provincial boundaries, and a number of challenges for local governance below the level of provinces require some thinking about multi-level regimes. Indigenous self-government presents another multi-level challenge for Canada, and the distinct needs and goals of the country's urban regions demonstrate that two autonomous orders of government may not be enough for the realization of self-government in this country.

Why Study Federalism?

Intellectual curiosity is ample reason for studying federalism. The lack of a single unified governance arrangement and the need for government units to negotiate and work together on the basis of consent make federalism both interesting and qualitatively different from other governmental and constitutional forms. How federal arrangements come into being, how they evolve, and why they persist are intriguing questions in their own right. At one point in the last century, when central government roles were expanding rapidly during the rise of the welfare state, some observers predicted that federalism would simply fade away (Laski, 1939). The reasons why it has in fact flourished, despite industrialization, globalization, and other developments, have sparked considerable discussion. At a minimum, most observers now agree that federalism has enormous staying power, even if they disagree on whether it makes for effective government and policy-making.

That staying power raises the practical question of whether federalism actually does make a difference. Would the type and nature of government services be qualitatively different in the absence of a federal system? Would particular policies have had different outcomes if only one government had been involved? Would the quality of health care in Canada, for example, be better, or worse, or at least different if the federal government had sole jurisdiction in this area? These questions are worth asking because they force us to think about the impact of intergovernmental relationships when we examine particular policy initiatives and the way federal structures and the intergovernmental process shape outcomes.

William Riker (1969) argued that federalism makes no difference whatsoever. Pairing federations with economically and culturally similar unitary systems—New Zealand and Australia, Britain and the US, for example—he noted that from an ordinary citizen's perspective it probably made little difference whether the system was federal or unitary, since the type and quality of services they would receive would likely be very similar. Furthermore, there was little difference between a federal and unitary system in terms of government spending in different policy areas.

Other writers, however, have seen things differently. Vincent Ostrom (1973), in a celebrated critique of Riker, notes that focusing strictly on levels of output is misleading. Federalism, according to Ostrom, allows particular communities to tailor their government services and their political lives much more closely to their specific needs. Citizens in one state or province, for example, may prefer to have fewer government services and pay lower taxes than those in other jurisdictions, or vice versa. Furthermore, federalism makes it possible to bring political accountability much closer to the people. A cabinet minister in Victoria, for example, who is accountable to the provincial legislature is much more meaningful to British Columbians in terms of access, transparency, and accountability than a cabinet minister based in Ottawa who is responsible for the same policy area but for the country as a whole.

Richard Vernon (1988) makes a similar point. Citing *The Federalist Papers* and James Madison's notion of the compound republic, he notes that different orders of government can act as checks on one another. He refers to Alexander Hamilton's notion that competition between two orders of government will make them more responsive to citizen preferences and demands. And he argues that the fixed boundaries and rules required by federalism help to protect minority rights and wishes against the excesses of majority rule. In the framework of a federal system, a group that exists as a minority in the nation as a whole can constitute a majority in the context of a state or province. If the regional government has jurisdiction over matters deemed crucial to the well-being of that national minority—education, for example—then federalism can make an important difference to that particular group.

Both Ostrom and Vernon stress that federalism also makes for a more complicated democracy, one that is probably less efficient and much more demanding of citizens than other types, though ultimately much more rewarding in terms of citizens' capacity to influence government decisions that affect them. In the absence of citizen engagement, or even basic citizen knowledge of how the system functions and affects government decision-making, federalism may not fully serve public interests. Particularly in Canada, the elite-centred nature of federalism and the secrecy surrounding intergovernmental processes suggest that federalism may not be fulfilling the promises claimed for it. Research suggests that citizens do have a hard time identifying who specifically is responsible for the policies that they live with (Cutler, 2004).

Therefore the question "Does federalism make a difference and in what way?" is an important one with respect both to specific policy areas and to the longer-term issues that will face the Canadian nation-state in the future. In this chapter we have looked at the basic architecture of federal systems and some of the crucial concepts and questions that we will examine more closely in subsequent chapters. Now that we have set the stage, we can briefly review the antecedents of the Canadian federation and the main factors—social, economic, and political—that have shaped its evolution over 140 years.

Questions for Critical Thought

1. What is the position of recent federal governments with respect to the preferred direction of the federation: more unitary and centralized, or more confederal and decentralized?

2. Do Canadians accept that Quebec is a nation and does it matter that the idea is not entrenched in the constitution?

3. Think about areas of public policy that matter most to you. How tolerant should we be of different policy outcomes in different provinces or territories? Do you trust the federal government to deliver a single national policy?

Notes

1. In this book we will generally use the term "order of government" rather than "level of government" to emphasize the independent and autonomous nature of governments in a federal system. "Level" implies a hierarchical relationship that may be apt in some circumstances but is generally not characteristic.

2. The United Kingdom has been evolving towards a type of federal arrangement for some time, given the devolved powers to the Scottish, Welsh, and Northern Ireland parliaments. Thus only England itself remains as a classically unitary system.

3. The metaphor comes from Lord Atkins's reasoning in the *Labour Conventions Reference*, A.C. 327 (1937).

4. Donald Smiley (1987) is credited with coining the term.

5. Elite accommodation is a key component in what is called "consociational democracy," a non-majoritarian mechanism for arriving at decisions in democratic political systems. See Lijphart (1977).

6. This definition draws from the work of Hooghe and Marks (2001), Brown (2002a), Bache and Flinders (2004), and Piattoni (2010).

References

Bache, I., and M. Flinders. 2004. *Multi-Level Governance*. Oxford: Oxford University Press.

Breton, A. 1985. "Supplementary Statement." *Report of the Royal Commission on the Economic Union and Development Prospects for Canada*. Ottawa: Supply and Services Canada.

Brown, D.M. 2002a. "Aspects of Multilevel Governance in Australia and Canada." Paper presented to Globalization, Multilevel Governance and Democracy: Continental, Comparative and Global Perspectives conference, Institute of Intergovernmental Relations, Queen's University, 3–4 May.

———. 2002b. *Market Rules: Economic Union Reform and Intergovernmental Policy-Making in Australia and Canada*. Montreal and Kingston: McGill–Queen's University Press.

Brunet-Jailly, E., A. Hurrelmann, and A. Verdun, eds. 2018. *European Union Governance and Policy Making: A Canadian Perspective*. Toronto: University of Toronto Press.

Cairns, A.C. 1971. "The Judicial Committee and Its Critics." *Canadian Journal of Political Science* 4, no. 3: 301–45.

———. 1977. "The Governments and Societies of Canadian Federalism." *Canadian Journal of Political Science* 10, no. 4: 695–725.

Cutler, F. 2004. "Government Responsibility and Electoral Accountability in Federations." *Publius* 34, no. 2: 19–38.

Diamond, M. 1961. "The Federalist's View of Federalism." In *Essays in Federalism*, edited by G.C.S. Benson. Claremont, CA: Claremont Men's College.

Dupré, J.S. 1988. "Reflections on the Workability of Executive Federalism." In *Perspectives on Canadian Federalism*, edited by R. Olling and M. Westmacott. Scarborough, ON: Prentice-Hall.

Elazar, D.J. 1962. *The American Partnership*. Chicago: University of Chicago Press.

Erk, J. 2007. *Explaining Federalism: State, Society and Congruence in Austria, Belgium, Canada, Germany, and Switzerland*. London: Routledge.

Gagnon, A. 2010. *The Case for Multinational Federalism: Beyond the All-encompassing Nation*. London: Routledge.

Grodzins, M. 1966. *The American System*. Chicago: Rand McNally & Company.

Gunlicks, A. 2003. *The Länder and German Federalism*. Manchester: Manchester University Press.

Harrison, K. 2006. "Provincial Interdependence: Concepts and Theories." In *Racing to the Bottom? Provincial Interdependence in the Canadian Federation*, edited by K. Harrison. Vancouver: University of British Columbia Press.

Hooghe, L., and G. Marks, 2001. *Multilevel Governance and European Integration*. Lanham, MD: Rowman & Littlefield.

Hueglin, T. 1999. *Early Modern Concepts for a Late Modern World: Althusius on Community and Federalism*. Waterloo, ON: Wilfrid Laurier University Press.

———. 2003. "Federalism at the Crossroads: Old Meanings, New Significance." *Canadian Journal of Political Science* 36, no. 2: 275–94.

King, P.T. 1982. *Federalism and Federation*. Baltimore: Johns Hopkins University Press.

Kymlicka, W. 1998. *Finding Our Way: Rethinking Ethnocultural Relations in Canada*. Toronto: Oxford University Press.

Ladner, K. 2003. "Treaty Federalism: An Indigenous Vision of Canadian Federalism." In *New Trends in Canadian Federalism*, 2nd edn, edited by F. Rocher and M. Smith. Peterborough, ON: Broadview Press.

Laski, H.J. 1939. "The Obsolescence of Federalism." *New Republic*: 367–9.

Lijphart, A. 1977. *Democracy in Plural Societies: A Comparative Exploration*. New Haven, CT: Yale University Press.

Lindquist, E.A. 1999. "Efficiency, Reliability, or Innovation? Managing Overlap and Interdependence in Canada's Federal System of Governance." In *Stretching the Federation: The Art of the State in Canada*, edited by R.A. Young. Kingston, ON: Institute of Intergovernmental Relations, Queen's University.

Livingston, W. 1952. "A Note on the Nature of Federalism." *Political Science Quarterly* 67, no. 1: 81–95.

———. 1956. *Federalism and Constitutional Change*. Oxford: Clarendon Press.

McRae, K.D., ed. 1974. *Consociational Democracy: Political Accommodation in Segmented Societies*. Toronto: McClelland and Stewart.

Ostrom, V. 1973. "Can Federalism Make a Difference?" *Publius* 3: 197–238.

Piattoni, S. 2010. *The Theory of Multi-Level Governance*. Oxford: Oxford University Press.

Riker, W. 1969. "Six Books in Search of a Subject or Does Federalism Exist and Does It Matter?" *Comparative Politics* 2, no. 1: 135–46.

Savoie, D. 1999. *Governing from the Centre: The Concentration of Power in Canadian Politics*. Toronto: University of Toronto Press.

Simeon, R. 2006 [1972]. *Federal–Provincial Diplomacy: The Making of Recent Policy in Canada*. Toronto: University of Toronto Press.

Simpson, J. 2001. *The Friendly Dictatorship*. Toronto: McClelland and Stewart.

Smiley, D.V. 1987. *The Federal Condition in Canada*. Toronto: McGraw-Hill Ryerson.

———and R.L. Watts. 1985. *Intrastate Federalism in Canada*. Toronto: University of Toronto Press.

Smith, J. 2005. "Institutionalism in the Study of Canadian Politics: The English-Canadian Tradition." In *New Institutionalism: Theory and Analysis*, edited by A. Lecours. Toronto: University of Toronto Press.

Taylor, C. 1991. "Shared and Divergent Values." In *Options for a New Canada*, edited by R.L. Watts and D.M. Brown, 55–76. Toronto: University of Toronto Press.

Vernon, R. 1988. "The Federal Citizen." In *Perspectives on Canadian Federalism*, edited by R. Olling and M. Westmacott. Scarborough, ON: Prentice-Hall.

Waite, P.B., ed. 1963. *The Confederation Debates in the Province of Canada, 1865*. Toronto: McClelland and Stewart.

Watts, R.L. 1999. *Comparing Federal Systems*, 2nd edn. Montreal and Kingston: McGill–Queen's University Press.

Wheare, K.C. 1963. *Federal Government*, 4th edn. London: Oxford University Press.

Chapter 2

The Economic, Social, and Institutional Bases of Canadian Federalism

Learning Objectives

- To understand the social, economic, and political underpinnings of the Canadian federal system.
- To understand why Canadians chose a federal form of government and how forces at play in the nineteenth century shaped the original federal constitution.
- To survey the changing population, economy, territory, and political culture of Canada, the effect of these changes on the evolving federal system since 1867, and how contemporary federal operations differ from the intent of the original constitution.
- To recognize the special cases of Quebec and Indigenous peoples as presenting unique challenges to the federal system.

How federations come into being and how they evolve over time are important questions. Examining them helps us understand how the legacies of previous political events, decisions, and institutions, as well as the socio-economic makeup of society, bear on the present and the dilemmas they pose for the future. In this chapter we identify the critical socio-economic, political, and institutional underpinnings of Canadian federalism and the factors that have shaped its development. In the course of this examination, three main themes emerge.

First is the asymmetry that underlies the Canadian federation. The largely French-speaking province of Quebec has made strong claims over the years for a special and, at times, separate status vis-à-vis the rest of Canada. A number of political practices and accommodations have evolved in recognition of this asymmetry, despite the absence of its formal recognition in the written constitution and the fact that at times other provinces, too, have asked for special treatment, if not status, in recognition of their own unique characteristics. The second theme is the awkward fit between the formal jurisdictions assigned to the two main orders of government, federal and provincial, and the realities of present-day social and economic life. Even though a number of major policy fields, including health care and education, belong to the provinces, the federal government uses its constitutional "spending power" (see Chapter 3) to play a role in those fields, partly because this is what citizens expect and partly for reasons of its own political and institutional self-interest. Finally, the third theme is the legacy of parliamentary institutions and executive federalism, which appears to limit both the opportunities for citizens to shape and participate directly in the making of public policy and, more generally, their capacity to exercise control over their political representatives.

Origins

In the previous chapter we discussed the rationale behind the adoption of a federal rather than a confederal or unitary form of government. Although there may be compelling reasons for choosing one form over another, the actual choice is usually determined by a variety of contingent, historical factors. Furthermore, once a formal federal arrangement is in place, subsequent developments may take it in a variety of directions. Both Australia and the United States were intended to be fairly decentralized federations. Instead, they evolved into relatively centralized ones, especially Australia. Canada, by contrast, was intended to be a highly centralized federation, with provinces representing little more than overgrown municipalities, at least in the eyes of John A. Macdonald. As we have seen, K.C. Wheare (1963: 19) labelled Canada's constitution "quasi-federal" since Ottawa had been assigned not only the residual powers but also the powers of disallowance and reservation. Over time, however, both powers fell into disuse, while judicial interpretation restricted the meaning of the residual powers, so that Canada, contrary to the intentions of at least some of the Founding Fathers, evolved into quite a decentralized federation.

As we noted in the previous chapter, some writers on federalism attribute both the choice of a federal form of governance and its character as it develops over time primarily to social and geographical factors. William Livingston (1952, 1956), for example, argued that federalism was largely a product of the society existing at the time. Other analysts, however, place the primary emphasis on the institutional framework. Foremost among these is the political scientist Alan Cairns. According to Cairns (1977: 698–9), "federalism, at least in the Canadian case, is a function not of societies but of the constitution, and more importantly of the governments that work the constitution." William Riker (1964), on the other hand, is much more inclined to emphasize political factors. He maintains that the US, Canada, and Australia were above all the products of the recession of empire. When colonies left the British Empire, whether through revolt or with Britain's approval (even encouragement), they needed to provide for defence and access to larger markets—necessities that until then had been supplied by the mother country.

Which perspective does more for our understanding is a question with no clear answer. The following review of some of the major points in Canada's development makes it clear that certain features of the 1867 constitution reflected the separate interests of the French- and English-speaking populations—first and foremost, of course, the creation of the separate provinces of Ontario and Quebec out of the United Province of Canada, in which Canada East and Canada West had lived together for more than 25 years. In some instances the Canadian constitution has perhaps taken us in unanticipated directions. Jurisdiction over natural resources has empowered a number of provinces and altered the dynamics of Canadian federalism in ways not anticipated by the Fathers of Confederation. Most developments seem to reflect some interaction between constitutional, political, and social factors. In part, the Canadian federation can be seen as the product of three empires—French, British, and American—each of which left a distinct legacy (Russell, 2017). The French legacy, obviously, is the francophone population and culture concentrated in Quebec but also present elsewhere. From Britain we inherited a set of political institutions that includes the Constitution Act of 1867 and the Westminster parliamentary model. The American influence can be seen in a variety of areas, but may be most evident in Canadians' expectation that as citizens they should be able to interact with government, despite the top-down form of representative democracy established by our constitutional makeup. Finally, one should keep in mind the role of Canada's Indigenous peoples and the manner in which they interacted with the three empires, sometimes as allies, at other times as subjugated people, and at yet other times as equals, especially at times when treaties were signed. These interactions, especially with British colonizers yielded important legacies, historical and legal (see Chapter 11), that are an important part of the framework within which Canadian governments and Indigenous peoples grapple with land claims and a host of other issues (Russell, 2017).

Before launching into the background of economy and geography, it is worth taking a closer look at the current day socio-economic features of the federation to see where we've come thus far. Table 2.1 provides data for each province and territory, including population, economic output and revenue dependency. The table illustrates the sharp differences between the larger and smaller provinces in population, and can also be compared with the spatial size differences illustrated in Figure 2.1. Just four provinces—Alberta, British Columbia, Ontario and Quebec—account for over 80 per cent of Canada's current population and 85 per cent of its national economy. And some provinces (not always the more populated ones) have much greater fiscal capacity than the others. All of these differences count in terms of the relative political clout and other resources that a provincial and territorial government can bring to their relations with other governments, especially the federal government, in the federation. These differences emerge frequently in the cases of intergovernmental relations covered in various chapters in this book.

Table 2.1 Provinces and Territories: Basic Socio-economic Features, 2017

	Population	Provincial Revenue from Federal Transfers%	Unemployment Rate	GDP per Capita
Canada	36,286,425	18.1	6.3	55,405
Newfoundland and Labrador	530,128	9.9	15.7	56,935
Prince Edward Island	148,649	33.5	10.0	42,157
Nova Scotia	949,501	30.7	7.9	42,640
New Brunswick	756,780	32.0	6.5	43,818
Quebec	8,326,089	20.3	5.8	46,126
Ontario	13,982,984	16.4	6.1	55,322
Manitoba	1,318,128	22.9	5.0	50,820
Saskatchewan	1,150,632	10.6	6.6	70,138
Alberta	4,252,879	12.6	7.8	78,100
British Columbia	4,751,612	13.1	5.3	53,267
Yukon	37,492	75.4	3.7	64,013
Northwest Territories	44,469	76.3	6.8	86,825
Nunavut	37,082	82.1	16.3	55,002

Sources: Authors' calculations based on data from Statistics Canada, accessed July 2017 at the following webpages: Labour force characteristics: https://www150.statcan.gc.ca/t1/tbl1/en/tv.action?pid=1410001702;
Population: http://www12.statcan.gc.ca/census-recensement/2016/dp-pd/hlt-fst/pd-pl/Table.cfm?Lang=Eng&T=101&S=50&O=A;
GDP: https://www150.statcan.gc.ca/t1/tbl1/en/tv.action?pid=3610022201;
Provincial revenue: Eisen and Lamman (2016).

Economy and Geography

One way of seeing how Canada's geography and economy have interacted with various social and political factors is to look at a map of North America (see Figure 2.1) and note how the northern part of the continent came to be colonized by France and Britain. For France, the St Lawrence was the main entry point into the North American interior, with trading routes eventually extending down the Ohio Valley, while British settlers concentrated on the Atlantic seaboard, using rivers such as the Hudson as their entry points into the interior. English and Scottish fur traders, in turn, entered the continent via Hudson Bay to compete with French fur traders in the West (Stevenson, 2012).

As a result of these geographic factors, two main competing trading routes developed. Conflict between the rival empires came to an end with France giving way to Britain after the latter had wrested away both its territory and its trading routes, first parts of Acadia in 1713, and then, in 1760, the rest of Acadia and New

Figure 2.1 Map of North America
Source: Map and Geospatial Information Collection, Dalhousie University.

France itself. By 1783, however, Britain itself was forced to recognize the new republican nation composed of the former 13 American colonies. Thus Britain in turn was compelled to give way, and ended up ceding most of the Ohio Valley.

Once the remaining British American colonies, including Quebec, had declined to join the 13 American colonies in revolt, their distinctive character was bolstered by the arrival of the Loyalists and affirmed by the War of 1812. Subsequent treaties between Britain and the United States confirmed the boundaries of 1783 and, beyond the Great Lakes, set the 49th parallel as the boundary all the way to the Oregon Country. In effect, these boundaries confirmed the presence of two separate economic and political systems.

What remained of the British North American west fell under the control of the Hudson's Bay Company. At the same time, in the St Lawrence River basin, trade in furs came to be replaced by trade in timber, grain, potash, and manufactured goods from the mother country (Creighton, 2002; Innis, 1956). In the latter half of the nineteenth century the transcontinental railway lines constructed in the US were replicated in Canada by the Canadian Pacific Railway, again reinforcing the pattern of dual economic–trading systems. Created out of the purchase of the North-Western Territory and Rupert's Land from the Hudson's Bay Company in 1870 and the ceding of the Arctic Islands by Britain to Canada in 1880, the Canadian North has been only sporadically involved in the development of the Canadian federation. As Frances Abele (1987: 311) has pointed out, for several decades after this purchase "the federal state was preoccupied with national consolidation south of the 60th parallel." It was only with the discovery of valuable minerals, such as gold in Yukon in the late 1890s, or when fears emerged that the US had designs on Canadian territory in the North, that authorities in Ottawa felt the need to create an administrative apparatus, beginning with the territorial government of Yukon, or to strike treaties with the Indigenous population. Otherwise, Canada had little incentive to integrate the North into the federation either economically or politically until the Second World War. Then the strategic importance of the North, both militarily and with respect to valuable mineral and energy deposits, became apparent. Later, in the post-war period, the need to recognize and accommodate the aspirations of Canada's Inuit became evident, a need that was partially met by the creation of the territory of Nunavut in 1999 by dividing the former Northwest Territories (NWT). Eighty-five per cent of Nunavut's population is Inuit, ensuring that the Indigenous people play the primary role in shaping the publicly elected government.

All three territorial governments are publicly elected and exercise powers comparable to those held by the provinces, except that—because of their limited fiscal capacities and the heavy administrative costs associated with small populations spread over vast territories—they are much more heavily dependent on Ottawa for financial support. In part because their political development took place much later and followed a different trajectory, the style of governance in the three territories is somewhat different from that in the rest of the country. Political parties play a much less important role and government legislation is much more likely to be developed and adopted on the basis of consensus (Cameron and White, 1995; Abele et al., 2009). Since the 1990s, as a result of the Charlottetown Accord process, the three territorial governments have participated in the various conferences of first ministers, premiers, and ministers, including the Council of the Federation founded in 2003. As we will see in Chapter 5, the consensus-based approach of territorial governments, together with their policy preferences on issues like climate change, has to some degree altered the character of these conferences.

Particularly since the advent of the Free Trade Agreement (FTA) in 1989 and the North American Free Trade Agreement (NAFTA) in 1994, the focus has been on north–south trade flows and linkages. Yet it is worth recalling that—except during a brief period of reciprocity between the US and British North America from 1854 to 1866—the predominant trading pattern in Canada has been east–west. The National Policy introduced by John A. Macdonald in 1879 had as its aim the opening up of the West through trade and immigration, the construction of the CPR, and tariff protection for local manufacturing. Thus east–west economic linkages were actively fostered well into the second half of the twentieth century. These east–west ties are still important for many Canadians and their governments. Even though, economically, Canada and its regions have become increasingly integrated into the North American economy as a whole—more than 75 per cent of our international trade is now with the US—we are still linked from east to west by our Canada-wide social safety net, the continuing importance of interprovincial trade, and, to a lesser extent, unique Canadian cultural institutions such as the CBC. Indeed, Courchene and Telmer (1998) have described our social programs as playing much the same role as the nineteenth-century CPR in linking the country together. Still, while our geography provides us with a common land mass, it also serves to attenuate linkages, if only because there is so much of it. As Mackenzie King stated in Parliament before the Second World War, when the storm clouds were gathering over Europe, "If some countries have too much history, then Canada has too much geography."

Now let us return to our map, and note that the main population centres of southern Ontario are separated from the vast expanse of thinly populated territory north of Lakes Huron and Superior. As anyone who has driven that stretch of the Trans-Canada Highway can testify, the landscape is mostly forested with many lakes and rock outcroppings—farms are rare and towns far apart. In many ways, this terrain of the Canadian Shield represents not only a physical but also a psychological and cultural barrier. By contrast, directly to the south of the lakes lies the heavily populated agricultural belt of the US Midwest.

The barrier that is the Canadian Shield also played a role in the settlement of the Canadian West. In the US, settlers gradually fanned out from the eastern seaboard through the Midwest and beyond, but in Canada many of the settlers who populated the West either moved north from the US or travelled directly there after arriving as immigrants, first from the UK and later from Eastern Europe. Except for those who moved west from other provinces in Canada or, until it joined the union in 1949, Newfoundland, there was little to tie the western Canadian settlers to the traditional political culture of eastern and central Canada. It is not surprising, therefore, that the old two-party system never really took hold in western Canada, a region that has instead tended to spawn sizable protest parties. The party system in the US has served to create a more unified and centralized federation, linking state parties with the national parties. In Canada, by contrast, the party system as such is not unified, although individual federal parties have been significant forces in national political integration. Indeed, at the provincial level Albertans founded the United Farmers of Alberta in the 1920s and the Social Credit Party in the 1930s, both of which made opposition to Ottawa and its basically central Canadian policies a mainstay of their election platforms and governing philosophy.

The Rocky Mountains have also been said to serve as a barrier, rendering British Columbia much more distinctive, as a society and a polity, than it might otherwise be. Still others have referred to the Ottawa Valley as a major demarcation line.[1] The five provinces to the east of the Ottawa River tend to lag behind the rest of the country economically; all five have depended on the federal government for equalization to compensate for the below-average fiscal capacities of their governments. Only Newfoundland and Labrador, as a result of offshore oil revenues, stopped qualifying for equalization, in 2008. In addition, especially in the Atlantic region, political practices until the 1990s followed a more traditional format, with more reliance on patronage and government grants as means of developing electoral support, and in three of the four provinces the traditional two-party system is still largely intact whereas in the West that system never really took root at all.

Provincial boundaries can reinforce geographic factors: the accidents of history have left the three Maritime provinces small in terms of territory, with no room for expansion. Quebec, Ontario, and Manitoba, however, started out small and grew large with additions from territory owned by the federal government, whereas Saskatchewan and Alberta were carved out directly from federal territory. Whether arbitrary or natural, provincial boundaries have a major effect in determining not only settlement patterns but provincial wealth, since each province owns and controls the natural resources within its borders.

Overall, Canada's economic makeup has been determined by its land mass, topography, and waterways. The country is heavily dependent on the production and export of basic commodities such as pulp, paper, lumber, energy products, and various metals. In every province, even highly industrialized Ontario, these sectors represent a significant proportion of the total economic activity, and in British Columbia and Alberta they are the dominant sectors by far. The same is true of the three territories (Yukon, NWT, and Nunavut). Much of the trade in these commodities involves exports to other countries, above all the United States. In 2015 more than 75 per cent of Canada's exports went to the US, a proportion that was only 55 per cent in 1985 (Statistics Canada, 2015).

Matters involving trade, both interprovincial and Canada–US, and economic development provide lots of fodder for intergovernmental debate (Hale, 2004; Skogstad, 2012). How should Canada handle trade disputes with the US? (Recent examples include softwood lumber, NAFTA, and agricultural supply management.) What can be done to reduce the remaining barriers to interprovincial trade, particularly since 2018 when the Supreme Court confirmed the narrow interpretation of section 121 of the Constitution Act, 1867 as it was originally intended, to allow the free movement of goods across provincial boundaries? What role should the provinces play in the crafting of international trade agreements? These are some of the issues currently on the intergovernmental agenda.

Canada's geography and economic life mean that transportation is another central theme. In fact, transportation in the form of railways was one of the driving forces behind Confederation, for under the Constitution Act, 1867 the federal government was to assume the public debt of each province when it joined the federal union. Both New Brunswick and Nova Scotia had gone heavily into debt subsidizing the construction of railways intended to link them with markets in central Canada and the US. Prince Edward Island, however, was virtually debt-free in 1867, and at first it declined the offer; but in 1871 it embarked on its own railway project, and by 1873 it too was ready to join Confederation, in part because Ottawa committed itself to providing "continuous steamship service" between PEI and the mainland. And it was largely on the strength of the promised transcontinental railway that British Columbia was enticed into joining Canada in 1871 (the Canadian Pacific Railway itself was not completed until 1885).

Transportation issues have frequently given rise to political discontent. Over the years, freight rates were a particular problem for manufacturers in the Maritimes and for prairie farmers. The high rates charged to transport grain were among the most important factors in the electoral success of protest parties: the Progressives in Manitoba, the United Farmers and Social Credit in Alberta, and the Co-operative Commonwealth Federation (CCF) in Saskatchewan. In some cases the governments formed by these parties found themselves in confrontation with Ottawa (over the printing of money in the case of Alberta); in others they introduced innovations that Ottawa eventually adopted (medicare in the case of Saskatchewan).

More generally, the West's greater vulnerability to international markets, the economic cycle, and climatic conditions, combined with perceived inequities in Ottawa's policies vis-à-vis the region, has traditionally led to tensions between the western provinces and the federal government. Although the arrival of free trade with the United States, beginning in 1989, effectively removed issues such as protective tariffs from the agenda and promoted north–south economic linkages, legacies from the past still make the western provinces sensitive to matters involving energy, transportation, environment, and trade, as illustrated by the highly acrimonious dispute between BC and Alberta over the Trans Mountain Pipeline (formerly owned by Kinder Morgan). When the US, for example, introduces substantial subsidies for agricultural producers, Ottawa is expected to provide remedies to enable Canadian producers to compete.

The opening up of the West through immigration, the provision of infrastructure by both federal and provincial governments, and the fostering of a domestic economy through tariffs and other measures meant that the creation of a transcontinental economy "was as much a political as an economic achievement" (Simeon and Robinson, 1990: 28). The federal government played a particularly active role in the early years—the era of the National Policy and the building of the transcontinental railway. It was Ottawa's liberal use of the declaratory and disallowance powers to take over provincial undertakings and overturn provincial legislation in this period that led Wheare to conclude that Canadian federalism was less than complete. After 1896, however, Ottawa took a more conciliatory approach in its relations with the provinces, helping to usher in what we might call the era of classical federalism, when governments really did try to maintain separate jurisdictions and the courts supported the "watertight compartments" approach to judicial interpretation.

In part, this development was a consequence of the position taken by Wilfrid Laurier's Liberal government, elected in 1896, which promised explicit recognition of provincial rights after its Conservative predecessor attempted to use remedial legislation to deal with the Manitoba Schools Crisis.[2] It was also the result, in part, of decisions by the Judicial Committee of the Privy Council (JCPC) of the United Kingdom, Canada's final court of appeal until 1949, which reflected a narrow interpretation of the "peace, order, and good government" clause in the 1867 Constitution Act (see Chapters 3 and 4) and took a more generous view of provincial jurisdiction over property and civil rights. Crucially, however, these interpretations also reflected changing economic imperatives.

By the turn of the twentieth century, natural resource extraction, steel production, and other manufacturing drew the provincial governments into a more important role in providing infrastructure such as roads and hydroelectric power. As well, since natural resources were owned by the provinces, forestry and mining companies increasingly needed to interact with provincial governments, making the latter more influential actors in the economic development process. Meanwhile, the urban growth that came with industrialization was also increasing the importance of the provinces, since municipal government was another area under provincial jurisdiction. The balance of power between federal and provincial governments was definitely beginning to shift towards the latter.

The Great Depression severely strained the finances of all provincial governments, pushing Saskatchewan and Alberta to the verge of bankruptcy. But this did not necessarily spell increased power for the federal government. The Conservative government of R.B. Bennett was only a late convert to the type of intervention introduced by the Roosevelt administration in the US. And even when the Bennett government did propose some New Deal–style measures, a number of them were rejected by the JCPC as going beyond federal jurisdiction. The Rowell-Sirois Royal Commission on Dominion–Provincial Relations, struck in 1938 to look at the financial implications of the Depression, did recommend some major changes to the distribution of powers and a greater centralization of fiscal power in Ottawa, along with what we now call equalization grants. However, that report was not released until 1940, and its recommendations were vigorously opposed by the three largest and richest provinces, Quebec, Ontario, and British Columbia (Smiley, 1978).

It was not until the arrival of the Second World War that the exigencies of a wartime economy shifted the balance back towards Ottawa. Among other things, a "tax rental" agreement was put in place under which the federal government effectively took over from the provinces a number of important tax fields, such as income tax, and then remitted a portion back to the provinces. After the war, it once again became evident that additional east–west infrastructure linkages were required—such as a cross-Canada highway network and a pipeline system to transport oil and natural gas from the western provinces to central Canadian markets. Also, the social and economic devastation and disruption of the 1930s and war years served as a major impetus to put in place a basic social safety net. Much of the proposed social programs were under provincial jurisdiction, but it was clear that Ottawa had both the will and the financial wherewithal to make them happen. Federal funding for post-secondary education was made available both to returning veterans and directly to universities. A Royal Commission on Arts and Letters (the Massey Commission) laid the groundwork for a more active federal role in the nation's educational and cultural activities: in addition to funding the government-owned CBC as a counterweight to American radio and television programming, in 1957 Ottawa created the Canada Council for the Arts (Black, 1975).

Support in the form of federal–provincial shared-cost agreements provided financing for the Trans-Canada Highway system, social assistance, and a variety of hospital and medical programs that ultimately became part of the full-scale medicare system introduced as a federal–provincial shared-cost program in all provinces from 1966 to 1970. This was the era of cooperative federalism, when officials at federal and provincial levels worked closely together to develop programs, whether the Trans-Canada Highway or labour market training programs (Dupré et al., 1973). In effect, these officials constituted policy communities of like-minded individuals who played a critical role in initiating and implementing joint federal–provincial programs. Although provinces such as Ontario and Alberta did not agree with the continuation of the tax rental agreements in the post-war period, they were happy to participate in a variety of federal programs. Quebec, however, did not always welcome federal funding. Among other things, Quebec ordered its universities not to accept direct funding from Ottawa, and for some time it refused to accept money available under the federally imposed tax rental agreements, arguing that such funds represented a federal intrusion in provincial jurisdiction.

This period of cooperative federalism was facilitated by Supreme Court decisions that made it possible for one government to delegate authority to an agency of another order of government under particular circumstances and provided a more liberal and centralist interpretation of the "peace, order, and good government" clause. Changing political and economic circumstances, along with the growing capacity of provincial governments to manage their political and economic affairs, made the post-war era of cooperative federalism relatively short-lived. During the 1960s Quebec, in particular, became more sophisticated in its demands for "opting-out" arrangements, based largely on what it considered its unique position in Confederation. On the economic front, perhaps the most important development was the first international oil shock, which came in 1973 when, as a result of actions initiated by the Organization of Petroleum Exporting Countries (OPEC) on behalf of oil-producing states, the world market for energy was radically altered and energy prices rose dramatically. Since energy in the form of oil, natural gas, and hydroelectric power is under provincial jurisdiction, this altered the balance not just between Ottawa and the provinces but also between provinces themselves, making some—notably Alberta, with its vast oil and gas reserves, and Quebec, with its hydro power—substantially better off than others (Doern and Toner, 1985). The oil shock ushered in a period of what has been labelled competitive federalism, which extended throughout the 1980s into the 1990s.

Efforts by the federal government, with the support of Ontario, to impose made-in-Canada pricing for oil and natural gas made for battles that were at times extremely bitter, most notably the fight over the National Energy Program introduced by the Trudeau government in 1980. The provinces began a counterattack to protect their jurisdiction, resulting ultimately in the natural resource amendment, section 92A, which was added in 1982 to the Constitution Act, 1867 and effectively saw the federal government concede primary control over natural resources to the provinces.

The imbalanced resource endowments of the provinces also strained the financial resources of the federal government, since Ottawa, through the Equalization Program introduced in 1957, was committed to raising the fiscal capacity of the have-not provinces to a level that would allow them to deliver basic public services comparable to those in the country as a whole. Despite efforts to control increases in provincial entitlements—by reducing the weight of energy revenues in the equalization formula, using a five-provinces standard that excluded Alberta rather than a national average; and by capping increases in social welfare transfers to the better-off provinces—Ottawa's deficit continued to grow.

Finally, in 1995 the federal government reduced its overall transfers to the provinces and at the same time, under the rubric of "program review," began systematically withdrawing from a number of program areas in the name of reducing overlap and duplication (Aucoin and Savoie, 1998). Although it was keen to maintain a strong presence in areas such as health care, it was willing to give the provinces more flexibility and authority in areas such as social assistance and the environment—in part because it recognized that it was now providing much less funding to the provinces than it had done in the past.

By the turn of the millennium Ottawa and the provinces did reach a rapprochement of sorts. Several provinces put forward the idea of committing themselves to the idea of a Canadian "social union" in recognition of both the importance of the social safety net and the primary responsibility of the provinces in this regard. In 1999 Ottawa and all the provinces except Quebec signed the Social Union Framework Agreement (SUFA), committing them to put more funding into areas such as health care and closer collaboration on future initiatives in the social policy field. (SUFA is explored in greater detail in Chapter 7.) At the time many argued that Canada was entering a new area of "collaborative federalism." Subsequently, however, skepticism grew over the fact that Ottawa and the provinces made little progress in resolving their differences over how best to reform the health-care system. Furthermore, although Quebec had refused to sign the agreement, it remained eligible for the benefits available to all the other provinces and territories. The unique positions within the federation of both Quebec and the Indigenous peoples, and the profound role that Quebec in particular has played in shaping the behaviour of all provinces, require closer discussion, found in Chapters 11 and 12. Here it will suffice to stress a few key points to complete our discussion of the general social and institutional setting of the federal system.

Two Special Cases of Diversity and Asymmetry: Quebec and Indigenous Peoples

Both Quebec and Indigenous peoples are special cases in the federation. Quebec, of course, is home to the largest concentration of Canada's francophones, our largest national minority. Moreover, the Québécois, who can be defined as all persons living in Quebec, are also considered a national community within Canada. The position of Indigenous peoples is also unique. As a collectivity they are a significant national minority. In addition, many Indigenous communities may be considered as nations. There are a variety of types of Indigenous governments and many Indigenous communities aspire to greater autonomy and more resources but, unlike Quebec and the other provinces, no Indigenous government is as yet a formal constituent partner in the federation.[3]

Quebec has had a tremendous influence on the creation and subsequent history of the Canadian federation. What is now the southern, most populated part of Quebec was part of the United Province of Canada from 1841 to 1867. As a predominantly French-speaking and Roman Catholic society, Canada East (as it was called) continued to demonstrate strongly separate features distinguishing it from Canada West (now Ontario). Its desire to return to a position of much greater autonomy, but within a federal union, provided a significant rationale for Confederation in 1867. Also, the particular needs of Quebec—to protect its majority language and religion, to preserve its unique code in civil law, and to secure control over education, health, and related matters—shaped directly the distribution of powers in the federation.

For much of Canada's first century, Quebec remained a strong defender of the original federal bargain with its emphasis on provincial autonomy. Quebec society was transformed during its "Quiet Revolution" of the 1960s, from an inward-oriented conservative society content with a small role for government to a more expansive, progressive society supporting enhanced powers for the Quebec state to promote and protect its French-majority society. This led Quebec into significant conflict with the rest of Canada, especially the federal government in Ottawa, over the nature and direction of national development, social programs, and fiscal relations, among other issues. Even where relations were not especially conflictual, Quebec continued to take positions in the intergovernmental arena that reflected its unique traditions and special characteristics, often with very different views and strategies compared with other provinces.

The provincial government of Quebec began a significant trend to buck the prevailing centralization of the Canadian state that had been building since the beginning of the Second World War, a trend that gradually included the other provinces. What's more is that the Quiet Revolution ushered a 30-year period of intense debate about Quebec's (and Canada's) very existence, as Quebecers explored a variety of potential options for major reform of the existing constitutional regime, including special status, independence, sovereignty-association, equal partnership, and asymmetrical federalism. The details of this profound debate are dealt with elsewhere in this book, including Chapter 12, but suffice here to say that Quebec became a catalyst for a major questioning of the federalism regime as it existed prior to the 1960s as well as for major reform. The Quebec agenda drove the process at first but was ultimately joined by other players and other agendas as well.

Indigenous peoples have been prominent in constitutional politics over the last half-century, dating to the federal government's failed White Paper on Indian Policy of 1969 (see Chapter 11). While today forming only a small minority—about 5 per cent—of Canada's overall population, their cultures and social conditions are unique and of a different order from the growing multicultural diversity of the general population, and their recognized Aboriginal rights because of having prior occupancy of the land, as well as historical treaties that many groups reached with France, Britain or Canada, have provided an increasingly significant role in the national polity. There are major problems but also much promise in the relationships of these peoples to the Canadian state. Many Indigenous communities remain marginalized with significant economic and social challenges. The promise is one of transcending the colonial past and of their peoples entering into a genuine political partnership, including power-sharing, with the other constituent communities of the federation.

A major relic of the colonial past, namely the Indian Act regime, continues to play an important role. Through this legislation, in place in one form or another since the 1870s, the federal government has managed reserve lands and resources in trust for many Indigenous groups and established the delegated authority of Indian band government. While the Indian Act continues to operate, there are now co-existing governance models including traditional governance; new self-governing arrangements authorized by modern land claim agreements; regional governments; and the territorial public government of Nunavut, which has a majority Inuit population. The 600-plus reserve/band councils structured under the Indian Act are also undergoing a degree of change. The role of all of these governing models and the extent to which they match the aspirations and needs of Canada's diverse Indigenous population are dealt with more fully in Chapter 11.

The movement towards greater Indigenous autonomy, self-determination, and control is part of a broader movement of Indigenous nationalism that receives inspiration from global post-colonial movements but also, closer to home, from the example of Quebec nationalism. It is too soon to tell if recently devised Indigenous governance arrangements will fit fully into the existing mould of inter-governmental relationships in the federal structure or if a more parallel form of relationship will emerge, such as expressed in the concept of "treaty federalism" (White, 2002). The challenge for Canada may seem less urgent and threatening than the Quebec secession movement has been, but the growth and development of Indigenous governance will transform multi-level governance and will remain an important set of issues in the intergovernmental agenda.

Summary

Geography, the legacies of empire both French and British, the presence of Indigenous peoples, the waves of immigration from the late nineteenth century onward, and the proximity of the United States—a country with nearly nine times our population and 10 times our GDP—have all left their imprint on the Canadian federation. To be sure, Canada's constitutional and institutional arrangements have helped to shape the way Canadian federalism has functioned over the years. And those arrangements largely continue to define the setting, arenas, and actors that constitute the Canadian intergovernmental system today.

But a good part of the original Constitution Act also reflected the socio-logical reality of Canada in 1867. Provincial jurisdiction over education and social and health needs, for example, was a major concern of the largely Catholic, French-speaking population of Canada East (Quebec). Linguistic duality has continued to be a major feature of the Canadian polity, and is directly reflected in the fact that Quebec has its own pension plan and blood collection agency (to cite but two examples), separate from the standard Canadian versions. Geographic distance and significant immigration from a variety of non-English-speaking countries starting in the late nineteenth century helped infuse western Canada with quite a different political character, which has also had a profound influence on its position in Confederation. Post-war immigration changed Canada's demographics even further, altering the character of major urban centres and giving rise to a set of demands for services that do not fit comfortably into the traditional federal framework (Gibbins, 1999). At times, all these linguistic and regional divisions appear to be fault lines that, under the right circumstances, could well open un-bridgeable chasms, though so far this has never quite come to pass.

Exploring the interaction between social forces and federal institutions re-veals significant disparities between the vision of federalism set out in 1867 and the practice of federalism in Canada today. The original Constitution Act may have reflected the societal norms and values and socio-economic conditions that prevailed in 1867, but the passage of time has made many of its provisions anachronistic. First, there is now an enormous gulf between the constitutional principle of provincial equality in relation to the federal government and the asymmetrical nature of the arrangements made to accommodate Quebec and the Indigenous peoples in practice today. Second, an equally enormous gulf exists between the formal responsibilities and jurisdictions of the two orders of gov-ernment as laid out in the constitution and the practical realities—in particular, what has come to be expected of Ottawa with respect to the costly responsibil-ities assigned to provincial governments. Ottawa has become intimately involved in these areas of provincial jurisdiction—albeit primarily as financier and with perhaps only modest influence—largely through the use of the federal spending power. Only in recent years, especially during the majority Conservative govern-ment in 2011–15, had the federal government actively promoted a more classical view of federalism with a more limited role for Ottawa. This position has not been as strongly embraced by the Justin Trudeau government since 2015, but thus far one could not say that it has been fully overturned. How the general imbalance between constitutional jurisdiction and political reality is reconciled in the con-text of federal–provincial negotiation is a frequent theme throughout this book.

Finally, a third disparity (often referred to as the "democratic deficit") is the one between the traditions of parliamentary democracy and the expectations of citizens that they should be able to influence policy and restrain executive power. The cornerstone of parliamentary democracy is the nineteenth-century notion of representative and responsible government—a notion appropriate to an era of strong political parties and limited citizen participation in political life (Sharman, 1990). As noted in Chapter 1, executive federalism is in large part rooted in this Westminster-style parliamentary government.

Among the most important societal changes over the past three decades has been a general increase in the numbers of well-educated, critically minded cit-izens. These people are much less deferential than their predecessors, and they are less accepting of the secretive and elitist nature of contemporary executive federal-ism (Nevitte, 1996). As will become evident in later chapters, executive federalism is still alive and well in many respects, despite warnings that its death is imminent. Nonetheless, changes in the environment in which executive federalism operates put considerable strain both on the actors directly involved in intergovernmental bargaining and on the system as a whole. In particular, the de facto understand-ings surrounding Quebec's position in Confederation largely reflect the views of intergovernmental elites, not the general public. The asymmetrical federalism exemplified by SUFA, the 2004 Health Care Accord (which included a codicil explicitly endorsing asymmetry for Quebec), and the 2006 House of Commons resolution recognizing the Québécois as "a nation within a united Canada" are all examples of such de facto understandings. They are also products of the elite accommodation that is still part of modern-day executive federalism in Canada.

Questions for Critical Thought

1. How would the federal constitution be designed if Canadians were to start over completely today?

2. How does globalization affect the way that Canadians relate to one another? Does it make us more united, or more diverse, than ever before?

3. How important is the concept of constitutional symmetry in our federation—i.e., that all constituent units have identical status? How far can or should Canadians go to accommodate "asymmetry," whether for Quebec, for the Indigenous peoples, or for some other community?

Notes

1. See Bliss (2000). Jennifer Smith (2002) has written a critical commentary on this perspective of "old versus new Canada," arguing that with respect to its assessment of political culture and dependency in Atlantic Canada that it is exaggerated or misleading.

2. In 1890 the Manitoba government abolished support for denominational schools, whose status had been protected under the Manitoba Act of 1870, which provided for the protection of the new province's largely French-speaking Roman Catholic minority. The same Act contained a provision that allowed Ottawa to intervene with remedial legislation in the event that the rights of either Catholics or Protestants were not respected by the provincial government. The province's abolition of denominational schools and use of French in the courts and the legislature was seen as a major affront to the rights of French Canadians throughout the country, resulting in a nationwide controversy. Although the federal Conservative government presented remedial legislation to Parliament in 1896, it was never passed and the government itself was defeated the same year. The subsequent Liberal government under Laurier brokered a compromise with Manitoba, under which limited support was provided for French-language instruction and religious education within the public school system.

3. Note that Nunavut has a so-called public government that happens to be largely controlled by Inuit, but it is not an Indigenous government per se.

References

Abele, F. 1987. "Canadian Contradictions: Forty Years of Northern Political Development." *Arctic* 40, no. 4: 310–20.

———, T. Courchene, L. Seidle, and F. St-Hilaire, eds. 2009. *Northern Exposure: Peoples, Powers and Prospects in Canada's North*. Montreal: Institute for Research on Public Policy.

Aucoin, P., and D.J. Savoie, eds. 1998. *Managing Strategic Change: Learning from*

Program Review. Ottawa: Canadian Centre for Management Development.

Black, E.R. 1975. *Divided Loyalties: Canadian Concepts of Federalism*. Montreal and Kingston: McGill-Queen's University Press.

Bliss, M. 2000. "The Fault Lines Deepen." *Globe and Mail*, 2 May.

Cairns, A.C. 1977. "The Governments and Societies of Canadian Federalism." *Canadian Journal of Political Science* 10, no. 4: 695–725.

Cameron, K., and G. White. 1995. *Northern Governments in Transition: Political and Constitutional Development in the Yukon, Nunavut and the Western Northwest Territories*. Montreal: Institute for Research on Public Policy.

Courchene, T.J., and C. Telmer. 1998. *From Heartland to North American Region State: The Social, Fiscal and Federal Evolution of Ontario*. Toronto: Centre for Public Management, University of Toronto.

Creighton, D.G. 2002. *The Commercial Empire of the St-Lawrence*, revised edn. Toronto: University of Toronto Press.

Doern, G.B., and G. Toner. 1985. *The Politics of Energy: The Development and Implementation of the NEP*. Toronto: Methuen.

Dupré, J.S., D.M. Cameron, G.H. McKechnie, and T.B. Rotenberg. 1973. *Federalism and Policy Development: The Case of Adult Occupational Training in Ontario*. Toronto: University of Toronto Press.

Eisen, B., and C. Lammam. 2016. "Federal Transfers to the Provinces at an All-Time High." *Commentary*, 12 Jan. https://www.fraserinstitute.org/article/federal-transfers-to-the-provinces-at-an-all-time-high.

Gibbins, R. 1999. "Taking Stock: Canadian Federalism and Its Constitutional Framework." In *How Ottawa Spends, 1999–2000*, edited by L. Pal. Toronto: Oxford University Press.

Hale, G.H. 2004. "Canadian Federalism and the Challenge of North American Integration." *Canadian Public Administration* 47, no. 4: 497–524.

Innis, H. 1956. *The Fur Trade in Canada*, revised edn. Toronto: University of Toronto Press.

Livingston, W. 1952. "A Note on the Nature of Federalism." *Political Science Quarterly* 67, no. 1: 81–95.

———. 1956. *Federalism and Constitutional Change*. Oxford: Clarendon Press.

Nevitte, N. 1996. *The Decline of Deference: Canadian Value Change in Cross-National Perspective*. Peterborough, ON: Broadview Press.

Riker, W.H. 1964. *Federalism: Origin, Operation, Significance*. Boston: Little, Brown.

Russell, P.H. 2017. *Canada's Odyssey: A Country Based on Incomplete Conquests*. Toronto: University of Toronto Press.

Sharman, C. 1990. "Parliamentary Federations and Limited Government: Constitutional Design and Redesign in Australia and Canada." *Journal of Theoretical Politics* 2, no. 2: 205–30.

Simeon, R., and I. Robinson, 1990. *State, Society, and the Development of Canadian Federalism*. Toronto: University of Toronto Press.

Skogstad, G. 2012. "International Trade Policy and the Evolution of Canadian Federalism." In *Canadian Federalism: Performance, Effectiveness, and Legitimacy*, 3rd edn, edited by H. Bakvis and G. Skogstad. Toronto: Oxford University Press.

Smiley, D.V., ed. 1978. *The Rowell-Sirois Report: An Abridgement of Book I of the Royal Commission Report on Dominion–Provincial Relations*. Toronto: Macmillan of Canada.

Smith, J. 2002. "Atlantic Canada at the Start of the New Millennium." In *Canada: The State of the Federation 2001: Canadian Political Culture(s) in Transition*, edited by H. Telford and H. Lazar. Montreal and Kingston: McGill-Queen's University Press.

Statistics Canada. 2015. "International Trade." https://www150.statcan.gc.ca/n1/en/subjects/international_trade.

Stevenson, G. 2012. "The Political Economy of Regionalism and Federalism." In *Canadian Federalism: Performance, Effectiveness, and Legitimacy*, 3rd edn, edited by H. Bakvis and G. Skogstad. Toronto: Oxford University Press.

Wheare, K.C. 1963. *Federal Government*, 4th edn. London: Oxford University Press.

White, G. 2002. "Treaty Federalism in Northern Canada: Aboriginal–Government Land Claims Boards." *Publius* 32, no. 3: 89–114.

Chapter 3

The Constitution and Constitutional Change

Week 4

Learning Objectives

- To understand the importance of constitutional jurisdiction to the foundation of government roles in a federation.
- To appreciate the most important written and unwritten constitutional elements that have influenced Canada's political development.
- To review why and how the constitution has been changed over the 150 years of the federation—and why constitutional reform is so difficult to achieve.

Intergovernmental relations are in large part a response to the constitutional relationship between the provincial and federal governments. The constitution serves as a blueprint for the assignment of governmental responsibilities and entitlements. Constitutionally defined jurisdiction, perhaps more than any other structural factor, determines the relative weights of the resources available to each order of government in its interactions with the other. With some notable exceptions, constitutional resources are generally quite stable. Provinces can grow and shrink in population or economic might (both of which constitute resources in the intergovernmental game), and they may have more or less influence on the leaders in the national legislature and government; but their constitutional resources remain fairly static. By specifying the procedures that would be required to alter those resources in the future, a constitution gives the deceptive impression that it would be easy to change. In Canada's case no clear formal procedures existed in the written constitution until the major amendments of 1982. Even since then, the original 1867 constitution has proven rather durable. Although constitutional issues have been a perennial preoccupation of the intergovernmental elite for much of Canada's history, the constitution itself, with some exceptions, has not been easily altered.

The constitution allocates legislative authority. For the federal and provincial governments alike, the scope of possible activity is limited to what the constitution permits their respective legislatures to do. If a government wants to embark on an ambitious new social program or grant permission for a large-scale resource-extraction project, it has to have the legislative authority to make the necessary laws. Otherwise it will be obliged to work cooperatively with the government that does have that authority. Legislative jurisdiction matters to intergovernmental relations because it defines the kinds of issues that will be hardest fought in the intergovernmental arena and the degree of influence that governments can have over one another's interests.

At the same time, jurisdiction can represent a substantial burden for a government with limited financial resources. The vertical fiscal imbalance characteristic of Canadian federalism (discussed at length in Chapter 6) is largely a product of the fact that the constitution assigned the provinces more legislative jurisdiction than fiscal capacity. Historically, the federal government has tried to use its spending power to help the provinces acquit their responsibilities. Constitutionally, this power is one of the federal government's most important assets, allowing it to play a creative role in areas over which the provinces have exclusive law-making control.

That Canada has a federal constitution is a result of the sociological, economic, and geographical factors discussed in Chapter 2. But the kind of federal constitution Canada has also reflects the lessons learned from pre-Confederation constitutional history and other nations' experience with federalism. The legacy of imperial arrangements and the Confederation-era experience of other federations, in particular the United States during its Civil War, shaped important features of the constitution that governments and citizens still encounter today (J. Smith, 1988; D.E. Smith, 1995). The same influences also account for the dominance of the executive level in Canadian intergovernmental relations. Although federal practice might be advertised as flexible and responsive, federal constitutions are reasonably fixed in character. This gives governmental actors a degree of certainty about the arrangements of the federation, and lets citizens know which government to hold accountable for particular aspects of public policy, good or bad (Trudeau, 1968). Even so, every constitution requires interpretation and adjustment from time to time. In most federations interpretation is provided by the innovative practices of governmental actors and by the authoritative readings of the legal language of the constitution by high courts (Baier, 2006). Formal adjustment through the alteration of constitutional text is usually provided for in a constitutional amendment procedure that gives some role to the subunits and central government in the development and approval of constitutional changes.

This chapter outlines the constitutional blueprint that informs present-day intergovernmental relations in Canada and explains some of the social and philosophical underpinnings of the choices made at the time of Confederation. While the evolution of the constitution through interpretation will be addressed in Chapter 4, this chapter includes a discussion of constitutional change, both achieved and otherwise, as it relates to the key jurisdictions affecting intergovernmental relations.

Canada's Constitutional Development

The Canadian constitution is perhaps not an ideal federal constitution. For starters, it is a mix of written and unwritten elements. The Constitution of the United States of America is much more codified and consequently even revered as a single, cohesive document. In the United Kingdom, unwritten rules and traditions play a more substantial role than any single document or charter. The Canadian constitution is a conscious amalgam of these two traditions. Although matters such as the exercise of legislative and executive power were spelled out in the British North America (now Constitution) Act, 1867, there was already an understanding that the institutions of government would work differently in practice. The unwritten elements of the constitution are referred to as conventions and the Canadian constitutional system relies heavily on them. Conventions are traditions and rules that are not legally binding but are enforced in the political sphere. That is to say, the only sanction for violating a convention is a political one (Heard, 2014). For example, the prime minister will generally respect the convention of appointing ministers to his or her cabinet in a way that represents all the provinces and regions of the country. A prime minister who failed to do so could not be legally penalized for ignoring this convention. Come election time, however, the prime minister's party might not fare so well in an unrepresented region. This would be an example of a political sanction.

Conventions are important in constitutional law because they serve to modify elements of the written constitution. This is especially true of the institution of responsible government, or the relationship between the executive and legislative branches of both provincial and federal governments. The Constitution Act, 1867 pledges Canada to a constitution "similar in principle" to that of the United Kingdom. With that simple phrase, the traditions of parliamentary government, particularly the reliance on convention to govern the behaviour of political actors, was imported wholesale into the Canadian constitutional order. The executive power in the written constitution is assigned to the governor general, who serves as the Crown's representative for Canada at the national level. Similar provisions exist for the provinces in the form of the lieutenant governors, who, though appointed by the federal government, represent the Crown proper—not the federal Crown[1]—and therefore enjoy considerable autonomy with respect to Ottawa.

On paper these offices appear to be very powerful. However, their occupants understand they exercise their authority only on the advice of a cabinet chosen from the elected branch. Thus, in practice, representatives of the Crown treat such advice as an order or instruction. The selection of the advisory cabinet is also a matter of convention: the role of providing advice to the Crown goes to the group or party most likely to enjoy the confidence of the legislative chamber. Even though none of these practices is clearly stipulated by the written constitution, they have enormous import for the practice of Canadian politics and federalism.

Because the cabinet secures its legitimacy by holding the confidence of the elected house, it is able to implement its programs and policies quite efficiently. This is particularly true when the advisers come from a party that has the majority of seats in the legislature and through strong party discipline can expect to maintain majority support. Under these circumstances the executive becomes extraordinarily free to direct the state and government policy in a direction commensurate with its goals. Since this is true for all governments in the Canadian system, it is executives, not legislators, who have the greatest say in what the public sector does. Not coincidentally, if there are coordination problems between governments, the executives of each order become the main conduits for their resolution. As discussed in Chapter 1, the responsible government model is the primary reason why executive federalism has become the dominant mode of intergovernmental interaction and accommodation in Canada. In this case the unwritten elements of the constitution may have as much influence on the shape and nature of the federal system as the written elements. This arrangement stands in contrast to the standard account of federal constitutionalism.

The written components of Canada's constitution still have some role to play, of course. Probably the most familiar of those components are what is often referred to as entrenched constitutional law, beginning with the Constitution Act, 1867 and its successor, the Constitution Act, 1982. Of the lesser-known pieces of Canada's entrenched constitutional law, some predate Confederation (e.g., orders from the imperial Crown and laws of the imperial Parliament such as the Royal Proclamation of 1763 and the Act of Union) and others were ratified after as amendments (e.g., the various terms of union under which individual provinces entered Confederation, the Statute of Westminster, 1931, and the Bill of Rights, 1960).

A second category of written constitutional law consists of ordinary statutes. These pieces of legislation deal with matters such as the electoral franchise, the creation of courts, and even human rights standards. Theoretically, these elements of the constitution are the most malleable, since they can be replaced by a simple Act of the legislature that created them. Together, these statutes make up a significant portion of what we might refer to as constitutional law. Some are recognized as a part of the written constitution (by section 52 of the Constitution Act, 1982) and others have such a status simply by the nature of their subject matter.

For the purposes of this chapter our focus will be on entrenched constitutional law, in particular the Constitution Acts of 1867 and 1982. Entrenched law, after all, is most formally relevant to the organization of the federal system. Conventions and ordinary statutes may play a critical role in the operation of the federal system, but they do not directly affect the apportioning of actual legal jurisdiction. Moreover, entrenched constitutional law also is responsible for some of the formal institutions of the federation, including the Senate and the constitutional amending formula.

Pre-Confederation Documents

Canada's constitutional history closely reflects its former status as a group of colonies in the British Empire. Both the 1867 and 1982 Acts were simple statutes of the United Kingdom's Parliament. Those Acts are still in operation today, but since their patriation in 1982 they have become wholly Canadian documents. Other imperial statutes and documents are no longer in effect, but in their time gave critical direction to the nature and substance of the present Canadian constitution. The most important of those documents are discussed below.

The earliest Canadian constitutional document is generally recognized to be the Royal Proclamation of 1763, which today is commonly cited as the first document to recognize the rights of Canada's Indigenous peoples. In addition to pledging the protection of the Crown to "the several Nations or Tribes of Indians" in their dealings with Europeans, the proclamation imposed British law over the former territory of New France, abolishing the practice of the French civil law in the new colony of "Quebec"—an area roughly consisting of the French-settled areas along the St Lawrence River. The Proclamation also provided for a representative assembly, although no such body ever had the opportunity to meet.

Nine years later, the Quebec Act, 1774 expanded "Quebec" to include much of what was later to be the province of Ontario. Importantly, it also restored the practice of the French civil law, at least until such time as the colony itself should choose to discontinue it, and provided freedom of worship for Roman Catholics in the colony. One other significant respect in which the Quebec Act differed from the 1763 document was that it failed to provide for an elected assembly, instead creating an appointed legislative council to advise the governor—a precursor to modern responsible government without the democratic foundation of an elected legislature (Russell, 2017).

The most immediate constitutional consequence of the American Revolution for Canada was the adoption of the Constitutional Act, 1791. The numerous Loyalists who repaired to the Maritimes and the colony of Quebec had bristled at some of the restrictions inherent in the governance structures provided by the Quebec Act, particularly the institution of an appointed council; the American dissenters were loyal to the Crown, but had become accustomed to electing a representative assembly and exercising some degree of control over their own community's affairs. The new Act divided the colony of Quebec into Upper and Lower Canada and provided for elected assemblies in each of these colonies.

After the rebellions of the 1830s, Lord Durham was sent to British North America to assess the state of the colonies. His famous report advised the adoption of responsible government and the reunification of Upper and Lower Canada in order to integrate and eventually assimilate the French-speaking population into the now larger English-speaking population. These recommendations were institutionalized by the Act of Union, 1840, which—motivated by the need to give greater self-governing powers to the colonies—provided for a representative assembly. With continued pressure for greater self-government from the colonists themselves, responsible government was achieved within a decade.

As we have noted before, responsible government is central to the way Canadian federalism has evolved. In January 1848 Nova Scotia became the first colony to dismiss its legislative council for failing to maintain the confidence of the elected assembly. Two other colonies followed suit within the same year: United Canada in March and New Brunswick in December (J. Smith, 1999). The achievement of responsible government did not come from a change in the written constitutional law, but from a change in how colonial governors interpreted their powers under the conventions of responsible government. While colonial law still gave the governor the ultimate legal power, the evolution of responsible government left the provision of advice to the governor in the hands of a delegation that held the confidence of the elected assembly.

Confederation and the British North America Act, 1867

The British North America (BNA) Act (renamed under Canadian law in 1982 as the Constitution Act, 1867) brought federalism to Canada. It united some (but not all) of the colonies of British North America, laid out a federal constitutional framework assigning different powers of legislation to the federal and provincial orders, and outlined the basic institutions of Parliament. Among the latter was the Senate of Canada, an institution intended to serve as a forum for the representation of regional interests at the national level.

From the viewpoint of intergovernmental relations, an important feature of the BNA Act was its pledge that Canada would have a constitution "similar in principle to that of the United Kingdom." This simple phrase transferred to the new Dominion government the majority of conventions and traditions of parliamentary government already in practice in the colonies. With those traditions came a logic that led to the eventual dominance of executives in both the national and the provincial orders of government. This early pledge to uphold British-style parliamentary values, in preference to congressional/presidential or other forms of government, created the structures that ensure executive dominance. Executive federalism, with all its democratic deficiencies, is the result not so much of the choice to implement federalism, as of the commitment to maintain a dominant parliamentary executive.

Nevertheless, perhaps the most significant feature of the BNA Act for intergovernmental relations was the division of powers contained largely in sections 91 and 92. Unlike many other federal constitutions, the BNA Act provides lists of legislative responsibilities for both the federal and the provincial levels of government.

Most other constitutional federations have enumerated the powers of one level of government and left the remainder or residue to the other. This was the American practice, later emulated by the Australians, who rejected the Canadian form. Still, any division of powers has to account for the unforeseen. The American and Australian form presumes to do so by leaving whatever is not enumerated to the states, which as colonies had unitary legislative power—that is to say that all matters open to a legislature could be enacted by that government. The Canadian model did not presume to cover every eventuality, but also sought to give greater clarity to what powers specifically belonged to each of the two orders of government. Thus section 91 of the Constitution Act lists 28 legislative responsibilities for the federal Parliament, including postal service, national defence, the regulation of trade and commerce, and the criminal law. Parliament is also assigned a general power to make laws for the "peace, order, and good government" of the country. This provision (often referred to as the POGG clause) has been generally understood to afford the federal government the capacity to legislate in areas beyond the 28 powers enumerated in section 91, including areas not otherwise identified by the constitution. In practice, as we will see in Chapter 4, this capacity has been interpreted much less expansively than the generality of the power involved would seem to suggest. Section 92 lists 16 matters in which the power to legislate is reserved for the provinces, among them municipalities, property and civil rights, and public lands, as well as the (now substantial) files of health and education.

The original BNA Act also specifies two categories of concurrent legislation, in which both the federal Parliament and the provincial legislatures are entitled to act. Immigration and agriculture are recognized as areas of joint jurisdiction with the proviso that federal legislation will be paramount in the event of conflict. This "paramountcy" rule ensures that concurrent jurisdiction does not result in deadlock, with different governments' laws cancelling one another out. Finally, the power to write criminal law is assigned to the federal government (hence the nationally uniform Criminal Code), but the enforcement of that law is left to the provinces. The discretion involved in the criminal law's application may amount to a kind of jurisdiction, but the federal government clearly has the upper hand in matters of criminal law (Baker, 2014). Several other features of the BNA Act are also relevant to the form and substance of the federal system, among them the clauses establishing the Senate, providing for the eventual creation of what would become the federal courts, including the Supreme Court of Canada, and making the federal executive responsible for the appointment of the members of all superior courts in the provinces.

The Character of the BNA Act

Scholars generally agree that Confederation was intended to create a strong national government with relatively weak provincial counterparts. Three provisions are commonly cited in support of this belief. The scope of federal powers, including the seemingly wide reserve powers provided under the POGG clause, is usually seen as the strongest evidence for centralist intent. The drafters of the Confederation settlement believed that they had remedied the singular weakness of the American federation by granting the reserve powers through POGG to the national (hence unifying) government rather than to the governments of the various subunits. At the time of Confederation the United States was still reeling from the Civil War—a disaster that many people believed could have been avoided if the American federation had not been so tilted towards the autonomy of the states. For the Canadians, secession of one or more subunits was conceivable only in a system as decentralized as the American one. By granting the residual power to the national government, the drafters thought they had eliminated the very premise on which the idea of secession had been conceived.

The national Parliament's powers of reservation and disallowance have also been seen as evidence of centralist intent. In effect, both of these powers amounted to vetoes over provincial legislation. Reservation allowed the federally appointed lieutenant governor of any province to withhold royal assent from legislation passed by that province until the Act had been reviewed and approved by the federal executive. Disallowance went even further, permitting the federal Parliament to nullify provincial legislation outright even after royal assent had been granted. Reminiscent of the restrictions under which the British North American colonies had operated as part of the British Empire, these provisions implied a hierarchy among Canadian governments that was antithetical to most formulations of federalism. The powers of reservation and disallowance may be taken as proof that some of the designers of Confederation were less than willing to give the provinces true autonomy. Whereas American federalism somewhat reluctantly turned power over to a central government, the Canadian version seemed to take the Empire as its model. One could argue that some oversight was necessary to ensure that provincial legislatures stayed within their constitutional jurisdiction. By the mid-1880s, however, Ottawa recognized that its ability to exercise its oversight power was limited. For the federal government to overrule a decision of a duly elected legislature was to risk its own political future. Moreover, supervising provincial legislatures was becoming an administrative burden for Parliament. The creation of the Supreme Court and its assumption of the power of judicial review over questions of constitutional jurisdiction can be traced to the political difficulties that Ottawa faced in its efforts to maintain a kind of colonial control over the provinces (J. Smith, 1983).

Finally, the matters assigned to the provinces were assumed to be less important than those assigned to the Parliament of Canada. Federal specialists often quote John A. Macdonald's claim that the Confederation settlement had "given the General Legislature all the great subjects of legislation" and "expressly declared that all subjects of general interest not distinctly and exclusively conferred upon the local governments and local legislatures, [should] be conferred upon the General Government and Legislature"; in so doing, he said, "we have . . . avoided that great source of weakness which has been the cause of the disruption of the United States"—namely, the states' rights problem (Waite, 1963). Today many of the matters assigned to provincial legislatures—public health, education, municipal affairs—have become central to the mission of the modern state, but at the time of Confederation they were genuinely minor concerns, involving services that were rarely provided by government and never on a large scale. That such matters would become so important was beyond the foresight of those who drafted the BNA Act.

Constitutional Change

Many of the constitutional changes that, over time, increased the status of the provinces were the result of judicial interpretation. Those developments will be considered in detail in the next chapter. Here we will simply note that judicial review may be considered a mechanism for informal or incremental constitutional change. In giving practical meaning to the provisions of a constitution, courts may effectively thwart its authors' intentions, or at the very least, change the expectations of governments and citizens about who should do what in a federation. There are certainly many who would argue that judicial interpretation has fundamentally altered the Canadian constitution, taking it in directions that its drafters never intended. At the very least, the courts played a part in slowly tipping important jurisdictional questions to the provinces (Laskin, 1947; Scott, 1951; Stevenson, 1989). Because judicial review proceeds slowly, little by little, the changes it brings about often go largely unnoticed. Formal amendment procedures generally command much more public attention and debate, sometimes even requiring public consent via referendum (as was the case in 1992 with the failed Charlottetown Accord).

There are times when formal constitutional change is necessary. In Canada such change has often been the product of the national government's efforts to expand its responsibilities or recover jurisdictional space lost as a result of judicial review. In the 1930s, for example, when the federal government was seeking to introduce various welfare-state programs, the JCPC objected, arguing that Parliament lacked the jurisdiction to implement programs to help the unemployed. In order to gain that jurisdiction it was necessary for the federal government to initiate an actual change to the constitution rather than just a change to an understanding of the constitution's provisions.

Most federal constitutions specify the formula to be used for any future amendment, but no such provision was included in Canada's 1867 constitution. Although Macdonald and others were confident that they had in fact anticipated every potential problem, this was not the reason behind the omission. Rather, they had simply failed to agree on a formula—and the fact that the power to amend the BNA Act remained with the imperial Parliament allowed them to set the issue aside for later consideration. Thus any government seeking a specific constitutional change first had to address the lack of an amending formula.

Changes made prior to the 1930s had focused mainly on central government institutions and the creation or admission of new provinces. They had done little or nothing to directly change the power of the provinces or to increase the power of the national government vis-à-vis the provinces. Since Canada's constitution was effectively an act of the imperial Parliament at Westminster, passed at the request of the colonies, any changes would have to follow the same pattern. This practice was mandated by the Statute of Westminster, 1931, under which the British Parliament was permitted to make laws for former colonies only at their request. What would constitute a legitimate request from Canada, however, was not clear. A simple request from the national Parliament would have sufficed if Canada had had a unitary system of government. But this was not the case. Because its system was federal, any attempt at constitutional change would have to take the provinces into account, particularly where the substance of the change would affect provincial powers.

It was only in the 1930s, when the need for new powers to address the consequences of the Great Depression became urgent, that the challenge of altering the division of powers in sections 91 and 92 was taken up. Ultimately, the federal government secured the unanimous agreement of the provinces to a number of changes, which it was then able to present to the British Parliament with a high degree of legitimacy. The need for provincial consent in such cases was never formalized. However, subsequent changes granting Parliament special legislative powers (for unemployment insurance in 1940, old age pensions in 1951, and supplementary benefits to old age pensions in 1963) all proceeded only with the unanimous approval of the provinces.

According to James Hurley (1996), by the time Ottawa and nine of the 10 provinces finally agreed to a domestic amending formula in 1982, at least 13 earlier efforts to that end had failed. The main points of dispute in those negotiations involved the precise requirements for determining provincial consent to fundamental constitutional change. The question of Quebec's special status as the only majority French-speaking province aside, the wide variations in size and population among the provinces made a wholly majoritarian amending formula unsuitable, but concessions for the older and smaller provinces also seemed unfair, given the growth of the western provinces since Confederation. Proposals varied among the following: (1) unanimity, which would have recognized a sort of provincial equality; (2) a weighted majority giving some consideration to population, but also recognizing the need to provide some protection to the smaller provinces; and (3) mechanisms that would recognize the binational nature of the country by giving some form of veto to Quebec. Various proposals tried to accommodate the provinces' differing interests, but none seemed likely to secure sufficient agreement.

The difficulty of finding an acceptable amending formula was evident in the process that eventually led to the adoption of the Constitution Act of 1982. After an initial threat to unilaterally submit changes to Westminster for approval, the federal government gave in to provincial pressure (and a Supreme Court ruling in the Patriation Reference) and sought "substantial provincial consent" for its proposal, which, in addition to giving complete control over future change to Canadian governments alone, would also entrench a bill of rights.[2] The final deal had the consent of all provinces except Quebec, which challenged the constitutionality of the document in the Supreme Court. The province argued that the Court's own standard of "substantial provincial consent" and Quebec's historical place in Confederation entitled it to a veto over constitutional change. The Court did not agree and the amendment plan proceeded, leading to the patriation of a new constitution that was accepted by every province except Quebec.

The 1982 Amending Formulae and Beyond

The Constitution Act, 1982 patriated the constitutional amendment process so that Canada would no longer depend on the UK for alterations to its fundamental law. The long-standing problem of provincial unanimity was resolved with an amending formula under which unanimity is required only for the most important changes to the constitution. In effect, the 1982 formula is really five separate formulae. The simplest changes are covered in sections 44 and 45, which deal with changes to the federal legislature or executive and the provincial constitutions, respectively. Such changes can be made by the relevant legislature acting alone. A slightly more complicated procedure is contemplated in section 43. Changes affecting one or more, but not all, provinces, or language rights within any of the provinces, require the approval of the provinces concerned and the federal government only. Such changes have been relatively straightforward since 1982 and account for the bulk of constitutional changes realized since 1982. In 1993, for instance, the terms of union for Prince Edward Island were changed to remove the requirement for subsidized ferry service to the province after the construction of the Confederation Bridge provided a fixed link to the mainland. Similarly, in 1997 and 1998 the provisions for denominational schools in Quebec and Newfoundland were changed using this procedure.

The two remaining formulae are reserved for more significant constitutional changes. The so-called general amending formula in section 38 would be required in cases involving subjects such as the division of powers, some changes to the Supreme Court, the addition of new provinces or transformation of territories into provinces, and some elements of Senate and House of Commons representation. The latter three categories of change are singled out in section 42 of the Constitution Act, 1982 as requiring the use of the general amending formula. While such changes are alterations to the structure of federal institutions alone and therefore would seem to qualify for coverage under section 44, those kinds of changes invoke important provincial interests that can be protected by provincial participation in their change. The general formula allows a change to be made if the federal Parliament and the legislatures of at least seven provinces representing, in aggregate, more than half of the national population agree. The formula does not offer a veto to any one province, but in effect it does allow regional groupings of provinces (western and Atlantic) to block change, as well as the most populous provinces because their support is mathematically required for the amendment hurdles to be reached. Finally, section 41 identifies a number of constitutional changes that would require the unanimous consent of the provinces, including any alteration in the role of the Crown; any reduction in the number of a province's MPs that would leave it with fewer representatives in the House than in the Senate; and changes in the composition of the Supreme Court or the constitutional status of the two official languages, as well as alterations to the amending procedures themselves.

The Harper Conservatives campaigned in 2004 on an elected Senate or, failing that, their preference was to eliminate the Senate rather than have it continue in its current unelected form. After Harper received his majority in 2011, he tried to push Senate reform through Parliament, instead of through negotiations with the provinces, since he finally had enough votes to pass a Senate bill in Parliament. However, Harper's vision of Senate reform was thwarted by the Supreme Court, which ruled that his proposed alterations of the Senate could not simply be enacted by the federal Parliament.

Both section 38 and section 41 of the Constitution Act, 1982 were invoked in the Supreme Court's ruling on the constitutionality of Stephen Harper's proposed reform of the Senate in 2014. The Court stated in its decision that a reform creating an elected Senate would have a significant enough impact on the provinces to fit under section 38, requiring the consent of at least seven provinces composing over 50 per cent of the Canadian population. Any move to abolish the Senate would be a significant alteration of the constitution, triggering section 41 and requiring unanimous consent from all 10 provinces. This ruling led Harper to drop his long-standing goal of Senate reform.[3]

Changes in the Division of Powers

The 1982 Constitution Act did not substantially change the division of legislative powers. In what was mainly a concession to the resource-rich western provinces, section 92A was added to the Constitution Act, 1867, conferring on the provincial legislatures the right to develop and regulate non-renewable natural resources and to raise revenues from their extraction through any means or mode of taxation. This section went some way towards resolving the conflicts with Ottawa that arose over the regulation and pricing of non-renewable natural resources following the federal government's adoption of the National Energy Program in 1980.

The amending formula aside, perhaps the most significant aspect of the 1982 constitutional changes for federalism was the fact that the Charter of Rights and Freedoms applied equally to the federal and provincial legislatures and governments. F.L. Morton has argued that the Charter had the potential to homogenize provincial policies by applying universal rights standards to areas where the provinces may have significant differences in their policies (Russell, 1983; Morton, 1995). It seems fairly clear that this was what Pierre Trudeau intended, believing as he did in the superiority of universal liberal guarantees like those in the Charter over the particular preferences of individual groups or provinces (Clarkson and McCall, 1990). It has even been suggested that the Charter was intended to give the national government the symbolic resources to compete with the provinces for the loyalty of citizens. According to this theory, by creating a generation of "Charter Canadians," aware of their universal rights and equipped with the legal mechanisms to protect those rights against provincial majorities, Trudeau hoped that the Charter might lead citizens to transfer their psychological attachments from their provincial communities to a national identity centred on rights. The validity of this theory is still hotly debated by constitutional analysts, but provincial legislatures are certainly aware that the laws they make must be consistent with the protections provided by the Charter (Cairns, 1992; Laforest, 1995). In that way the Charter is no less effective a limit on legislative activity than is the division of powers.

Attempted Amendments after 1982

Because Quebec had refused to accept the 1982 constitutional changes, securing its agreement became a priority for the federal government of Brian Mulroney, elected in 1984. Three years later, after the Liberal government of Robert Bourassa had replaced the Parti Québécois (PQ) in Quebec City, Mulroney succeeded in persuading all 10 provincial premiers to sign the Meech Lake Accord: a set of constitutional amendments that met Quebec's minimum demands, including increased legislative power for all the provinces regarding immigration and a greater role for all provinces in the appointment of senators and Supreme Court justices. In addition, the Accord promised Quebec a veto over future constitutional change and, most controversially, recognition as a distinct society in a new section 2 to be added to the Constitution Act, 1867.

The nature of these terms (particularly the veto, which was effectively a change to the amending formula and a guarantee of three seats on the Supreme Court for Quebec) meant that adoption of the Accord would require unanimous consent as outlined in section 41 of the Constitution Act, 1982: not only the federal Parliament but all provincial legislatures would have to pass resolutions adopting the constitutional change. Furthermore, once a resolution to amend the constitution has been passed by one legislature, section 39 imposes a time limit of three years for all the other legislatures to pass their own resolutions. The first province to adopt the Meech Lake Accord was Quebec, in June 1987. Several other provinces soon followed suit. Manitoba and Newfoundland, however, changed governments before their legislatures had a chance to vote on the proposed changes, and the new governments decided to reopen the issue for debate. Despite last-minute efforts to salvage the Accord, it failed to secure the necessary legislative support and thus expired in June 1990.

After the Meech Lake failure there was still substantial support in Quebec for sovereignty or, at the very least, for greater autonomy within the federation. Bourassa's Liberals bought time by passing a law committing the government to either holding a referendum on sovereignty within two years or bringing to a referendum new proposals for constitutional reform to meet Quebec's traditional demands. This led to a second round of constitutional negotiations that culminated in the Charlottetown Accord, reached in August 1992 and put to a Canada-wide referendum in October of that year.

The architects of the Charlottetown agreement were keenly aware that the Meech Lake process had been deservedly criticized as elite-dominated and more focused on the concerns of governments than of citizens. The Charlottetown process consequently was much more inclusive, and although it offered Quebec many of the same changes proposed in the Meech Lake Accord, it added considerably more to the reform package. If Meech Lake was the "Quebec round" of constitutional reform, aimed at making Quebec a full partner in the post-1982 constitution, Charlottetown was to be the "Canada round," meeting Quebec's demands but also taking into account demands from other parts of Canadian society: thus the Accord included proposals for Senate reform, Aboriginal self-government, and even changes to the House of Commons. Governments hoped that the referendum would secure a majority in each province and thus fulfill the unanimity requirement. But in the end only four provinces voted to accept the Accord, one of them—Ontario—by the slimmest of margins. Thus the second round of mega-constitutional change also ended in failure (Russell, 2004).

Post-Charlottetown Constitutional Politics

In the years since Charlottetown, governments have been wary of comprehensive constitutional change. Only small changes have been made to the constitution since 1992, almost all of them on the initiative of the provinces directly concerned. Although Stephen Harper relaunched the debate over Senate reform soon after his election in 2006, no government since 1992 has proposed even beginning discussions of constitutional amendment. In fact, Prime Minister Harper made it clear that it was in order to avoid any formal constitutional change that his government chose to seek incremental reforms to the Senate rather than a Charlottetown-style overhaul (Senate of Canada, 2006). However, as noted above, Harper's work on

Senate reform was abandoned after the Supreme Court prevented him from using his majority in Parliament to pass laws reforming the Senate without the consent of the provinces. Feeling that it would be impossible to get the provinces to agree on a Senate reform package, Harper dropped the issue.

Justin Trudeau, leading a Liberal majority government has, like Harper, shown little interest in reopening any constitutional debates. His electoral reform proposals, which stalled in committees before officially being abandoned by the government in February 2017, composed the only significant policy plank that would have impacted the structure of government. However, the Liberal government has worked around the constraints imposed by the constitution by introducing its own version of Senate reform, where new senators are officially independent and non-partisan but still chosen by the prime minister with the advice of an independent advisory board, a change that does not require the consent of the provinces. Trudeau's unwillingness to risk the messy infighting of a constitutional negotiation was clearly illustrated when, in June 2017, he bluntly rejected Quebec Premier Phillippe Couillard's attempt to reopen negotiations that would see Quebec become a signatory to the 1982 constitution in exchange for that province's traditional constitutional demands being met.

The Federal Spending Power

One of the key areas for intergovernmental discussion that involves the constitution without necessarily amending the constitution has been the federal spending power. New students of intergovernmental relations in Canada may be forgiven if they are puzzled to find that the list of federal powers in section 91 of the constitution makes no reference to "spending power." According to Peter Hogg (2015), the federal spending power is not explicit; rather, it is *inferred* from the constitutional power granted to Parliament to raise revenue by whatever means it chooses (in the language of the constitution, by "any mode or system of taxation'). For Hogg, and for generations of free-spending federal governments, the corollary of the revenue power is the power to spend the revenue collected wherever the federal government wishes—regardless of legislative jurisdiction. When provinces (particularly Quebec) protest that the power to raise revenue does not imply a power to spend, supporters of the spending power reply that Ottawa may condition provincial priorities, but ultimately the provinces are free to refuse the money. The provinces retain their autonomy because they are not truly compelled to participate in the program.

The fiscal reality of Canadian federalism, as other chapters explain in detail, is that the provinces do not have revenue-raising capacities commensurate with their legislative obligations. Hence their freedom to choose is not always as great as defenders of the spending power suggest. The spending power gives the federal government a way to exploit the fiscal-capacity gap. Some of the most expensive public services provided to Canadians—education, welfare, health care—are the responsibility of provincial governments. Yet the provincial taxation power is more limited than that of the federal government. In essence the provinces are required to share the most important revenue sources—income and consumption taxes—with the federal government. The result has been that a significant portion of provincial spending, on average about 30 per cent, is paid for from federal revenues.[4] Although today such funding comes with many fewer conditions than it did in the past, some of it still has at least nominal strings attached. The federal government has routinely seen fit to use the power of its purse to promote its goals for the country. Provinces have often been offered funding for new programs on the condition that they meet certain federal standards. Generally, once programs are established for shared funding they become regularized and the provinces are given considerable latitude to implement policy as they see fit. But that does not mean that provinces can rely on Ottawa to uphold its commitments indefinitely.

During the fiscally challenging 1990s, when the federal government needed to balance its books, it did so in part by reducing its transfers to the provinces. As we will see in Chapter 7, on the "social union," the federal cuts forced the provinces to rationalize some parts of their health-care systems, reduce social benefits, and raise university tuitions in order to keep their own books in order. The cutback era demonstrated that federal spending power can mean effective control over matters of provincial jurisdiction. However, the Supreme Court has ruled that it is not strictly an invasion of provincial responsibilities, since the provinces have always been free to reject the funds (*Reference Re: Canada Assistance Plan*, 1991). In response to this uncertainty, the provinces demanded that the federal government establish clearer rules for the use of the federal spending power in the future.

Without explicitly engaging the constitutional file, the two orders of government negotiated a protocol for new social programs initiated by Ottawa. The Social Union Framework Agreement (SUFA) was designed to give the provinces more input into federal spending. An unusual document, SUFA is more than a garden-variety intergovernmental agreement, but it does not amount to a constitutional restriction on the activity of either order of government. The overall strategy was to address some of the outstanding intergovernmental issues raised in the constitutional battles of the late 1980s and early 1990s without actually changing the constitution. Governments have not been especially faithful to the terms of the agreement—perhaps not surprising, given the absence of any legal obligation— and Quebec never fully committed to the project. Consequently, SUFA has not been a resounding success (Noël, St-Hilaire, and S. Fortin 2003). The attempt to deal with the spending power in this quasi-constitutional manner having failed, the provinces in recent years have shifted their attention to bringing provincial revenues more in line with provincial responsibilities by addressing what has become known as the "fiscal imbalance." In its 2007 Speech from the Throne, the Harper government promised a new, perhaps constitutional, solution to limit the spending power in the future, but no proposal ever appeared. The essence of the Harper doctrine of both open federalism and the spending power remained in his government's practical intergovernmental relations and not in attempted constitutional reform (these issues are discussed further in later chapters).[5]

Constitutional Change Redux

Quebec Secession

The most significant changes to Canada's constitution were undoubtedly those made in 1982. Those changes were motivated in large part by the threat that without them Quebec might leave the federation. Quebec is not the only province to have reconsidered its commitment to the union; in the early years of Confederation secessionist sentiment was strongest in the Maritime provinces. In modern times, however, threats of secession have come almost exclusively from Quebec.

The Parti Québécois has long been committed to independence for Quebec. Since the federal constitution provides no mechanism for a province to secede, the PQ has been obliged to seek ways of showing that popular support for independence is sufficient to justify initiating such a process. In 1980 the PQ government held a referendum on a proposal for a sort of soft independence that they called "sovereignty association," which would have kept some ties to Canada, but essentially was intended to put the province on the road to sovereign nationhood. That proposal was rejected by roughly 60 per cent of the voters. Nevertheless, during the campaign leading up to the referendum Prime Minister Trudeau pledged that a "No" vote in the referendum would not be a vote for the status quo. In effect, Trudeau offered Quebecers—and all Canadians—a new constitution if the referendum failed.

The relative strength of the movement for independence thus presented not just a threat but also an opportunity to revisit some of the basic terms of Canada's constitutional structure. Trudeau was able to use the threat of secession to persuade other provinces that the basic constitutional bargain needed updating, and he capitalized on popular support for other possible changes—notably the inclusion of a bill of rights—to keep the premiers at the negotiating table. The eventual product of that process, the Constitution Act, 1982, as we have seen, failed to satisfy the Quebec legislature, and the result was another decade of efforts to blunt the force of arguments for separation and bring Quebec into the constitution.

That the Charlottetown Accord was put to a nationwide referendum was also motivated by the continuing threat of Quebec secession. As we noted above, Quebec Premier Robert Bourassa had committed his government to holding another referendum, either on secession or on a new constitutional proposal, after the failure of the Meech Lake Accord. Since Quebec was going to vote on the proposed changes, other provinces wanted a similar opportunity. When the Charlottetown Accord was rejected, the PQ was returned to power with the promise that it would once again take the question of Quebec's relationship with Canada to the Quebec electorate. It held a referendum in 1995 on a vague proposal for a new relationship with the rest of Canada; once again the goal might not necessarily have been complete independence, but there was no doubt that the future of the Canadian state was at stake. Support for the secessionist proposal was much greater in 1995 than it had been in 1980, falling just short of a majority.

The close result obliged the Liberal government of Jean Chrétien to consider new strategies. "Plan A" was to appease Quebec by meeting at least some of its outstanding constitutional demands and thereby demonstrating that federalism could work. "Plan B" was to prepare for contesting a future sovereignty vote. One element of the Plan B strategy was to clarify the legal implications of a move towards secession by Quebec or any other province. To this end the federal government asked the Supreme Court of Canada for its opinion on whether Quebec had the right, under Canadian constitutional law or international law, to secede from the federation. In its 1998 decision, *Reference Re: The Secession of Quebec*, the Court essentially replied that no province had the right to unilateral secession. At the same time, however, it suggested that if a province could demonstrate that secession was in fact the democratic will of the people, then the rest of the federation would have a moral obligation to negotiate such an arrangement in good faith (Schneiderman, 1999). The Court further suggested that such a will could be demonstrated by securing a "clear majority" of voters in support of a "clear question" in a referendum—though as Gagnon and Erk (2002: 326) note, in failing to specify what might constitute a "clear question" or a "clear majority," the decision included "a fair degree of studied ambiguity." Two years after the Court's ruling, in 2000, the federal Parliament passed the Clarity Act, which provided for Parliament to have a role in determining whether a question and result were clear, and setting out the conditions under which the federal government would negotiate the secession of a province from Canada.

Federalists and secessionists alike initially declared the Supreme Court's judgement to represent a victory for their side. Although the latter eventually contested some aspects of the ruling, and in particular the Clarity Act, Plan B tactics have served to define the parameters within which secession by a constituent unit could be considered. Some observers have even suggested that the Reference decision amounts to a constitutional amendment itself. In outlining a process through which a province might secede under terms consistent both with other constitutional principles and with the standards of international law, the Supreme Court made more transparent what had been an extremely murky discourse of competing scenarios for the future, particularly in the years immediately before and after the 1995 referendum (Young, 1999; Choudry and Howse, 2000). It seems obvious, even if it is difficult to demonstrate a strong causal linkage, that support for sovereignty in Quebec has dropped in part because the implications of secession are better understood. What is more certainly known is that there is less political support since 1995 for another referendum. Quebec's nationalist parties have stated that a third referendum will not be held until "winning conditions" are in place—that is, until they can expect a majority of voters to support secession.

The "Regional Veto"

Another outstanding constitutional issue since patriation has been the role of the provinces in approving constitutional change. Following the 1982 amendments, Quebec continued to argue that its unique status entitled it to a veto over constitutional change. The parts of the constitution that can only be changed with the unanimous consent of the provinces effectively give every province a veto. Meech Lake and Charlottetown seemed to prove that comprehensive constitutional change would almost always require unanimity from the provinces. But the general amending formula still allows changes to go ahead without the approval of as many as three provinces. In the present amending formula, the only government with the guaranteed power to veto constitutional change is the federal Parliament, whose consent is required for all amendments except those to provincial constitutions. As part of its Plan A strategy, in 1996 the Liberal government in Ottawa passed legislation providing for Ottawa to require five-region consent—the "regions" being British Columbia, the Prairie provinces, Ontario, Quebec, and the Atlantic provinces—before the federal Parliament would consent to a constitutional amendment. This statute, the Act Respecting Constitutional Amendments, was one of several non-constitutional measures designed to demonstrate that the federation was in fact flexible enough to accommodate Quebec's needs. The fact that it was not entrenched in the constitution, and could therefore be rescinded by a simple parliamentary majority, might have made it meaningless for Quebec nationalists, but the "regional veto" did seem to satisfy some segments of the Quebec public.

Quebec as a "Nation"

Appealing to Quebec voters was no less important for Stephen Harper's Conservative government than for his Liberal predecessors. Lacking a parliamentary majority from 2006 until 2011, and well aware of the national reluctance to reopen the constitution, Harper tried to accommodate Quebec without disturbing the constitutional status quo. Thus in the fall of 2006, the Harper government initiated a parliamentary recognition of the Québécois as a nation within Canada. In the spirit of the once controversial distinct society clause, this parliamentary resolution was designed to recognize the differential status of Quebec within Canada. Specifically, the motion asked: "[t]hat this House recognize that the Québécois form a nation within a united Canada" (*Hansard*, 22 Nov. 2006). Whether this amounted to a grant of new or different powers for the province is unclear. What the recognition did do was continue the post-Charlottetown tradition of taking reversible action on constitutional questions and avoiding formal amendment.

Summary

This chapter illustrates the importance of constitutional structure to the conduct of intergovernmental relations. The constitution provides governments and citizens with a blueprint for the distribution of power within the federation. That plan is subject to ongoing adjustment, and is not necessarily the best guide to who does what, but it does provide a baseline from which governments can work. Constitutional jurisdiction and control of revenue sources are precious assets in any intergovernmental system—bargaining chips that can be used in the negotiating struggles that characterize intergovernmental relations—and they are allotted by the constitution. As we have seen, the constitution itself is also an important subject matter for intergovernmental relations. Constitution-making and constitution-changing in Canada have almost always been the exclusive preserve of governments. Despite the pressure exerted on governments to open up and consult more widely on constitutional issues, since the failure of the Charlottetown Accord, decision-making in that area is once again in the hands of government.

At times it seems as though governments have spent almost as much time discussing the rules of the federalism game as they have spent playing it. The meaning and form of the Canadian federal system are constantly under pressure, contested by different parts of the federation. For William Livingston, as we saw in Chapter 1, the institutions that constitutions establish were simple "instrumentalities": mere reflections of pre-existing diversities within the federation. Thus, when those diversities change, the instrumentalities will be pressured to change as well. A federation that lacks the capacity to change instrumentalities will experience increasing tension as the pressure for recognition of new diversities builds. Canada's federal experience suggests that institutions are not as neutral as Livingston suggested—but that only makes the process of altering them all the more likely to become the focus of the nation's doubts, fears, and jealousies.

That said, the Canadian constitution has proven remarkably durable. It is one of only a few constitutions in the world to have lasted more than a century—and to have survived substantial revision in that time. For all the constitutional self-doubt that Canada has experienced since 1982, the federal system keeps clicking along. Indeed, an important part of Canada's constitutional culture may be the ability to live with some uncertainty or lack of specificity (Thomas, 1997). All of this suggests a certain tension among the formal, legalistic characteristics of federalism as a form of government, the more pragmatic model of parliamentary government, and the particular challenges that arise in a multinational society with numerous competing visions of what constitutes the ideal Canadian political community.

Questions for Critical Thought

1. Is Canada a country of equal nations, equal provinces, or equal citizens?

2. If you were to redraft the federal constitution today, how would you divide powers between the federal Parliament and the provinces?

3. Is a referendum an appropriate way to amend a constitution? What are the arguments in favour and against such a majoritarian vote, and should a simple majority at a particular point in time prevail?

Notes

1. A point established in *Liquidators of the Maritime Bank v. Receiver General of New Brunswick* [1893], A.C. 487.

2. This became the Canadian Charter of Rights and Freedoms, which is Part I of the Constitution Act, 1982. The Charter is distinct from and much more far-reaching than the earlier 1960 Bill of Rights, a federal statute that applies only in regard to matters under federal jurisdiction.

3. See *Reference re Senate Reform*, SCR 2014, Part 3, Vol. 1, at 704.

4. See Table 2.1 in Chapter 2, which shows, among other things, the proportion of provincial revenues derived from federal transfers.

5. For a thorough analysis of the Harper approach and discussion of the political and legal issues surrounding the spending power, see Courchene et al. (2012).

References

Baier, G. 2006. *Courts and Federalism: Judicial Doctrine in the United States, Australia and Canada*. Vancouver: University of British Columbia Press.

Baker, D. 2014. "The Temptation of Provincial Criminal Law." *Canadian Public Administration* 57, no. 2: 275–94.

Cairns, A.C. 1992. *Charter Versus Federalism: The Dilemmas of Constitutional Reform*. Montreal and Kingston: McGill-Queen's University Press.

Choudry, S., and R. Howse. 2000. "Constitutional Theory and the Quebec Secession Reference." *Canadian Journal of Law and Jurisprudence* 13, no. 2: 143–69.

Clarkson, S., and C. McCall. 1990. *Trudeau and Our Times*, vol. 1, *The Magnificent Obsession*. Toronto: McClelland and Stewart.

Courchene, T.J., et al., eds. 2012. *Canada: The State of the Federation 2008: Open Federalism and the Spending Power*. Montreal and Kingston: McGill-Queen's University Press.

Gagnon, A.-G., and J. Erk. 2002. "Legitimacy, Effectiveness, and Federalism: On the Benefits of Ambiguity." In *Canadian Federalism: Performance, Effectiveness, and Legitimacy*, edited by H. Bakvis and G. Skogstad. Toronto: Oxford University Press.

Heard, A. 2014. *Canadian Constitutional Conventions: The Marriage of Law and Politics*, 2nd edn. Toronto: Oxford University Press.

Hogg, P.W. 2015. *Constitutional Law of Canada*, student edn. Scarborough, ON: Thomson Carswell.

Hurley, J. 1996. *Amending Canada's Constitution: History, Processes, Problems and Prospects*. Ottawa: Government of Canada.

Laforest, G. 1995. *Trudeau and the End of a Canadian Dream*. Montreal and Kingston: McGill-Queen's University Press.

Laskin, B. 1947. "Peace, Order and Good Government Re-Examined." *Canadian Bar Review* 25, no. 10: 1054–87.

Morton, F.L. 1995. "The Effect of the Charter of Rights on Canadian Federalism." *Publius* 25, no. 3: 173–88.

Noël, A., F. St-Hilaire, and S. Fortin. 2003. "Learning from the SUFA Experience." In *Forging the Canadian Social Union: SUFA and Beyond*, edited by A. Noël, F. St-Hilaire, and S. Fortin. Montreal: Institute for Research on Public Policy.

Russell, P.H. 1983. "The Political Purposes of the Canadian Charter of Rights and Freedoms." *Canadian Bar Review* 61, no. 1: 30–54.

———. 2004. *Constitutional Odyssey: Can Canadians Become a Sovereign People?* 3rd edn. Toronto: University of Toronto Press.

———. 2017. *Canada's Odyssey: A Country Based on Incomplete Conquests*. Toronto: University of Toronto Press.

Schneiderman, D. 1999. *The Quebec Decision: Perspectives on the Supreme Court Ruling on Secession*. Toronto: J. Lorimer.

Scott, F.R. 1951. "Centralization and Decentralization in Canadian Federalism." *Canadian Bar Review* 29, no. 10: 1095–125.

Senate of Canada. 2006. "Proceedings of the Special Senate Committee on Senate Reform." 7 Sept. https://sencanada.ca/en/Content/Sen/committee/391/refo/02ev-e.

Smith, D.E. 1995. "Bagehot, the Crown and the Canadian Constitution." *Canadian Journal of Political Science* 28, no. 4: 619–35.

Smith, J. 1983. "The Origins of Judicial Review in Canada." *Canadian Journal of Political Science* 16, no. 1: 115–34.

———. 1988. "Canadian Confederation and the Influence of American Federalism." *Canadian Journal of Political Science* 21, no. 3: 443–63.

———. 1999. "Responsible Government and Democracy." In *Taking Stock of 150 Years of Responsible Government in Canada*, edited by F.L. Seidle and L. Massicotte. Ottawa: Canadian Study of Parliament Group.

Stevenson, G. 1989. *Unfulfilled Union: Canadian Federalism and National Unity*. Toronto: Gage.

Thomas, D.M. 1997. *Whistling Past the Graveyard: Constitutional Abeyances, Quebec, and the Future of Canada*. Toronto: Oxford University Press.

Trudeau, P.E. 1968. *Federalism and the French Canadians*. Toronto: Macmillan of Canada.

Waite, P.B., ed. 1963. *The Confederation Debates in the Province of Canada, 1865*. Toronto: McClelland and Stewart.

Young, R. 1999. *The Struggle for Quebec*. Montreal and Kingston: McGill-Queen's University Press.

Chapter 4

Judicial Review and Dispute Resolution

Weell 5

Learning Objectives

- To understand the importance of the process of judicial review in the legal arbitration of intergovernmental disputes.
- To examine the major historical schools of thought on how to interpret the constitution and the significance of applying those differing approaches to the resolution of intergovernmental litigation.
- To explore the growing practice of alternative methods for resolving intergovernmental disputes.

As the preceding chapter suggests, formal alteration of Canada's constitution is by no means easy. The difficulty of constitutional change is an indication of the difficulty of intergovernmental negotiation—and of the degree to which the federation depends on it to manage tensions and policy-making. The simple fact that 11 governments must agree to any substantive amendment makes change difficult. Throw in the need for public consultation and in some cases popular approval through a referendum and the constitution seems even more resistant to major alteration. The dynamics of negotiation and compromise in intergovernmental relations do not easily lend themselves to the kind of definitive resolution necessary for changing the country's supreme law. Provincial premiers and federal prime ministers alike tend to stake out symbolic positions and points of principle that make compromise almost impossible. Fighting over money for social programs or regional development seems easy by comparison. After all, a dollar can be broken down into pennies and distributed more or less equally. It is not so easy to provide every province or region with an equal share of dignity, or to reconcile completely different visions of the purpose of the federation (Dupré, 1988).

Because the constitution itself cannot easily be adapted to new circumstances, the responsibility for ensuring effective operation of the federal system falls heavily on intergovernmental relations. The main vehicles of intergovernmental relations are negotiations between members of the executive branches of the federal and provincial governments—first ministers, cabinet ministers, and senior bureaucrats—conducted at formal meetings and even in more mundane or ceremonial interactions. Lower-level bureaucrats and officials also work out compromises and approaches that require intergovernmental negotiation, often in the course of delivering programs and services. As a federation, Canada is not unique in having difficulties with constitutional change. Consequently, whether by accident or by design, federations have developed more incremental ways of adjusting their constitutional arrangements without formally amending them. Although the resulting adjustments may not be permanent, the fact that they occupy a middle ground between formal amendment and the handshake-style informality of intergovernmental relations may in itself offer certain advantages.

The primary mechanism of incremental change is judicial review. In democracies, the main function of courts is adjudicative: to settle disputes between contending parties. In the simple act of resolving a dispute, a court may be obliged to give a more definitive or authoritative meaning to a particular legislative provision or to the constitution that governs the law-making process. In other words, dispute resolution itself requires interpretation and elaboration of the meaning of legislative and constitutional provisions. Judicial review holds a particular law or government action up to the standard of the constitution and in the event of a conflict may find some or all of that law or action to be unconstitutional. In federations, judicial review takes on the added task of determining appropriate jurisdiction. Legislation and government action can be ruled either *intra* or *ultra vires*—that is, within or outside the constitutional mandate of the order of government enacting the legislation. Judicial review of this sort is commonly initiated by governments challenging one or another's apparent invasion of what they see to be their legislative jurisdiction.

Legal challenges to the constitutionality of legislation represent an alternative front in intergovernmental relations (Russell, 1985). This is especially true in Canada because of the reference power that governments have inferred from the constitution. A provincial government may refer questions of constitutionality to the highest court of appeal in the province, and the federal government may do the same with the Supreme Court of Canada. Authoritative decisions on the meaning of constitutional powers help to shape the envelope of activities in which governments can legitimately engage. When the constitutionality of a legislature's actions is in doubt, the government whose authority has been questioned can refer the matter to its highest court for a definitive ruling. The reference procedure is thus a kind of fast track for constitutional review.

But governments are not the only bodies that can initiate the judicial review process. Citizens accused of breaking a law can contest the constitutionality of that law by arguing that the government responsible for the law lacked the jurisdictional authority to legislate in that area. This approach was famously used against the Duplessis regime in Quebec in what were Canada's earliest civil rights cases (Scott, 1959). Similarly, companies subject to regulation by either order of government may challenge the legislative authority of that government to impose rules or sanctions on them. When the federal government began to play a much more active role in regulating the economy and society in the 1930s, companies whose interests were affected turned to the courts to enforce constitutional limitations on those incursions. In the United States as well as Canada, jurisdictional limitations became the principal constitutional grounds cited in legal arguments against regulation. Such challenges were initially successful in hampering government activity. Constitutional amendments and changes in courts and their approaches were necessary before federal governments in both countries were able to play a more active role in social and economic policy.

Judicial review is a unique type of intergovernmental activity because in the courts, unlike other forums of intergovernmental relations, decision-making is based on legal rather than political arguments. That is not to say that there are no politics involved in the decision to take an issue to court, or that judges are wholly apolitical in the way they function. Nonetheless, moving an intergovernmental conflict into court introduces a whole new set of variables and incentives for the governments involved to consider. First, the stakes in judicial review are relatively high. The rulings of Canada's Supreme Court, as authoritative interpretations of the constitution's text, are really no less binding than constitutional amendments. As we noted in Chapter 3, the *Reference Re: The Secession of Quebec* has essentially altered the amending formula of the constitution by clarifying the legal procedures that would be required for a province to leave the federation. Most intergovernmental agreements can easily be changed to adjust to new conditions or concerns. Constitutional interpretation is more lasting, and its results are much more "zero-sum." Jurisdiction is a difficult thing to divide or give back. Courts generally prefer to award their decisions to one party or another, so a court's ruling rarely allows for compromise between contending interpretations of the constitution. Jurisdiction in any particular area belongs to one government or the other. In practice, governments can and do agree to compromise, but legal interpretation of the constitution does not allow for much sharing. However, and this reflects more of a political if not moral role of the court, the Supreme Court over the past 10 years, in delivering its judgements in federalism cases, often has called upon the parties in dispute to cooperate to sort out complex overlapping issues (a prominent example is the 2011 *Reference re Securities Act*).[1] In referring to widespread practice for pragmatic outcomes in intergovernmental relations in Canada, the Supreme Court in its 1987 judgement in *Ontario v. OPSEU*, [1987] 2 SCR 2, went so far as to call cooperative federalism "a dominant tide." Whether this contributes to a parallel doctrine of interpretation, as some legal scholars suggest, is uncertain (Brouillet, 2017; cf. Daly, 2015).

Second, courts are obliged to respect the results of prior cases and in most cases to feel bound by such precedents. This doctrine of *stare decisis* obliges courts to abide by the findings of higher courts and the judgements in previous cases. While there is always room for new interpretations of constitutional language and even moderate reinterpretations of earlier cases, judges have a much narrower compass for decision-making than politicians do (Hogg, 2015). The adversarial nature of legal argument and the need to articulate a single interpretation of the constitution, one that fits within the parameters of previous interpretations, limits the creativity of judges when they address constitutional issues. Likewise, governments may think twice before taking a jurisdictional dispute to court. A positive result may mean total victory, but a negative one would mean a total loss or a complete concession of jurisdiction to the other order of government.

As a consequence, governments use legal resources very strategically. When they feel that they have a strong claim to jurisdiction based on past judicial rulings, they are much more likely to take a bold position and risk taking the dispute to court. A strong legal claim also gives a government a stronger position in negotiations. For example, if the Supreme Court has supported a provincial government's claim to jurisdiction, this is likely to strengthen the province's position in negotiations with Ottawa regarding a shared program that the federal government has previously claimed some legislative authority over. On the other hand, it may be in the strategic interest of a government to take a jurisdictional claim to court even if its chances of winning are slim. In the 1990s, several provinces opposed to the federal government's firearms registry challenged the federal authority in that area. Even though most legal experts believed that the claimants' case was weak, the provinces in question had strong constituencies hostile to the legislation—constituencies that the governments in question hoped to appease by exhausting the legal avenues available to frustrate the federal plan. Likewise, the NDP government of British Columbia pledged to use every "tool" it could to try to stop the Trans Mountain Pipeline, including a constitutional reference over jurisdiction of some elements of pipeline regulation. In the *Reference Re: Firearms Act (Canada)*, 1998, the Supreme Court ruled in favour of the federal government under the auspices of its criminal law power, but the provinces that objected at least could claim they tried everything they could to challenge an unwelcome federal policy.

The scope of the powers outlined in the constitution has been fleshed out by government initiatives and the approval or disapproval arrived at through judicial review. Governments, both provincial and federal, have pushed the envelope of their respective powers to the limits they think are acceptable. It has fallen to the courts to tell them when they have exceeded their legitimate jurisdiction or to confirm the appropriateness of their judgement (Smith, 1983). In Canada's early history the task of authoritative interpretation was left to the

Judicial Committee of the Privy Council—a colonial holdover composed not of Canadian judges but of Law Lords belonging to the upper house of the British Parliament. The JCPC remained Canada's highest court long after Confederation, hearing its last Canadian appeals in 1949. Because the JCPC adjudicated Canada's earliest constitutional challenges, its influence on the interpretation of the constitution's provisions regarding the powers exercised by the provincial and federal legislatures has been profound. In addition, the JCPC affirmed the decentralizing direction in which Canadian federalism was independently evolving, thereby reinforcing what was naturally happening in the federation (Cairns, 1971). Since the end of the JCPC era the final arbiter of Canadian federalism and intergovernmental relations has been the Supreme Court of Canada. The Supreme Court's role in the federal system was greatly increased after the passage of the Constitution Act, 1982, in particular impacting the federal system with judicial review under the Charter of Rights and Freedoms, and the provisions respecting Aboriginal rights. By interpreting and defining the scope and limits of legislative powers in the constitution, Canada's courts continue to play an important role in intergovernmental relations.

Increasingly, however, Canada's court system is not the only site of dispute resolution between governments. Mindful of the courts' broad interpretive power and the finality of their decisions regarding the relative powers of provincial and federal legislatures, Canada's governments have become increasingly wary of submitting their disputes to judicial review. For either party in an intergovernmental dispute, the risk of losing is substantial enough that both sides often prefer to avoid legal confrontation if at all possible. Periods of intergovernmental disharmony will still see governments resort to formal challenges in the courts, but in recent years a number of parallel institutions have been developed to resolve disputes. These institutions and their implications for intergovernmental relations are discussed in the latter part of this chapter.

Judicial Review and the Division of Powers

Among the powers listed in the Constitution Act, 1867 are three that have been substantially influenced by judicial interpretation: (1) the preamble to section 91, the POGG clause, which grants the federal Parliament the power to implement laws for the general welfare of the country; (2) the provinces' general power over property and civil rights; and (3) the federal power over trade and commerce. Courts have differed over time in their treatment of these three provisions, but cumulatively their interpretations are in large part responsible for the relatively decentralized nature of Canadian federalism. Legislatures have been conditioned to a significant degree by the permissiveness or lack thereof that courts have shown when testing the limits of their jurisdictional spheres.

The JCPC Era

Critics of the JCPC have generally blamed it for the limited powers of the federal government (Cairns, 1971; Laskin, 1947; Scott, 1959). In retrospect, it was perhaps rash to attribute the direction in which Canadian federalism evolved entirely to the Law Lords. That said, however, the success of the provinces in expanding their jurisdiction through the rulings of the JCPC, often at the expense of the federal government, certainly did not disappoint those who favoured a provincially dominated federal system.

The JCPC made its decentralist influence felt mainly by giving narrow interpretations to the federal POGG and trade and commerce powers and expansive ones to the provincial powers over property and civil rights. In so doing, the JCPC has been seen as contradicting the intentions of the Fathers of Confederation. The Fathers, it is argued, sought to create a more centralized union of the provinces. Why the JCPC would undermine that intention is not quite clear. What can be said is that its findings in favour of the provinces were not out of step with the way the provinces were evolving in the late nineteenth and early twentieth centuries.

Bora Laskin, one of the more eminent constitutional scholars and jurists of the last century, described the POGG clause as "the favourite whipping boy of constitutional commentators" (Laskin, 1947). Critics such as Laskin pointed to what they thought was the JCPC's misinterpretation of POGG as the primary culprit for Canadian federalism's misdirection. A more generous interpretation would certainly have represented a potential threat to provincial autonomy, since POGG is by nature so general that it could be applied to just about any subject of legislation. It has often been remarked that the challenge of POGG is not to decide what it includes, but to figure out what its limitations are. The JCPC erred on the side of more limitations. Cairns (1971) has also suggested that the JCPC was more comfortable with statutory interpretation where the approach is to focus on specifics rather than broad meanings.

POGG is found in the preamble of section 91, the clause that enumerates the powers of the federal Parliament. Theoretically, it could be interpreted in either of two ways. A more centralist view would see POGG as a general grant of power, with the enumerated powers in section 91 serving simply as examples of how the general power might be exercised. Thus to promote peace, order, and good government, the federal Parliament can make laws related to weights and measures, as in section 91(17), or fisheries, as in section 91(12), but is not limited to those headings of legislation alone. In other words, the list of 28 powers accorded Parliament in section 91 is not meant to be exhaustive, but merely to illustrate the scope of the federal power. The Privy Council supported this vision of POGG for a short period following Confederation. In a series of decisions the Judicial Committee endorsed a "two-compartment" theory according to which federal jurisdiction consisted of POGG and the list of matters enumerated in section 91, and provincial jurisdiction consisted of the section 92 matters. Not many years later, POGG came to be understood as one of three compartments in the constitution. In that instance, the section 91 list and the section 92 list made up the main compartments for the federal and provincial legislatures respectively and POGG existed as a third compartment—an extra grant to the federal Parliament for use in extraordinary circumstances.[2]

Extraordinary circumstances, in the collective mind of the JCPC, basically came to mean national emergencies. Justifications based on the POGG power were available to the federal government, but only in cases where it could be proven that, for the sake of a nationwide crisis, provincial autonomy had to be overridden. The JCPC's first opportunity to define the emergency power came with *In Re: Board of Commerce Act*, 1922, in which the Lords did not support the broad powers incorporated in the federal anti-profiteering legislation before them, but hinted that a more dire form of extraordinary circumstances might actually qualify for a POGG justification. A year later, in *Fort Frances Pulp & Power Co. v. Manitoba Free Press* (1923), they found such a situation with a case involving newsprint prices, which remained under the control of the recent wartime regime. However, the JCPC narrowed the scope of emergency two years later in *Toronto Electric Commissioners v. Snider* (1925), which struck down the federal Industrial Disputes Investigation Act because it sought to control labour disputes within a peacetime context.

The JCPC briefly indicated that potential justification for federal legislation under POGG outside of emergencies might exist in *Re: Regulation and Control of Aeronautics in Canada* (1932). The Committee upheld legislation creating a national regime for the control of air travel and safety under section 132—the so-called Empire treaties clause. The real reason for seeking such control was that the federal government needed it to fulfill the terms of an international treaty. But the Committee hinted that a subject like aeronautics might also be considered a matter of national interest that could be handled under the POGG power. The reference *Re: Regulation and Control of Radio Communication in Canada*, A.C. 304 (1932) gave similar hope to centralists.

In that case a treaty implementation power was accorded to Parliament on the basis of a national interest alone. The apparent potential for increased central government activity in the name of the national interest encouraged the government of R.B. Bennett to commit Canada to uphold international standards on a number of matters such as labour regulation, in the hope of adding them to the list of policy areas under federal jurisdiction (Saywell, 2002). The POGG power did not fare well, however, when these efforts were constitutionally tested. With respect to the "Bennett New Deal" legislation, designed to help Canadians cope with the dire economic and social conditions of the Great Depression, the JCPC refused to recognize any emergency justification.[3] It also rejected the federal government's argument that unemployment insurance was a matter of national concern (*Employment and Social Insurance Reference*, 1937), establishing that power would ultimately require a constitutional amendment. Another key case in the 1930s, however, set out clear limits of the treaty power for the federal Parliament. In the 1937 *Labour Conventions* case the federal power to enter into treaties was found not to extend to their implementation where matters of provincial jurisdiction were concerned. The JCPC encouraged the federal government to cooperate with the provinces to achieve joint implementation where possible. The ruling has never been overturned and still prevents the unilateral federal implementation of international treaties, including free trade agreements and the climate change protocols.

The JCPC's hostility to expansive readings of federal powers spurred an effort by the federal government in the 1940s and 1950s to actually amend the constitution in key social program areas, as well as to demand reform of a system in which the final court of appeal for Canadians was the Privy Council of Great Britain. Furthermore, that the federal government should have to prove the existence of an emergency before it could exercise the POGG powers made a mockery of the centralists' belief that POGG was a comprehensive residual power. Despite its rejection of the Bennett New Deal legislation, in its last days as Canada's court the JCPC changed course a little and expanded the POGG category to include matters of national concern or dimensions. One of the last major cases to be heard by the JCPC opened up a space for POGG that did not depend on the existence of an emergency. In *Attorney General of Ontario v. Canada Temperance Federation* (1946) the JCPC refuted much of its earlier POGG jurisprudence and created a national concern "branch" or justification (in addition to an emergency branch) for POGG.

Overall, however, the JCPC was much more generous in its interpretation of provincial powers. Its rulings significantly expanded the scope of the provinces' property and civil rights power, usually at the expense of the federal power over trade and commerce. In *Citizens Insurance Co. v. Parsons* (1881), the JCPC found that the regulation of fire insurance was not within the scope of the federal trade and commerce power, but rather a provincial matter under the heading of property and civil rights. It even went so far as to suggest that the federal power over trade and commerce did not include general commercial relations within the provinces and was effectively limited to the regulation of trade with other nations, interprovincial trade, and "the general regulation of trade affecting the whole Dominion." A quarter-century later, in *Attorney General of Canada v. Attorney General of Alberta* (1916), the federal power with respect to trade was even more narrowly interpreted as "essentially an auxiliary power incapable of serving on its own as a primary source of legislative capacity." A similar approach was used to place the power over matters such as industrial disputes in the property and civil rights category. By the end of the JCPC era the scope of provincial jurisdiction was much broader than the founders seem to have envisioned, while the federal government faced very strong limitations on its presumed powers under the general POGG power.

All of this happened in a period when the scope of government activity was increasing and the ambitions of the federal government in particular were very broad. The federal government has recognized from a very early stage that its range of activity is limited by restrictive interpretations of the constitution. Thus the system of intergovernmental relations that exists today is in important respects a consequence of the JCPC's narrow interpretation of some federal powers. Since the federal government was not allowed free rein to intervene in the economy, it was unable to create employment and social programs on a broad scale, as its American counterpart did. Instead, Ottawa was compelled to cooperate and negotiate with the provinces.

The Supreme Court Era

The federal Parliament's luck seemed to change in 1949, when the Supreme Court of Canada replaced the JCPC as the final arbiter of disputes for the federation. The Supreme Court quickly expanded the notion of national concern first suggested in the *Canada Temperance* case and began to define a broader scope for the POGG power. Added to the POGG list of matters under federal control were aeronautics (in *Johannesson v. West St. Paul*, 1952), atomic energy (in *Pronto Uranium Mines, Ltd. v. O.L.R.B.*, 1956), a national capital region (in *Munro v. National Capital Commission*, 1966), and seabed natural resources (in *Re: Offshore Mineral Rights of B.C.*, 1967). Nevertheless, the Court was moderate in its approach. Although it put an end to the trend towards aggressive decentralization, it did not attempt to reverse direction and move towards centralization, as many legal commentators had hoped a wholly domestic court would (Laskin, 1951).

This difference in approach can be attributed in part to the nature of the questions the Supreme Court has been asked to rule on. One key example of a matter on which the JCPC never ruled was the practice known as delegation. This occurs when one order of government lends its legislative power to another—either because it lacks the interest or capacity to deal with the matter in question, or because the other order makes it an offer it cannot refuse. This practice of delegating power could potentially allow both orders of government to use negotiated agreements to skirt the constitutional division of powers. Thus, even though incremental change through bilateral and multilateral agreements is in some ways the trademark of Canadian federalism, the Supreme Court has not been an unalloyed booster of such arrangements. The Court forbade a cooperative scheme put together by the Nova Scotia and federal governments in the so-called interdelegation case of 1951 (*Attorney General of Nova Scotia v. Attorney General of Canada*, 1951), but it did permit a slightly different form of delegation to pass a year later. In *PEI Potato Marketing Board v. H.B. Willis* (1952), the federal Parliament was permitted to delegate responsibility to an administrative board created by the provincial legislature, without having to transfer any law-making power to the provincial legislature.

Andre Bzdera (1993) argues that an institution whose members are appointed by the federal government and based in Ottawa (Supreme Court justices are obliged by law to live in the National Capital Region during the term of their appointment) is likely to be biased in favour of the national government. On the whole, however, commentators generally describe the Supreme Court's approach to the division of powers as balanced (Hogg, 1979; Baier, 2002, 2008). Conflicting reasoning in some of the Supreme Court's rulings on the division of powers suggests that the balance has sometimes required significant contortions on the part of Supreme Court justices. The *Reference Re: Anti-Inflation Act*, which tested the constitutionality of federal wage and price control legislation passed in 1976, offers an almost painful example of the Court's efforts to avoid favouring one order of government over the other (Russell, 1977). It also suggests how the different perspectives represented by individual members of the Court can sometimes have the effect of cancelling each other out. The federal government had hoped for a strong endorsement of its policies from a court led by a chief justice who was a noted centralist, but what it got was a welter of opinions and dissents that scarcely managed to uphold the Act. A bare majority on the Court endorsed the legislation on the grounds that rampant inflation constituted a national emergency. Part of the reason the Court had been reluctant to accept "national concern" arguments in support of POGG in the past had always been the seemingly potential limitlessness of such reasoning. If routine matters could be promoted to the status of "national concern," expansionist central governments would be encouraged to define any number of areas in those terms. The "national emergency" doctrine represented a less risky option for the Court. Thus, even though the *Anti-Inflation* decision ultimately defended the federal government's intervention, it limited the scope for future use of the "national concern" justification.

With *Anti-Inflation* as the precedent, the Supreme Court began a tradition of somewhat ambivalent jurisprudence in questions involving federalism. Many observers consequently believed that judicial review was of limited importance for the politics of Canadian federalism (Monahan, 1987; Weiler, 1974). By taking the middle ground, the Court had merely endorsed the model of Canadian federalism already in operation. Instead of reshaping it, judicial review simply mirrored the existing system. Some critics even suggested that, in framing its endorsement of the status quo in legalistic terms, the Court was essentially acting in a political manner, pretending that its decisions were based only on what the law demanded (Russell, 1977). Governments appeared to accept this critique and became less interested in litigating their conflicts. Although governments always reserve the option of challenging each other in court, the use of judicial review to work out kinks in the federal system became less frequent because governments were increasingly uncertain about the results and more comfortable negotiating with one another to achieve mutually acceptable outcomes.

The Supreme Court's influence never disappeared, however, and events led the Court to revisit POGG questions in a series of cases through the 1990s. In several cases concerning environmental jurisdiction, the Court had the opportunity to expand the "national concern" doctrine. In *R. v. Crown Zellerbach Canada Ltd.* (1988), the Court developed what has become known as the "provincial inability" test, referring to situations in which the inability of a province to act in some particular area might have adverse effects on other provinces. In instances where provincial inability might be shown to exist, there was potential for the expansion of federal power. In a number of cases since *Crown Zellerbach*, the Court has shied away from any significant expansion of Parliament's jurisdiction under POGG (Baier, 1998). It has, however, expanded the federal power in the area of criminal law by including under that rubric matters such as toxic dumping (*R. v. Hydro-Québec*, 1997). The Court further emphasized the scope of the criminal law when it upheld the national firearms registry despite vehement provincial opposition, in *Reference Re: Firearms Act (Canada)*, 1998.

Another potentially important area of federal jurisdiction is trade and commerce. Like POGG, the trade and commerce clause has considerable potential for expansion of federal responsibilities. In the United States, the federal legislature's jurisdiction over commerce has been quite generously interpreted to allow a very wide range of regulatory and program activities. The JCPC never gave much scope to Ottawa's power in that area, preferring to emphasize the provincial property and civil rights category. But the Supreme Court has flirted with expanding the federal trade and commerce power in cases of national interest. International trade is generally recognized as falling under federal control, and the federal government has proceeded accordingly, though it has regularly involved or consulted the provinces in negotiations involving provincially regulated industries (such as forestry) or industries with particular regional concentrations (such as fisheries).

What has been controversial is the prospect that the trade and commerce power might be used to justify federal regulation of internal trade among the provinces. In the relevant cases, the Court has insisted that the power be used only for general purposes, not targeted at a specific industry or activity. The test to be applied in such cases is similar to the "provincial inability" test: for example, Ottawa might be justified in imposing a general regulation in cases where one province's failure to regulate might have negative consequences for other provinces or for the federation as a whole. Federal anti-combines legislation designed to curb anti-competitive and monopolistic corporate behaviour was upheld under the trade and commerce heading in *General Motors of Canada v. City National Leasing* (1989), in which the Court implied that the federal Parliament needed to be able to regulate the national market because provinces might not always do their best to ensure an open market throughout the country. More recent signs suggest that the Court may be moving in a different direction, more tolerant of provincial protectionism than presumed in the past. In 2018 the Court's decision in *R. v. Comeau* cited the principle of federalism and the ability to protect regional diversity as grounds for rejecting a challenge to limits on interprovincial importation of beer and liquor based on the free movement of goods cited in section 121 of the Constitution Act, 1867.

The federal government, until very recently, has had reason to believe that it could be more aggressive in its regulation of trade and commerce and still survive a legal challenge. Thus, whenever the provinces have been lackadaisical about negotiating the removal of internal trade barriers, the federal government has not hesitated to threaten unilateral action under the trade and commerce power (Brown, 2002). Federal proposals for a national securities regulator were grounded in the belief that there is ample room in the trade and commerce power to justify such an exercise. This belief turned out to be not so well grounded, however, at least when it comes to the Supreme Court. In 2011, the Supreme Court was asked to weigh in on the constitutionality of a proposed unified federal regulatory body for securities that would replace the individual provincial bodies. The Court ruled that such a change would indeed be unconstitutional, as securities are under the regulatory jurisdiction of the provinces, and the Harper government could not demonstrate a pressing need for federal involvement. In their ruling, the justices argued that the "main thrust" of the proposed Securities Act "does not address a matter of genuine national importance and scope going to trade as a whole in a way that is distinct and different from provincial concerns" (SCC Reports, part 4, 2011, vol. 3, *Reference re National Securities Act*).

The Court's interpretation of the trade and commerce power is actually an excellent example of the indirect effect that judicial review can have on intergovernmental relations. The real impact of the Court's decisions on the character of Canadian federalism can be seen not in the changing extent of federal power but rather in the way that governments interpret those decisions and conduct themselves.

This is especially apparent in the case of the Charter of Rights. Many observers have maintained that the Charter was designed to override Canada's federal character and impose national standards on the provinces, homogenizing much of their public policy (Morton, 1995; Russell, 1983). In Canada, unlike some other federations, the rights guarantees in the national constitution apply not just to federal laws and activities but to provincial ones as well. Prime Minister Trudeau, the chief architect of the Charter, seemed intent on establishing a sense of national community, based on national values that the legal guarantees set out in the Charter would impose across the country. Those with a less centralist bent feared that the enforcement of those standards by the Supreme Court would prevent the provinces from realizing their diverse preferences in public policy (Morton, 1995). Other observers have found that the Supreme Court's Charter jurisprudence has probably not been as homogenizing as skeptics predicted, though there is controversy about the proper way to measure the effects of the Charter on legislative diversity. Numbers alone don't always tell the whole story. Advocates of the Charter point out that the most frequent loser under the Charter is the federal government, not the provinces. But given the scope of federal activities that is not necessarily surprising. It is not clear that Canadian federalism has become more centralized since 1982, or that provincial legislatures have been unduly restricted in the choices they have made (Kelly, 2001, 2008; Kelly and Murphy, 2005). To borrow from James Kelly and Michael Murphy, the Supreme Court has become something of a "meta-actor" in Canadian federalism. By interpreting the Charter and the division of powers in the ways that it does, the Supreme Court does have some effect on the framework in which intergovernmental relations are conducted. But judicial review seldom determines the final shape of policy outcomes. Ultimately, governments act in an environment conditioned by the Supreme Court, but it is up to governments to decide what they will make of the judiciary's findings (Baier, 2006). Unlike the role of judicial review in federalism cases, where the tendency is for zero-sum results, in cases involving the Charter judicial review often provides room for legislatures to fix a Charter violation while preserving the original purpose of the legislation.

As discussed more fully in Chapter 11, a similar situation exists for judicial review of Indigenous rights. Just as with individual citizens, the courts have served as a crucially important tool for Indigenous governments and non-governmental organizations, which, despite their great difficulty in advancing Indigenous concerns in the political arena, have won highly significant victories in the interpretation (and often expansion) of their rights, at the expense of both the federal government and provincial and territorial governments. While one might argue that the jurisdiction in the federal system as such that has been the most commonly affected has been that of Parliament, in fact the evolving interpretation of Indigenous rights, land claims, and treaties has been impacting the entire intergovernmental system—including, of course, the Indigenous governments themselves.

The Limits and Potential of Judicial Review

The limitations of judicial review in the context of intergovernmental relations were illustrated in the early 1990s, when the federal government made some (now modest-seeming) cuts to provincial transfers. The main target was the Canada Assistance Plan (CAP), which paid 50 per cent of the cost of provincial social assistance and welfare programs. In the past the program provided that transfers would increase in tandem with provincial spending on social assistance, but in 1990 Ottawa decided that the so-called "have" provinces—Alberta, British Columbia, and Ontario—should receive increases of no more than 5 per cent per annum, regardless of how much their spending increased. When this "cap on CAP" was enacted, rising costs soon ensured that the federal contributions in those provinces amounted to considerably less than 50 per cent.[4]

The British Columbia government referred the legislation, the Government Expenditures Restraint Act, to the BC Court of Appeal, asking whether Parliament had the authority to limit its obligations under the CAP without the consent of the provinces affected. The Court of Appeal found that such a change did indeed require provincial consent, but the Supreme Court of Canada in the 1991 *Reference Re: Canada Assistance Plan (B.C.)* overruled the BC decision, largely on the grounds that to do otherwise would compromise the sovereignty of Parliament. Any sanctions against the federal government for reneging on its commitments, the Court found, would have to be political, not legal.

In its unanimous judgement, the Court ruled decisively that Parliament, not cabinet, is responsible for the design of intergovernmental agreements. So even if a prime minister makes a promise to the provinces, the authority to back up that promise in actual spending and legislation lies with Parliament, not the executive. If Parliament wishes to alter the provisions of a commitment to the provinces (such as the CAP), a previous pattern of cost-sharing or even a promise from the federal government cannot be binding. Similarly, the Court argued that a province's legitimate expectation of funds could not override parliamentary sovereignty by requiring that transfers continue regardless of the wishes of Parliament. The logic of parliamentary sovereignty means that no Parliament can bind the law-making authority of a future Parliament through the passing of an ordinary statute. Financial commitments like those contained in the CAP can be made, but it is well within the authority of a future Parliament to change those commitments when circumstances change. Intergovernmental agreements, by their nature, must rest on these impermanent foundations.

The Court may not have intended to discourage provincial governments, or for that matter, citizens, from seeking judicial resolution of intergovernmental disputes involving the appropriate transfer of funds. However, its (quite proper) decision to defer to Parliament on the changes to the CAP offered them little hope. Intergovernmental agreements, according to the Court's reasoning, are essentially political commitments, outside the authority of the judiciary. While legislation such as the CAP may create obligations to the other governments, those obligations are only as lasting as the legislation itself. If Parliament or a provincial legislature wants to change a law there is little the courts can do to stop them, even if other governments have come to rely on the programs that the old law created. The CAP case has had serious implications for the political use of legal resources in intergovernmental relations because it demonstrated that there are real limits to the usefulness of judicial review as a remedy in a significant share of intergovernmental disputes.

The CAP case has provoked observers to think more carefully about how effectively intergovernmental agreements can be legally enforced. Governments often have to pressure one another to live up to the terms of an agreement (internal enforcement), but citizens and others also have an interest in governments living up to the terms of an agreement (external enforcement) (Swinton, 1995). If the courts are not able or willing to help enforce informal commitments between governments, a major route for accountability and legitimacy in the federal system may be blocked off. In short, enforcement of intergovernmental agreements appears to be a political matter, and that generally means that governments can ignore their obligations if they feel that the political cost of doing so will not be severe.

Dispute Resolution

Jurisdictional conflicts are not unusual in a federation. The country's high court can serve as an umpire in such cases, impartially applying the constitution (or its reading of the constitution) to resolve the dispute. But jurisdiction is not the only thing that federal and provincial governments disagree about. Historically, in Canada, disagreements about financial commitments or even ambitious new programs to regulate the economy or society have sometimes been massaged into disputes over jurisdiction, but not all conflicts are amenable to settlement on the basis of the constitutional division of powers.

In recent years, for example, some media commentators have suggested that the premiers of Nova Scotia and Newfoundland and Labrador could take legal action to compel the federal government to live up to its obligations under accords reached with those provinces for the development of offshore oil and gas resources, and Lorne Calvert, the former premier of Saskatchewan, began legal proceedings against Ottawa regarding the Equalization Program (Galloway, 2007; Galloway and Alphonso, 2007). The federal government's carbon tax, based on an intergovernmental agreement with the provinces, has also been the basis of a constitutional challenge, first, by the single non-signatory province, Saskatchewan, followed by Ontario, which withdrew its support of the tax after a change of government following the June 2018 provincial election. Cooperative programs and agreements, by their nature, are relatively untroubled by strict constitutional categories, so looking to the constitution as a guide for enforcement may not be all that helpful. From a practical point of view, as we have already noted (and will note again) elsewhere in this book, strict observance of constitutional jurisdiction would make it impossible for the federation to function. If the constitutional division of powers can be seen as a contractual arrangement between governments establishing who will do what to deliver services to their citizens, judicial review might be conceived as a means of enforcing that contract and clarifying its terms for the signatories. Intergovernmental agreements can be seen in a similar contractual light, although the degree of formality involved varies widely: from a simple handshake agreement to a specific financial commitment to a full-blown accord with multiple chapters and institutionalization of offices and staff. These are contracts of a different kind from the constitution; nevertheless, they too occasionally need clarification or enforcement. Since the courts, as we saw with the CAP case, have declined that role, other means of dispute resolution have been required, including in some cases provisions internal to intergovernmental agreements themselves. The role of such provisions should not be overstated, however: negotiation is still the principal method of dispute resolution. One reason is that formal dispute resolution mechanisms by nature require governments to give up some of the bargaining room they have traditionally used to advance their interests.

Informal signals and negotiations are sometimes conducted in the full glare of the national media. When he was premier of Newfoundland and Labrador from 2003 to 2010, Danny Williams was well known for his skill at using the media in his battles with Ottawa: placing advertisements asking "Steve" (Harper) to be fairer to Newfoundland and Labrador, calling the prime minister to task on talk shows, walking out of first ministers' meetings, and even lowering the Canadian flag to half-staff at provincial government buildings. Williams was hardly the first Canadian premier to stage publicity stunts; all first ministers must make some effort to court public opinion. We should not overestimate either the frequency or the impact of such efforts. Much more often, disputes between the two orders of government are dealt with in private, through quiet accommodation on the part of officials and advisers. Examples discussed elsewhere in this book, such as the negotiation of the Millennium Scholarship fund and Labour Market Development agreements, are just the proverbial tip of the iceberg. Every day, Canadian governments resolve disputes over their respective roles in joint and collaborative programs through simple discussion.

That said, not all matters lend themselves to the behind-the-scenes approach. When governments differ substantially in their views, compromise may not be possible. Even when they can find room for agreement, they may want stronger guarantees of one another's obligations in the future than can be assured by handshakes or goodwill. When tensions between governments are high, such as the heated battle over the Trans Mountain Pipeline between Alberta and British Columbia, norms might get tossed out the window. Despite considerable doubts about the "legality" of an Alberta ban on British Columbia wine, the government of Alberta proceeded with the ban to pressure its neighbour regardless of the trade guarantees that exist in agreements.

Canadian governments since the 1960s have become accustomed to making relatively informal arrangements with one another, and the flexibility of those arrangements has left something of a vacuum for enforcement. As the Supreme Court made clear in the *Canada Assistance Plan Reference*, a court cannot prevent a legislature from operating within the scope of its constitutional powers. The consequences for reneging on intergovernmental commitments are more often political than legal, and are generally diffuse rather than specific. Hence governments may see little need to be especially faithful to such agreements, especially if they feel they have strong electoral support for their actions. In recent years, some corners of intergovernmental relations have become a little more formalized or institutionalized, and mechanisms for the resolution of disputes have increasingly been incorporated into agreements themselves. Thus, recent intergovernmental structures have included quasi-judicial mechanisms for the resolution of disputes between the parties. The Agreement on Internal Trade (AIT, replaced in 2017 by the Canadian Free Trade Agreement), for example, had a chapter devoted to provisions for dispute resolution in the event of a complaint that some jurisdiction created trade barriers contrary to the agreement. Despite criticisms, those provisions were used to resolve several significant disputes. (Indeed, to a large degree, Canada's trade dispute mechanism is modelled on international practice, which was the impetus for the new 2017 agreement.) The Social Union Framework Agreement proposed a model of dispute resolution that included more formal reporting of disputes between the federal and provincial governments, and outlined various collaborative procedures to resolve them. The Social Union model has also been proposed as a method of dispute resolution in intergovernmental conflicts over health care. In correspondence with the Alberta government in the 1990s, federal Minister of Health Anne McClellan pledged to use informal dispute procedures based on the SUFA model. In general, though, the SUFA provisions have hardly been used at all. In the AIT and SUFA, ad hoc tribunals or panels must be appointed to hear the cases of the governments involved, but in no case does the tribunal or panel have the authority to ensure that governments abide by their rulings.

Despite their relative formality, the new approach to dispute resolution suggests that the old habits of negotiation and compromise between governments die hard. The procedures are specified in writing, but they are still relatively informal, preferring compromise and behind-the-scenes dispute avoidance. Ultimately, they seek to preserve a certain amount of discretion for governments, perhaps to avoid the zero-sum results associated with legal rulings. Though a court may be balanced over time in its treatment of different orders of government, individual cases and hence individual policy outcomes cannot be balanced the same way. As Douglas Brown (2002) notes, many (if not all) of the governments that negotiated the Agreement on Internal Trade were reluctant to hand over too much authority to an independent secretariat to settle disputes. The Council of the Federation, a cooperative organization of the provinces designed both to communicate provincial concerns to Ottawa and to promote greater cooperation among the provinces, highlighted the improvement of dispute resolution procedures in the AIT as a priority. The Council has gone so far as to recognize that its own member governments have probably given themselves too much discretion to decide how disputes would be handled and rulings implemented. In addition, numerous delays and opportunities for renegotiation were built into the AIT dispute process. If disputes are settled by a tribunal, it remains up to the violating government to voluntarily comply with the ruling. Some provinces, such as Alberta, have been enthusiastic supporters of the processes of dispute resolution and have tried to lend the AIT legitimacy by abiding by the tribunals' decisions. Other provinces, such as Quebec, have been less enthusiastic, or at least less prompt to comply with rulings or even properly acquit their responsibilities under the dispute procedures (Council of the Federation, 2004). In short, while the intergovernmental apparatus has experimented with ways of making agreements more enforceable, these efforts are still at an early stage and very likely received a setback with the tensions over the Trans Mountain Pipeline involving BC and Alberta. Federal theory relies on judicial review to maintain constitutional supremacy and keep governments accountable to the constitutional order. Non-judicial mechanisms for solving disagreements are less final and authoritative, even if they do offer some of the other advantages of more formal mechanisms.

Summary

The activism of the JCPC in promoting decentralization and the more conscious efforts of the Supreme Court of Canada to balance power between provincial and federal governments indicate that neutrality is not always a trademark of the judicial function in a federation. Some Canadian legal scholars have suggested that the Court's role in federalism is illegitimate and cannot be justified in the present democratic age (Monahan, 1987; Weiler, 1974): the judiciary, they argue, makes decisions on political grounds behind the veil of an artificial impartiality and is immune from the standards of accountability that political actors in a democracy should be subject to. The merits and demerits of this argument are beyond the scope of this chapter. Nevertheless, the CAP case gives us some idea of the limitations of judicial review in the present age of Canadian federalism.

If the role of judicial review in Canadian federalism is less central today than it was in the past, this has little to do with the perceived legitimacy of the judiciary as an actor in federal–provincial relations. Rather, it is a reflection of the prevalence of cooperative and collaborative intergovernmental agreements that circumvent constitutional niceties such as jurisdiction. The Court occasionally proves its relevance with a case like the *Reference Re: Firearms* or *Hydro-Québec*, and it certainly affects federalism through its enforcement of standards in the Charter of Rights and Freedoms. It is in the role of interpreter of the division of powers or umpire in disputes over what is legitimate federal or provincial activity that the Court's importance has decreased since Confederation.

The consequences of this development for the federation are open to debate. The essential accountability concern is not whether the Supreme Court is properly accountable to the electorate, but whether it is still capable of enforcing governments' accountability for properly exercising their constitutional jurisdiction. In the increasingly complex world of intergovernmental relations it has become more difficult for citizens to know who is really supposed to be doing what and whose feet they should hold to the flame if they are unhappy. The decreasing profile of the judiciary as umpire and enforcer of responsibilities can only serve to make the lines of accountability even more obscure.

Questions for Critical Thought

1. When is it a good idea to take another government to court, even if you are advised that you could lose the case?

2. In Switzerland, jurisdictional disputes between governments are settled not by the courts, but by the citizens in a referendum. Is this a better approach?

3. Should the Supreme Court of Canada always try to balance federal and provincial power, or does it have a more important role to play in promoting pan-Canadian rights and standards?

Notes

1. In the Securities Reference, a unanimous court counselled cooperation, but still recognized that at the same time "the constitutional boundaries that underlie the division of powers must be respected."

2. In *A.G. Ontario v. A.G. Canada (the Local Prohibition Case)*, A.C. 348 (1896), the JCPC ruled that "the exercise of legislative power by the parliament of Canada, in regard to all manners not enumerated in sect. 91, ought to be strictly confined to such matters as are unquestionably of Canadian interest and importance, and ought not to trench upon provincial legislation with respect to any of the classes of subjects enumerated in sect. 92." Determining what qualifies as a matter of "Canadian interest and importance" continues to occupy the Court. The effect of the last part of the quotation above makes POGG a third compartment. There is a prior claim to section 92—legislation must first be found to not fit a section 92 heading before it can qualify for POGG justification.

3. The New Deal package was originally referred to the Supreme Court of Canada in November 1935 by an ambivalent Mackenzie King, who had replaced Bennett as prime minister that October. The package of cases included the *Labour Conventions Reference*, A.C. 327 (1937), the *Employment and Social Insurance Reference*, A.C. 355 (1937), and the *National Products Marketing Act Reference*, A.C. 377 (1937). Five of the eight legislated reform measures presented to the JCPC were rejected as *ultra vires* the federal government.

4. By the end of the five years that the "cap on CAP" existed, federal funding for CAP programs in Ontario had dropped from 50 to 29 per cent. See Maslove (1996: 288).

References

Baier, G. 1998. "Tempering Peace, Order and Good Government: Provincial Inability and Canadian Federalism." *National Journal of Constitutional Law* 9, no. 3: 277–306.

———. 2002. "Judicial Review and Canadian Federalism." In *Canadian Federalism: Performance, Effectiveness, and Legitimacy*, edited by H. Bakvis and G. Skogstad. Toronto: Oxford University Press.

———. 2006. *Courts and Federalism: Judicial Doctrine in the United States, Australia and Canada*. Vancouver: University of British Columbia Press.

———. 2008. "The Courts, the Division of Powers, and Dispute Resolution." In *Canadian Federalism: Performance, Effectiveness, and Legitimacy*, 2nd edn, edited by H. Bakvis and G. Skogstad. Toronto: Oxford University Press.

Brouillet, E. 2017. "The Supreme Court of Canada: The Concept of Cooperative Federalism and Its Effects on the Balance of Power." In *Courts in Federal Countries: Federalists or Unitarists?*, edited by N. Aroney and J. Kincaid, 135–64. Toronto: University of Toronto Press.

Brown, D.M. 2002. *Market Rules: Economic Union Reform and Intergovernmental Policy-Making in Australia and Canada*. Montreal and Kingston: McGill-Queen's University Press.

Bzdera, A. 1993. "Comparative Analysis of Federal High Courts: A Political Theory of Judicial Review." *Canadian Journal of Political Science* 26, no. 1: 3–29.

Cairns, A.C. 1971. "The Judicial Committee and Its Critics." *Canadian Journal of Political Science* 4, no. 3: 301–45.

Council of the Federation. 2004. *Council of the Federation: Internal Trade Workplan*. Ottawa: Council of the Federation.

Daly, P. 2015. "Cooperative Federalism Divides the Supreme Court." Accessed 16 July 2018. http://www.iconnectblog.com/2015/03/cooperative-federalism-divides-the-supreme-court-of-canada-quebec-attorney-general-v-canada-attorney-general/.

Dupré, J.S. 1988. "Reflections on the Workability of Executive Federalism." In *Perspectives on Canadian Federalism*, edited by R. Olling and M.Westmacott. Scarborough, ON: Prentice-Hall.

Galloway, G. 2007. "Calvert Threatens to Take Ottawa to Court; Saskatchewan Opens Second Front in Revenue Dispute." *Globe and Mail*, 14 June.

——— and C. Alphonso. 2007. "I'll See You in Court, PM Tells Atlantic Premiers; Defiant Harper Says Atlantic Accord Hasn't Been Broken and Challenges Newfoundland and Nova Scotia to Legal Fight." *Globe and Mail*, 12 June.

Hogg, P.W. 1979. "Is the Supreme Court of Canada Biased in Constitutional Cases?" *Canadian Bar Review* 57, no. 4: 721–39.

———. 2015. *Constitutional Law of Canada*, student edn. Scarborough, ON: Thomson Carswell.

Kelly, J.B. 2001. "Reconciling Rights and Federalism during Review of the Charter of Rights and Freedoms: The Supreme Court of Canada and the Centralization Thesis, 1982 to 1999." *Canadian Journal of Political Science* 34: 321–55.

———. 2008. "The Courts, the Charter, and Federalism." In *Canadian Federalism: Performance, Effectiveness, and Legitimacy*, 2nd edn, edited by H. Bakvis and G. Skogstad. Toronto: Oxford University Press.

——— and M. Murphy. 2005. "Shaping the Constitutional Dialogue on Federalism: The Canadian Supreme Court as Meta-Political Actor." *Publius* 35, no. 2: 217–43.

Laskin, B. 1947. "Peace, Order and Good Government Re-Examined." *Canadian Bar Review* 25, no. 10: 1054–87.

———. 1951. "The Supreme Court of Canada: A Final Court of Appeal of and for Canadians." *Canadian Bar Review* 29, no. 10: 1038–79.

Maslove, A.M 1996. "The Canada Health and Social Transfer: Forcing Issues." In *How Ottawa Spends 1996–97: Life under the Knife*, edited by Gene Swimmer, 283–302. Ottawa: Carleton University Press.

Monahan, P. 1987. *Politics and the Constitution: The Charter, Federalism and the Supreme Court of Canada*. Toronto: Carswell.

Morton, F.L. 1995. "The Effect of the Charter of Rights on Canadian Federalism." *Publius* 25, no. 3: 173–88.

Russell, P.H. 1977. "The Anti-Inflation Case: The Anatomy of a Constitutional Decision." *Canadian Public Administration* 20, no. 4: 632–65.

———. 1983. "The Political Purposes of the Canadian Charter of Rights and Freedoms." *Canadian Bar Review* 61, no. 1: 30–54.

———. 1985. "The Supreme Court and Federal Provincial Relations: The Political Use of Legal Resources." *Canadian Public Policy* 11, no. 2: 161–70.

Saywell, J. 2002. *The Lawmakers: Judicial Power and the Shaping of Canadian Federalism*. Toronto: University of Toronto Press.

Scott, F.R. 1959. *Civil Liberties and Canadian Federalism*. Toronto: University of Toronto Press.

Smith, J. 1983. "The Origins of Judicial Review in Canada." *Canadian Journal of Political Science* 16, no. 1: 115–34.

Swinton, K. 1995. "Courting Our Way to Economic Integration: Judicial Review and the Canadian Economic Union." *Canadian Business Law Journal* 25, no. 1: 280–304.

Weiler, P.C. 1974. *In the Last Resort: A Critical Study of the Supreme Court of Canada*. Toronto: Carswell/Methuen.

Chapter 5

Executive Federalism: Back to the Future?

Weeks 6 & 7

Learning Objectives
- To understand the many settings and levels of executive federalism.
- To appreciate why and how governments choose to interact with one another.
- To explore the evidence of a reported decline in executive federalism over the past decade.

Introduction

Executive federalism has been a hallmark of the functioning of the Canadian federation for well over half a century, with its most notable feature being the predominance of political and bureaucratic elites from both orders of government and the interactions among them. There have been many flavours and phases of executive federalism, such as cooperative federalism (predominant in the early post-war period), competitive federalism, and collaborative federalism. Over the years, numerous questions have been raised about the legitimacy and efficacy of executive federalism. In the 1970s and 1980s a number of academics, most notably Donald Smiley (1979), argued that it contributes to "undue secrecy," "an unduly low level of citizen participation," and "dilutes the accountability of governments to their respective legislatures," among other attributes serving to undermine Canadian democracy. Others have pointed to the frequent stalemates between governments, preventing the implementation of needed programs or adjustments in the balance of responsibilities between governments, what Fritz Scharpf (1988) has termed the "joint-decision trap."

Both considerations have led various authors to speculate not just on the need for reform but also on the possible demise of executive federalism, a theme that resurfaced in the Harper era. In 1995 Kathy Brock wrote a thought-provoking piece—"The End of Executive Federalism?"—suggesting that in light of the open and inclusive processes used with the failed 1992 Charlottetown Accord it would be next to impossible to go back to the old closed processes in future years. Then, in 2011, Geoff Norquay argued—on quite different grounds, namely Prime Minister Harper's embrace of classical federalism and disinclination to meet with fellow first ministers under almost any circumstances—that the new "Harper doctrine" had resulted in "the death of executive federalism" (Norquay, 2011: 46). In the case of Brock's prognosis, the negotiation of the Social Union Framework Agreement (SUFA) in 1999, using many of the traditional forums and practices, including closed-door meetings and exclusion of non-government groups, suggests that, if not mistaken, she was at least premature in her views. As for Norquay's pronouncement, relying as it does on an assessment of Prime Minister Harper's view on federalism and his behaviour up to 2011, there is ample evidence that his judgement is premature as well.

Why Executive Federalism?

The Canadian federal model is premised on distinct federal and provincial jurisdictions, "watertight compartments" to use the classic metaphor, which are spelled out in the constitution and often reinforced, as well as redefined, by court decisions. At the same time, the interdependencies of modern policy-making and financing of programs have given rise to extensive coordination and collaboration across governments, and a recognition of the need for flexibility to overcome the rigidities of the constitutional framework. Such flexibility is a crucial element in what Inwood, Johns, and O'Reilly (2011) have called "intergovernmental policy capacity." It further implies a need for institutions and a set of agreed-upon rules to manage such interactions. Intergovernmental institutions such as first ministers' conferences and ministerial councils can facilitate interaction, which ideally should lead to increased trust among governments. Yet, problematically, they also allow governments to protect their jurisdiction, which typically pits both orders of government and individual governments against each other.

Further characteristics of the system of executive federalism also can be seen as problematic. As noted in earlier chapters, it is dominated by executives at the top of what is essentially a set of rather narrow, hierarchically organized pyramids, representing the federal, provincial, and territorial governments. If the expectation is that the intergovernmental system as a whole will function in a reasonably collaborative fashion, then the overall tone and the spirit of cooperation, through necessity, will need to be set by those at the top, that is, the prime minister and the 13 premiers. As will be noted in this chapter, however, this spirit of cooperation is often lacking. Crucially, during Stephen Harper's term, support for the system was under considerable strain from no less than the prime minister himself. At the same time, when Harper's successor, Justin Trudeau, tried to bring a more collaborative "sunny ways" style to intergovernmental negotiations, this new approach was not necessarily always reciprocated by other first ministers.

To the extent that we are seeking to resolve some of the problems stemming from these contradictory forces and developments, it is not at all clear where the solutions might lie. The key problem, in the eyes of many, is that of developing the system's capacity to generate trust ties and policy capacity among first ministers, ministers, and those below them. In their suggestions for improving the capacity of the first ministers' conference in particular, Papillon and Simeon (2004) make recommendations such as having regular meetings of first ministers, linking these meetings to the parliamentary and legislative process, and creating a more open and transparent process. Overall, they argue, "the case of institutionalizing the FMC [First Ministers' Conference] is . . . a strong one" (Papillon and Simeon, 2004: 132). But this seemingly powerful argument for enhancing institutionalization and adopting a firmer set of decision-rules is challenged by another long-time student of Canadian federalism, who argues that one of the key features of the Canadian system—ambiguity, and by implication the lack of institutionalization—is what helps makes the system work (Lazar, 2004). In his words, "AMBIGUITY was the mid-wife of Canada's birth. And AMBIGUITY remains central to the Canadian politics of today" (Lazar, 2004: 4).

A further element is that the federal government under Stephen Harper, using the rubric of "open federalism," sought in many ways to unwind many of the interdependencies among governments that had evolved over the years. As prime minister, he never convened a first ministers' conference or meeting other than two brief informal sessions and a somewhat longer session in 2009 to discuss Canada's economic action plan during the financial crisis. Also, in a number of areas, the prime minister sought to reduce or even eliminate Ottawa's presence. Take the case of health care, for example, a field in which Ottawa deliberately cultivated a high profile through the Canada Health Transfer (CHT) and the Canada Health Act. Upon coming to office Prime Minister Harper indicated that while CHT transfers would continue, albeit at a reduced rate of growth, the government of Canada was no longer interested in directing or influencing how the money was to be spent by the provinces, seeing this policy and delivery responsibility as provincial, with the federal government playing a minimal role at most. In brief, for a good part of the Harper era (2006–15), the thrust of the federal government favoured a reversion towards a more classical form of federalism (Bakvis, 2014).

This chapter does not claim to resolve the debate over the merits of a more classical approach or greater or lesser institutionalization. But the ensuing discussion of the machinery of executive federalism does serve to elucidate some of the unwritten rules and regularities that exist and outlines some of the practices that, in conjunction with other factors, either promote or hinder the generation of trust ties, an important condition for intergovernmental effectiveness (see the discussion of this term later in this chapter). The present chapter does so by examining first ministers' conferences (FMCs) and meetings, ministerial councils, meetings of officials, and the Council of the Federation (COF), as well as the contradictory elements embedded within the overall system. We will review briefly the different sites, the formal structures, and the forces that shape or drive how these different intergovernmental bodies function. We also address the issue of the future direction of executive federalism, whether the federal government will remain disengaged from formal intergovernmental relations, and whether the perennial topic of the closed and anti-democratic nature of executive federalism continues to resonate or is only visible at times of major crises.

The Settings of Executive Federalism

The original 1867 Constitution Act made no provision for intergovernmental relations. Neither did judicial interpretation help matters. Indeed, as noted in Chapters 3 and 4, the thrust of many of the decisions by the JCPC implied that interaction between governments should be limited—essentially, that each level of government should stick to its own watertight compartments. When interactions did occur it was often in the courts. Wilfrid Laurier, elected as federal Liberal prime minister in 1896 on a platform that included respect for provincial rights, did bring together the premiers for the initial meeting of all first ministers in 1906, although the next such meeting did not take place for another 12 years. Furthermore, the 1906 meeting was called only after persistent badgering from the premiers. In the meantime the provincial premiers had already taken the initiative, led by Quebec, to hold meetings among themselves, without the federal prime minister, in 1887 and 1902.[1] Only in the 1930s at the height of the Depression did a pattern emerge of FMCs being used on a regular basis as a vehicle for discussing the responses of governments to economic crises.

Things changed dramatically in the post-war period with the arrival of the welfare state. With Ottawa providing a considerable portion of the financing, and also to a fair degree the necessary leadership, but lacking the constitutional authority, a high level of coordination was required. As well, the levels of taxation required to support these new initiatives necessitated cooperation between governments in order to avoid the excessive overlap and competition that occurred between governments over income tax and other taxes in the 1920s and 1930s. All these forces led to a dramatic increase in the frequencies of meetings, primarily of officials, and led to what Donald Smiley (1987) termed "executive federalism": the relations between elected and appointed officials from the two orders of government. In examining the settings, institutions, and processes involved in intergovernmental relations it is again worth stressing the point made by many observers, namely, the fluidity of the rules and norms and the overall low level of institutionalization. While there is the Canadian Intergovernmental Conference Secretariat (CICS) created in 1973 and based in Ottawa, it has relatively few staff and provides only limited administrative support. Essentially, it plays a service role, handling the logistics of meetings. Thus, while it is responsible for distributing materials for conferences (and also maintains a valuable archive), it is not involved in drafting or shaping any of this material.[2] In contrast, the European Union, what many see as a federation in the making, has a secretariat numbering in the thousands. The secretariat for the Council of Australian Governments (COAG) also appears to play a more active role, providing support for the various ministerial councils, among other things.[3] In Canada, the most institutionalized forum for intergovernmental relations—the Council of Atlantic Premiers (previously the Council of Maritime Premiers)—is a regional body, serving a population of less than two million, with a staff that is responsible not only for logistics but also the conduct of research and analysis in support of the Council's deliberations.

First Ministers' Conferences and First Ministers' Meetings (FMCs/FMMs)

The pre-eminent body, the one that sits at the top of the intergovernmental pyramid, is the First Ministers' Conference, also referred to by its more formal title, the Federal–Provincial Plenary Conference. Its origins go back to the first such meeting, called by Wilfrid Laurier in 1906, which at the time was rather awkwardly titled "Conference of the Representatives of the Government of Canada and the Various Provinces." Only one further conference took place under that label (1918) and then, in 1927, they came to be called, variously, Dominion–Provincial, Federal–Provincial, and First Ministers' conferences. The term "First Ministers" began to be used in 1974 with a conference on energy, but the term can likely be traced back to the ill-fated Victoria Charter of 1971, whose formal provisions, among other things, would have provided for annual meetings of "first ministers."

Since the early 1990s the FMC has been superseded by first ministers' meetings (FMMs), the latter implying less formality and more flexibility. All meetings held under Jean Chrétien's stewardship were FMMs. This format reached a new level of informality when the about to be anointed Prime Minister Paul Martin held a session with the premiers over breakfast at the time of the Grey Cup in November of 2003. The term "Conference" in conjunction with "first ministers" had become very much associated with constitutional conferences, constitutional wrangling, and the spectre of the failed Meech Lake Accord. Prime Minister Chrétien, in seeking to distance himself from any suggestion of reopening constitutional talks, held seven FMMs but not a single FMC in his 10 years in office. While Paul Martin held a number of FMMs, as noted at the outset Stephen Harper held only one FMM plus two brief informal meetings with the premiers in his nine years as prime minister, favouring instead one-on-one meetings with them when circumstances warranted. The days of high-level summitry involving delegations composed of premiers, ministers, "spin doctors," and advisers, meeting under the glare of extensive media coverage, appear to be long past, associated in the main with acrimonious and largely failed exercises in constitutional negotiation. It should be kept in mind that even during their heyday the FMCs were seen as more a forum for discussion than for decision-making. Only under exceptional circumstances, as during the constitutional negotiations in the 1980s, did first ministers agree on a specific proposal or set of proposals. Votes were rarely held and few clear-cut decisions were taken.

As noted by Papillon and Simeon (2004), FMMs are less formal and more private. In the 1990s they certainly reflected the style of the then new Chrétien government and, more generally, a new mindset by all the participants in wishing to de-emphasize the all-encompassing FMC and emphasizing more collaboration and a low-key approach to solving intergovernmental issues between governments. In doing so, the expectation was no doubt that it would also help to take first ministers' sessions out of the glare of media attention and make them less accessible to outside actors. Given the spectacular failures of both Meech Lake and Charlottetown, and the resulting opprobrium that came to be attached to first ministers' summitry, this development was not surprising. As well, in taking more of a gradualist approach, many high-level activities were channelled through ministerial councils, on which there will be more said below. FMMs, however, continued to play an important albeit rather different role relative to the FMCs of the 1980s and early 1990s. At the same time, some of the FMMs held during the 1990s came to resemble good old-fashioned FMCs.

FMMs were now more likely to be scheduled as a culmination of a long process that started elsewhere, most likely in a ministerial council. For example, the Social Union Framework Agreement originated with discussions among provincial governments, including annual premiers' conferences starting in 1995. It was then advanced at federal–provincial meetings of ministers of justice and social policy. Finally, in February of 1999, when ministers had taken the file as far as possible, the prime minister sat down with the premiers to make the final compromises for the package that came to be known as SUFA. While Quebec was not a signatory, the agreement was carefully structured so that Quebec could receive the extra health-care funding that was part of the SUFA package. Also, the SUFA first ministers' meeting, in scale and attendant publicity, resembled a traditional FMC. Thus while FMMs, like FMCs, are not frequent, and concrete results are even less frequent, they are still very important; no major change or new major policy that cuts across federal and provincial/territorial jurisdiction is likely to occur without the involvement of first ministers.

Jean Chrétien, during his tenure as prime minister, introduced a variant of the FMM, namely his "Team Canada" trade missions abroad, which included the premiers. Ostensibly about trade rather than federal–provincial issues, like the informal breakfasts and dinners associated with FMMs and FMCs, these missions allowed for free-flowing discussion across a whole range of issues. As trade promotion exercises, the success of these half-dozen missions remained unclear, but as sessions in promoting understanding and tackling problematic issues between and among the first ministers, the trade missions were among the more productive activities hosted by the prime minister.

In his short-lived tenure (2004–6) Prime Minister Paul Martin held four FMMs, including a major one on health care in November 2004, as well as an elaborate conference of first ministers and Aboriginal leadership, which resulted in the Kelowna Accord of November 2005. As noted earlier, in contrast, Prime Minister Harper held only two brief informal meetings with the premiers, an informal dinner shortly after taking office, and another more formal session, again over dinner, in January 2008. His only full-day meeting with the premiers occurred in January 2009 at the height of the recession, where Harper outlined a stimulus package that included significant federal support for municipal and provincial infrastructure projects. His philosophy of "open federalism" notwithstanding, Prime Minister Harper clearly had limited interest in hosting collective gatherings of first ministers, whether in the form of an FMM or FMC. Instead, he had a much stronger penchant for bilateral sessions with premiers or communicating with them by phone or e-mail. To the extent that his approach constituted a deliberate strategy, it limited even further the prospects of the first ministers' forum becoming, any time soon, "the centrepiece . . . of the machinery of intergovernmental relations in Canada" (Papillon and Simeon, 2004: 113).

Justin Trudeau partially reversed this trend, pledging in the 2015 election to hold frequent FMMs. He had criticized the Harper government for what he saw as an unwillingness to engage constructively with provincial leaders. Crucially, several of Trudeau's most important policy promises, like cannabis legalization and a new carbon tax, would require federal–provincial cooperation, and provided the new Liberal government with good reasons to continue with regular FMMs. To mid-2018 he had met with the premiers (and for part of at least one meeting, national Indigenous leaders) on a variety of intergovernmental issues. This includes a meeting in November 2015 shortly after the election; two meetings in 2016 on the topic of climate change; a conference call briefing on Canada–US trade relations in April 2017, and a one-day meeting in October 2017 on two federal priorities—Indigenous reconciliation and NAFTA—and two issues added by the provinces—tax-sharing around the legalized sale of cannabis and proposed federal small business taxes (Tasker, 2017).

The outcomes of these meetings, which were all closed to the public, are difficult to summarize or even to determine. As discussed in Chapter 9, the FMMs on the climate change issue seem to have been important milestones towards reaching the pan-Canadian agreement released in December 2016. On other topics, however, firm results were not forthcoming and communiqués were not released—but that is not to say that the meetings were not a useful part of the ongoing process of reaching consensus and ironing out difficulties on a variety of issues. On the whole, one would have to note that the Justin Trudeau approach as prime minister is to continue with FMMs as a useful form of intergovernmental cooperation, but that it is not a fundamentally significant part of the government's strategic approach.

Premiers and the Council of the Federation

In addition to FMCs and FMMs, there also is the Council of the Federation, pre-viously known as the Annual Premiers' Conference (APC), consisting of all first ministers *minus* the federal prime minister. This conference actually has a longer history than the FMC, with the first provincial premiers' conference being con-vened in 1887 by the premier of Quebec, two decades before the first FMC hosted by Wilfrid Laurier. The premiers' conference continued to meet sporadically until 1960, when it became an annual event largely at the instigation of newly elected Quebec Premier Jean Lesage. In 2003 the APC took a monumental leap forward, at least by the standards of Canadian intergovernmental relations, by remaking itself into the Council of the Federation (COF), complete with a steering commit-tee composed of provincial deputies, a secretariat, and a provision for the striking of ad hoc committees of ministers to examine specific topics. In addition to its regular summer meeting, the founding agreement of the COF also commits the premiers and territorial leaders to at least one additional meeting a year.

The COF stands as the only senior national intergovernmental body that meets on a regular basis (the regional Council of Atlantic Premiers and the West-ern Premiers' Conference also meet regularly). The annual gathering in July or August, hosted by one of the premiers on a rotating basis (who also serves as chair of the COF for the year), attracts considerable media attention; it has also become ritualized to a degree. At one stage the norm was for the annual event to focus largely on interprovincial issues—securities regulation, interprovincial trucking, consumer legislation, and the like. And although neither the federal prime min-ister nor federal ministers would be present, there was usually a federal observer. In the late 1980s, however, the tenor changed. The federal observer was no longer welcome to sit in on meetings and the focus, or at least certainly the attention, of the event shifted to strategic consideration of federal–provincial issues. Espe-cially with issues such as health care and fiscal transfers generally, the premiers tended to join together and issue declarations to the effect that Ottawa needs to be more responsive in dealing with these matters. Through the 1980s and 1990s the recourse of the premiers to ritualistic demands for more federal funds became predictable and thus less effective. On the other hand, the addition of the leaders of the three territories, including Nunavut created in 1999, has altered the char-acter of the body, as these representatives are clearly more sympathetic to issues such as those of Indigenous peoples and climate change.

Over the years a number of premiers have used the premiers' conference as a venue in which to air, and garner support for, issues of particular relevance to them or their province. In 1996, for example, Premier Mike Harris of Ontario tried to promote the idea of the provinces taking primary responsibility for set-ting national standards in the social policy area and at the same time becoming less dependent on Ottawa for financing these programs.[4] Premiers from have-not provinces proved to be decidedly lukewarm to the idea, fearing the further loss of money from Ottawa. Similarly, a few years later BC Premier Glen Clark's efforts to have the premiers collectively pressure Ottawa to take more decisive action on the US–Canada salmon fisheries dispute also met with failure. So, too, did the efforts of Nova Scotia in 2001 for support on special treatment for offshore revenues in the equalization formula, although when Newfoundland took up the cause a few years later the issue did attain momentum, with both provinces obtaining significant concessions from the Paul Martin government in 2005 (see discussion in Chapter 6). And in 2002, Alberta's call for the premiers to oppose collectively the signing by the federal government of the Kyoto Protocol on global warming, a call that the Alberta government promoted in full-page ads in the national press in the lead-up to the meeting, was publicly rejected by a significant proportion of the premiers at the post-meeting press conference, including by all three territorial leaders (McCarthy, 2002).

By various criteria the old annual premiers' conference appeared less effective than it might have been. At the same time, discussion by the premiers among themselves in the mid-1990s, in the aftermath of the drastic cuts in fiscal transfers imposed by Ottawa, eventually led to the Social Union Framework Agreement. As is the case with FMMs, however, much of the work leading up to SUFA was done by ministerial subcommittees and committees of officials. But the essential idea of a framework agreement on the social union was stimulated by the active role of the premiers.

The question remains whether the COF represents a significant development. Some have argued that the premiers missed a valuable opportunity in 2003 by not including a set of decision-rules akin to those used by the European Union or by not creating a more permanent body that would either include the federal government or serve as a replacement for the Senate. The original idea and the actual title of the Council date back to constitutional discussions of the late 1970s and early 1980s, when the annual meeting of premiers was seen either as a replacement for the Senate or as a variation on the German Bundesrat, a body composed of all state premiers and an integral part of the German parliament where it constitutes the second chamber. This latter Bundesrat-type model was recommended by the Task Force on Canadian Unity (Pepin-Robarts) when it proposed what it called, coincidentally, the Council of the Federation in 1979.[5] In 1980 the Quebec Liberal Party under leader Claude Ryan proposed an entity called the Federal Council that would be constituted as a separate intergovernmental body and not, in contrast to Pepin-Robarts, as part of the federal Parliament. It did, however, include the federal government as a full participant and had a set of decision-rules that included a regional veto. In the fall of 1980 after a constitutional patriation resolution was tabled in Parliament, the Standing Senate Committee on Legal and Constitutional Affairs proposed a federal–provincial council to play a coordinating role, which, according to Peter Meekison (2003), probably came closest to what the Quebec Liberal Party outlined in its Council of the Federation model in 2001. The 2001 Quebec proposal also had the federal government included as a partner.

In the present era, the Quebec government, under Liberal Premier Jean Charest and his minister of intergovernmental relations, Benoit Pelletier, pressed hardest for a new body. The model announced by the premiers in late 2003, however, remained purely confederal with no role for Ottawa, other than as respondent to the claims put forward by the new Council, much like the old premiers' conference. Yet there was more to it than that. Jean Charest in 2003, freshly elected as premier of Quebec, was the leader of a non-sovereignist but nonetheless Quebec-first Liberal Party. His agenda included two issues that in his view were important to Quebec: dealing with the fiscal imbalance and asymmetrical federalism, with the latter implying a unique status for Quebec within Confederation. Both issues became important COF agenda items, with the COF launching a special task force to review fiscal federalism and, in 2004, endorsing a special arrangement between Ottawa and Quebec with respect to the health-care accord, which saw Quebec exempted from certain conditions and affirmed that province's unique position (Maioni, 2008). In many ways, the latter was the more important, denoting acceptance by all the premiers of a position that was of considerable symbolic significance; the actual "conditions" from which Quebec gained exemption were, in reality, relatively minor.

The creators and supporters of the COF publicly stated that regular and more frequent meetings, as well as institutional support in the form of a secretariat not only to the COF but to the various subcommittees, would lead to the development of common positions to be presented to Ottawa on issues where there was a strong consensus among all the premiers. Rather than premiers negotiating among themselves and, individually, with Ottawa, as typically occurs in the context of an FMC or FMM, it would mean the federal government negotiating directly with the COF or its representatives, that is, transforming a multilateral process into essentially a bilateral one between a single entity and a collective one. At a later stage, under this optimistic scenario, it is conceivable that the COF would occupy something comparable to the German Bundesrat, perhaps even displacing the present Senate, though this would require a constitutional amendment. The possibility was also raised that at some stage Ottawa would play a formal role within the COF, albeit on terms largely defined by the COF rather than Ottawa. With sufficient discipline and commitment it is conceivable that the COF could displace the FMC/FMM system and perhaps even Ottawa from atop the intergovernmental pyramid.[6] Certainly with the promise of stronger leadership and a high degree of institutionalization, at least relative to what was in place before with the Annual Premiers' Conference and presently with the FMC/FMM, the promise was high. In brief, for a number of people it appeared that here was an opportunity for the provinces collectively to take control of the intergovernmental agenda and gain a long-term strategic advantage vis-à-vis Ottawa. Others, however, with the benefit of hindsight would probably have labelled this as wishful thinking.

Crucially, for the COF to be effective in the way many hoped, it would have to have its act together. Specifically, it would necessarily need to adopt a set of decision-rules that ensured ample support for COF decisions yet at the same time afforded protection to significant minority opinion, but not so that it would require the unrealistically high threshold of unanimity (Brown, 2003). No decision-rules were ever adopted; instead, the norm of "consensus" continued to prevail, which for all intents and purposes meant "unanimity." Given that the odds of at least one province or territory being offside at any one time, the lack of a more realistic decision-making process would sooner or later spell trouble.

The test of the COF as an institution arrived with the fiscal imbalance issue, one of the two main items on Charest's agenda. Matters began promisingly enough. A blue-ribbon panel was commissioned by the COF to examine the issue and to make recommendations. Fiscal federalism proved to be a dangerous terrain on which to prove the COF's mettle, however. As will become evident in Chapter 6, aside from the intrinsic zero-sum dimensions relating to fiscal imbalance—under any new arrangement there are bound to be winners and losers—the field was further complicated by the issue of the equalization clawback and the offshore accords agreed to by the Martin government. The end result was that the recommendations of the blue-ribbon panel—as outlined in the Gagné-Stein Report (Council of the Federation, 2006)—received only a lukewarm response from most provinces and outright rejection by at least three provinces. A meeting of the COF scheduled to discuss Gagné-Stein was abruptly cancelled, as many governments feared that the rifts among them were far too deep. In brief, the Council, which initially appeared to be one of the more significant developments in Canadian intergovernmental relations, now looked a lot less promising. At one level, the failure to deliver on that initial promise can be seen as a failure of provincial leadership. On another level, however, it suggests that there is simply no will or capacity in the system that tolerates, let alone promotes, regularization and institutionalization of intergovernmental relations. Or further, this failure simply speaks to the distinctive interests of the provinces that no tinkering with rules can easily overcome (Lazar, 2003).

Ministerial Councils and Civil Society

Perhaps nothing provides a better insight into intergovernmental relations as an activity and preoccupation—that is, the locus of intergovernmental activity—than the Canadian Intergovernmental Conference Secretariat (CICS) website. If FMCs or FMMs occur only every couple of years, or even less frequently as was the case under Harper, and premiers' meetings once or twice a year, ministerial meetings occur almost on a weekly basis. Simply by clicking on "Find a past conference" on the CICS website (http://www.scics.ca/en/), one will find listings of all the major meetings and teleconferences in recent years, including news releases, communiqués, and other statements, with the exception of those involving departments and ministries of Finance.[7] In any given month, there will be on average about six different ministerial meetings, ranging from fisheries ministers to those responsible for seniors. Conferences involving ministers of Finance and provincial treasurers are the most important meetings since they deal with fiscal and financing issues that affect all policy areas. They also tend to attract considerably more attention. Much like FMMs or FMCs, relatively few deals or agreements are struck at these meetings. Typically, reports will be reviewed, discussions will take place, and commitments will be made to examine various issues further and to work towards developing a consensus on matters deemed important to Canadians.

Ministerial councils are noteworthy in three further respects. Much more so than FMCs/FMMs, many ministerial councils are to a degree institutionalized, with full-time secretariats as well as regularly scheduled meetings.[8] Furthermore, in these bodies one is most likely to find a level of trust among both ministers and officials. And, at the ministerial level, one is most likely to find connections with civil society in the form of public interest groups, trade associations, and the like—in brief, a variety of stakeholders who have a significant interest in the outcomes of intergovernmental negotiations. The Canadian Council of Forest Ministers (CCFM), for example, conducts much of its work through the National Forest Strategy Coalition (NFSC), which has overseen the development of three national forest strategies since 1985. The NFSC, significantly, comprises not only the ministers of the provinces and territories, as well as the federal minister, but also industry organizations and conservation and Indigenous groups. According to Simmons (2008, 2012), its significance lies in the fact that the signatories to the accords that accompany the national forest strategies include both ministers and non-government representatives and, further, these accords contain up to 100 separate "commitments to action" and are the result of a broadly based deliberative process. The 2003–8 accord had the backing of 63 signatories, though the signatories did not include the provinces of Quebec, Manitoba, and Alberta.

Simmons (2008) also identified the Canadian Council of Ministers of Environment (CCME) as a body and forum that routinely incorporates non-governmental actors into its policy development. It also has a full-time secretariat, multi-year business plan, formalized task groups, and a publications program, and represents, in Simmons's view, "the most institutionalized of all the intergovernmental bodies" (Simmons, 2008: 367). Like the CCFM, the deliberations of the CCME have resulted in a number of accords, though the overall record is mixed. Winfield and Macdonald (2008) argue that little progress has been made in the area of developing standards for handling toxic substances, for example. They also point to the example of the 1998 Canada-Wide Harmonization Accord, which they note was heavily criticized by environmental non-governmental organizations, academics, and the Parliamentary Standing Committee on Environment and Sustainable Development for, among other things, the apparent abandonment of Ottawa's regulatory role in the environmental field.

Ministerial councils and their meetings can be federal–provincial–territorial or interprovincial–territorial. They can also involve just a subset of ministers, for example, the Atlantic Council of Fisheries and Aquaculture Ministers. One of the more important committees is the Council of Ministers of Education of Canada (CMEC), which deals with an area in the main exclusively under the jurisdiction of the provinces, although the federal government has a significant interest in this field, especially post-secondary education (Wallner, 2014). Except on rare occasions the federal minister is not invited, and then only outside of the normal business of the meeting. In other areas provincial and territorial ministers meet by themselves. Particularly given the wide array of services the provinces have a responsibility for delivering, there is ample reason for provinces and territories to meet frequently to ensure coordination in areas such as the administration of justice, transportation, and health care.

In brief, a number of ministerial councils are part, and at times even at the epicentre, of distinct policy communities. As Simmons (2005, 2012) has noted, the character of these policy communities varies considerably from council to council, with some displaying extensive participation of various non-governmental stakeholders and demonstrating that the development of trust ties can extend beyond the level of governments, while others are somewhat more removed from civic society. It is also at the ministerial council level that much of the real work is accomplished. Though capped at the end by a meeting of the first ministers, most of the work that went into the making of SUFA was conducted at the level of officials working under the auspices of the council of social union ministers.[9] It was an exception that proved the rule.

It is important to keep in mind, however, that whatever consensus emerges at the level of these ministerial councils and associated bodies can easily be over-ridden by developments at the broader political level, as illustrated by the 1998 Harmonization Accord on the environment. In this instance, within the federal government at the highest level it was decided that the necessity of an agreement with the provinces overrode strong misgivings by the federal Department of the Environment and even the minister herself (Winfield and Macdonald, 2008). As will be noted below, tensions between central agencies and departments and agencies can be greater than between those departments and their counterparts in other governments.

It remains an open question of how best to measure the effectiveness of inter-governmental bodies, whether FMMs or ministerial councils. Focusing exclusively on the presence or absence of formal agreements may not necessarily be the most appropriate criterion to use in assessing them. Maintaining good communication to ensure a shared understanding of the issues at hand is an important consideration.

Furthermore, in the communiqués issued at the end of conferences or meetings, one can find signs of implicit if not explicit agreement on various matters through phrases such as: "Ministers expressed support for this legislation" (referring to federal legislation), "ministers commended the federal minister's recent decision," or the federal "Minister agreed to take the matter of . . . costs . . . to his Cabinet colleagues later this year." In brief, meetings that indicate support for a federal activity or eventually lead to a new or revised piece of federal or provincial legislation can be seen as evidence of both progress and collaboration. Conversely, the failure to issue a post-conference communiqué can be seen as a sign of a significant impasse. In fact, the wording and content of the post-conference communiqué occupies a fair amount of time of council members and officials; in effect, it represents an important indicator for assessing where things stand with respect to consensus and commitment, and for outside observers—after the careful parsing of words and phrases—it can be a useful guide on whether progress has been made or where a policy area may be heading.

Meetings of Officials

Along with meetings of ministers, the CICS site also lists meetings of deputy ministers, both federal–provincial and interprovincial. In reviewing the list, a pattern is often discernible: meetings of ministers will be preceded by meetings of their deputies by a few days or weeks. On occasion ministers and deputies will meet simultaneously or their meetings will overlap. Essentially, officials do the preparatory work, and in the process of doing so they play an important role in shaping the agenda and the tenor of the discussion. Among other things, officials will be responsible for drafting reports on outstanding issues in various policy domains, will collect and standardize data in connection with drafting these reports, and, more generally, will develop a common set of tools and concepts to facilitate discussion during meetings of ministers and/or deputies, that is, if the process is working well. Officials working in support of these meetings will be below the level of deputies and will typically meet on their own, and will be in constant communication with each other by phone and e-mail. Meetings of officials, in fact, are the most frequent if unheralded intergovernmental events. As in the case of cabinet meetings or the management of departments, ministers for all intents would be paralyzed without the support of officials. This is not to say that ministers lack power or the capacity to give direction, but simply that they are not in a position to manage the minutia and intricacies of the positions they take into intergovernmental meetings.

Equally crucial, officials are also largely responsible for orchestrating consultative exercises and liaising with non-government actors. As noted above, in efforts to open up the intergovernmental process over the past decade—if only in response to criticism of the closed nature of the process—most ministerial councils have developed ties and networks with non-government stakeholders, as well as third governments such as municipalities and First Nations. These consultative exercises can be quite elaborate and require considerable resources to manage properly, especially if they are going to be perceived as legitimate by the relevant policy communities and interested observers. Often these consultative excises are outsourced to specialized consulting firms or think-tanks with interests and expertise in the policy area in question, but the overall process and the key participants in these exercises will be officials from federal and provincial line departments involved in the particular sector.[10]

The increase in consultative exercises, while generally seen as a positive development, can still trigger misgivings by governments, officials, and politicians. First, there is the long-standing fear of losing control of a process that in the eyes of many officials still works best when conducted in private. Second, governments also may use consultative mechanisms as a way of engendering support in the broader community for their position and as a means of bringing pressure to bear on other governments. For example, in 2005, when the Liberal government of Paul Martin negotiated a series of bilateral agreements with the provinces and territories on child care and early childhood learning, one of the conditions attached to most of the agreements was that the provincial governments involved undertake a consultative process with their stakeholders. Some of the provincial governments suspected that this was simply a ploy on Ottawa's part to allow various public interest groups, whose views were more likely to be aligned with the federal government's aspirations, an opportunity to shape the configuration of the programs that the provinces would deliver.

On the whole, it is at the level of officials where ties between governments are likely to be closest and where communication is best. While the meetings may be numerous, the total number of people involved in intergovernmental relations constitutes a relatively small community. Particularly when Ottawa launches a new program, which increasingly tends to be done on a bilateral basis, these officials will be in constant touch with each other, sharing information and perspectives. And when Ottawa proceeds on a bilateral basis, negotiating agreements with each province individually, provincial governments are understandably anxious to discover what other provinces may be asking for, receiving, or not receiving. Provincial officials are usually quite frank with each other, especially with people with whom they have developed close working relations over the years. At the same time, they are never totally frank; there is always a strategic element that dictates the withholding of some crucial information, if only because decisions are imminent or because cabinet confidences may be involved. In addition, even within a common sense of Canadian loyalty and relationships, a diplomatic culture and posture has developed over time.

At a much earlier stage several decades ago, during the era of cooperative federalism, officials likely did exercise more power, especially senior officials, mainly since political leadership at the time was less engaged in the intergovernmental process and was more willing to defer to their officials in line departments for handling what were seen as the rather arcane details concerning road construction or tax administration. In many instances, ministers and premiers were interested primarily in the fact that they could construct roads and schools with Ottawa providing 50 per cent of the costs. Especially the political leadership was not that keen in looking gift horses in the mouth. It was left to officials on both federal and provincial sides to negotiate what were seen as the technical details, a situation that permitted officials to shape programs that fitted their conceptions of what constituted appropriate standards and priorities. As noted in Chapter 2, all this began to change during the 1960s, with Quebec setting the lead in creating an infrastructure that simultaneously allowed ministers, and especially the premier, to have more say over policy and at the same time bring more sophisticated expertise to bear on the issues at hand. Even before Quebec introduced these innovations, certain provinces were beginning to realize that they needed the expertise not only of engineers but also of economists and lawyers familiar with the broader framework within which federal–provincial agreements were reached and how to gain maximum advantage.

Intergovernmental Agencies, the Intragovernmental Dimension, and Trust Ties

This newly acquired economic and legal expertise was institutionalized and brought to bear on the intergovernmental process through what came to be known as "intergovernmental affairs agencies" (IGAs). These agencies were not only the product of the changed nature of relations between governments but also due to changes within governments. In an earlier era of what Dupré (1988) and Smiley (1987) have referred to as the era of the "departmentalized" cabinet, relations between governments were handled through interactions between first ministers or by ministers and senior officials. It was an era in which the key unit tended to be the line department at both the federal and the provincial levels and where often-larger-than-life ministerial figures such as J.G. (Jimmy) Gardiner, long-time minister of agriculture, and C.D. Howe, "minister of everything," both in the King and St Laurent cabinets, predominated. Intergovernmental issues were typically managed within the sectoral confines of the two like-minded federal and provincial departments, with cost-shared programs providing the fuel for cooperative programs arranged between them.

The departmentalized cabinet, however, came to be displaced by the "institutionalized" cabinet (Dunn, 1995; Dupré, 1988; Smiley, 1987), a transition beginning in the 1960s. It involved a series of administrative reforms, essentially driven by some significant political changes that sought a more integrated, whole-of-government approach right at the top, at the level of cabinet.

Line departments and ministers were, and still are, important actors, but now direction and perspective were provided by cabinet and cabinet committees as a whole, amply supported by central agencies. While these developments applied to all government programs and operations, intergovernmental programs and activities were especially affected, if only because they related to some of the most salient political issues at the time, such as public pensions and medicare in the 1960s. These new, specialized IGAs at both the federal and the provincial levels were tasked with handling not only relations between governments but also the internal *intra*governmental relations within governments. These new agencies, then, became part of the strategic apex.

Quebec was the first to set up a Department of Federal–Provincial Relations in 1961 (renamed and reorganized as the Department of Intergovernmental Affairs in 1967 and adding responsibility for international affairs). Ontario created a new Department of Treasury, Economics and Intergovernmental Affairs in the mid-1960s. Later, in 1978, when the constitutional debate became the dominant issue, the Intergovernmental Affairs portion was hived off and became a separate agency. The federal government created a Federal–Provincial Relations Office (FPRO) separate from the Privy Council Office (PCO) in 1975. By the end of the 1970s virtually all governments had some kind of specialized intergovernmental affairs agency in place. IGAs reached their apotheosis in the 1970s and 1980s, largely as a consequence of their crucial role in constitutional talks. It was also when a particular kind of expertise— that of constitutional lawyers and political scientists—tended to predominate within IGAs, which is not surprising since the constitution was the main item on the agenda. And when the constitution is the primary item, the main concern will be protecting and extending the government's jurisdiction and to link related issues to the government's broader objectives. All of this led Donald Smiley (1980: 115) to make the interesting observation that "Intergovernmental affairs agencies appear to contribute to federal–provincial conflict rather than accommodation."

With the cooling of interest in constitutional change, the role and scope of IGAs came to be much reduced. FPRO was placed back in PCO in 1995, and is now referred to as the Intergovernmental Relations Secretariat. There is still a separate minister of Intergovernmental Relations, though in the Harper government it was seen as a relatively junior portfolio.

Shortly after his election, Justin Trudeau named himself as minister of Intergovernmental Affairs as well as Youth. This seemed to be intended to send a message about the importance Trudeau places on working with the provinces, and to end the view that Intergovernmental Affairs is a role of little significance given to second-tier ministers. However, this decision has also put him under some criticism, as members of other parties have claimed that those ministries are underserved because of not having a designated minister.

In some provinces the premier assumes the additional portfolio of minister of Intergovernmental Affairs, in others a separate minister assumes that function, but in all the provinces and territories the premier dominates the tone and substance of intergovernmental relations, akin to the way a prime minister dominates foreign policy despite the need for a separate minister of Foreign Affairs.

Being part of the strategic apex, it is the role of IGAs to promote a government-wide perspective on executive decisions and to provide the requisite coordination and support in pursuit of this objective. Particularly in some of the larger provinces, IGAs also have the responsibility of looking after offices located abroad serving the interests of the province and acting as a conduit for contacts with the academic and business community in the province who have expertise or interests in the province's relations with Ottawa (Elton and McCormick, 1997). At the same time, the manner in which these agencies perform their various roles, and how they are organized, can vary considerably. Some, like Alberta's, carry much more weight, having as part of their legal mandate the right to participate in all intergovernmental negotiations conducted by line departments. Other IGAs play more of an advisory and less of a coordinating role (Pollard, 1986). These variations in part reflect the personal preferences and approach of the incumbent first minister. They are also in good part a function of the environment and political climate. If the environment is uncertain or turbulent, there will be more emphasis on centralized control.

The role played by central agencies, particularly by IGAs, and by the institutionalized cabinet as a whole has had important implications for what J. Stefan Dupré (1988) in one of the classic pieces on Canadian federalism has labelled the "workability of executive federalism" and the factors that help promote more effective intergovernmental relations. In deciding what constitutes "effective" it is worth noting that Dupré has in mind a fairly minimal definition. For him the important criterion is that the two sides are able to have a dialogue and perhaps reach some understanding of what needs to be done. Actual decisions resulting from the process should not be a criterion for judging the success or failure of an intergovernmental process.

In his analysis Dupré draws a distinction between what he calls functional relations and summit relations. The original Canada Assistance Plan (CAP) of the 1960s, the social security review, regional economic development, and labour market training he sees as functional issues, that is, issues in distinct policy areas. Under summit relations he places issues such as constitutional review and fiscal relations, areas where "summitry" in the form of FMCs is a frequent occurrence. Success is more likely in the former category than the latter. However, even within each category there is variation, and this variation can be due in good part to the presence or absence of "trust ties."

According to Dupré, trust ties are more likely to be generated when representatives from both sides tend to have similar professional backgrounds. When, in the case of labour market training agreements, one side is composed largely of economists and the other of educationists, there is bound to be tension, with the former looking at training issues from the perspective of net economic benefits and the latter more concerned about educating the whole person, not just with economic outputs. In the area of summit relations, Dupré notes that while negotiations over fiscal relations are not always successful, there is at least some common ground in that departments of Finance or provincial treasury departments tend to be populated by the same kind of people, and that ministers of Finance tend to be somewhat more in tune with, or feel more dependent on, their officials. At the end of the day there is usually at least some understanding if not agreement.

All of this, according to Dupré, points to the extent to which intergovernmental relations is a product of relations within governments, that is, the intragovernmental dimension. In his view, to a large extent corroborative of Smiley's perspective, when functional or line departments are displaced by central agencies such as IGAs, this will tend to undermine the existing trust ties that serve as the essential lubricant of intergovernmental relations. These ties can take many years to develop and represent a commodity that should not be discarded lightly. When contemplating a shift in strategy a government needs to consider whether this new strategy will undermine previously generated goodwill.

More generally, the *intra*governmental dimension draws attention to the fact that how governments are organized internally has a considerable bearing on the conduct of *inter*governmental affairs, something that involves more than just IGAs. It is often the case, for example, when the federal government wishes to launch a new program or perhaps off-load responsibilities on to provincial governments, the latter may be set up quite differently in relation to the programs or functions in question. At a minimum the result will be delays as one or more provincial governments may need to reorganize and be brought up to speed to even think about tackling these new functions. The reverse can also be true. The federal government may wish to retrieve certain functions (often for reasons related to political credit and visibility) but then discover it lacks the organizational capacity to handle them. In brief, if there is a mismatch in the organizational interface between the two levels of government, then the result can be highly problematic.

Finally, it should be noted that major shocks or fundamental shifts in government policy can seriously undermine trust ties, even if the representatives of the different orders of government share a common background. Thus, Program Review in the mid-1990s, the major initiative by the Chrétien government to reduce the deficit through, among other things, substantial cuts to federal–provincial transfers (see Aucoin and Savoie, 1998), led to a "general decline in trust levels" (Inwood, Johns, and O'Reilly, 2004: 269). The example of Program Review also points to an important development over the past decade: the increasing independence of departments and ministries of Finance and the erosion of trust ties among them. As Harvey Lazar (2005) has noted, both orders of government have become more responsible for, and dependent on, their own revenue-raising capacities with the growth in the value of the tax points at the provincial level and the cuts in federal transfers to the provinces relative to the revenues provinces raise by themselves. This development has led to less inter-action and a lessening of interdependence among departments and ministries of Finance of both orders of government. These entities have both central agency and line functions, and constitute one of the main guardians in the budgetary process. As will be discussed in Chapter 6 on fiscal federalism, they are also major players in intergovernmental relations, especially when financial issues are at stake, and most intergovernmental programs have a financial dimension to them. Under Program Review, the guardian role of finance agencies became pronounced. Furthermore, the more adversarial stance, particularly of the federal Department of Finance, has affected not only federal–provincial but also intra-governmental relations, that is, between Finance and line departments. Within the federal government and, to some extent, the provinces, program review is now a continuing process, and therefore is less prone to unilateralism and surprise for intergovernmental partners.

One final point worth making is that, while finance agencies have always been involved in summit relations, a common background and the shared lan-guage of economics among Finance officials has meant that there is plenty of opportunity to work through problems and generate a high level of trust. More recent developments suggest that these opportunities are less available and that the stability previously imparted through high levels of trust within and among the Finance and Treasury community has been significantly undermined. Federal line departments looking to cement relations with their provincial counterparts are more likely to see finance agencies as obstacles rather than facilitators.

Regional Bodies

As noted earlier, a large number of meetings involve subsets of representatives from the 14 federal, provincial, and territorial governments. As also noted, sev-eral interactions are of a bilateral nature, often as part of longer-term strategy by Ottawa to achieve national objectives in the form of a series of separate but still linked agreements with each of the provinces, a pattern that was common to the Chrétien and Martin era. There are, however, also interprovincial meetings or bodies with a distinct regional mandate, most specifically the Council of Atlan-tic Premiers (the Council of Maritime Premiers until 2000, when the province of Newfoundland and Labrador joined) and the Western Premiers' Conference. While not organized into a regular council or conference, there are frequent meet-ings of Ontario and Quebec first ministers, ministers, and officials on a broad range of bilateral issues.

The Council of Atlantic Premiers in particular enjoys a much higher degree of institutionalization than just about any other intergovernmental body in Canada. Born out of a recommendation of the Deutsch Commission on Maritime Union in 1970, the original Council of Maritime Premiers came into being in 1971, endowed with a legal mandate to foster cooperation among the three maritime governments and with a permanent secretariat based in Halifax. Some hoped that the Council would be a step towards more full-scale union of the three provinces. Others, however, suspected that it was in good part a symbolic gesture on the part of the three premiers with the actual if unstated intention to stave off such a possibility. Nonetheless, over the years this body has served as an umbrella and an enabler for a number of regional administrative agencies and policy activities, and the secretariat has provided support for regularly scheduled quarterly meetings for the now four premiers. It has direct responsibility for managing a number of administrative agencies providing services to the three Maritime provinces, or all four Atlantic provinces, including the Maritime Provinces Higher Education Commission (MPHEC), the Atlantic Provinces Education Foundation, and the Maritime Provinces Harness Racing Commission. In the past it has also had responsibility for the Maritime Municipal Training and Development Board and the Land Registration Information System.[11]

One final point about the Maritime/Atlantic premiers' council is that the record of cooperation is limited to technical and administrative matters and falls short on issues of higher political salience. Thus, for example, the council has had much less success in resolving differences and achieving regional cooperation in such key areas as energy policy, a regional electricity grid, oil and gas development, and fisheries. The institutions of regional cooperation, as developed as they are, have not been able to overcome the much stronger institutional and political forces of the provincial governments themselves when key provincial interests are at stake.

The Western Premiers' Conference (WPC) can be seen as the western counterpart of the Council of Atlantic Premiers, except that the WPC lacks a permanent secretariat. The seven governments involved in the annual event take turns hosting it and the hosting government also provides support for that year for the informal secretariat. Just as the Council of Maritime Premiers was first launched as a result of federal government urgings for the three provinces to consider closer cooperation if not amalgamation, the WPC arose out of a special Western Economic Opportunities Conference organized by Ottawa. The western premiers felt the results of the conference were sufficiently worthwhile that they decided to meet on a regular basis. It currently includes the three territories as well as the four western provinces. Like the Council of Atlantic Premiers, the WPC has its limitations when it comes to dealing with issues where one province stands to gain or lose.

As illustrated by a communiqué from the 2016 conference, the premiers have reached a rough consensus on, among other issues, resource development, immigration, and Indigenous relations. They also took a common stand that the federal government will need to increase its health-care funding to the provinces.

And they outlined more specific goals that the provinces will seek to reach collectively, such as investing in resilient infrastructure that can withstand the effects of climate change, and grid expansion and an improvement in energy infrastructure, which would facilitate improved access to renewables like wind, solar, and hydro. On the other hand, the WPC appears to have played no role at all in helping to resolve the dispute between BC and Alberta and Saskatchewan over the Trans Mountain Pipeline. Nor does it appear to play any role in trying to protect the integrity of the New West Partnership Trade Agreement struck between the three provinces in 2010.

Finally, one area where both the WPC and the Council of Atlantic Premiers play an interesting role is in relations with the US, specifically with neighbouring states. The Council of Atlantic Premiers has a primary role in organizing the Annual Conference of the New England Governors and the Eastern Canadian Premiers (which includes Quebec). Since September 2001, border issues—both access for trade purposes and security—have been prominent in this conference and in the joint session of the WPC and the Western Governors' Association (which takes place as a single session of the WPC Conference).

Multilateralism, Bilateralism, and Unilateralism

The above discussion may lead the reader to conclude that most relations between governments involve either all 13 or 14 governments, or a significant subset of them, as in the Council of the Atlantic Premiers, for example. This is the multilateral approach. However, much of intergovernmental relations are not multilateral. Rather, government-to-government interaction—especially that between Ottawa and individual provinces or territories—is often conducted on a bilateral basis. A hallmark of the Harper approach to executive federalism had been both his eschewal of first ministers' meetings and his propensity for one-on-one meetings with individual premiers, either in person or by phone. Unilateralism implies one government—which in virtually all instances tends to be the federal government—giving direction to another government or set of governments with little consultation and limited opportunity for bargaining. Typically, it involves Ottawa informing the provincial and territorial governments what it intends to do in an area such as equalization where it holds most of the cards and all of the purse strings. It is possible for provinces to push back—Quebec has often done so, for example—but when it comes to financial matters, where the money flows from Ottawa to the recipient governments, the latter have little choice in the matter. Over the past several decades both Liberal and Conservative governments in Ottawa have, after some discussion and debate, simply announced that they were trimming back or restructuring federal transfers or programs and that was the end of the matter.

The decision of whether to pursue a unilateral, bilateral, or multilateral approach can have significant consequences for the policy areas in question.

Keith Banting (2012), in analyzing the development of Canada's social safety net in the post-war period, notes that whether a new program was the result of a joint decision resulting from multilateral negotiations or a unilateral decision by Ottawa can have an impact not only on the configuration and generosity of the program but also on its subsequent management, governance, and capacity to change and adapt in the future. The choice of a single government or set of governments to pursue one or the other approach (and it should be stressed that the choice need not be mutually exclusive) is conditioned in part by factors such as who has jurisdiction and in part by strategic considerations. In the 1990s the Liberal government in Ottawa pioneered an approach that can be called sequential bilateralism, which was used to negotiate a set of Labour Market Development Agreements (Bakvis and Aucoin, 2000). After announcing it was willing to turn over to the provinces responsibility for a good portion of labour market training, as well as funding and federal staff to be absorbed by provincial governments into their relevant ministry or department, it began negotiating with individual provinces, allowing them to shape an agreement that fit their particular needs. Alberta and New Brunswick were the quickest off the mark. When these two initial agreements were struck Ottawa then used them as models or templates for discussions with other provinces. The first agreements also included an innovative "me too" clause whereby the provinces in question could go back to Ottawa and negotiate a new feature that another province in a subsequent agreement had successfully negotiated. This feature reduced the risk of being "first mover" by later allowing the province to opt into a benefit it may have missed initially.

Unlike Chrétien or Martin, Prime Minister Harper seemed to have little use for sequential bilateralism as a strategy in pursuit of national goals. Geoff Norquay (2011) noted that, overall, the federal–provincial relations scene had been relatively quiescent, with few divisive issues, since the Conservatives came to power in Ottawa. The Martin government's 10-year accord with the provinces on health care reached in 2004 meant there was at least one highly contentious file that required less attention. As well, with a few exceptions—the attempt to create a single national securities regulator; more recently a new cost-shared program in labour market training—there was a disinclination to launch new national programs. And in the case of either new programs or the renewal of old ones, there was a tendency to rely on unilateral action. The federal–provincial meeting in January 2009 was the only instance where the prime minister met with first ministers collectively to discuss an important issue (the global financial crisis) and to share with them details on one of the government's plans for dealing with it (such as the infrastructure program). More typical of the pattern was the government's cut-and-dried approach to the renewal of the health-care accord. In that case the minister of Finance, James Flaherty, tabled a letter at a meeting of Finance ministers in Victoria in November 2011 outlining the government's intent to continue until 2014 the increase in transfers as per the 2004 accord, and thereafter tying increases to inflation with no new conditions. It is as good an example as any of that government's aversion to any kind of discussion or dialogue on major programs. Prime Minister Harper's communication with the provinces was restricted to an interview with Peter Mansbridge on the CBC, in which he let it be known that in his view provinces were responsible for the delivery of health care and that his government had no wish to interfere.

While Harper was averse to using bilateralism in pursuit of national programs, as well as to FMMs, he did meet frequently with premiers on a one-to-one basis. In late 2012 the PMO, in response to criticism of the lack of FMMs, noted that the prime minister had held 74 bilateral meetings with first ministers between 2010 and 2012. Several of these meetings concerned serious issues and resulted in significant federal commitments—federal support for the bailout of the auto industry in Ontario and federal support for the Muskrat Falls hydroelectric project in Labrador, with its associated Maritime Link underwater transmission line to Nova Scotia, are but two examples of such outcomes. There are no comparable data for earlier periods, but the level of reported activity in this respect is likely similar to that of earlier prime ministers.

At the ministerial and sub-ministerial levels there have been changes in the degree of activity but not nearly to the extent found with FMCs and FMMs. Figure 5.1 depicts changes in the number of meetings from 2000 to 2012. Note that while 52 federal–provincial–territorial (FPT) meetings at the ministerial level took place in 2000, only 34 such meetings were held in 2012. And although there were fluctuations over time, a definite downward trend occurred at the ministerial level. Activity at the interprovincial–territorial ministerial level and sub-ministerial level (deputy ministers) has also declined. Furthermore, in the case of FPT ministerial meetings, there are indications that with the arrival of the Harper government in 2006 such meetings became more tightly scripted and controlled, with federal ministers given little scope for independent action. Looking at the array of meetings and networks more broadly, a survey of Ontario government ministries in 2009 reported that their staff were involved 790 FPT and PT committees and working groups and participated in more than 5,000 meetings, both virtual and face-to-face, that year. There are no data for other years, but assuming 2009 was reasonably representative, there still appears to be a lot of intergovernmental activity at the officials' level.

Overall, then, while FMMs and FMCs effectively ceased after 2009, and ministerial councils are also meeting less frequently and under more constrained circumstances, there is still considerable activity at lower levels as both orders of government grapple with the coordination of interdependencies at the federal–provincial–territorial and interprovincial–territorial levels that are invariably found in any federation. At the same time, there is no doubt that the Harper government's approach, not just to federalism but to governance more generally, changed the tenor of executive federalism.

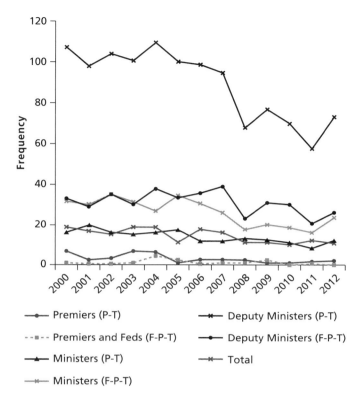

Figure 5.1 Frequencies of Intergovernmental Meetings and Conferences, 2000–12

Source: Bakvis (2014), compiled from data available on the Canadian Intergovernmental Conference Secretariat (CICS), http://www.scics.ca/en/.

Finally, from the record thus far of its first two years, the Liberal federal government led by Prime Minister Justin Trudeau has adopted a mixture of unilateral, bilateral, and multilateral approaches. As discussed more fully in the chapters that follow, the approach differs according to the policy area. On the contentious file of health-care funding, the Trudeau government began with a take-it-or-leave-it unilateral offer to the provinces, but relented under considerable provincial pressure. Consequently, through a bilateral approach the federal government made revised offers tailored to individual provinces' needs (some might say a "divide-and-conquer" approach). On the two issues of climate change and child care, the Trudeau government has adopted a mixture of multilateral and bilateral tactics, seeking a general accord with all provinces and territories (but not achieving unanimity) on broad principles in a framework agreement, while pursuing the detail—particularly of funding arrangements—in flexible bilateral agreements with each province or territory.

Summary

In the introduction to this chapter we identified the issues and debates encircling executive federalism, including questions concerning the closed and allegedly undemocratic nature of the intergovernmental process, the potential for stalemate and deadlock, whether intergovernmental relations would be better served through greater institutionalization and rules, especially at the level of first ministers, and the kind of changes that the government of Stephen Harper brought to executive federalism. (In our concluding chapter we address the broader approach and assessment of the Harper era on Canadian federalism, encompassing more than just its approach to the executive federalism process.) We also raised the possibility of whether major changes in the nature of executive federalism might be in the offing, either by way of greater institutionalization or, conversely, by increasing irrelevance.

This chapter reviewed the critical settings and arenas of executive federalism and addressed the debate over the institutionalization and strengthening of one of the key bodies in the federation, namely the first ministers' conference (FMC) or meeting (FMM). We discussed specific factors in the intergovernmental system, such as the role of central agencies and the importance of trust ties, and the limitations of bodies such as the Council of the Federation. We also examined some data on meetings of various intergovernmental bodies and committees and briefly reviewed three policy areas, with the view to assessing whether there have been changes over time in light of allegations that Prime Minister Harper was much less interested and engaged in the federal process and more interested in disengaging the federal government from provincial jurisdiction as part of his philosophy of open federalism. It is clear that the Conservative prime minister convened far fewer FMMs compared to his predecessors, including Jean Chrétien, who was also known to have an aversion to FMMs. This aversion seems to have been lifted in the early days of the Trudeau government, but it remains to be seen whether a collaborative spirit (at least publicly) continues. There has been some decline in the frequency of meetings at the ministerial and officials' levels, and there have been suggestions that ministers are being kept on a much tighter leash, making for less flexibility and autonomy for the ministerial councils in question. The tighter leash is not surprising given the highly controlled environment the prime minister and the Prime Minister's Office have created to manage government communications, policy, and operations. As discussed more fully in our conclusion, the federal government's overall disinclination to engage the provinces on major policy files to a large extent makes moot the question of whether we are likely to see greater institutionalization of the intergovernmental process. In sum, there remains slim basis for declaring the end of executive federalism. Indeed, notwithstanding the lack of engagement between the prime minister and the provincial and territorial governments, the continuing extent of activity below the level of first ministers indicates that the executive federalism model is not about to expire any time soon.

Questions for Critical Thought

1. What are the arguments for and against greater public scrutiny and transparency in the closed-door practices of executive federalism?

2. Should the prime minister of Canada take the lead to establish more formal, institutionalized first ministers' meetings?

3. Should the federal government roll back the disentangled approach known as "open federalism," or is any of that approach still relevant?

Notes

1. The terms "prime minister" and "premier" mean the same thing in their institutional origins. In the early periods of the Canadian regime they were interchangeable. Gradually, conventional usage has settled on the federal head of government being called "prime minister" while the provincial heads of governments have been called "premiers." After the late 1970s, the government leaders of the territories have also been called "premiers." In Quebec and in the French language, the premier is known as "premier ministre." The generic term "first minister" has been adopted since the 1970s.

2. See http://www.scics.ca/en/ for how CICS sees its role.

3. See https://www.coag.gov.au/ for an outline of the organization and functions of the Council of Australian Governments.

4. To this end, the Ontario government commissioned Queen's University economist Thomas Courchene to author a detailed working paper on this subject (Courchene, 1996).

5. For a review of the history and the various proposals related to the Council of the Federation, see Meekison (2003).

6. For a discussion of the promise, and limitations, of the Council of the Federation shortly after it was launched, see the series of working papers commissioned in 2003 by the Institute of Intergovernmental Relations, entitled Council of the Federation Series 2003: http://www.queensu.ca/iigr/publications/working-papers. For a recent assessment, see Simmons (2017).

7. There is an important exception in that meetings of Finance ministers and their officials are not serviced by the CICS, and no record of their meetings appears on its website. Instead, the administration of those meetings is done directly by the federal Department of Finance.

8. Detailed analysis of ministerial councils can be found in the work of Julie Simmons (2004, 2005, 2008, 2012).

9. The official title of this ministerial council was the Federal–Provincial–Territorial Council on Social Policy Renewal.

10. See Simmons (2005) for a superb analysis of different ministerial councils and associated networks.

11. See Tomblin (1995) for a more detailed discussion of the origins and development of the Council of Maritime Premiers.

References

Aucoin, P., and D.J. Savoie, eds. 1998. *Managing Strategic Change: Learning from Program Review*. Ottawa: Canadian Centre for Management Development.

Bakvis, H. 2014. "Changing Intergovernmental Governance in Canada in the Era of 'Open Federalism.'" Paper presented to Conference on Variety and Dynamics of Multilevel Governance in Canada and Europe. TU Darmstadt, 12–13 June.

———and P. Aucoin. 2000. *Negotiating Labour Market Development Agreements*. Ottawa: Canadian Centre for Management Development.

Banting, K. 2012. "The Three Federalisms Revisited: Social Policy and

Intergovernmental Decision-Making." In *Canadian Federalism*, 3rd edn, edited by H. Bakvis and G. Skogstad. Toronto: Oxford University Press.

Brock, K. 1995. "The End of Executive Federalism?" In *New Trends in Canadian Federalism*, edited by F. Rocher and M. Smith. Peterborough, ON: Broadview Press.

Brown, D.M. 2003. "Getting Things Done in the Federation: Do We Need New Rules for an Old Game?" Kingston, ON: Institute of Intergovernmental Relations, Queen's University.

CBC. 2012. "TRANSCRIPT | Peter Mansbridge Talks with Stephen Harper." Posted 18 Jan. http://www.cbc.ca/news/politics/story/2012/01/17/pol-mansbridge-interview-harper-transcript.html.

Council of the Federation (COF). 2006. "Advisory Panel on Fiscal Imbalance: Reconciling the Irreconcilable: Addressing Canada's Fiscal Imbalance." Ottawa: COF.

Courchene, T.J. 1996. *Access: A Convention on the Canadian Economic and Social Systems*. Toronto: Government of Ontario.

Dunn, C. 1995. *The Institutionalized Cabinet: Governing the Western Provinces*. Montreal and Kingston: McGill-Queen's University Press.

Dupré, J.S. 1988. "Reflections on the Workability of Executive Federalism." In *Perspectives on Canadian Federalism*, edited by R. Olling and M. Westmacott. Scarborough, ON: Prentice-Hall.

Elton, D., and P. McCormick. 1997. "The Alberta Case: Intergovernmental Relations." In *Public Administration and Public Management: Experiences in Canada*, edited by J. Bourgault, M. Demers, and C. Williams. Ste Foy, QC: Institute of Public Administration of Canada.

Inwood, G.C., C. Johns, and P. O'Reilly. 2004. "Intergovernmental Officials in Canada." In *Canada: The State of the Federation 2002*, edited by J.P. Meekison, H. Telford, and H. Lazar. Montreal and Kingston: McGill-Queen's University Press.

———, ———, and ———. 2011. *Intergovernmental Policy Capacity in Canada: Inside the Worlds of Finance, Environment, Trade, and Health*. Montreal and Kingston: McGill-Queen's University Press.

Lazar, H. 2003. "Managing Interdependencies in the Canadian Federation: Lessons from the Social Union Framework Agreement." Kingston, ON: Institute of Intergovernmental Relations, Queen's University.

———. 2004. *Canadian Social Union: Reality and Myth*. Kingston, ON: Institute of Intergovernmental Relations, Queen's University.

———. 2005. "Trust in Intergovernmental Fiscal Relations." In *Canadian Fiscal Arrangements: What Works, What Might Work Better*, edited by H. Lazar. Kingston, ON: Institute of Intergovernmental Relations, Queen's University.

McCarthy, S. 2002. "Premiers Derail Klein Plan: Nunavut Leader Warns Colleagues of Lasting Damage from Climate Change." *Globe and Mail*, 3 Aug., A1.

Maioni, A. 2008. "Health Care." In *Canadian Federalism: Performance, Effectiveness, and Legitimacy*, 2nd edn, edited by H. Bakvis and G. Skogstad. Toronto: Oxford University Press.

Meekison, J.P. 2003. "Council of the Federation: An Idea Whose Time Has Come." Kingston, ON: Institute of Intergovernmental Relations, Queen's University.

Norquay, G. 2011. "'The Death of Executive Federalism and the Rise of the 'Harper Doctrine': Prospects for the Next Health Accord." *Policy Options* (Dec.): 46–50.

Papillon, M., and R. Simeon. 2004. "The Weakest Link? First Ministers' Conferences in Canadian Intergovernmental Relations." In *Canada: The State of the Federation, 2002: Reconsidering the Institutions of Canadian Federalism*, edited by J.P. Meekison, H. Telford, and H. Lazar. Kingston, ON: Institute of Intergovernmental Relations, Queen's University.

Pollard, B.G. 1986. *Managing the Interface: Intergovernmental Affairs Agencies in Canada*. Kingston, ON: Institute of Intergovernmental Relations, Queen's University.

Scharpf, F.W. 1988. "The Joint-Decision-Making Trap: Lessons from German Federalism." *Public Administration* 66: 239–78.

Simmons, J.M. 2004. "Securing the Threads of Co-operation in the Tapestry of Intergovernmental Relations: Does the Institutionalization of Ministerial Conferences Matter?" In *Canada: The State of the Federation, 2002: Reconsidering the Institutions of Canadian Federalism*, edited by J.P. Meekison, H. Telford, and H. Lazar. Kingston, ON: Institute of Intergovernmental Relations, Queen's University.

———. 2005. "Executive Federalism after Charlottetown: Understanding the Role of Non-Governmental Actors." PhD dissertation, University of Toronto.

———. 2008. "Democratizing Executive Federalism: The Role of Non-Governmental Actors in Intergovernmental Agreements." In *Canadian Federalism: Performance, Effectiveness, and Legitimacy*, 2nd edn, edited by H. Bakvis and G. Skogstad. Toronto: Oxford University Press.

———. 2012. "Democratizing Executive Federalism: The Role of Non-Governmental Actors in Intergovernmental Agreements." In *Canadian Federalism: Performance, Effectiveness, and Legitimacy*, 3rd edn, edited by H. Bakvis and G. Skogstad. Toronto: Oxford University Press.

———. 2017. "Canadian Multilateral Intergovernmental Institutions and the Limits of Institutional Innovation." *Regional & Federal Studies* 27: 573–96.

Smiley, D.V. 1979. "An Outsider's Observations of Federal–Provincial Relations among Consenting Adults." In *Confrontation and Collaboration: Intergovernmental Relations in Canada Today*, edited by R. Simeon. Toronto: Institute of Public Administration of Canada.

———. 1980. *Canada in Question: Federalism in the Eighties*. Toronto: McGraw-Hill Ryerson.

———.1987. *The Federal Condition in Canada*. Toronto: McGraw-Hill Ryerson.

Tasker, J. 2017. "Premiers Resist Federal Proposals for Excise Tax on Legal Cannabis." *CBC News*, 3 Oct. https://www.cbc.ca/news/politics/first-ministers-meeting-indigenous-1.4318370.

Tomblin, S. 1995. *Ottawa and the Outer Provinces: The Challenge of Regional Integration in Canada*. Toronto: Lorimer.

Wallner, J. 2014. *Learning to School: Federalism and Public Schooling in Canada*. Toronto: University of Toronto Press.

Winfield, M., and D. Macdonald. 2008. "The Harmonization Accord and Climate Change Policy: Two Case Studies in Federal–Provincial Environmental Policy." In *Canadian Federalism: Performance, Effectiveness, and Legitimacy*, 2nd edn, edited by H. Bakvis and G. Skogstad. Toronto: Oxford University Press.

Chapter 6

Fiscal Relations: Basic Principles
and Current Issues

Week 8

Learning Objectives

- To understand the role played by financial arrangements between governments in enabling the federation to achieve its goals and to adapt to change.
- To grasp key concepts in public finance and "fiscal federalism," including the significance of tax and expenditure structure, and vertical and horizontal balance.
- To review the most important continuing issues in fiscal relations such as equalization, funding for national programs such as health care, and management of public finances.

Fiscal relations are an indispensable part of a federal system. In this chapter we examine three aspects of fiscal relations. First is their *function*—what they are intended to achieve—in theory and in practice. In all federations fiscal relations are a vital means of intergovernmental interaction; they provide for flexibility within an often rigid constitutional framework and for ongoing, pragmatic implementation of federation-wide objectives. Second is the specific *structure* of fiscal relations. In Canada this structure is relatively decentralized, reflecting the high value that the country places on provincial autonomy. Third is the way fiscal relations *change*. Fiscal relations are a subset of broader fiscal policy decisions, designed ultimately to fit into changing budgetary priorities and to reflect changing economic realities. They can also be intensely symbolic and political, representing broad political values and strong partisan positions. Also in this chapter we examine major recent issues—debt control and deficit reduction, tax cuts, economic stimulus, health-care costs, equalization and oil revenues, the fiscal imbalance—all of which affect our current understanding of the function and structure of fiscal relations and how these relations change.

The Functions, Principles, and Dynamics of Fiscal Federalism

Fiscal relations are a key part of the operation of all federal systems[1]—indeed, of any relationship among governments of any kind (Bird and Vaillancourt, 2006). They are, in effect, a family of relationships that work to ensure that all the governments within a given political community have the fiscal ability to match their legal autonomy and expenditure responsibilities. Whether the system is federal, as in Canada, or unitary, as in France, and whatever the levels involved—provincial–municipal, federal–provincial, federal–Indigenous—the financial arrangements underpinning the relationship go a long way towards defining it. If one level of government has the money and another is always begging for it, no constitutional principle of independence or autonomy is going to change the practical fact of dependency. One is always balancing the ideal relationship with realistic facts.

Fiscal arrangements give practical effect to the distribution of power in a federal system. Formal constitutional provisions—such as sections 91 and 92 of the Constitution Act, 1867—would be irrelevant if revenues could not be collected and spent to support those functions. Moreover, fiscal relations are one of the most important means by which a federal constitution—especially one that is relatively old, as Canada's is—can remain flexible enough to adapt to changing conditions of governance and meet changing demands on the state. It was by adjusting their fiscal arrangements that governments were able to provide relief during the Great Depression, tax and spend as necessary in wartime, develop the post-war "welfare state," and, more recently, balance their budgets and reduce their debts.[2]

Fiscal relations also play a major role in the realization of the federation's overall objectives, especially those that reflect the values encompassed by the concepts of "social union" and "economic union" (discussed in detail in Chapters 7 and 8). The social union seeks to achieve common social policy standards and entitlements (to varying degrees depending on the policy), which requires fiscal relations that share wealth, in other words, that redistribute fiscal resources from richer individuals and regions to poorer ones. The social union is mainly, therefore, about achieving equity goals, but unless it also does so as efficiently as possible, there would be less wealth to distribute in the first place. The economic union (also often called a "common market") provides for the efficient movement of goods, services, capital, and labour throughout the federation. Common tax treatment and similar levels of public services contribute greatly to those efficiency goals. Harmonized fiscal policy also contributes to equity, by ensuring that similarly situated persons or corporations receive the same treatment.

Efficiency and equity are not the only important values in a federation, however, and a fiscal policy with these as the only goals would tend to uniformity and unity. Thus, they must be traded off against federal values such as flexibility, diversity, autonomy, and accountability. To promote these latter values, fiscal arrangements also need to take into account three other objectives. The first is to ensure that the government that makes expenditures also raises at least some of the revenues to pay for them. The second is to ensure that local, regional, and national preferences in redistribution and equity are met. And the third is to ensure that governments have sufficient fiscal autonomy to make their own choices about public goods and services and levels of taxation. In effect, then, fiscal relations have to pursue simultaneously several competing values and objectives.[3]

"Fiscal balance" is another important part of fiscal relations. There are two types of fiscal balance in a federation: vertical and horizontal.[4] *Vertical fiscal balance* (or *imbalance*) refers to the relative positions of the central government and the constituent units. In Canada this usually means the federal and provincial orders of government, but the same term can be applied to federal–territorial, provincial–local, federal–Indigenous, and even federal–local relationships. A vertical fiscal imbalance thus is like a funding gap between the central government and the constituent governments because the central government's authority over the entire country allows it to tax mobile economic resources—wealth, profits, income, and consumption—wherever they occur. From an efficiency perspective it makes sense that the central government has a greater fiscal capacity than the units, which usually have neither full legal taxing power nor the practical means to access national wealth in order to fund their expenditures. The result is a gap between federal revenues and provincial expenditure needs (Lazar, St-Hilaire, and Tremblay, 2004). In every federation this gap is filled, at least in part, by cash transfers from the centre to the units. But this is not the only method available. A central government can also reallocate or transfer a larger share of taxes to the units, or even shift an entire tax field to them, permanently reducing part of its own superior fiscal capacity. Another way of closing the gap is simply to transfer the expenditure responsibility upwards, to the federal government. The Canadian federation has used all three of these methods over its history, but has relied most frequently on the cash transfer approach.

The term *horizontal fiscal balance* (or *imbalance*) refers to the relative fiscal position of the units themselves: more specifically, in Canada's case, the differing fiscal capacities of the various provinces and territories to fund their own expenditure responsibilities. Gaps or imbalances arise primarily because of differences in economic activity and accrued wealth: in short, regional economic disparities. Virtually all federations find some way to even out horizontal imbalances, both for general equity reasons, to ensure a measure of fiscal equality across the country, and for constitutional purposes, to ensure that all the units are able to manage the responsibilities allocated to them. In some federations, such as Germany, rich provinces make direct payments to the poorer ones. More commonly, though, correction of horizontal imbalances is left to the federal government, which uses its fiscal capacity to redistribute wealth, most often through intergovernmental grants but also in some cases through transfers to persons: in Canada, for instance, payments made to individuals through the employment insurance program have the effect of redistributing wealth from the richer provinces to less prosperous ones. It's important to note that the federal government's ability to correct horizontal imbalances depends on the existence of the vertical gap—that is, the fact that the federal government is able to collect more revenue than it needs to fulfill its responsibilities—since vertical transfers are the chief means of bridging the horizontal gaps. This means that the federal level would still need a superior revenue capacity even if provincial expenditure responsibility and revenue capacity were, on average, evenly matched.

In sum, then, a system is said to be in balance when a government's revenue capacity matches its expenditure responsibilities. It is in imbalance when one government—almost always the central one—has an excess of revenue capacity over expenditure responsibility. And it is in imbalance when different constituent governments have widely differing fiscal capacities but are expected to deliver similar public services.

At this stage, readers familiar with the real world of government budgets and fiscal policy would probably say that the concept of revenue–expenditure balance outlined here is rather abstract. They would be right. Actual balance is in the eye of the beholder. What one person sees as excess revenue capacity another will see as a prudent budget surplus, and what looks like a revenue deficit to one observer may look like a preference for low taxes to another. Nonetheless, in most federations governments collectively try to overcome the worst effects of imbalance. And the magnitude of that task will change over time. How a given federation tries to achieve that balance (or to live with imbalance) says a lot, as well, about its underlying values as a political community.

Finally, fiscal federalism requires more or less lasting structural components to give life to the objectives and values just discussed.[5] These include the legal powers to raise taxes and other revenues, to spend money, and to borrow money—powers that different federations will allocate to their various governments in different ways—and a set of mechanisms for sharing revenues and expenditure costs and otherwise transferring financial resources from one government to another. These features are often outlined in the federal constitution, in which case they can be formally changed only by constitutional amendment—a difficult task. This is not to say that the basic allocation of taxing and spending power is set in stone: change can take place informally, as modifications grow into political conventions, are incorporated into intergovernmental agreements and legislation, or gradually become accepted practice. Nevertheless, these processes do tend to take rather a long time, as even the smallest change in fiscal relations engenders a lot of debate. Thus the basic allocation of taxing and spending power does change, but slowly.

In other respects the stuff of fiscal relations is changing all the time. This is true in two senses. First, the revenues and expenditures of any government are in constant flux in response to economic growth or shrinkage, annual budgetary decisions, and changes in interest rates, bond ratings, exchange rates, and so on. These changes have immediate consequences for the effectiveness of specific intergovernmental arrangements to share revenues or costs. Fiscal arrangements, therefore, often turn out to be more costly than planned, or insufficient to meet growing needs. Arrangements that have been especially well designed will anticipate external changes and automatically adjust to them. But, as we shall see, that situation is rare, despite the best efforts of policy planners.

The second sense in which change is a constant is that formal fiscal arrangements in most federal systems, including Canada, are designed usually for the medium term only—for example, five years—in the knowledge that the changing conditions discussed above will sooner or later force adjustments. Many fiscal arrangements are based on some kind of formula that makes annual calculations about shared revenues or costs more or less automatic, providing yet more flexibility over time. Thus—in principle at least—fiscal arrangements, like intergovernmental relations as a whole, are among the means by which a federation provides for a moderate degree of change and adaptation without constitutional reform. Even so, any particular incremental change can still give rise to enormous controversy.

The Structure of Fiscal Relations in Canada

Constitutional Powers

Three aspects of Canada's constitutional allocation of powers play an important role in shaping fiscal relations within the federation. First, the fact that most fields of jurisdiction are exclusive to either the federal or the provincial order of government makes the two orders more independent of one another than they would be with a concurrent scheme of powers.

It also means that Ottawa has less scope than other federal governments to legislate specific conditions for programs to be delivered by the provinces (Watts, 2008). The requirement that fiscal arrangements respect the jurisdictional autonomy of the provinces—even if there is debate about what this requirement entails—is especially problematic because three of the major expenditure fields over which the provinces have jurisdiction are ones that have become central to advanced industrial societies over the past 60 years: health care, education, and social services/assistance.

The second aspect of the division of powers relevant to fiscal relations is the fact that both the federal and the provincial governments have full access to the most important and most broadly based sources of tax revenue. Both can levy not only personal and corporate income taxes but also general sales or consumption taxes, as well as payroll taxes. The capacity of the Canadian provinces to pay for their expenditure responsibilities from their own revenue sources is greater than that of their counterparts in most other federal systems. However, because key tax bases such as personal income and consumption of goods and services are shared, there is a risk that taxpayers will be subjected to conflicting demands and overwhelming tax burdens. Therefore the two orders of government must find ways to harmonize their taxes.

Finally, there is the fact that the federal government's "spending power," though recognized by the courts, is not spelled out in detail by the constitution (see discussion in Chapter 3). The spending power has been the means by which Ottawa has promoted a national (pan-Canadian) approach to social programs, including direct payments to individuals and to organizations for redistributive purposes. This practice has been controversial, however, particularly in Quebec, where there is strong support for the principle of strict provincial autonomy. Also, many Canadians do not see the need for much redistribution, and thus would oppose the use of the federal spending power on those grounds.

Revenue Sources and Tax Structure

As noted above, the federal government and the provinces share the most important and broad-based tax sources. The most important revenue types are:

- Personal income tax (PIT): PIT is levied by both the federal and the provincial governments. The federal government collects the provincial tax together with its own, except in Quebec where there are parallel collection systems. Usually the provincial tax base is defined as a portion of the federal, but recently there has been some movement towards more independence in the definition of the tax base. For example, Alberta has used a "flat" rate for its income tax: the percentage charged does not rise as income rises.
- Corporate income tax (CIT): Corporate taxes also are levied by both governments, and also are collected by the federal government for most provinces. Here, too, there has been some movement towards independent tax bases.
- Consumption or sales taxes: These are levied by Ottawa and all the provincial governments except Alberta. The federal government levies the Goods and Services Tax, which is harmonized with the provincial sales tax in Newfoundland and Labrador, Nova Scotia, New Brunswick, and Ontario. In Quebec, where the provincial government collects the federal GST as well as its own provincial sales tax, the two taxes are determined on a nearly identical basis.
- Natural resource revenues in the form of mineral royalties, stumpage fees for logging, and other specific taxes: Resource revenues are a significant source of provincial-only taxes.

- Property taxes: These are levied by municipalities (under the authority of provincial law), although in some provinces revenue from property tax is directed to school boards on a province-wide basis.
- Payroll taxes: Both the federal and the provincial governments collect premiums from employers and employees for each person employed to pay for programs such as employment insurance, the Canada or Quebec Pension Plan and, in some provinces, health care.
- Customs and excise duties: Important tax sources at the time of Confederation, these are exclusively federal. The federal taxes on alcohol, tobacco, and gasoline are excise taxes.
- Gaming revenues: The provinces receive significant revenues from gaming (lotteries, casinos, horse racing, charity bingo, video lotteries, etc.).
- Alcoholic beverages: Provinces get the lion's share of revenue from alcoholic beverages, partly through direct taxes on products, and partly through monopoly profits from provincial liquor corporations.

The overall trend for all revenue sources has been to an increasingly larger share for the provincial governments, in other words, increasing fiscal decentralization.

Table 6.1 provides an overview of the main types and shares of taxes collected by the federal and combined provincial–local governments in Canada in 1990 and in 2011. It aggregates the tax and revenue types listed above into four main categories. In 1955, when Ottawa exercised strong central control over revenue generation, the federal government levied approximately 70 per cent of all taxes. By 1990, however, its share had declined to 48 per cent, falling further to 45 per cent by 2011. The main reason for this decline was that provincial

Table 6.1 Federal, Provincial–Territorial, and Local Own-Source Revenues ($ millions)

	1990			2011		
	Federal	Prov./Terr./ Local	Total	Federal	Prov./Terr./ Local	Total
Income taxes	69,078	43,927	113,005	151,691	95,956	247,647
Consumption and production taxes	27,160	42,685	69,845	46,995	99,669	146,664
Payroll taxes for social insurance	13,027	5,800	18,827	18,585	11,463	30,048
Local government taxes including property taxes	—	24,848	24,848	—	53,929	53,929
Total	109,265	117,260	226,525	217,271	261,017	478,288

Note: Payroll taxes do not include CPP/QPP contributions.
Source: Statistics Canada, adapted from Treff and Ort (2013: Table A.4).

expenditure responsibilities (e.g., health care) were rising much more quickly than federal expenditure responsibilities (e.g., defence). In response to this trend, the federal government ceded considerable tax room on corporate and personal income to the provinces in the 1950s, 1960s, and 1970s. Since there are few constitutional prohibitions to provincial revenue-raising, taxes both big and small have proliferated at the provincial level.

Intergovernmental Transfers

Canada—like other federal systems—uses intergovernmental fiscal transfers (sometimes referred to as "grants") to reduce vertical and horizontal fiscal imbalances. Despite our relatively decentralized tax structure, in which the provinces get a fairly significant share of total revenues, a gap remains between the provinces' expenditure responsibilities and their ability to raise the revenues to fund them. There is also a wide disparity among the provinces in their potential to raise revenues. Table 6.2 provides an overview of the magnitude of these transfers for every fifth fiscal year from 1992–3 to 2012–13.

There are two basic types of transfer. *Conditional transfers* are payments made for specific purposes, usually introduced to induce provinces to participate in national social programs with similar entitlements across the country. The last major attempt to introduce a new social program in this way took place in 2004–6, when the Martin federal government negotiated with some provinces and territories to establish a national child-care program, but the Harper government cancelled the agreements when it came to office. A more successful conditional program in place since 1994 has been for funding public infrastructure projects, now called the Investing in Canada plan, under which the Liberal federal government since 2015

Table 6.2 Major Federal Cash Transfers to Provinces and Territories, Selected Years, 1992–3 to 2017–18 ($ millions*)

	1992–3	1997–8	2002–3	2007–8	2012–13	2017–18
Social program transfers**	18,396	12,500	19,100	31,065	40,428	50,898
Equalization	7,784	9,738	8,859	12,925	15,423	18,354
Territorial Funding Formula	1,076	1,229	1,616	2,313	3,111	3,682
Total	27,256	23,467	29,575	46,303	58,962	72,934

*Dollar amounts are nominal and reflect actual transfer amounts in the years indicated.
**Social program transfers for 1992–3 consist of the EPF and CAP cash transfers; since 1997–8 they consist of the CHT/CST cash transfer.
Sources: Authors' calculations based on data from the following sources: Finance Canada (2006: Annex 3, Tables A.3.1–A.3.3); updated by Finance Canada (2008, 2012, 2018). Budget documents prior to 2014 are available in the following archived webpages, accessed July 2018: https://www.budget.gc.ca/pdfarch/index-eng.html; for the 2017–18 data, see https://www.fin.gc.ca/fedprov/mtp-eng.asp.

offers conditional transfers to the provinces for spending on municipal infrastructure. The Canada Health and Social Transfers (see below) are conditional, but loosely so.

Unconditional transfers come with no expenditure strings attached, although there are specific formulae that determine which provinces get what proportion of funds. Equalization is the most important of these programs.

There is a further important distinction between:

- *cash transfers*, i.e., the payment of actual cash from the federal government to the provinces; and
- *tax transfers*, i.e., the ceding of tax room to the provinces, taking the form of a specific portion or points of personal income or corporate income tax. The tax points have a nominal value when first ceded, but afterwards grow or shrink with the provincial tax base.

As we will see below, tax transfers are controversial in that once they are ceded they are hard to get back. The classic example is the negotiated end to the wartime tax rental program in the 1950s, under which the provinces gained additional tax room that they have continued to enjoy ever since. Once a tax transfer has been established, the provinces tend to consider that money to be part of their own-source revenue rather than an ongoing federal contribution, whereas the federal government will usually continue to count a tax transfer in its overall calculation of support to the provinces.

On the whole, there are probably fewer conditions attached to intergovernmental cash and tax transfers in Canada than in any other federal system. In fiscal year 2018–19 the three biggest programs, accounting for more than 95 per cent of all federal cash transfers, were the equalization program and the Canada Health and Social Transfers (CHT and CST). Equalization is wholly unconditional. The CHT and CST include a few conditions (e.g., about meeting the five basic principles of medicare as required under the Canada Health Act and ensuring that migrants from other provinces can qualify for welfare payments after a reasonable waiting period), but they still leave considerable room for provincial interpretation, and the medicare conditions in particular are difficult to enforce.

Moreover, neither the CHT nor the CST is tied to the provinces' own expenditure programs. This is not the case in most other federal countries. Nor was it the case in Canada until the late 1970s. In the past, federal payments were conditional on matching provincial expenditure for specific purposes: thus, if Ontario, for example, spent $100 million to build hospitals or universities, the federal government would match that expenditure with another $100 million. Elsewhere, such as in the United States, Australia, and Germany, most federal transfers still take the form of matching funds or are otherwise very specific as to purpose.

Equalization is by design the least conditional of the transfer programs. Its purpose is to ensure that all provinces have, at least in principle, the capacity to deliver comparable services at comparable rates of taxation. Introduced in 1957, with many minor adjustments since, the program tries to bring provinces with a fiscal capacity below the national average up to a national standard. Commitment to the principle of equalization, but not an actual formula, was incorporated into the constitution in 1982.[6] Equalization does not take funds from the richer provinces directly. Rather, the funds for this purpose come from the federal budget. Thus, they are collected throughout the country, and individual taxpayers in the poorer provinces contribute, according to their income, as much as their counterparts in the richer provinces. Despite what some provincial political leaders may imply, there are no direct transfers between provincial governments; equalization payments are made by the federal government, not the richer provinces as such; and provincial legislatures do not vote funds for these purposes.

From 1982 to 2007 the "standard" used to determine entitlement to equalization payments was the average of the tax yields from more than 30 different revenue sources of five provinces—British Columbia, Saskatchewan, Manitoba, Ontario, and Quebec. In 2007 the federal government reduced the number of revenue groups used in the calculation to five and adopted a 10-province standard. Against this standard each province's actual fiscal capacity is measured to determine the extent of its entitlement. In 2018–19 six of the 10 provinces fell below the standard and therefore received equalization payments. The four provinces ineligible to receive payments were Alberta, Saskatchewan, British Columbia, and Newfoundland and Labrador.

Most transfers to the territorial governments are based on what is known as the Territorial Funding Formula (TFF). Based on expenditure patterns rather than revenue, the TFF reflects the special expenditure needs of the territories. Although territorial governments also receive the CHT and CST, these funds are deducted from their TFF entitlements. In 2018–19 the three northern territories together received a total of $3.5 billion from the TFF (see Table 6.3).

The Process and Politics of Fiscal Relations

Intergovernmental relations on financial matters exhibit most of the main characteristics of executive federalism, as discussed in Chapter 5. The key discussions are restricted to governments, and are jealously guarded by cabinet ministers and their senior officials. Of course, the subject matter of intergovernmental fiscal relations is highly technical and necessarily complex. The apparent requirement within each government for secrecy in the preparation of budgets reinforces the usual tendency to treat the details of intergovernmental negotiation as confidential, not open to public scrutiny. Together, the complex nature of the issues under discussion and the lack of transparency make for a murky accountability that governments sometimes exploit to avoid accepting the blame for cutbacks in funding or program entitlements.

Intergovernmental relations involving fiscal issues are also highly bureaucratic and thus hierarchical. The structure is topped by the federal–provincial–territorial conferences of finance ministers, who usually meet twice a year, on an agenda heavily determined by the federal chair (unlike other intergovernmental forums, these conferences do not include a provincial or territorial co-chair). Preparations for these meetings are made by deputy ministers (i.e., unelected officials), who report to the ministers and meet as the Continuing Committee of Officials (CCO). Several other committees, dealing with economic and fiscal data, fiscal arrangements, taxation, and the Canada and Quebec Pension Plans, report to the CCO. They meet much more frequently but no less privately than their superiors.

First ministers also take part in fiscal relations, but there is no established decision-making structure or pattern of meetings. Instead, the first ministers become involved as political priorities dictate: examples include the meetings held in the 1970s to seek consensus on anti-inflation measures, or after 1995 to determine how to restore funding to health-care programs. In any case, routine interaction is left to the finance ministers and their officials.

As with most other Canadian intergovernmental arrangements, fiscal relations occur across a spectrum from competitive to cooperative behaviour, with stops along the way at such points as mutual argument, loosely determined consensus, and jointly implemented programs. Fiscal policy as a whole is only loosely coordinated. More often than not, decisions on fiscal arrangements are not the result of formal intergovernmental agreement, but rather reflect the final determination of the federal government alone. There will be extensive meetings in which government representatives will argue their positions and agree on some general approaches and principles, but the final decision is made by individual governments in their cabinets. Sometimes this occurs simply because there is no consensus possible among the differing interests and positions of the provinces and territories, leaving the federal government to dictate a solution. Yet it can also be the case that the federal government deems it should act contrary even to the unanimous position of the provinces. Indeed, the provinces often resent what they deem to be "unilateral" actions. In 1981, 1982, 1990, 1995, and 2011, for example, the federal government announced—with little or no advance notice— significant cuts (or cuts to the growth rates) to intergovernmental transfers for established social programs, essentially downloading budgetary restraint onto the provinces and territories.

Nonetheless, in some cases, political success depends on much tighter agreement. A recent example is the series of health accords negotiated between 1998 and 2004, wherein each of the provincial and territorial governments agreed to very specific amounts and purposes for renewed health transfer payments. Finally, there are also examples (they are exceptions) of detailed rules requiring that any changes be formally agreed to according to a fixed voting formula—such as those governing the Canada and Quebec Pension Plans.[7]

Despite their technical nature and the secrecy, and the ambiguity about who gets to decide fiscal matters and how that is done, fiscal arrangements remain at the heart of federal–provincial relations and of the budget-making process in every government. Thus they are not immune to politics: in fact, they are among the most hotly contested political issues, reflecting real ideological differences and regional interests. The lack of formality in fiscal policy-making means that the federal cabinet, for example, has more leeway (but also more vulnerability) to give in to other political interests who may not agree with the provincial–territorial consensus, such as social policy interest groups who would push for stronger federal intervention in provincial spending programs. Finally, it bears repeating that intergovernmental fiscal issues always reflect broader political and economic concerns of the day.

Changing Objectives and Outcomes, 1945–2018

In fiscal federalism, form follows function. The shape of programs reflects economic, social, and political priorities of the day. So the fiscal relations of 2018 are very different from those of 1945. But that is not the only reason why Canada's contemporary fiscal relations look the way they do. A contributing factor is what has come to be known as path dependency: governments become accustomed to certain patterns of taxation and expenditure, and various political interests (government departments, social interest groups, the regional business communities, etc.) get vested in the existing design, flow, and magnitude of transfer payments and tax regimes. Thus, despite the occasional "big bang," change usually takes longer than many would like, and we often have to settle for yesterday's solutions because there is no consensus on what to replace them with today.

The interplay between continuity and change has followed several distinct historical periods. These include an era of strong central power, 1945–59; an era of decentralization to the provinces and a maturing of the welfare state, 1960–76; a period of consolidation and gradual cutbacks, 1976–95; a period of very deep retrenchment eased gradually through program redesign, 1995–2007; and finally a period of recession and austerity, 2008 to the present (this last period is discussed more fully at the end of this chapter).

From the early 1990s, governments in Canada were preoccupied with the need for a more sustainable fiscal policy. Budgetary deficits had become chronic, and public debt was escalating. At the same time, tougher international competition and neo-liberal political trends sharply limited the scope for tax increases, and Canadian taxpayers in general were less confident than they had been that government would spend their money wisely. For the first time in many decades, a consensus emerged in favour of eliminating budget deficits and reducing public debt. Support for reducing public services was less strong, but in general Canadians were willing to accept tough measures.[8]

The Liberal government elected in 1993 faced a huge budgetary deficit and debt payments unprecedented in peacetime, based on deficits that had been accumulating since 1976. After its first year in office the Chrétien government was warned by the international financial community that its financial position was perilous. The turnaround effort that followed was to have a huge and continuing impact on fiscal federalism. Finance Minister Paul Martin's February 1995 budget has become a milestone in Canadian politics. It reversed the growth of budgetary deficits, which had peaked at $42 billion in the previous fiscal year (1993–4), and laid the groundwork for a balanced budget that was eventually achieved in 1998. Based on the findings of a wide-ranging Program Review, federal spending was dramatically reduced: most programs experienced deep cuts and many were eliminated altogether. In addition, transfer payments to the provinces were sharply reduced, and the remaining programs (EPF and CAP) were combined to create a single Canada Health and Social Transfer (CHST). The equalization program, however, was not affected.

The 1995 budget had the following consequences. First, it helped improve Canada's overall fiscal position, setting a general Canadian trend towards balanced budgets. Second, it forced a cascade of expenditure cuts onto provincial, territorial, and municipal governments, and contributed to eroding trust in Ottawa's ability to keep long-term funding commitments. Third, it led gradually to calls from the provinces and territories to rebalance the system. Fourth, it led to a renewed debate over conditions to federal transfers. And finally, the fact that the equalization program was left unscathed while social transfers were cut gave rise to questions about the value of regional redistribution.

While the provincial premiers and their governments acknowledged the need for tough federal measures in 1995 and beyond, they all shared the view that the transfers they counted on were cut more deeply than any other federal program.[9] As the federal surplus grew, so too did provincial pressure for correction of the vertical fiscal imbalance (VFI). In fact, although the concept behind the term had been familiar in public finance and academic circles for decades, the term "vertical fiscal imbalance" did not enter the political discourse in Canada until 2002, when Quebec's Commission on Fiscal Imbalance detailed the nature of a VFI from both the Quebec and the broader provincial and territorial perspectives (Quebec, 2002). With the formation of the Council of the Federation in 2003, the issue of fiscal imbalance (both vertical and horizontal) became a continuing part of the new institution's agenda and work plan.

In 2005 the Council established an advisory panel to provide an independent assessment of fiscal balance issues. The report of that panel (called the Gagné-Stein Report after its co-chairs) found that for the previous decade the provinces had indeed had "insufficient resources to accomplish the tasks for which they are constitutionally responsible," while the federal government had been "running budgetary surpluses and . . . spending significantly in areas that the Constitution of Canada has assigned to the Provinces" (Gagné and Stein, 2006: 9). Furthermore, the panel predicted that the overall fiscal prospects of the provinces would worsen in future, particularly as a result of population aging and rising health-care costs. Yet the federal budgetary surplus was projected to continue growing.

A variety of solutions to the VFI were proposed, by the Gagné-Stein panel and others. They included transferring the entire tax proceeds of the GST to the provinces (Quebec, 2002); transferring more income tax points to the provinces (Quebec, 2002); significantly increasing the health-care transfers (Romanow, 2002; Gagné and Stein, 2006); and increasing federal equalization and TFF payments, even if that would not benefit all provinces (Senate, 2002; Gagné and Stein, 2006; O'Brien, 2006a, 2006b). Few experts argued for a wholesale realignment of federal and provincial spending responsibilities. Among the provinces, Alberta became the only unambiguous proponent of tax transfers. Quebec eventually favoured increasing equalization payments as the best way to bridge both the vertical and the horizontal gaps. However, Ontario took a hard line against enhanced equalization, seeking a specific solution to the unique features of its own position (Ontario, 2006).

Liberal governments from 1993 to 2006 used direct federal spending to make up the gaps in provincial funding adequacy—not a cooperative approach, but one that did address VFI to a degree. But the right-of-centre opposition parties (Reform, Alliance, and their successor, the new Conservative Party) had generally opposed such program realignment.

Of course, provincial or territorial perspectives alone do not determine how fiscal federalism works: the federal view determines the outcome. And the federal perspective on the fiscal imbalance issue was for many years quite different from that of the provinces—especially under the Liberal Prime Ministers Jean Chrétien and Paul Martin. Their governments mounted arguments to counter most of the provincial positions.[10] For example, they maintained that the federal surpluses were not huge in relation to the deficits that had preceded them and they reminded the provinces that the federal debt burden was roughly twice the size of all the provincial debts combined. Moreover, they argued, the provinces had plenty of access to revenues; some of their revenue sources (e.g., gaming) were growing rapidly; and Ottawa, too, faced spending pressures in areas such as security, the needs of on-reserve Indigenous populations, and seniors' pensions.

Complicating the VFI issue is the wide range of provincial policy preferences and needs. What if the provinces have different expenditure needs and preferences? What if one province wants publicly funded daycare and another doesn't? What if one province is prepared to impose a retail sales tax and another isn't, or if one prefers better social programs over tax cuts, or vice versa? It is natural in a federation for provinces to differ on matters such as these. But the federal government argues that until a province makes at least an average effort to raise taxes, or to keep its expenditures within an average range of federal national standards, then it cannot claim imbalance.

If the Liberal position on vertical fiscal imbalance was defensive, the federal Conservative Party was more supportive. The Harper government made VFI a prominent part of its "open federalism" approach, which included commitments to respect provincial jurisdiction and to retreat from areas of provincial responsibility in which Ottawa had intruded, such as housing and university scholarships. Moreover, on fiscal federalism as such the Conservatives instituted new arrangements in the 2007 budget following four principles: improved accountability by obtaining greater clarity of roles and responsibilities; fiscal responsibility and budget transparency; predictable and stable long-term fiscal arrangements; and effective collaborative management of the federation.[11]

In summary, the overall legacy of the 1995 budget earthquake was a long and often bitter debate over vertical fiscal imbalance. Yet, by the year 2000, transfers for social programs were at their lowest point in 50 years in terms of their contribution to expenditures on provincial programs (Banting and Boadway, 2004). Just as significantly, the relative decline in those transfer programs meant that provincial governments were less dependent on federal transfers than at any point in the past half-century—and therefore less willing to let Ottawa define national social standards. In fact, the provinces are less dependent on intergovernmental transfers than their counterparts in any other federation, and those transfers came with fewer conditions in Canada than anywhere else. The current situation is well illustrated by the debate over health-care funding, which leads us now to the CHT/CST.

Transfers for Social Programs: The Evolution of the CHT/CST

The federal government created the Canada Health and Social Transfer in 1995 by combining two earlier transfer programs: the Established Programs Financing (EPF) for health and post-secondary education, and the Canada Assistance Plan (CAP) for welfare and social services. The purpose of this change was twofold. First, Ottawa sought to complete the process, begun in the 1970s, of simplifying federal–provincial transfer programs and minimizing the conditions attached to them, in the process decoupling federal financial commitments from actual program costs. Second, it needed to cut the level of transfer payments in general to meet its deficit reduction targets. Since, as we have seen, the equalization program was left more or less intact, the remaining programs took the brunt of the cuts. As a result, the public debate about the CHST was first and foremost about those cuts and, after 1998, about restoration of the funding that had been taken away.

The CHST was not unconditional, but it was not fully conditional either. Rather, it was a hybrid that inherited two very general conditions from the old CAP and EPF programs. The first was that the provinces would impose no restrictions on the eligibility for welfare of new residents arriving from other provinces. The second was that the provincial health services would meet the five broad principles of the Canada Health Act.[12] As long as these conditions were met, the provinces could spend the money transferred from Ottawa as they saw fit. At a first ministers' meeting in February 1999, where the federal government committed to begin restoring a portion of the funds cut in 1995, all provincial and territorial premiers undertook to spend any incremental CHST funds on health care. This was hardly a difficult decision politically, since provincial governments for a decade had made it their policy to increase health-care funding while either holding post-secondary and welfare funding constant or cutting deeply in these areas.

In fact, funding for health care so dominated intergovernmental discussions that the federal government was eventually persuaded to separate it from other social spending. Thus, in 2004 the CHST itself was restructured to create two new programs: the CHT and the CST. In the 12 years between 1995 and 2007, all the funding increases went to health, but at least the CST (which is not earmarked for any particular social program) has not suffered any further erosion. Since 2007 the key issue has been how to maintain CHT and CST funding levels through a major recession and how to tame their growth (and, for the provinces, how to constrain social program spending more generally) in the context of continuing post-recession austerity. Table 6.3 shows the details of the major transfer payments to each province and territory in fiscal year 2018–19.

The CHT and CST have been at the centre of three major controversies. The first issue was allocation—how much money each province would get. The second was the overall level of cash funding; discussions in this area usually focused on restoration of the funds cut in 1995. The third was the issue of conditions on federal funding, which were commonly defined as national standards for social programs. The original programs that predated the CHT and CST provided transfers to the provinces and territories on the basis of matching funds, driven by differing needs and commitments across the provinces. For example, because Quebec and Newfoundland spent more per capita on social assistance and services than Ontario or New Brunswick, they received more in the form of matching funds under the CAP. By the mid-1990s, the four provinces with below-average entitlements—British Columbia, Alberta, Saskatchewan, and Ontario—began a campaign for equal per capita shares, to which the federal government responded with a plan to eliminate the per capita differences over a decade. The campaign for "equal shares" drove a further wedge between the "have" and "have-not" provinces. The battle was waged as much among the provinces as it was with the federal government. It was the Harper government that finally acted on the issue,

Table 6.3 Major Federal Cash Transfers to Provinces and Territories, Estimated Entitlements, 2018–19 ($ millions)

	CHT	CST	Equalization	TFF	Offshore Accords	Total
Newfoundland and Labrador	548	201				750
Prince Edward Island	161	59	419			638
Nova Scotia	996	366	1,933		(95)	3,201
New Brunswick	792	291	1,874			2,956
Quebec	8,791	3,226	11,732			23,749
Ontario	14,964	5,492	963			21,420
Manitoba	1,410	518	2,037			3,965
Saskatchewan	1,224	449				1,673
Alberta	4,504	1,653				6,157
British Columbia	5,066	1,859				6,925
Nunavut	40	15		1,579		1,637
Northwest Territories	46	17		1,256		1,319
Yukon	40	15		950		1,006
All provinces and territories	38,584	14,161	18,958	3,785	(95)	75,393

Source: Authors' calculations based on data from Finance Canada (2018). Data available at https://www.fin.gc.ca/fedprov/mtp-eng.asp.

making adjustments in the budgets of 2007 and 2008 before putting the CHT on an equal per capita basis in 2012. This move proved to be highly beneficial for the "have" provinces, with Alberta, for example, seeing its annual entitlement rise by almost 40 per cent (Wingrove, 2012). It also had repercussions for debates over equalization, as later on Alberta and Saskatchewan argued that half the transfers for equalization should be allocated to all provinces on a per capita basis since a good part of the money came from the "have" provinces rather than federal coffers (Yakabuski, 2018). It was an argument little grounded in fact, but it illustrates the ongoing efforts by some provinces to move the narrative away from citizen equity to provincial equity (Béland et al., 2017).

Unlike the allocation issue, the provinces and territories found more common ground on the issue of funding cuts. All charged that the federal government was unfairly offloading its accumulated 1995 deficit onto them. They claimed that cuts to transfer payments through the CHST between 1994–5 and 1998–9 amounted to 35 per cent, whereas federal programs in general were cut by only 7 per cent in the same period. As a result of this disproportionate degree of off-loading, the provinces were forced to cut their funding to municipalities, universities and colleges, school boards, and hospitals.

The provinces' primary goal was to see federal cash payments restored to EPF/CAP levels, from the initial CHST allocation of $11.5 billion to $18.5 billion. This they achieved in September 2000, when the premiers secured Prime Minister Chrétien's agreement that the CHST would be increased to match the combined total of EPF/CAP funds in 1995 ($18.5 billion) and would reach $21 billion by 2005–6. Of the additional money, $2.2 billion was earmarked for "early childhood development" initiatives, and the rest for health care. An additional federal grant of $2.3 billion over five years was also promised on the condition that it would go to health information technology, medical equipment, and a transition fund for primary care reform. All the additional cash transfers to the provinces were to be distributed on an equal per capita basis.

The federal government agreed to an even more significant restoration of health-care funding in the 2004 Health Care Accord. In that agreement, Prime Minister Martin and the provincial and territorial premiers established a framework for increasing the federal contribution over a period of 10 years by $41.2 billion in new investments, bringing the overall federal contribution on an annual basis by the end of the 10-year period to $30.5 billion.[13]

Finally, in introducing the CHST the federal government invited the provinces to work with it to develop by mutual consent a set of shared principles and objectives that would underlie the operations of the new transfer. This commitment eventually led to the signing of the Social Union Framework Agreement in February 1999, discussed more fully in Chapter 7. In those negotiations the federal government sought to reimpose conditions on its funding, in an effort both to preserve the principles of medicare and to promote specific federal priorities such as primary care reform (i.e., where people go first for treatment or advice, such as the doctor's office or an emergency clinic), reduction of surgery wait times, and early childhood education. The more it pressed on these priorities, however, the more the provinces and territories insisted that federal funding match or be directly related to their actual costs.

Progress was made, eventually. In the 2000 agreement to restore CHST cash, all the provinces and territories, including Quebec, had agreed to a general statement of vision, a set of principles, and an action plan for health-care reform; all except Quebec had also agreed to a plan for early childhood development. The 2004 agreement was much more substantial. It provided another set of broad principles, but went beyond that to set out an elaborate work plan on issues such as human resource planning, wait-time reduction, primary care reform, home care, a national pharmaceuticals strategy, and health promotion. More important, it required not only that governments report on their progress to a Canada Health Council, but that they report to citizens on an annual basis. The agreement finessed the issue of Quebec's reluctance to enter into joint social policy determination by including a side deal on "asymmetrical federalism" that allows Quebec additional flexibility in interpreting the specifics and timing of the intergovernmental commitments (Graefe, 2005).

The Conservative federal government under Stephen Harper rejected the use of the federal spending power to establish new national social programs. They continued the broader commitment to longer-term, more stable and predictable transfers. And as discussed next, their enhanced commitment to the equalization program was in line with Quebec's view that Ottawa should deal with the VFI issue mainly through increased equalization payments (which also help to correct horizontal imbalances). The disadvantage of this approach was that the richer provinces demanded, as a quid pro quo, a renewed emphasis on equal per capita shares in the remaining transfers (Courchene, 2007). Thus, in their 2007 budget the Conservatives reworked the CST transfer to provide equal per capita shares across the provinces, stripping away some built-in equalizing features, and signalled their intention to do the same with the CHT when the current 10-year plan for health-care funding expired in 2014–15 (which they did). This marked a momentous shift in fiscal federalism, away from the concept of differential need and the principle of regional redistribution, towards the electoral clout and political opportunity offered by the richer and more populous provinces of Ontario, British Columbia, and Alberta. Finally, since 2007, the CHT and CST issues have not been as controversial, nor have changes been as dramatic (see further discussion below regarding the impact of the 2007–8 financial crisis). The Harper government essentially rolled over the 2004–14 commitments, albeit with some important constraint in terms of the rate of growth of the funding transfers. In 2011 they committed to maintain the 6 per cent annual increase until 2016, with the intention to reduce it to 3 per cent starting in April 2017.

The issue of health transfers became one of the first major challenges for Justin Trudeau's Liberal government. The provinces were not satisfied by the Trudeau government's offer of a 3.5 per cent increase in health-care funding for all provinces, arguing that rising health-care costs would necessitate more federal funding to sustain the system. All 10 provinces formed a block and refused to sign an agreement with the federal government until they received a 5.2 per cent increase.

The Liberal government got around this issue by negotiating special deals with each individual province, starting with the provinces that were most friendly with the federal Liberals, namely the Liberal governments of Nova Scotia, New Brunswick, and Newfoundland and Labrador. After this initial success the Trudeau government was able to slowly chip away at provincial resistance and sign deals with each province, most of which received over 3 per cent annual increases. Also, as a deal sweetener in August 2017, the federal government announced the addition of $5 billion in supplementary funds over 10 years starting in 2018–19 to contribute to the joint priorities of improving access to mental health and addiction services and to home and community care.

Equalization: Still the Glue that Binds the Federation?

Equalization is the second largest intergovernmental transfer program in Canada, costing the federal government $18.9 billion in 2018–19. In that fiscal year it was distributed to all but four provinces (Alberta, British Columbia, Saskatchewan, and Newfoundland and Labrador). The importance of the equalization program to its recipients varies widely. In 2012–13 equalization payments were projected to amount to 22 per cent of total revenues in the province of Prince Edward Island; 17 per cent in Nova Scotia; 23 per cent in New Brunswick; 11 per cent in Quebec; 3 per cent in Ontario; and 17 per cent in Manitoba (Treff and Ort, 2013: Table 7.3).

The fact that the equalization program fared better than other federal programs in the 1990s was a reflection of the federal government's recognition that cutting equalization as well as transfer funds would amount to cutting payments to the poorer provinces even more deeply than to the rich, with the result that minimum national standards in public goods and services (loosely defined) would be even more seriously undermined. Thus the nominal budgetary allocation for equalization was never cut. Indeed, funding for the program was increased by 5 per cent in 1994. More important, however, was the fact that entitlements had not yet hit the ceiling built into the formula in 1982, according to which the overall year-to-year growth in entitlements was not to exceed the growth rate in the national economy. Together, tax cuts, out-migration in some provinces, and a narrowing of provincial fiscal disparities kept entitlements below that level until the late 1990s. By 2000, however, the ceiling was becoming a serious problem, and the provinces put pressure on Finance Minister Paul Martin to lift it. After Martin became Prime Minister, in late 2003, his government did just that. But other, more significant changes to equalization were in the works.

Throughout the 1990s, concerns about equalization had fallen into two categories. On the one hand, the richer provinces, together with some neo-liberal commentators and analysts, criticized the equalization program as being too expensive and therefore as preventing Ottawa from reducing taxes to the degree they believed it should. They also claimed that it promoted fiscal dependency and therefore prevented the recipient provinces from adjusting to economic realities.[14] They were supported in these views by a number of social policy analysts who questioned why regional redistribution should remain so relatively generous and why it needed to be done at all outside the equalization program (Banting, 1995; Milne, 1998). These arguments were influential. Many provisions aimed at regional redistribution, such as the differing per capita payments to provinces for health and social programs, were eliminated from intergovernmental transfer programs. And there were major cuts in the regional redistribution features of other major federal funding programs such as (un)employment insurance.

These changes gave rise to concern that cuts to the core equalization program would be next on the agenda.

A second set of concerns had to do with the overall design of the program from the perspective of the recipient provinces, which maintained that it did not work to fully equalize fiscal capacity; that it did not take into account differing expenditure needs; and that it discouraged resource development. Another problem was that the formula was overly complex and opaque. Such concerns led some to propose simpler and more transparently fair models to fulfill the constitutional commitment to equalization.

From 1982 until 2004 the equalization formula was based on a five-province standard. Excluded from this equation were Alberta (because of its volatile, often enormous, petroleum revenues) and the four Atlantic provinces (to counterbalance in population terms the exclusion of Alberta). By excluding Alberta, the federal government got off the hook for bringing every province up to Alberta's oil-driven fiscal capacity. The problem was that, by 2005, the five-province average only achieved 92 per cent of the equalization that a full 10-province standard would have, even if one excluded petroleum revenues from the formula. This reflects Alberta's overall superior fiscal capacity even without counting oil and gas revenues (O'Brien, 2006a, 2006b). After 2000 and the renewed escalation of petroleum prices, Alberta in particular reaped a huge increase in resource revenues, on top of its already enviable fiscal position. As a result, the overall fiscal capacity gap between Alberta and the other provinces widened, reversing what since the mid-1980s had been a trend towards convergence.

At the same time, Nova Scotia, Newfoundland and Labrador, and Saskatchewan have seen their equalization entitlements reduced or eliminated as their own resource revenues have increased.[15] The technical rules of the equalization formula often penalized individual provinces when, by virtue of bringing on new resources, their resource revenues alone were well above the average national tax yield for that resource category, but in other respects their fiscal capacity remained low. In these cases, provinces could make very little or no net gain, as for each dollar of new resource revenue they could lose as much as a dollar in equalization entitlement. Various side agreements and other provisions in the formula tried to limit this effect, but provinces such as Newfoundland and Labrador and Nova Scotia in particular found it hard to accept that there should be any "clawback" when their overall per capita revenues still fell so far behind those of other provinces.

Another problem with the equalization program was that it did not take into account actual disparities in program needs or differing costs in meeting the same program needs. It concentrated only on revenue capacity, assuming that per capita expenditure needs are the same. Yet some provinces clearly have significantly greater expenditure needs than others in key social program categories (disabled, sick elderly, university students, etc.). Also, the constitutional commitment to equity may not be fully satisfied without some compensation for these differences, since otherwise the levels of public services may not be "reasonably comparable" across all provinces.[16] The equalization program in Canada has never taken these differences into account.

In summary, since the millennium there have been pressures both to refine and expand the equalization program, and to contain and reduce it. In 2004 Prime Minister Paul Martin announced a new framework for equalization and the Territorial Funding Formula, which suspended altogether the formula for determining entitlements and instead provided for moderate increases in transfers based on recent historical trends. At the same time the federal government launched a review of equalization policy to be carried out by an expert panel. A second step came in February 2005, with the signing of the Offshore Petroleum Resources Accords: two eight-year agreements, one with Nova Scotia and one with Newfoundland and Labrador, intended to deal with their specific grievances in relation to resource revenues and the equalization program. Overall the new arrangements, though ad hoc and not structured by a formula, did provide for years of stability and growth in the recipient provinces and territories. The re-negotiation of the offshore accords with the two Atlantic provinces proved to be more controversial. The bilateral agreements essentially arranged for significant off-set payments to be made separately out of federal revenues, to compensate for the clawed-back equalization entitlements. Other provinces, notably Ontario and Quebec, criticized these bilateral arrangements as entailing yet more redistribution outside the confines of the formal equalization program.

As the Harper Conservative era began, the issue of horizontal imbalance, or equalization, generated significant debate. In 2006 the provinces were at odds over what should be done (Harding, 2006). Some wished to see significant improvements in the program while others opposed the inclusion of any resource revenues if that would mean a significant reduction in their entitlements. What made it hard to find common ground was the unavoidable trade-off, with finite federal resources, between fixing the vertical imbalance and fixing the horizontal one. Common ground was achievable on health care in 2004, because all provinces and territories got nearly the same per capita share of an expanding fiscal pie.

With the provinces at odds with one another, fortunately independent analysts seemed to be coming together. The two major independent panels noted above, one appointed by the provinces (Gagné-Stein), the other by the federal government (O'Brien), presented their reports in 2006, proposing ways to return the horizontal equity programs to a firmer foundation. Both reports called for a 10-province standard, one that includes Alberta. Gagné-Stein advocated that 100 per cent of resource revenues be included in the equalization formula, while O'Brien advocated 50 per cent. But both reports also acknowledged that the level of entitlements that such a new formula would generate could be more than the federal government could afford. They recommended scaling back the allocations accordingly, while still retaining what they hoped would be a more transparent and fairer determination of provincial entitlements.[17] Both reports offered positive assessments of the program—as have most observers for the past 20 years (Boadway, 2006). The reports noted that public support for the equalization program is relatively strong, and O'Brien in particular noted how effectively the program has worked to correct the horizontal fiscal imbalance:

> Without Equalization payments, the fiscal capacity of the least well-off province was between 58 and 68 per cent of the national average. With Equalization, the fiscal capacity of that province was raised to between 91 and almost 100 per cent of the national average. (O'Brien, 2006a: 30)

These are important findings. They mean that despite its technical complexity and the often rancorous debate and ideological division that have surrounded the equalization program, it works. Canadian federal governments are likely to stick with the fiscal glue that has helped to hold the federation together for the past 60 years.

The March 2007 budget adopted most of the O'Brien report's recommendations. It placed both the equalization and the Territorial Funding Formula programs back on the foundation of a long-term, transparent formula. By adopting the 10-province standard it provided for a significant increase in overall equalization entitlements (worth roughly $1 billion). It also simplified the estimates process, payment scheduling, and representative tax system used to determine fiscal capacity. On the issue of natural resources revenues, it decided to include 50 per cent of natural resource revenues in the formula for calculating fiscal capacity.

These changes in the architecture of the program have stood the test of time over the past several years, including the transition of the federal government from the Conservatives to the Liberals in 2015, with little apparent appetite to revisit the controversies of 2004–7. By 2009, however, two rather symbolic changes occurred as a result of shifting economic and fiscal fortunes: for the first time since the origins of the program in 1957, Ontario received equalization payments while Newfoundland and Labrador did not. Finally, and significantly, in late 2008 the federal government announced that it would limit future growth in total equalization payments to growth in the national GDP.

Responding to the 2008–9 Recession and the Continuing Period of Austerity

The deep recession of 2008–9 played havoc with public finances in Canada, forcing some changes in fiscal federalism. Indeed, the recession raised many concerns about how and whether the federal system would adapt. Would there be sufficient intergovernmental coordination of macroeconomic policy? Did all of the debt and deficit cutting of the previous two decades put us in a better position? Did the short-term and longer-term economic effects of the recession change the intergovernmental balance of power in Canada?

The recession had an immediate impact on public finances because of declining revenues and rising costs related to unemployment and welfare, an overall loss of about $20 billion in combined government revenue in Canada (TD Economics, 2009). Yet it became clear very quickly that all governments would have to be involved in economic stimulus—the spending of funds to halt growing unemployment and to maintain some degree of consumer demand. Even so, when added to the $20 billion hole the recession had already punched into public finances, such expenditures contributed to a substantial deterioration in budget balances. Thus, short-term economic stability was purchased by long-term fiscal pain.

From the events during the recession and in the difficult recovery since, one can make four observations to summarize their impact and interaction with fiscal federalism. First, as noted, the recession reversed a hard-won position of all governments from financial surplus to budgetary deficits. In August 2010 TD Economics forecasted that the federal budgetary position deteriorated in just two years from +$9.5 billion in 2007–8 to –$53.8 billion in 2009–10, and the net position of all the provinces and territories went from +$11.3 billion to –$26.8 billion in the same period (TD Economics, 2010). Among the provinces, historic debt legacies combined with the recession to produce significant differences, from Quebec with a debt of nearly 50 per cent of GDP to Alberta with no debt at all, and in terms of budgetary deficit with Ontario having the most serious ongoing budgetary position (the highest annual deficit as a percentage of GDP, approaching 3.5 per cent). While it is perhaps cold comfort to Canadians, international comparisons demonstrate that our deficit and debt hangover from 2008–9 were among the least burdensome among OECD countries. Clearly, the difficult choices made in the 1990s contributed to a stronger fiscal position going into the recession (IMF, 2010; TD Economics, 2010).

All governments indicated that their position was to restore their budgets to a balanced position within two to four years following the end of the recession in 2009. Getting there was less than easy. The federal government's own fiscal position took six years to recover, finally achieving a small budgetary surplus in 2014–15, while also making substantial improvements in its debt burden. The provinces, on the whole, have been less fortunate. British Columbia, Alberta, and Saskatchewan achieved a surplus position after five years; Quebec, Prince Edward Island, and Newfoundland and Labrador were just balancing their budgets by 2014–15. Ontario and Nova Scotia took three more years to do the same, in 2017–18, and New Brunswick is still a few years away from eliminating its budgetary deficit (PBO, 2017). This history of post-recession recovery reflects the relative fiscal positions of the provinces by 2014. Just a few years later, in 2018, key aspects of that positioning have already changed: Alberta is in a deficit position and Quebec has a strong surplus. Thus, provincial positions change with changing economic conditions as well as the ideological or fiscal policy positions of the provincial governments in power.

Second, the objectives of balanced budgets (whether a short- or longer-term goal) have entailed a substantial degree of restraint on program expenditures at all levels: in some respects, a return to the difficult years of the early 1990s. The axe has not fallen primarily on intergovernmental transfers, however; when one considers the extra funds put into infrastructure programs, transfers were still increasing overall as late as 2010–11. The federal budget of 2009 did place a new ceiling on equalization payments, as noted above. During the 2011 election campaign the Conservatives promised to maintain the 6 per cent annual growth in health transfers for at least two years past the expiry of the 10-year accord in 2014, but confirmed their intention, over the objections of the provinces and territories, to reduce the rate of growth of the CHT payments, as noted, to 3 per cent starting in 2017.

Thus there arose a post-recession tension between, on the one hand, a federal government intent on both tax and expenditure cuts and its deficit elimination and debt reduction goals and, on the other hand, provinces whose revenues had not recovered and who faced difficult challenges in restraining expenditures, especially in light of rising health-care costs for an aging population. Even with the substantial differences among provinces, their collective position was sufficiently severe for them to return to the vertical fiscal imbalance debate of a decade ago. Through the Council of the Federation the premiers called on Ottawa to reverse its unilateral cuts to transfer payment projections, bolstered by independent analysis of the Parliamentary Budget Office (Council of the Federation, 2014; PBO, 2012). For its part the federal government pointed out that actual payments (as opposed to growth rates) continue to increase year by year and that, in any case, the provinces have both the tax room and the jurisdictional capacity to fix their own fiscal problems (Finance Canada, 2015).

Third, and on a happier note, the recession demonstrated a generally cooperative and functional relationship among the governments. Perhaps because all regional economies were impacted by the downturn, there was no evidence of discord on the overall macroeconomic stance to be taken. All provinces undertook a similar degree of countercyclical budgeting in sync with the federal position; all participated readily in a major acceleration of existing infrastructure programs to stimulate the construction and related sectors. The provinces may not have been thrilled with the conditional nature of the federal funds, but they seemed to swallow their objections (Young, 2009).

Summary

Fiscal federalism changes frequently—indeed, the arrangements for revenue-sharing within a federation are among the most important means it has for responding to changing economic, social, and political conditions. Exactly how Canada's fiscal relations will change in the next few years is impossible to predict. The major economic and social factors that will come into play seem clear enough. Whether our major trading partners recover from the current period of low growth and near-recession, whether commodity prices recover, and whether the Canadian dollar remains lower than the US dollar are key uncertainties, as well as the ultimate effects of a growing but aging Canadian population on social program costs. There is no way of knowing how even one of these issues will affect fiscal policy in Canada, let alone how they will interact in the context of Canadian fiscal federalism. All we can say with any certainty is that much of the information on current programs and issues presented in this chapter will be out of date in a few years.

As for the process of fiscal federalism, the general trends towards more public participation, greater accountability, and transparency in policy-making are beginning to be felt in the area of fiscal relations, if only sporadically. In many governments the budgetary process is now also more open and consultative. But simplicity is not attainable—or even desirable—in fiscal federalism, where one size rarely fits all, and complex problems require complex solutions.

Meanwhile, fiscal federalism is no more or less collaborative a process than it has ever been. In the absence of more formal working rules for intergovernmental relations, Canadian governments are limited in their ability to solve common problems cooperatively. No one government has the authority to act, yet the incentives to cooperate are often missing (Painter, 1991). Occasionally, when—as in the case of the 2004 Health Accord—there is a high level of policy convergence, good-faith negotiation can produce significant results. More often, "consensus" amounts to little more than platitudes about common goals and agreement on lowest-common-denominator action. On major issues, intergovernmental activity is—more often than not—still limited to the consultation stage: the final decisions continue to be left to individual governments' first ministers and cabinets. This certainly continued to be the case with both the Conservative federal governments and the Liberal government since 2006.

In summary, fiscal federalism remains highly political, in that it lies at the heart of the most strategic choices that governments face. In the past decade we have seen major challenges to the overall framework of fiscal relations and some momentous changes. Nonetheless, in no federation do specific fiscal arrangements last for long, and they must all adapt to new economic and political realities. These new realities can come months after the ink has dried on a hard-won agreement or carefully fine-tuned budget. Canada is no exception.

Questions for Critical Thought

1. What is the link between intergovernmental transfers and common standards of health care? Can those standards be achieved without fiscal transfers?

2. What are the consequences of Canada being the most fiscally decentralized federation in the world?

3. Does the equalization program promote equity at the cost of economic efficiency? What are the alternatives?

Notes

1. Fiscal federalism theory predicts strong similarities in the nature of intergovernmental fiscal relationships in federations around the world. These similarities have been confirmed by comparative studies. For classic literature and recent updates, see Musgrave (1969); Oates (1972); Bird (1986); Ter-Minassian (1997); Boadway and Shah (2009); and Anderson (2010).

2. For a comprehensive historical and structural study of Canadian fiscal federalism to about 1990, see Boadway and Hobson (1993).

3. There is an enormous literature on competing values in Canadian fiscal federalism—a literature that in itself reflects those tensions. For overviews, see Boadway and Hobson (1993) and Lazar (2000). In addition, two recent public reports provide excellent overviews of competing values: see Gagné and Stein (2006) and O'Brien (2006a, 2006b).

4. Our analysis here is informed by Lazar, St-Hilaire, and Tremblay (2004) and Boadway (2005); see also Courchene (2004); Dion (2005); and Gagné and Stein (2006).

5. Economists specializing in public finance take a keen interest in fiscal federalism, seeking to determine what specific combination of taxing and expenditure responsibilities is optimal from the perspective of important economic principles such as efficiency, utility, and welfare. Should the federal government be responsible for collecting all taxes on mobile factors such as personal or corporate income? Should the federal government be primarily responsible for redistribution? Should the fiscal capacity of all governments in a federation be the same? Should revenue

capacity match expenditure responsibility? These are questions that have engaged theorists and empirical researchers for decades. See references cited in note 1 above, as well as Breton and Scott (1978).

6. The text of section 36(2) reads as follows: "Parliament and the government of Canada are committed to the principle of making equalization payments to ensure that provincial governments have sufficient revenues to provide reasonably comparable levels of public services at reasonably comparable levels of taxation." For a discussion of the history and effect of section 36, see Brown (2007).

7. For a thorough review of executive federalism in the finance area, see Leslie, Neumann, and Robinson (2004).

8. The issues of debt reduction and balanced budgeting are contested politically, but we stand by our assessment that the majority of the Canadian public supported strong fiscal medicine in the 1990s. For various perspectives on the 1995 budget and changing political and public opinion perspectives on fiscal policy in the 1990s, see MacKinnon (2003).

9. See, for example, the joint position paper prepared for the 1998 Annual Premiers' Conference: Provincial–Territorial Finance Ministers, *Redesigning Fiscal Federalism*.

10. For an enduring version of the argument for fiscal balance, see Dion (2005).

11. For discussion of the various options open to the Harper government and an analysis of its potential approach to fiscal relations, see *Policy Options* 27, 7 (Sept. 2006). On "open federalism," see the discussion and associated references in the concluding chapter of this book.

12. The five principles of medicare incorporated in the Canada Health Act are universality, comprehensiveness, accessibility, portability, and public administration. The Act also prohibits extra billing and user fees for hospital and medical care services, and authorizes the use of financial penalties to enforce these prohibitions. The provinces continue to endorse these principles, although there is some pressure within and outside governments to reinterpret them.

13. The 2004 Health Accord was officially titled "The 10-year Plan to Strengthen Health Care," and is available in Fierlbeck and Lahey (2013: Appendix 2).

14. See, for example, Courchene (1995) and Boessenkool (1996). A broad survey of views in the literature, with a comprehensive bibliography, is available in O'Brien (2006a, 2006b).

15. The case for Newfoundland and Labrador was made in the report of the Royal Commission on Renewing and Strengthening Our Place in Canada (see Government of Newfoundland and Labrador 2003); Nova Scotia's case—a "campaign for fairness"—was best summarized by its submission to the O'Brien report (see O'Brien, 2006a: Appendix A). Saskatchewan's case was made by Courchene (2004).

16. See note 6 above.

17. Another key difference between the two reports is that the federal expert panel (O'Brien) would impose a cap on equalization payments to any province whose per capita fiscal capacity is greater than that of a province not receiving equalization. This proposed equalization cap responds to concerns that the offshore resources agreement with Newfoundland and Labrador could soon move that that province's per capita fiscal capacity, after equalization, ahead of Ontario's.

References

Anderson, G. 2010. *Fiscal Federalism: A Comparative Introduction*. Toronto: Oxford University Press.

Banting, K.G. 1995. "Who 'R Us?" In *The 1995 Federal Budget: Retrospect and Prospect*, edited by T. Courchene and T.Wilson. Kingston, ON: John Deutsch Institute for the Study of Economic Policy, Queen's University.

———and R. Boadway. 2004. "Defining the Sharing Community: The Federal Role in Health Care." In *Money, Politics and Health Care*, edited by H. Lazar and F. St-Hilaire, 1–78. Montreal: Institute for Research on Public Policy.

Béland, D., A. Lecours, G.P. Marchildon, H. Mou, and M.R. Olfert. 2017. *Fiscal Federalism and Equalization Policy*. Toronto: University of Toronto Press.

Bird, R.M. 1986. *Federal Finance in Comparative Perspective*. Toronto: Canadian Tax Foundation.

———and F. Vaillancourt, eds. 2006. *Perspectives on Fiscal Federalism*. Washington, DC: World Bank Institute.

Boadway, R. 2005. "The Vertical Fiscal Gap: Conceptions and Misconceptions." In *Canadian Fiscal Arrangements: What Works, What Might Work Better*, edited by H. Lazar. Montreal and Kingston: McGill-Queen's University Press.

———. 2006. "Two Panels on Two Balances." *Policy Options* 27, no. 7: 40–5.

———and P. Hobson. 1993. *Intergovernmental Fiscal Relations in Canada*. Toronto: Canadian Tax Foundation.

———and A. Shah. 2009. *Fiscal Federalism: Principles and Practice of Multiorder Governance*. Cambridge: Cambridge University Press.

Boessenkool, K. 1996. *The Illusion of Equality: Provincial Distribution of the Canada Health and Social Transfer*. Toronto: C.D. Howe Institute.

Breton, A., and A. Scott. 1978. *The Economic Constitution of Federal States*. Toronto: University of Toronto Press.

Brown, Douglas M. 2007. "Integration, Equity and Section 36." *Supreme Court Law Review* 37 S.C.L.R (2d).

Council of the Federation (COF). 2014. "Communiqué of 29 August from the 55th Annual Premiers Conference, 26–30 August, Charlottetown." http://www.canadaspremiers.ca/en/meetings-events/71-2014/359-summer-meeting-august-26-30-2014-charlottetown-prince-edward-island.

Courchene, T.J. 1995. "Redistributing Money and Power: A Guide to the Canada Health and Social Transfer." *Observation* 39. Toronto: C.D. Howe Institute.

———. 2004. "Hourglass Federalism: How the Feds Got the Provinces to Run out of Money in a Decade of Liberal Budgets." *Policy Options* 24, no. 4: 12–17.

———. 2007. "A Blueprint for Fiscal Federalism." *Policy Options* 28, no. 4: 16–24.

Dion, S. 2005. "Fiscal Balance in Canada." In *Canadian Fiscal Arrangements: What Works, What Might Work Better*, edited by H. Lazar. Montreal and Kingston: McGill- Queen's University Press.

Fierlbeck, K., and W. Lahey, eds. 2013. *Health Care Federalism: Critical Junctures and Critical Perspectives*. Montreal and Kingston: McGill-Queen's University Press.

Finance Canada. 2006. *Restoring Fiscal Balance in Canada* (Budget Papers, 2006). Ottawa: Finance Canada.

———. 2007. *Restoring Fiscal Balance for a Stronger Federation* (Budget 2007 Paper). Ottawa: Finance Canada.

———. 2008. *The Budget Plan, 2008*. Ottawa: Finance Canada.

———. 2012. *Budget Plan, 2012–13*. Ottawa: Finance Canada.

———. 2015. *The Budget Plan, 2015*. At: https://www.budget.gc.ca/2015/home-accueil-eng.html.

———. 2018. *Budget Plan, 2018–19*. Ottawa: Finance Canada.

Gagné, R., and J. Stein. 2006. *Reconciling the Irreconcilable: Addressing Canada's Fiscal Imbalance: Report of the Advisory Panel on Fiscal Imbalance*. Ottawa: Council of the Federation.

Government of Newfoundland and Labrador. 2003. *Main Report of the Royal Commission on Our Place in Canada* [Young Report]. St John's: Government of Newfoundland and Labrador.

———, Department of Finance. 2008. "Budget Address, 2008."

Graefe, P. 2005. *The Scope and Limits of Asymmetry in Recent Social Policy Agreements*. Working Papers on Asymmetry, No. 10. Kingston, ON: Institute of Intergovernmental Relations, Queen's University.

Harding, K. 2006. "Premier's Bid for Unity Turns to Acrimony: No Deal Achieved on Equalization Plan." *Globe and Mail*, 6 June.

International Monetary Fund (IMF). 2010. *Fiscal Monitor*. Washington, DC, 14 May.

Lazar, H. 2000. "In Search of a New Mission Statement for Canadian Fiscal Federalism." In *Canada: The State of the Federation 1999–2000*, edited by H. Lazar. Kingston, ON: Institute of Intergovernmental Relations.

———, F. St-Hilaire, and J.-F. Tremblay. 2004. "Vertical Fiscal Imbalance: Myth or Reality?" In *Money, Politics and Health Care: Reconstructing the Federal–Provincial Partnership*, edited by H. Lazar and F. St-Hilaire. Montreal: Institute for Research on Public Policy and Institute of Intergovernmental Relations.

Leslie, P., R. Neumann, and R. Robinson. 2004. "Managing Canadian Fiscal Federalism." In *Reconsidering the Institutions of Canadian Federalism*, edited by P. Meekison et al. Kingston, ON: Institute of Intergovernmental Relations, Queen's University.

MacKinnon, J. 2003. *Minding the Public Purse: The Fiscal Crisis, Political Trade-Offs and Canada's Future*. Montreal and Kingston: McGill-Queen's University Press.

Milne, D. 1998. "Equalization and the Politics of Restraint." In *Equalization: Its Contribution to Canada's Economic and Fiscal Progress*, edited by B.A. Hobson. Kingston, ON: John Deutsch Institute for the Study of Economic Policy, Queen's University.

Musgrave, R.A. 1969. *Fiscal Systems*. New Haven, CT: Yale University Press.

O'Brien, A. 2006a. "Achieving a National Purpose: Improving Territorial Formula Financing and Strengthening Canada's Territories." Ottawa: Finance Canada, Expert Panel on Equalization and Territorial Formula Financing.

———. 2006b. "Achieving a National Purpose: Putting Equalization Back on Track." Ottawa: Finance Canada, Expert Panel on Equalization and Territorial Formula Financing.

Oates, W.E. 1972. *Fiscal Federalism*. New York: Harcourt Brace Jovanovitch.

Ontario. 2006. *Strong Ontario: Seeking Fairness for Canadians Living in Ontario*. Toronto: Intergovernmental Affairs.

Painter, M. 1991. "Intergovernmental Relations: An Institutional Analysis." *Canadian Journal of Political Science* 24: 269–88.

Parliamentary Budget Officer (PBO). 2012. *Fiscal Sustainability Report, 2012*. Ottawa: Parliament of Canada.

———. 2017. *Fiscal Sustainability Report, 2017*. Ottawa: Parliament of Canada.

Quebec. 2002. *A New Division of Canada's Fiscal Resources*. Report of the Commission on Fiscal Imbalance [Seguin Report]. Quebec: Government of Quebec.

Romanow, R. 2002. *Building on Values: The Future of Health Care in Canada*. Ottawa: Commission on the Future of Health Care in Canada.

Senate. 2002. *The Effectiveness and Possible Improvements to the Present Equalization Policy*. Ottawa: Senate of Canada.

TD Economics. 2009. "The Coming Era of Fiscal Restraint." TD Economics Special Report, Toronto, 20 Oct.

———. 2010. "Canada's Fiscal Exit Strategy." TD Economics Special Report, Toronto, 3 Aug.

Ter-Minassian, T., ed. 1997. *Fiscal Federalism in Theory and Practice*. Washington, DC: IMF.

Treff, K., and D. Ort. 2013. *Finances of the Nation: A Review of Expenditures and Revenues of the Federal, Provincial, and Local Governments of Canada*. Toronto: Canadian Tax Foundation.

Watts, R.L. 2008. *Comparing Federal Systems*, 3rd edn. Kingston, ON: Institute of Intergovernmental Relations, Queen's University.

Wingrove, J. 2012. "Ottawa's Per-Capita Health Transfers a Windfall for Alberta." *Globe and Mail*, 17 Jan.

Yakabuski, K. 2018. "Another Equalization Spat? Blame Stephen Harper." *Globe and Mail*, 26 June.

Young, R. 2009. "Subnational Governments and the Stimulus Packages in Canada and the United States," panel remarks. American Political Science Association annual meeting, Toronto, Sept.

Chapter 7

The Social Union

Week 9

Learning Objectives
• To understand the concept of social union and how social policy depends on the cooperation of all governments.   • To assess the different intergovernmental arrangements for three key sets of social policies: pensions, health care, and children.   • To understand how the federal spending power works in practice, and the distinction between the legal power to spend and actual expenditure levels.

Introduction

In the past decade one of the most contentious issues in Canadian federalism has been the state of the social union. We noted in Chapter 5, discussing executive federalism, that the Harper Conservative government had taken a decentralist approach, claiming to respect provincial autonomy and jurisdiction and to favour a reduction in the entanglements between the federal and the provincial–territorial orders of government. It was suggested that Prime Minister Harper's position was driven not just, or even primarily, by his philosophy on federalism, but also by his deeply held beliefs on social and economic policy. Certainly, the social policy initiatives undertaken on Harper's watch ran against the grain of what federal governments in the preceding 50 years had understood by Canada's social union. A continuing benchmark, by which many will judge the federal government under Justin Trudeau, is to what extent it will seek to restore the sense of social union.

This chapter will focus on four sets of issues: first, the main developments over the past decade in federal–provincial social policy initiatives; second, the Harper government legacy with respect to the social union; third, the Trudeau government's social policy initiatives; and fourth, the way in which social policy outcomes are influenced by the different types of federal–provincial decision rules operating in different social policy arenas. In tackling these issues we will focus on three policy areas in particular—children, pensions, and health care.

Before turning to these issues it is important to define the concept of "social union." The term is a broad concept denoting the nature of the social entitlements of citizens. In Canada it encompasses programs that are part of our social safety net, such as child care, employment insurance, social assistance, and old age support, and, what for many people constitutes the most important program by far: publicly funded and universal medical care. Post-secondary education, and access to it, is also generally considered part of our array of social programs, even though it can also be placed under the heading of "economic union" with its implications for labour markets and economic productivity. More so than in any other area, the role of provincial governments in delivering social programs is crucial since they have primary constitutional responsibility for many of them. At the same time, as noted in previous chapters, the federal government also plays a major role, mainly by providing financial support. As well, it does have jurisdiction over unemployment insurance and old age security and shares jurisdiction with the provinces over contributory pensions (Banting, 2012). Equally important, federal governments generally have placed a high value on having a visible and active role in maintaining and enhancing the social safety net in general. However, the prominent role the federal government has staked out for itself in this area and the centrality of the provinces in jurisdictional terms has set the stage for innumerable and highly public conflicts over the years, especially in the field of health care.

The term "social union" implies more than the social safety net. It is also indicative of the extent to which most, though not all, governments in the federation seek to promote a Canada-wide approach to those entitlements and a shared sense of social purpose. As such, the social union is a latecomer to the federal system. In 1867, neither the state nor its citizens intended a social policy role for government; and most of the building blocks of the social safety net were not in place until after the Second World War. The term "social union" itself was coined only relatively recently, in the early 1990s at the time of discussions leading to the Charlottetown Accord. For many years after 1945, robust federal leadership and funding of social programs, either solely by the federal government or together with the provinces, helped build up the basis for what later came to be called the social union. However, since the severe budget cuts of the mid-1990s and strained federal–provincial relations over social programs, governments and citizens began thinking of ways to recast the nation's social safety net. These discussions and negotiations among governments culminated in what became known as the Social Union Framework Agreement (SUFA) of 1999. In contrast to the constitutional negotiations earlier that decade, the negotiations provided limited involvement by citizens or key constituencies such as Indigenous peoples. SUFA also lacked one key signatory, namely the province of Quebec. While Quebec was an early advocate of an increased federal–provincial commitment to social program, it pulled out of the negotiations when it felt the agreement would entail unacceptable federal intrusions into Quebec's jurisdiction.

The Canadian social union covers an enormous variety of social programs. Different policy fields tend to have their own approaches and internal logics (Boychuk, 2004; Esping-Andersen, 1990). Furthermore, provinces have tended to have different designs and ends in mind in the delivery of social programs. In the case of health care, Canada does not have one single system but in effect 13 separate provincial and territorial systems, each with its own particular interpretation of the broad principles found in the Canada Health Act of 1984. Most provinces cover the cost of prescription drugs for those on social assistance and, to a lesser extent, those over the age of 65. Quebec, in contrast, has a comprehensive pharmacare program covering all its citizens. In the field of social assistance, certain provinces have tended to follow a more redistributive regime while others have focused more on incentives to encourage labour market participation (Boychuk, 1998). In the area of disability assistance, some provinces claw back all monies recipients receive under the Canada Pension Plan disabilities provision. Other provinces do not (Prince, 2015).

Yet most provincial programs have evolved within the context of a variety of federal programs. In the past these tended to be cost-shared in nature. With the demise of the Canada Assistance Plan in 1995, when it was folded into what was then the Canada Health and Social Transfer (CHST), virtually all social programs have been supported by Ottawa through block funding, an approach with fewer conditions and restrictions. According to Lazar (2006), while interdependence is greater in some sectors than others, most sectors are characterized by non-hierarchical relationships between governments.

The one exception has been health care. While funded on a block transfer basis under the Canada Health Transfer (CHT), this transfer still has restrictions placed on it as a result of the Canada Health Act of 1984, as discussed below. It is true, nonetheless, that during the Harper era the federal government paid much less attention to enforcing these restrictions, and the Trudeau government has also turned a blind eye to what appear to be some obvious transgressions. Health care (and in particular the universal medical insurance program) is special because it is by far the most visible and important, emotionally and in practical terms, of the various programs delivered by governments. Election and other surveys typically place it at or near the top of issues that voters consider most important. An Ipsos Public Affairs poll in June 2016, for example, indicated that 37 per cent of Canadians ranked it as their most important concern, just behind unemployment and jobs at 38 per cent (Ipsos Public Affairs, 2016). In many respects health care constitutes its own distinct field, separate from other social programs, a fact recognized by the Canada Health Transfer (CHT) carved out of the Canada Health and Social Transfer (CHST) in 2004.

The presence of the health-care gorilla, and its voracious appetite for tax dollars, has, and will continue to have, major consequences for how the other components within the social union are handled and supported, or not supported. This chapter provides a summary of the development of Canada's social safety net, culminating with the Social Union Framework Agreement (SUFA) in 1999 and the subsequent erosion in both the acceptance of the social union concept in intergovernmental circles and the programs encompassed by it. We look briefly at the three current policy fields noted above to illustrate important differences in the way various programs are negotiated and shaped and the factors responsible for these differences.

Social Union and the Federal Spending Power

As noted, the term "social union" is relatively new in Canada, dating to the early 1990s. According to Margaret Biggs (1996: 1), it refers to "the web of rights and obligations between Canadian citizens and governments that give effect and meaning to our shared sense of social purpose and common citizenship." Bob Rae, at the time premier of Ontario, is often credited with popularizing the term during the negotiations for the Charlottetown Accord as a parallel to, and as a way of counterbalancing, the emphasis on the economic union. More generally, the term arose in the 1990s from a perceived lack of something rather than the presence of something, that is, a growing sense that the welfare state, built up in Canada since 1945 through intergovernmental cooperation and the strong use of federal spending, was under siege. In Chapter 6 we reviewed the context of reduced funding for Canada-wide social programs and a widespread perception (if not always reality) that it was becoming impossible to introduce new programs because of funding constraints as well as the absence of a framework or set of rules that would allow governments to reach decisions. Many Canadians came to worry that social programs to which they feel entitled no longer have consistent characteristics across Canada and that provincial concentration on economic competitiveness is creating a social policy race to the bottom.

Thus policy thinkers, and some political leaders, came to use the term "social union" as a way of rethinking how to achieve social rights and obligations without major federal funding and conditional programs. The social union debate, however, has been wrapped up not only in fiscal federalism issues but also in constitutional law and issues about constitutional reform, crucially including Quebec's status in the federation. The Constitution Act, 1867, a mid-nineteenth-century creation, foresaw a very limited role for the state in the social lives of its citizens. When the federal government gradually began to take on a leadership role in social policy and to help create the welfare state by the mid-twentieth century, it found itself without much legislative power to do so. One solution was to amend the constitution to strengthen the federal role, which happened in the case of unemployment insurance (1940) and old age pensions (1951, 1964). But the federal government also began simply to spend money on its own programs or to share the costs of provincial programs, regardless of its legislative jurisdiction. It did so for the very practical and political reason that a substantial majority of Canadians wanted it to do so. And, as noted in Chapter 3, in constitutional terms, the federal government based its actions on what has been called the spending power (Watts, 1999; Banting, 2012).

Until the 1960s, Quebec governments resisted a number of federal programs, particularly ones that bypassed the Quebec government and transferred money directly to non-government institutions. For example, the Quebec government flatly prohibited its universities from accepting direct federal funding in the 1950s. It did so in part as a means of preserving more conservative social values. This resistance has continued since the 1960s, although no longer for conservative reasons. Rather, Quebec has sought to use autonomous and progressive social policy and programs as a chief means of promoting French language and culture. The Quebec government has a history of seeking to opt out of Canada-wide programs that the federal government and the other provinces were introducing in favour of its own program designs.[1] The province has argued in such cases that the federal government should compensate Quebec for its share of federal funding—after all, Québécois pay federal taxes too. The debate that often ensued was under what conditions Quebec should be able to opt out. For example, should it be only from cost-shared programs or also from direct federal programs?

From the late 1960s until the Charlottetown Accord of 1992, the issue of the spending power and social policy was never far from centre stage in Canada's constitutional reform debate. It counts as part of Canada's continuing constitutional impasse that our governments have not yet been able to pass amendments or, in the case of the Charlottetown Accord, to obtain public consent to settle the spending power issue. In 1969, Prime Minister Pierre Trudeau proposed constitutional amendments to consolidate and regulate the use of the spending power, but ultimately did not succeed. The proposed changes would have recognized and legitimized the use of the power while making it subject to provincial consent in some cases. The issue returned again in the 1978–81 negotiations, as well as being one of Quebec's five original demands in the Meech Lake Accord of 1987. There the proposal was to create a new section 106A of the Constitution Act, 1867 with the following wording:

> The Government of Canada shall provide reasonable compensation to the government of a province that chooses not to participate in a national shared-cost program that is established by the Government of Canada after the coming into force of this section in an area of exclusive provincial jurisdiction that is compatible with national objectives. (Meech Lake Accord, 3 June 1987, Part 7)

After the Meech Lake Accord's failure to be ratified in 1990, negotiations on a renewed constitutional settlement took place, leading to the Charlottetown Accord of 1992. Part of the controversy surrounding the Meech Lake Accord had been the perception, largely from outside Quebec, that the new provision on the spending power would prevent the federal government from ever again making major progress on national social programs. There were opponents to any kind of decentralization or diminution of federal power, as well as fears over the proposed free trade agreement with the US.[2] Nonetheless, the text in the Charlottetown Accord was similar to Meech, if somewhat watered down: it limited the principle of compensation to new, Canada-wide, shared-cost programs and also called for an intergovernmental agreement or framework to govern the use of the spending power more broadly. After the demise of that Accord, the idea of a constitutional amendment, as such, was put on ice, but the device of a new intergovernmental framework would be revived after the landmark 1995 federal budget.

The previous chapter outlined the fiscal background that led to the next phase in the social union/spending power issue. The prelude to what Keith Banting (2012) calls the "crisis in the post-war social union" involved the various attempts of the federal government to decouple its funding commitments from actual provincial spending in cost-shared programs. This came in the form of "block grants" of the Established Programs Financing (EPF) arrangement (1977) and in the consolidation of the EPF and the CAP into the CHST (1995). The introduction of the CHST in the 1995 federal budget underscored the chief federal priorities at the time: reducing the deficit, paring back the welfare state, and withdrawing from heavily conditional funding programs with the provinces. Moreover, a decade of federal cuts and unilateral changes to their funding programs had left the provinces reeling, distrustful of the federal government, and determined to pursue the social union on their own terms. By the mid-1990s, the debate over the spending power seemed very old hat: the issue then was not federal spending but federal de-spending.

Even though the SUFA is not often cited or seemingly employed today, 20 years after its conclusion it remains an important development in Canadian federalism. It illustrates the fundamentally different positions regarding the social union of three key sets of players: the government of Canada (and many Canadian interest groups), the government of Quebec (and many interests in Quebec), and the provincial and territorial governments apart from Quebec. It also illustrates that with some flexibility, Canadian governments can come to agreement on social union issues.

The long negotiations saw the provinces concerned with restoring social program funds from Ottawa, moving towards joint decision-making on social programs including the interpretation and enforcement of policy objectives and standards, and the placing of constraints on the spending power. The federal government shared these goals to an extent, but did not want to get too boxed in, while also improving accountability and transparency and encouraging mobility within the federation. Finally, Quebec had its more traditional concerns, which, while generally supportive of the provincial goals, insisted that it should continue to be able to opt out of new national social programs with full financial compensation. The highlights of the final agreement reached in 1998 are that the basic principles and values of the social union were defined, the federal spending power was explicitly recognized, and this power could be invoked for new national social programs so long as there was a threshold of provincial support.

The dynamics of the negotiations need not be dwelled upon here, but it is worth noting that Quebec Premier Lucien Bouchard did play an active role in building consensus among the provinces and with the federal government, even if, at the end of the day, the Quebec government chose not to enter into the final agreement with Ottawa (Noël, 2001). It did, however, reach an understanding with Ottawa so that, de facto, it would receive the same benefits and levels of transfers as the other provinces. The asymmetrical nature of the deal and the process by which it was reached came to define a pattern that Gibbins (1999) labelled 9-1-1 federalism, a process by which all the provinces absent Quebec reached a deal with Ottawa, which in turn would then negotiate separately with Quebec as to how the terms of the agreement would or could be applied to that province.

SUFA constituted an important step—if very tentative—towards a new model of intergovernmental collaboration, a model in which the federal government and the provinces and territories are supposed to be equal partners in policy formation and implementation, and in which the rules are more jointly determined and executed. However, in the nearly two decades since SUFA was signed, most observers would concur that this agreement has had very limited impact. The Chrétien Liberals and Harper Conservatives have both introduced policies that can be seen as contrary to the intent of SUFA, such as the Millennium Scholarship Foundation in the case of the Chrétien Liberals and the cancellation of the federal–provincial child-care agreements in 2006 by the Conservatives.

We now turn to three policy areas—child care and children's benefits, pension reform, and health care—to see what developments in these areas have to tell us about the continuing evolution of the Canadian social union.

Child Care and the Children's Benefit

The National Child Benefit (NCB) of 1998 and the Early Learning and Child-Care (ELCC) program of 2005, the products of intensive negotiations by the federal and the provincial governments, were two exceptions to what was otherwise a rather sparse decade for the launch of new social initiatives. The NCB, implemented shortly before the signing of SUFA, was seen as a model and likely an inspiration for new forms of collaboration promised by SUFA. The NCB was innovative primarily in the way that federal and provincial programs in support of low-income families with children were linked together. Rather than Ottawa transferring funds to the provinces to support provincially delivered programs, Ottawa used the income tax system and direct payments to recipients to deliver its contributions to the program in coordination with the provinces and territories. The new program built on the 1993 Child Tax Benefit, which saw the replacement of federal family allowance cheques and a number of child tax credits with a single income-dependent payment, and targeted benefits to those in need rather than being a universal entitlement paid to all families. The 1998 NCB featured an agreement between Ottawa and the provinces so that the latter would begin reinvesting the savings from their welfare-based child benefits (in light of increased transfers from Ottawa for those programs) into programs targeting the working poor. The aim was "an 'integrated child benefit': all low-income families, regardless of their major source(s) of income, would receive the same amount of federal child benefits" (Battle, 2015: 5). Quebec was not a formal participant in the program but, foreshadowing SUFA, in practical terms it was. According to Ken Battle, a social policy expert and founder of the Caledon Institute, the NCB largely succeeded in its aim.

The other program, one that was barely launched in 2005 before the Paul Martin government was defeated, was the Early Learning and Child-Care program (ELCC). Beginning in 1984 with a federal-initiated ministerial task force on child care and continuing with the Mulroney government's special parliamentary committee and proposed (never passed) legislation, there had been plenty of discussion on the possibility of a national child-care program by the time Ottawa and the provinces agreed to the Multilateral Framework Agreement on Early Learning and Child Care (ELCC) in 2003. Ottawa committed to provide $900 million over five years on the understanding that the provinces in turn would commit $5 billion over the same time period and adhere to four basic principles related to universality, quality, accessibility, and programming with a developmental focus (Friendly and White, 2008: 189). There were also commitments to annual reporting and government regulation of ELCC programming. As Friendly and White (2008) note, moving from the broad framework agreement to specific details required a shift from multilateralism to a bilateral approach or, more accurately, sequential bilateralism that saw the federal Social Development minister negotiating separate agreements with each of the provinces, taking into account the different needs and ideologies of the various provincial governments.

Back to the Future, Part 1, under Harper

In 2006 the newly elected Harper government, acting on its election promise, immediately began the process of dismantling the ELCC program, giving the required one-year notice while providing transitional payments, even to those provinces that did not have a formal agreement. By July of 2006 it had begun mailing out cheques to families with children under age six as part of its own election commitment to provide families taxable payments of $1,200 per child. This annual cash payment, the Universal Child Care Benefit (UCCB), was no longer targeted at just low-income families and in many ways was a throwback to the old system of family allowance cheques. There was no obligation for recipients to spend the money on child care. Not too long before the 2015 federal election the age limit was extended to age 17. There were other wrinkles added along the way, such as the revival of the non-refundable $2,000 child tax credit and income-splitting between spouses. The net effect of this complex web of benefits, exemptions, and tax credits, according to Ken Battle, is that it was of benefit to only about 13 per cent of Canadian households, primarily "one-income couples with children and two-income families in which one parent has significantly more income than the other parent" (Battle, 2015).

The Harper government also committed itself to something entitled the Childcare Spaces Initiative, based on offering financial incentives to employers and private child-care operators to create spaces. As Friendly and White (2012: 190) note, it was a strange policy choice for a government with a hands-off social policy and a non-interference stance on provincial jurisdiction. It was also at odds with the rules and norms of SUFA. No effort was made by either federal or provincial governments to track the number of spaces created as a result of this program. There was also little effort made to assess whether the new UCCB helped recipients to gain access to whatever spaces were available. According to the Conservatives in their 2006 election platform, "Only the Conservatives believe in freedom of choice in childcare. The best role for government is to let parents choose what's best for their children . . . whether that means formal childcare, informal care through neighbours or relatives, or a parent staying at home" (quoted in Friendly and White, 2012: 190). Battle (2015) notes that the full annual payment per child (initially $1,200 and then $1,920 in 2015) before taxes bought little in the way of child care, especially since these amounts were before taxes and, in the case of the increase in 2015, this was reduced not by taxes but by the simultaneous removal of the $345 Child Tax Credit. The only families that gained significantly were those with high incomes and only one parent working under the family income-splitting provisions.

Back to the Future, Part 2, under Trudeau

Rolling back most of the Harper child-care and family income provisions under the slogan of "real change for the middle class" was a central plank in the 2015 Liberal election platform, with the promise that 90 per cent of families would be better off. The focus on the middle class was hammered home in the 2016 budget, entitled *Growing the Middle Class*, which introduced the new Canada Child Benefit (Finance Canada, 2016). Much like the changes in the 1990s, which saw the consolidation of several transfer programs into the National Child Benefit of 1998, the CCB lumped together the Universal Child Care Benefit, the Canada Child Tax Benefit, and the Family Tax Cut (income-splitting for families). As well, the children's fitness and arts tax credits were to be phased out by the end of 2016. The new benefit represented a significant increase over the Conservative program, $2,300 on average. In another key difference from the Conservative approach, the CCB was made non-taxable. Still another major difference was configuring the new CCB so that it was of much greater benefit to lower-income families, with the value of the benefit declining with increased income so that families with combined incomes over $150,000 would not collect any of the CCB. The budget legislation was passed in June 2016 and the new benefit rolled out in July of that year. It's worth noting that the money under the UCCB, the major feature of the Conservatives' child-care program in 2006, was then also rolled into the new CCB.

Two additional features merit discussion. First, although the Liberal government committed itself to spending $22.5 billion over five years on the program, the payments themselves are not indexed to inflation, which suggests that the value of the program to recipients would erode by about 10 to 12 per cent over that period. Second, since many of the low-income recipient families would also be receiving benefits through provincial programs such as social assistance or income support programs for those employed, there was the danger of some or all of the new CCB being clawed back by provincial governments. What was noteworthy was that by launch time in July 2016 all provincial and territorial governments had committed themselves to not claw back any of the CCB monies in the hands of social assistance claimants, though the status of working poor families in this respect was less clear (McGregor, 2016). In effect, Ottawa had been engaging the provinces through traditional back channels to persuade them not to use their power to claw back the payments.

As for actual child care and early learning, the Liberal Party in its 2015 election platform promised that this would be part of another major commitment to invest in infrastructure, including social infrastructure, which would include affordable housing and cultural and recreational infrastructure as well as child care. The 2015 platform promised that a Liberal government would work collaboratively with the provinces to develop a National Early Learning and Child Care Framework (NELCCF); the platform also recognized unique differences among provinces as to how child care was delivered and funded. After a $500 million investment in child care in the 2016 budget for the 2017–18 fiscal year, the 2017 budget promised an additional $7 billion over 10 years to "support and create more high-quality, affordable child care spaces across the country." The government anticipated this new funding could support up to 40,000 new subsidized child-care spaces.

If the Conservatives' UCCB of 2006 represented a throwback to the old system of family allowance cheques, then the new NELCCF hearkens back to the 2003 Multilateral Framework Agreement on Early Learning and Child Care negotiated under the previous Liberal government of Jean Chrétien. That agreement became the basis for negotiating a series of specific bilateral agreements with the individual provinces. This template is being used again. Of course, the overall policy environment has changed since 2003. Most provinces and territories continued to develop and extend their own child-care programs, albeit on a limited basis, doing so in a variety of ways, in part with the view to capturing some of the monies stemming from the complex mishmash of tax credits and direct transfers to families introduced by the Conservatives. In other words, the starting point for the NELCCF negotiations was quite different from what it was back in 2003.

In June 2017 the federal, provincial, and territorial ministers responsible for early learning and child care completed a framework agreement designed to guide bilateral agreements with each province and territory in the coming year.[3] The agreement provides the principles to guide federal funding contributions, noted above, and aims at "inclusive" programming by provinces in early childhood education and child care by regulated provincial facilities, targeting to high-needs groups under six years of age. Quebec did not sign the agreement because of its stance on autonomy, but supports the general principles and expects to receive its share of federal funding.

What lessons can we draw from the past decade and a half of federal–provincial interaction in the child care, child and family support, and early learning field? The NCB of 1998 was regarded by many as the ideal model of what collaborative intergovernmental relations should look like, and no doubt it had a positive effect on the consummation of negotiations over the 2003 ELCC agreement and the child-care agreements that followed. Given the technical nature of the NCB and the child-care agreements, through necessity there was extensive involvement of officials in the negotiations, which by the time the discussions were successfully completed left a solid reservoir of goodwill. In addition, over the years an extensive network of academic experts and practitioners have helped to develop and deploy various tax measures and expenditures as instruments for the delivery of, first, the National Child Benefit and, later, the Canada Child Benefit.

All evidence points to the fact that this accumulated intergovernmental policy capacity, to use the term developed by Inwood, Johns, and O'Reilly (2011), remained intact over a full decade, a time during which the Harper government deliberately attempted to disengage itself from interactions with other governments, especially in the social policy field. When the Liberals returned to power in October 2015, it took only nine months for Ottawa and the provinces to pick up the threads, hammer out a revised framework agreement, and have the funds flowing to recipient families. It is conceivable at the time of the negotiations that the federal government could have attached conditions to its contributions to the CCB, by withholding monies from the Canada Social Transfer for example, to ensure that no province or territory would claw back the new benefits. However, that proved unnecessary. Employment and Social Development Canada, the lead federal department on the file, was able to state that "negative interactions" were avoided through collaboration with the provinces (quoted in McGregor, 2016). And, as just noted, collaborative progress is also clearly being made towards a series of bilateral agreements with the provinces and territories on early learning and child care. To the extent that collaboration, underpinned by comity and fair dealing, is one of the hallmarks of SUFA, then one can conclude that at least part of the SUFA legacy is alive and well in this particular sector.

Canada/Quebec Pension Plan Reform—Joint-Decision Federalism in Action

Like medicare, the Canada/Quebec Pension Plan (CPP/QPP) was the product of the 1960s, an era that was probably the most critical of the post-war era for the launch of most of the important social programs. Most programs, such as medicare and the Canada Assistance Plan, were developed on a shared-cost basis between Ottawa and the provinces, with the provinces responsible for delivery with financial assistance from Ottawa. The CPP was one of the very few that was based on joint responsibility, that is, both the federal and the provincial governments had a role in ensuring the adequate delivery of compensatory pension plans, something made possible by constitutional amendments in 1951 and 1964 (Banting, 2012). Critically, the 1964 amendment also specified a set of decision rules for making changes to the plan—two-thirds of the provinces (de facto seven provinces) with at least two-thirds of the population had to agree to any changes—making the CPP unique in a federal system characterized mainly by the lack of formal decision-rules, other than the formula for amending the constitution.

Two other noteworthy features: first, the fact that it was the CPP/QPP, and not just the CPP, was a strong endorsement of asymmetrical federalism (even though the two plans largely mirrored each other). Second was the fact that this asymmetry became enshrined, with some conditions. As well, the 1960s negotiations that led to the CPP/QPP were the first visible demonstrations of Quebec's newfound prowess in the intergovernmental arena. Quebec proposed a public pension scheme that was in many ways more sophisticated than what Ottawa had in mind. The result was a joint CPP/QPP that covered a greater proportion of earnings than what Ottawa originally had in mind, and helped to overcome resistance from the Ontario government and from the Ontario-based insurance industry that had been largely opposed to any kind of public pension plan (Simeon, 2009 [1972]; Little, 2008).

At the same time, the CPP/QPP has been regarded as a relatively modest program, certainly when compared to public pension schemes in most other advanced industrialized countries. As well, analysts such as Keith Banting (2012) have regarded the multiple veto points because of the relatively high thresholds in the amending formula as limiting the ability of the program to respond to changing circumstances—whether that is perceived as the need to cut back or expand the program. Certainly in comparison, medicare, launched only a little later than CPP/QPP, was far more comprehensive in what it covered and, with its shared-cost funding arrangement, appeared to promise a lot more flexibility.

According to Banting (2012), efforts in the mid-1970s to expand CPP/QPP went nowhere. By the mid-1990s major problems in CPP/QPP became evident once again. Benefits being paid out would begin outstripping contributions in the not-too-distant future, so that in 20 years CPP would end up in a permanent deficit situation without an increase in the contribution rate, a reduction in benefits, or a combination of both. Given that all governments were in retrenchment mode, there was little appetite for major expansions in QPP/CPP, except for BC and Saskatchewan, both under NDP governments. At the same time, Quebec and some of the other provinces were adamantly opposed to seeing any reductions in benefits. The end result of these discussions was, according to Banting (2012), some modest changes that were subsequently implemented in 1998. These changes provided an increase in contribution rates for both employers and employees and the investment of CPP contributions not immediately needed for benefits in equity markets through a new Canada Pension Plan Investment Board (CPPIB), all with the aim of improving the long-term financial viability of the plan. The QPP was already investing a portion of its contributions through the Caisse de dépôt et placement du Québec. These modest changes, according to Banting, were in keeping with the conservative nature of the plan and the need for a broad consensus to meet the requirements of the two-thirds/two-thirds majority formula.

Another analyst, Bruce Little (2008), however, saw the changes, in particular the creation of the CPPIB, as rather more significant. In addition to demonstrating that executive federalism could be made to work (eight of the 10 provinces encompassing 82 per cent of the population concurred), in his view the changes made the CPP/QPP model "extraordinarily robust for its own purposes" and that, subsequently, "[t]he CPP reforms have worn their first decade well" (Little, 2008: 310). It can be further argued that the creation of the CPPIB and the investment fund it manages helped set the stage for the next round of changes, this time involving the expansion of CPP/QPP.

Over the years critics have pointed out that CPP/QPP benefits are far less generous compared to public pension schemes in other countries, including the US, where the Social Security program benefits are roughly twice those of CPP/QPP. As noted by Moscovitch, Lochead, and Falvo (2016), the "Canadian pension model is often viewed as being good in terms of poverty reduction, but 'under developed' in terms of income replacement for middle-income—and especially higher-income—earners." Various interests groups and trade unions, as well as some provincial governments, have argued that CPP/QPP should raise both the proportion of earnings and the overall level of earnings covered by the plan. This argument gained considerable impetus with the fact that employer pension plans were becoming less and less generous, especially after the 2008–9 financial crisis, with the most highly valued and secure "defined benefit" plans becoming almost extinct in the private sector.

Beginning in 2010, federal and provincial Finance ministers began consultations on CPP/QPP expansion, with the federal government indicating that it was open to the idea. Among the provinces, PEI and Ontario were most strongly supportive, with the long-time PEI minister of Finance presenting by far the most detailed proposal, which would expand CPP at earnings of $25,000 up to $100,000, resulting in a replacement rate of 33 per cent up to $100,000. Six provinces publicly indicated support for CPP expansion; Alberta was the most adamant in opposing the proposed changes. In general, opposing provinces argued that CPP expansion would impose increased burdens on contributors—both employees and employers—and that voluntary schemes involving the private sector would be preferable if there was an identifiable need for Canadians to save more for retirement.

By late 2013, shortly before a scheduled meeting of Finance ministers, federal Finance Minister James Flaherty announced that CPP expansion was off the table; he felt that there was simply insufficient consensus among the provinces and, as well, cited the still weak economy. At about this time the government of Ontario began indicating an interest in setting up its own pension scheme in the absence of CPP expansion. In 2014 these musings became a reality when Ontario Premier Kathleen Wynne made it a prime issue in the provincial election that year. Following a decisive win she announced plans for the Ontario Retirement Pension Plan (ORPP), which would be more generous than what had been mooted for the CPP up to that point (Lee, 2016: 277). Legislation for the ORPP was passed, an administration corporation created, and staff hired, including a CEO. Even after the defeat of the Harper government in 2015 the Ontario premier stated that until there were clear indications that a CPP expansion was in the cards it was full steam ahead for rolling out the ORPP.

As well as a change of government at the federal level in October 2015 there was also change at the provincial level, most notably in Alberta where the NDP came to power in May 2015, a party more sympathetic to public pensions, and in Manitoba, where the Progressive Conservatives replaced the NDP in April 2016. By the summer of 2016, to the surprise of most observers, eight of 10 provinces, including Ontario, agreed to an enhanced CPP (Lee, 2016: 267), which met the seven provinces/two-thirds population threshold. Manitoba demurred, largely because, the newly elected PC government claimed, it had not yet had the opportunity to review the proposed changes. For Quebec, the main problem was that the changes would actually result in those in the lower income brackets (the working poor) receiving less in the way of pension benefits, a criticism that had been made of the proposal by those who thought it was geared too much to the middle class (Lee, 2016; Milligan and Schirle, 2016). The deadline for all concurring governments to provide their formal approval was 15 July 2016, and this appeared to be a relatively simple matter since legislative approval at neither provincial nor the federal level was required. At the last moment, however, the BC government balked, stating that before giving its approval in principle it needed to conduct a public consultation, which it proceeded to do via an online website through which individuals and groups could submit their views. Three months later, on 4 October 2016, the BC government announced that it was then able to give its full approval in light of the public feedback received (British Columbia, 2016). By coincidence, its approval came a week after Ottawa announced its approval of the Pacific Northwest liquefied natural gas (LNG) proposal (subject to 190 separate conditions), a project that was at the top of the BC government's list of development priorities.

What are some of the possible lessons that could be drawn from the CPP/QPP case? First, as with the National Child Benefit, one can cite the importance of trust ties as well as an extensive network of outside experts generally supportive of CPP expansion, again evidence of strong intergovernmental policy capacity (Inwood, Johns, and O'Reilly, 2011). But robust strategic manoeuvring also played a role. The government of Ontario under Wynne made a clear and credible threat that the province would simply proceed—as the constitution allows—with its own provincial version of CPP under the rubric of the Ontario Retirement Pension Plan, in the face of Ottawa and the other governments failing to reach agreement.[4] The spectre of Ontario with 38 per cent of the population going it alone was enough to persuade even reluctant governments, such as Saskatchewan, to come on board. A third and perhaps most important lesson was the presence of a distinct formula for making binding decisions. As Saskatchewan Premier Brad Wall put it: "When it became clear the federal government had the numbers they needed for a deal [i.e., seven provinces and 67 per cent of the population] Saskatchewan worked to achieve a compromise by delaying the start date of the enhancement until 2019 and the phased-in implementation by one year to 2025" (quoted in Wherry, 2016). In other words, the one or two holdout provinces could not veto the entire deal.

Health Care: From Unilateralism to Multilateralism to Bilateralism

In 2016, shortly before Christmas, a *Globe and Mail* editorial stated: "it's been a long time since federal–provincial health funding 'negotiations' involved actual negotiations. Negotiations imply an exchange—you give me X, and in return, I will give you Y. That's not really what's up with federal–provincial fiscal arrangements on health care. You can make demands of Santa Claus, but you aren't exactly negotiating" (*Globe and Mail*, 2016). The Trudeau government had offered annual increases of 3 per cent, identical to what the Harper government had offered, down from 6 per cent under the previous health accord negotiated by then Prime Minister Paul Martin back in 2004, plus (in contrast to Harper) additional funding for mental health and home care should the provinces accept conditions imposed by Ottawa to ensure those funds were actually spent in those two areas. The provinces had collectively responded with a request for 5.2 per cent with no strings attached other than those spelled out in the Canada Health Act of 1984.

Almost exactly five years previously, then Finance Minister James Flaherty announced to a meeting of federal and provincial Finance ministers that in five years' time the annual increases of 6 per cent under the Canada Health Transfer would be reduced to 3 per cent annually or to growth in GDP, whichever was greater. Notwithstanding the fact of a change of government in 2015, with the new Liberal governing party having promised in the election that it would not be taking the same approach to health-care funding as the Harper government, the basic message presented to provincial Finance and Health ministers was fundamentally the same: an increase only slightly higher than what the Harper government promised, with some conditional sweeteners attached.

The spectre of one of Ottawa's largest transfer programs continuing to increase at more than twice the rate of inflation for a decade or more no doubt played a major role in the decision of both the Harper and Trudeau governments to hold the line. The failure of the two meetings to result in comprehensive agreements also points to the fact that health care—its financing and delivery—is one of the most challenging policy issues facing the Canadian federal system. Variously labelled the health-care monster or the devourer of government budgets (e.g., Simpson, 2012), for all provinces the field constitutes the largest single budgetary item, with unrelenting cost pressures. For Ottawa it represents a field in which, traditionally, it has desired a strong and visible presence but lacks meaningful forms of leverage other than its spending power. In sum, on the one hand the provinces lack the fiscal resources and are often overwhelmed by the program responsibilities; on the other hand, Ottawa has more fiscal resources but no authority under the constitution.

Health care is by far the most publicly visible area in social policy, with all the attendant expectations of advocacy groups and the public as a whole. This public scrutiny restricts the capacity of governments to come to agreements.[5] Federal–provincial–territorial meetings have all the hallmarks of summit-style federalism, taking place under the close scrutiny of the media and other interested parties. The often bitter wrangling—where terms like "deceitful" are routinely fired at the federal government by provincial ministers, including premiers—also involves the public clash of two competing narratives. And in this clash, the provinces over the years have gained the upper hand, arguably at the expense of a more adaptive and effective health-care delivery system (Bakvis, 2017).

In the intergovernmental discourse on health-care funding, particularly up to 2004, governments argued about what the federal contribution to provincial expenditures actually was as well as what it should be (see Commission on the Future of Health Care in Canada, 2002; Lazar and St-Hilaire, 2004). This was a debate complicated by and tied into the debate over vertical fiscal imbalance discussed in the last chapter. The provinces were arguing that the federal cash contribution was only 18 per cent of actual costs; the federal government in turn argued that its contribution included not just the cash transfers but also the value of tax points turned over in the 1970s expressly to pay for mature social programs.

Prior to 1977 most major social programs, other than equalization, were supported by Ottawa on a shared-cost basis, at the time colloquially referred to as 50 cent dollars. The essence was that Ottawa would match provincial expenditures roughly on a fifty–fifty basis. There were three major areas so funded: post-secondary education (PSE), social assistance, and health care. In 1977 Ottawa and the provinces agreed that PSE and health care were sufficiently mature that the provinces could be expected to maintain standards in those two fields without conditions being attached to transfers by Ottawa. As long as the provinces agree to the five basic principles (public administration, comprehensiveness, universality, portability, and accessibility) with respect to health-care delivery to citizens, there would be much greater flexibility on how federal funding could be spent. In fact, as long as each province adhered to those basic and broadly defined standards, it was free to spend as little or as much of the federal transfers as it wished. Part of the 1977 settlement was that half the amount was in cash, the other half in the form of tax points. That is, the federal government partially ceded room in the income and corporate tax fields to create additional tax room for the provinces that was roughly the equivalent of half the cash it had been transferring prior to 1977.

The new arrangements enacted in 1977, under the prosaic title of Established Programs Financing (EPF), flowed more money to provinces than Ottawa anticipated, to the benefit of the poorer provinces especially. As a proportion of total provincial health expenditures, federal EPF transfers reached a peak of somewhat over 50 per cent in 1980. From 1982 onward, however, Ottawa started to cut back the cash portion but not the tax points (which would have been difficult to retrieve in any event). In every annual budget statement, the federal government dutifully noted the overall amount for each province, including the value of the tax points. Over time it also became clear that the tax portion of the transfer was growing while the cash transfer part was shrinking. Because Quebec has more tax room than the other provinces because of earlier opting-out arrangements, its cash portion for health care was shrinking even faster. In order to ensure that actual cash would continue to flow to the provinces, and to Quebec in particular, as well as to give the provinces more flexibility to compensate for the overall decline in transfers, Ottawa in 1995 collapsed payments for health and PSE under EPF and for the Canada Assistance Plan (which up to that point was the last major conditional grant program) into a single Canada Health and Social Transfer (CHST). The Canada Health Act still applied but the provinces could now redirect some of the money formerly dedicated to social assistance, for example, to health care or other areas.

Not too long before the 1997 federal election the Liberal government began to restore some of the cuts made in 1994–5. In 1999, as part of the SUFA negotiations, Ottawa and the provinces reached a five-year accord on health funding that restored most of the previous cuts and provided for a basic CHST floor that would rise over time (Boismenu and Graefe, 2004). Provinces made a commitment to greater accountability and new forms of health-care delivery, but there were no formal requirements for reporting on results other than to their citizens. In 2003 Ottawa and the provinces reached another agreement on a $34.8 billion health-care renewal accord over five years, with almost half the money focused on primary health care, home care, and catastrophic drug coverage (Fafard, 2013: 36). This accord included additional commitments to reporting and the development of further performance indicators, provisions consistent with the recommendations of the 2002 Royal Commission on the Future of Health Care (Romanow Report), which had urged that increased health transfers be linked to greater transparency and accountability. The year 2003 also saw the creation of the Health Council of Canada, composed of representatives appointed by the provincial and federal governments, which was tasked with reporting on the implementation of the 2003 and, later, the 2004 accords, including the performance indicators. Alberta and Quebec declined to participate in the reporting aspects.

The single most important development in that decade was the 2004 health accord, often referred to as the Martin accord after the prime minister at the time. It featured a *10-Year Plan to Strengthen Health Care* (Health Canada, 2004) with federal commitment to boost the health transfer to the provinces and territories annually by 6 per cent over the 10-year period, plus a Wait Times Reduction Fund of $4.5 billion over six years. The 2004 accord was even more explicit on the issue of performance indicators with a commitment by all parties to develop specific indicators on wait times. Two other important features are worth noting. First, Quebec was given more latitude in how the additional transfers could be spent and how the performance indicators were to be interpreted, a provision that was not only agreed to by Ottawa but also accepted by the other provinces and territories. Second, Ottawa agreed to an annual escalator of 6 per cent in CHT transfers over a 10-year period.

After the 2006 federal election the Harper government left the Martin health accord intact (unlike the 2004 Kelowna Accord with Canada's Indigenous peoples, largely about health care, which was rescinded), including the 6 per cent escalator. Indeed, in the 2007 budget the Conservative government provided an extra $612 million to help provinces implement more quickly the wait-time guarantees in the Martin accord. However, as Fafard (2013) notes, Ontario was the only province to implement anything remotely resembling a wait-time benchmark with a protocol allowing patients to complain. The Health Council, the third-party agency ostensibly tasked with overseeing the implementation and monitoring of performance measures relating to wait times, among other factors, was left in the dark as to definitions and expectations pertaining to these guarantees. After the 2008 election the Conservatives ceased engaging in any discussions about wait times, guarantees, or performance measures. Coupled with the prime minister's statement in 2009 that "I don't lecture the provinces publicly on how they should be running their health care systems" (quoted in Fafard, 2013: 40), it was clear that the Harper government had little or no interest in holding the provinces feet to the fire regarding wait times or even the Canada Health Act. In March 2014 the Health Council of Canada was abolished.

Bending the Cost Curve?

The single most important act of the Harper government in the health area came in December 2011 when, during a federal–provincial meeting of Finance ministers, the federal minister of Finance handed each provincial minister an envelope containing a summary of the amount in CHT transfers their province could count on over the next decade. While the specific sums varied for each province, the basic message was the same: maintenance of the 6 per cent escalator till 2017; thereafter it would be reduced to either 3 per cent or the rate of increase in nominal GDP, whichever was greater. It was also made clear that the offer was non-negotiable. Rather than heralding a long, drawn-out negotiation process involving federal and provincial/territorial governments, with lobbying and public interventions by various advocacy groups, the Conservative government held true to its original promise and declined any further discussions.

Despite the surprising announcement, the initial reaction from the provinces was far from universally negative. The Ontario premier indicated dismay with the halving of the 6 per cent escalator, stating that his province would be willing to accept specific conditions if the escalator was restored or additional money would be invested, for example, in more home care and seniors' care (*CBC News*, 2012). The BC premier, on the other hand, while regretting the reduction in the escalator, at the same time noted that Ottawa was essentially "vacating the policy field for premiers. . . . To me, this is really a huge opportunity for premiers to step up and to take the reins on health care" (Kennedy, 2012). When it became apparent that the Harper government was unlikely to budge, the premiers began to adjust to a new fiscal reality, both on their own and through the Council of the Federation (COF). One area tackled by the premiers was generic drugs, where Canada has traditionally had among the highest prices in the world.[6] While the COF had begun to address the issue in 2010, it was not until after the December 2011 announcement on the reduction in the escalator that these efforts gained momentum.

A Health Care Innovation Working Group, chaired by the premiers of PEI and Saskatchewan, besides considering generic drug costs, was tasked with examining clinical practice, team-based health care, and human resource management initiatives with the view to achieving better outcomes at lower costs. This led to the launch of the Pan-Canadian Competitive Value Price Initiative for Generic Drugs covering a limited number of generics, 14 by 2015. The result has been major reductions in what provincial plans pay for generics (i.e., plans funded directly by provincial governments for seniors or those on social assistance). However, there is considerable variation from province to province. In some provinces the cap on pricing applies to private plans as well, but not in others. And some provinces, BC for example, allow for exemptions for certain generics (Lexchin, 2015).

Critics have claimed that the provinces could have gone a lot further, particularly in missing the opportunity to implement a national competitive bidding process for generics, but taken as a whole the moves on generic pricing can be seen as a significant development in cost containment. So, too, was the tougher stance a number of provinces took in their negotiations with health-care providers, mainly physicians. Whether there was a causal link or it was merely a matter of coincidence, national health expenditures began trending downward from a peak reached in 2010. According to data compiled by the Canadian Institute for Health Information, the average annual growth rate for the period 2010–16 was only 0.1 per cent (CIHI, 2016: 9). Prime Minister Harper himself was well aware of the slowdown in health expenditure increases when, in a 2015 campaign stop in New Brunswick, he criticized the province for failing to spend all the money that Ottawa had been transferring under the CHT on health care (*CBC News*, 2015).

Trudeau: From Multilateralism to Sequential Bilateralism

According to the Liberal Party's 2015 election platform, a Liberal government would strike a new health accord with the provinces that would "make home care more available, prescription drugs more affordable, and mental health care more accessible" (Liberal Party of Canada, 2015). It spoke to the issue of a long-term agreement on funding and promised to invest $3 billion over four years into "more and better home care." It also signalled an intention to help to improve access to prescription medications while stopping short of promising pharmacare. It further stated that collaborative leadership, the factor "missing during the Harper decade," would be the critical ingredient in bringing about the new accord.

Following the change in government in October 2015, negotiations between Jane Philpott, the new federal minister of Health, and her provincial counterparts proceeded on a positive note, with the provinces expecting Ottawa to abandon the previous government's decision to reduce the escalator down to 3 per cent of nominal GDP growth. At a certain point, however, it became apparent that the new Liberal government was taking a position much closer to the Harper one than what the provinces were requesting (5.2 per cent), offering 3.5 per cent plus additional funding for home and community care and for mental health and addiction services. Negotiations hit a low point when, in December 2016, the provinces rejected the federal government's offer of health-care funds and took a unified position that the money was not enough to address rising costs. The provinces intended to pressure the federal government into raising its offer.

The premiers' argument centred on the fact that health expenditures in Canada are rapidly increasing as the population ages, and provincial fiscal capacity has simply not kept up with the increasing costs. This is especially problematic because health-care costs are a huge chunk of provincial budgets, ranging from 35 to 45 per cent depending on the province or territory.[7] The Parliamentary Budget Officer has released reports indicating that provinces will need to either cut spending or raise taxes in the coming years to handle this increase in costs.

The Trudeau government was able to work around the impasse by signing individual deals with all the provinces and territories over a one-year period. It reached the bilateral agreements by being flexible on supplementary cost-shared funding for specific provinces (as an example, special funds to assist British Columbia in dealing with the opioid crisis), as well as agreeing to a general $5 billion fund over 10 years, separate from the CHT, to improve access to mental health and addiction services and to community and home-care services. The overall federal approach preserved the principle of asymmetrical federalism, as Quebec is still allowed to invest the health funds it receives according to its own priorities. This pleased Quebec Premier Philippe Couillard, who was also generally content with the final agreement, although he did not appreciate the "divide and rule" style of negotiating that the federal government had implemented. Couillard told reporters, "I regret that they had this approach of dividing the agreement into individual deals for each province and territory. They chose instead to take a province-by-province approach. Fine. We maintained and watched out for our interests, and each province did the same thing" (quoted in Galloway, 2017).

Summary

Social policy in the Canadian federation is a highly dynamic field, as the past decade has shown. Practically all social policy areas have been affected by political imperatives for governments to respond to key challenges—such as fiscal consolidation after the financial crisis of 2008–9, the aging population, increased urbanization, and changing family values and circumstances. Our social policy framework, with the programs and entitlements that Canadians receive through this framework, is highly intergovernmental, demonstrating many aspects of the federal system at work. We have titled this chapter the "social union" because it reflects the significance of evolving social policy and program arrangements to Canadian integration and unity, and the fact that so much social policy emerges from intergovernmental debate, negotiation, and agreement.

Indeed, one of the major historic debates about Canadian federalism since the 1960s has been about which government should take the lead on social policy, and about the constitutional values and rules to determine federal and provincial roles. This debate centred on Quebec's concerns about the federal spending power, but against a backdrop of the development in the 1960s and over the next few decades of very ambitious new national social programs—national in the sense of being joint enterprises of both federal and provincial/territorial governments. These include the three key cases discussed in this chapter: children, contributory pensions, and health care.

The most recent attempt by Canadian governments to settle their differences over social policy roles was the Social Union Framework Agreement of 1999. That agreement is still valid, but its impact has been limited. Neither order of government was quite ready to constrain its independence of movement, retaining a large degree of competitiveness to their ongoing interactions. Moreover, the Harper era of 2006–15 was marked by less federal intrusion than in the recent past on provincial and territorial social policy turf, reducing the need for SUFA application. As Tom McIntosh has noted, the nuts and bolts of social policy development must take place at the ground level, and the shape of the social union will depend much more on evolving Canadian public opinion about the role of social policy and the evolving fiscal policy framework than on a general intergovernmental agreement (McIntosh, 2002: 11).

The nuts and bolts of three key cases of social policy have been reviewed in this chapter. The checkered history of child benefits policy over the past 20 years presents some key lessons, not least of which is that ideological positions regarding the role of the state in social policy play a big role, particularly in the nature of federal leadership. It is also a field that illustrates how well differing federal and provincial programs can be coordinated, with each order of government concentrating on roles that they can do best. Both this field and the pensions area illustrate the continuing importance of networks of officials and technical experts who have useful and constant discussion. However, as the pensions case reveals, clear decision rules can also be a significant factor in overcoming major regional and governmental differences. Finally, health care illustrates many key characteristics of our federation at work. It shows how independent each order of government is to run their own programs and, in the federal government's case, to make virtually unilateral decisions about how much it can afford to contribute to rising health-care costs. At the same time, the health field illustrates well the effectiveness of informal executive federalism in sharing enormous amounts of information about reforming the complicated health-care delivery system. Governments learn from one another in the context of still very strong common Canadian expectations of their health-care systems. Thus, a part of this reality is that it is not Ottawa but public opinion across the federation that enforces the common principles of medicare.

Questions for Critical Thought

1. What are the arguments for and against common social programs across Canada?

2. Does it matter that the federal government should have a direct role in the provision of some social programs, and how best is that done?

3. In what ways does the health-care field represent a unique intergovernmental policy area that is distinct from other social policy fields?

4. Should the Social Union Framework Agreement be revived?

Notes

1. This position has not been universal and was often subject to negotiation. For example, Quebec generally embraced the federal proposals for medicare funding in 1970.

2. Richard Simeon (1990) makes the point that defenders of Meech argued that the new provision would, in fact, strengthen the federal spending power by constitutionally recognizing it and notes that many observers thought the critics' views were unfounded and overblown.

3. See https://www.canada.ca/en/employment-social-development/programs/early-learning-child-care/reports/2017-multilateral-framework.html.

4. Ontario had gone as far as actually putting in place the infrastructure for the ORPP, including the hiring of senior officials to run it, and had spent around $70 million up to the point when the revamped CPP agreement was announced in June 2016 and the nascent ORPP scrapped (Ferguson, 2016).

5. The difficulty in attaining agreement on resolving issues related to health care—not only in relation to funding but also on how to reform the system—has led a number of analysts to note that the system has remained virtually unchanged since universal health care was introduced nationally in 1966. For an excellent analysis of this "paradigm freeze," see Lazar et al. (2013).

6. Generic drugs are ones no longer under patent and are priced and regulated differently from those drugs still enjoying patent protection. While patented drugs are regulated by the Patented Medicines Prices Review Board, generics are not. Thus, patented drugs sold in Canada are only somewhat higher compared to a set of other countries, generics tend to be two to three times higher. See Lexchin (2015).

7. For comparisons on the basis of per capita expenditures across the provinces and territories, see CIHI (2014); for analysis of the proportion of budgeted expenditures, see Barua, Palacios, and Emes (2017).

References

Banting, K.G. 2012. "The Three Federalisms: Social Policy and Intergovernmental Decision-Making." *Canadian Federalism: Performance, Effectiveness, and Legitimacy*, 3rd edn, edited by H. Bakvis and G. Skogstad. Toronto: Oxford University Press.

Bakvis, H. 2017. "Federalism and Universal Healthcare: Policy Drift, Two-Level Games, and the Power of Narrative". Paper presented to ACSUS Biennial Conference, Las Vegas, NV, October.

Barua, B., M. Palacios, and J. Emes. 2017. *The Sustainability of Health Care Spending in Canada*. Vancouver: Fraser Institute.

Battle, K. 2015. *Child Benefits in Canada: Politics versus Policy*. Ottawa: Caledon Institute.

Biggs, M. 1996. *Building Blocks for Canada's New Social Union*. Ottawa: Canadian Policy Research Networks.

Boismenu, G., and P. Graefe. 2004. "The New Federal Tool Belt: Attempts to

Rebuild Social Policy Leadership."
Canadian Public Policy 30, no. 1: 71–89.

Boychuk, G.W. 1998. *Patchworks of Purpose: The Development of Provincial Social Assistance Regimes in Canada*. Montreal and Kingston: McGill-Queen's University Press.

——. 2004. *The Canadian Social Model: The Logics of Policy Development*. Ottawa: Canadian Policy Research Networks.

British Columbia. 2016. "B.C. Confirms Support for Canada Pension Plan Enhancement." Press release, 4 Oct.

Canadian Institute for Health Information (CIHI). 2014. *National Health Expenditure Trends, 1975 to 2014*. Ottawa: CIHI.

——. 2016. *National Health Expenditure Trends, 1975 to 2016*. Ottawa: CIHI.

CBC News. 2012. "McGuinty Wants Conditions on Health Transfers: Federal Government Should Set National Standards, Ontario Premier Says." 9 Jan. http://www.cbc.ca/news/canada/toronto/mcguinty-wants-conditions-on-health-transfers-1.1143022.

——. 2015. "Stephen Harper Defends Health Funding, Criticizes Province." 17 Aug. http://www.cbc.ca/news/canada/new-brunswick/stephen-harper-defends-health-funding-criticizes-province-1.3193704.

Commission on the Future of Health Care in Canada. 2002. *Building on Values: The Future of Health Care in Canada* (Romanow Report). Ottawa: Commission on the Future of Health Care in Canada.

Esping-Andersen, G. 1990. *The Three Worlds of Welfare Capitalism*. Princeton, NJ: Princeton University Press.

Fafard, P. 2013. "Intergovernmental Accountability and Health Care: Reflections on the Recent Canadian Experience." In *Overpromising and Underperforming: Understanding and Evaluating New Intergovernmental Accountability Regimes*, edited by P. Graefe et al. Toronto: University of Toronto Press.

Ferguson, R. 2016. "Ontario Spent $70 Million on Scrapped Pension Plan." *Toronto Star*, 28 July.

Finance Canada. 2016. *Budget 2016—Growing the Middle Class*. Ottawa: Department of Finance.

Friendly, M., and L. White. 2008. "From Multilateralism to Bilateralism to Unilateralism in Three Short Years: Child Care in Canadian Federalism." In *Canadian Federalism: Performance, Effectiveness, and Legitimacy*, 2nd edn, edited by H. Bakvis and G. Skogstad. Toronto: Oxford University Press.

——. 2012. "'No-lateralism': Paradoxes in Early Childhood Education and Care Policy in the Canadian Federation." In *Canadian Federalism: Performance, Effectiveness, and Legitimacy*, 3rd edn, edited by H. Bakvis and G. Skogstad. Toronto: Oxford University Press.

Galloway, G. 2017. "Health Accord Nearly Sealed as Ontario, Quebec, Alberta Reach Deals." *Globe and Mail*, 10 Mar.

Gibbins, R. 1999. "Taking Stock: Canadian Federalism and Its Constitutional Framework." In *How Ottawa Spends, 1999–2000*, edited by L. Pal. Toronto: Oxford University Press.

Globe and Mail. 2016. "Globe Editorial: On Health Funding, Ottawa Is Giving Provinces a Take-It or Take-It Offer." 20 Dec.

Health Canada. 2004. *10-Year Plan to Strengthen Health Care*. Ottawa: Health Canada.

Inwood, G., C. Johns, and P. O'Reilly. 2011. *Intergovernmental Policy Capacity in Canada: Inside the Worlds of Finance, Environment, Trade, and Health*. Montreal and Kingston: McGill-Queen's University Press.

Ipsos Public Affairs. 2016. *Report to Health-CareCAN and Canadian College of Health Leaders*. 6 June. http://www.nhlc-cnls.ca/assets/2016%20Ottawa/NHLCIpsosReportJune1.pdf.

Kennedy, M. 2012. "Premiers Divided over Harper's Approach to Medicare." *National Post*, 15 Jan.

Lazar, H. 2006. "The Intergovernmental Dimensions of the Social Union: A Sectoral Analysis." *Canadian Public Administration* 49, no. 1: 23–45.

——and F. St-Hillaire, eds. 2004. *Money, Politics, and Health Care: Reconstructing the Federal–Provincial Partnership*. Montreal and Kingston: McGill-Queen's University Press.

——, J.N. Lavis, P.-G. Forest, and J. Church. 2013. *Paradigm Freeze: Why It Is So Hard to Reform Health Care in Canada*. Montreal and Kingston: McGill-Queen's University Press.

Lee, Ian. 2016. "Canada Pension Plan Enhancement: Issues and Unexpected Outcomes." In *How Ottawa Spends, 2016–17*, edited by G.B. Doern and C. Stoney. Ottawa: Carleton University Press.

Lexchin, J. 2015. "Drug Pricing in Canada." In *Pharmaceutical Prices in the 21st Century*, edited by Z.-U.-D. Babar, 25–41. New York: Springer.

Liberal Party of Canada. 2015. "A New Health Accord." https://www.liberal.ca/realchange/a-new-health-accord/.

Little, B. 2008. *Fixing the Future: How Canada's Usually Fractious Governments Worked Together to Rescue the Canada Pension Plan.* Toronto: University of Toronto Press.

McGregor, J. 2016. "Canada Child Benefit Seen as Fighting Poverty—As Long As Provinces Co-operate." *CBC News*, 14 July. http://www.cbc.ca/news/politics/ccb-social-assistance-clawback-provinces-campaign-2000-1.3675873.

McIntosh, T. 2002. "As Time Goes By: Building on SUFA's Commitments." In *Building the Social Union: Perspectives, Directions and Challenges*, edited by T. McIntosh. Regina: Saskatchewan Institute of Public Policy.

Milligan, K., and T. Schirle. 2016. "The Pressing Question: Does CPP Expansion Help Low Earners?" Toronto: C.D. Howe Institute. Accessed 6 Dec. 2016. https://www.cdhowe.org/sites/default/files/attachments/research_papers/mixed/e-brief_241.pdf.

Moscovitch, A., R. Lochead, and N. Falvo 2016. "Ten Things to Know about the CPP Debate." *Behind the Numbers* (Canadian Centre for Policy Alternatives). Accessed 3 Nov. 2016. http://behindthenumbers.ca/2016/10/27/ten-things-know-cpp-debate/#comments.

Noël, A. 2001. "Without Quebec: Collaborative Federalism with a Footnote?" In *Building the Social Union: Perspectives, Directions and Challenges*, edited by T. McIntosh. Regina: Canadian Plains Research Centre.

Prince M.J. 2015. "Prime Minister as Moral Crusader: Stephen Harper's Punitive Turn in Social Policy Making." *Canadian Review of Social Policy* 71: 53–69.

Simeon, R. 2009 [1972]. *Federal–Provincial Diplomacy: The Making of Recent Policy in Canada.* Toronto: University of Toronto Press.

———. 1990. "Why Did the Meech Lake Accord Fail?" In *Canada: The State of the Federation, 1990*, edited by R.L. Watts and D.M. Brown. Kingston, ON: Institute of Intergovernmental Relations, Queen's University.

Simpson, J. 2012. *Chronic Condition: Why Canada's Health Care System Needs to be Dragged into the 21st Century.* Toronto: Penguin Canada.

Watts, R.L. 1999. *The Spending Power in Federal Systems: A Comparative Study.* Kingston, ON: Institute of Intergovernmental Relations, Queen's University.

Wherry, A. 2016. "How the Federal and Provincial Governments Made a Deal on CPP." *CBC News.* 21 June.

Chapter 8

The Economic Union and Economic Policy

week 10

Learning Objectives

- To understand the concept of economic union and its importance to the founding of Canada.
- To review how the federal and provincial governments contribute to macro-economic policy.
- To explore the tension between national and regional economic development.
- To assess the movement to freer internal and international trade.

Canada came into existence in 1867 as a federal community in good part to create a single new economy out of the old colonial economies, and these regional economies continue to coexist both with the national economy and with a continental and global economy. The definition of what constitutes a particular economic space—regional, national, global—matters a lot in terms of the rules that apply and who gets to set them (one only has to think of the controversy over Greece and the Eurozone). At the same time, economic interests differ greatly within the society, depending on class, occupation, gender, urban–rural locale, and province or region. And since Canada is a federation of regions with different economic conditions and interests, federal politics reflects those differences.

Governments rely on a variety of instruments to pursue economic policy in areas such as the money supply, taxation, spending, the regulation of trade (internal and international), contracts and property rights, labour standards, resources, transportation, energy, and communications. Policy outcomes reflect the nature of federal institutions, including the legal jurisdiction and fiscal powers of the two orders of government under the constitution and the way those powers have been exercised over time. Specific policies reflect both the governing instruments available and the way that jurisdiction is distributed across the different levels of government. For example, the federal government is restricted in its ability to regulate the securities industry because the provinces have primary jurisdiction in this area. Some areas of economic policy require the cooperation of federal and provincial governments, and economies can suffer if that cooperation is lacking.

Changes in economic conditions and economic thinking both have a major impact on the type of policies pursued. In the early years of Confederation, the Canadian economy was still developing: the vast lands of the Canadian West had barely begun to be opened up; resources were just beginning to be exploited systematically; and the track was still being laid for the transcontinental railway that would be completed in 1885. The policy requirements of a developing agricultural or resource economy differ considerably from those of a manufacturing or diverse urban economy. As well, policies can and do change in response to economic boom-and-bust conditions, changes in the nature and intensity of trade (who we trade with, and the importance of trade to the economy overall), and the terms of trade (e.g., are prices for commodities such as wheat or oil high or low?). Also, it matters where the attention of policy-makers is directed. Is it on macroeconomic indicators such as growth, inflation, unemployment, or productivity? Or is it on microeconomic factors such as comparative advantage of specific sectors (oil sands or automobiles), the training of the labour force, technological innovation, or the promotion of sustainable development and the reduction of pollution?

The interests of the society and the state tend to crystallize into broader ideological positions on economic policy. The largest and most deceptively simple issue in this ideological context is the role of government intervention in the economy. Should government actively intervene in the marketplace to pursue objectives such as equality of opportunity, full employment, acceptable living standards, or environmental quality? Or should government stay on the sidelines and intervene only to secure personal safety, protect property rights, and provide essential public goods and services? There have been enormous differences of view on this issue over the course of Canadian history. The dominant economic issue of the day might be inflation control, a made-in-Canada oil price, a trade war with the United States, reducing regional disparities, or expanding interprovincial pipelines. Regardless of the goal, if there is a jurisdictional division of authority over the subject matter and a regional difference of interest in the policy outcome, federal–provincial politics will play a part in determining how this goal will be pursued, or even whether it will be pursued at all. In the Canadian federation these differences play themselves out in intergovernmental arenas on a regular basis.

This chapter outlines four of the most important concerns of economic policy-making in the current federal system: maintenance of the economic union; management of the national economy as a whole; regional equity; and the challenges of remaining competitive in the face of globalization.

The Economic Union

One of the primary goals of Confederation in 1867 was to create a larger market than was available in the three colonies that first joined the union (the United Province of Canada, Nova Scotia, and New Brunswick) and to lay the groundwork for its expansion, with the addition of new provinces and territories, into a genuinely continental economy extending from the Atlantic to the Pacific. In this sense, economic union represents a form of economic and political integration: creating a whole out of a set of parts. New political institutions are created to establish economic space and to regulate the activity within that space (Trebilcock, 1987). Both before and after Confederation, Canada's economy was integrated within that of the British Empire. Yet since 1921 we have had more trade and investment with the United States than with Britain, and since the 1980s in particular our economy has become increasingly integrated with the American and global economies.

As a form of integration, full economic union is quite advanced (even more so than the common market of the European Union). It assumes the creation of a single new political community and it assumes political institutions that can shape the boundaries of economic activity. Some of the means used to this end are "negative," such as legal constraints against intervention in the marketplace; others are "positive," such as the pursuit of unified or harmonized regulation and the creation of joint public works or other public goods and services that help sustain the new, larger economy (Tinbergen, 1965; Scharpf, 1996). In the process, economic unions create significant benefits for the community:

1. *market integration*: the expanded economic space realizes economies of scale and specialization over time;
2. *increased bargaining power*: a larger economic unit exercises greater influence or market power in relation to external countries and markets;
3. *sharing of costs*: spreading costs over a larger population enhances the ability to undertake defence expenditures and large developmental projects and other public goods; and
4. *pooling and sharing of risks*: federation, in this sense, is an insurance scheme, particularly in the context of regional economic diversity (ECC, 1991: 31–3).

All federal constitutions provide for an economic union, with varying degrees of precision. Arguably the most powerful constitutional provisions are those that prohibit barriers to free trade within the union. In 1867 the former colonies turned over the right to impose tariffs to the newly created federal Parliament. According to section 121 of the Constitution Act [1867], "All articles of the Growth, Produce, or Manufacture of any one of the other provinces shall . . . be admitted free into each of the other Provinces"; in other words, no tariffs can be imposed on goods moving from one province to another. Historically, this provision has been narrowly interpreted as applying only to discriminatory taxes, and only on goods. But economic union is about more than the elimination of tariffs on goods; it is also about the free movement of services, labour, and capital. Over the years various provincial governments, and even the federal government, have found ways to hamper the free flow of all three of those items, justifying their restrictions on a variety of non-trade-related grounds. Although Canadians did acquire the explicit right to move and to take up a livelihood in any part of the country in 1982, under the Charter of Rights and Freedoms (section 6), the lack of a broader constitutional guarantee to domestic free trade has been of concern for some decades.

Certainly the 1867 Constitution Act granted the federal Parliament control over key factors affecting "positive integration," such as jurisdiction over trade and commerce (the courts later ruled that this power covered only international and interprovincial trade, not intraprovincial trade), the raising and borrowing of money, banking, bankruptcy, patents, and interprovincial works (what we would now call infrastructure) such as railways, canals, and telegraph installations. These jurisdictional powers ensured that the federal government controlled all the chief levers of economic power deemed necessary in the nineteenth century to build a national economy, even if they do not substitute entirely for a specific guarantee of domestic free trade (see also discussion in Chapter 4 regarding the recent Supreme Court judgement in *R. v. Comeau*). Meanwhile the provinces retained considerable legal jurisdiction of their own over other important economic matters, such as the ownership and management of Crown land and other natural resources, civil law (including contracts and labour law), and the sale of securities. They also had control of social services such as health, education, and welfare. In the nineteenth century, however, the latter were not the major areas of public expenditure they are today; rather, they were provided mainly by private organizations such as churches, and the provinces' responsibility amounted mainly to regulating those organizations.

In 1867 and for many years thereafter, creating the Canadian economic union called for a lot more than constitutional provisions: it also required bold and visionary action. The "fathers" of Confederation foresaw a transcontinental economy. Building that economy took some 50 years of western expansion and consolidation activity on the part of the new Dominion (federal) government, following an economic strategy that entailed the acquisition of the Hudson's Bay Company's lands, agricultural settlement and industrial growth facilitated by massive immigration, the construction of a transcontinental railway, and the imposition of high external tariffs for the protection of domestic manufacturers. This basic strategy was embodied in Prime Minister John A. Macdonald's "National Policy," announced in 1878, which remained more or less in place until the Second World War (Eden and Molot, 1993). Politically, western expansion of the agricultural and industrial economy in the nineteenth century had a major impact on the Indigenous peoples, and ushered in a radically different relationship with the settler population (see Chapter 11).

Thus the economic union created a new pattern of economic activity. The east–west economy came to be characterized by a distinctly regionalized division of labour, which in turn generated or perpetuated significant disparities in wealth and population densities (Mackintosh, 1939; Shearer, 1985). While all provinces participated in the country's staples-based export economy (fish, fur, timber, paper, grain, and minerals demanded by markets in the US and overseas), the long-term goal was to develop a more advanced manufacturing economy. The three Maritime provinces initially did well in the new national economy, benefiting from significant new industrialization. But as the centres of both population and economic life moved westward, manufacturing became concentrated in central Canada, especially southern Ontario and Quebec. Meanwhile the territories and provinces west of Ontario remained in essence an economic colony of the east, exploited by the railways and banks controlled in Montreal and Toronto, but receiving few of the benefits of the protected manufacturing economy.

By the 1930s a variety of regional and ideological protest movements had emerged in response to these economic developments, demanding a reorientation of federal economic policy and compensation for the effects of past policies.[1] The federal government responded with the series of important national policies put in place between 1945 and 1975, including national income security programs such as the old age security and unemployment insurance, fiscal equalization, and shared-cost social programs (see Chapters 6 and 7). Meanwhile, the provinces began to build their own economic development strategies around the ownership and management of natural resources and other regional advantages. Some of these provincial strategies reinforced the national economic design, but just as many sought to thwart it (Simeon and Robinson, 1990; Brown and Leslie, 1994).

By the 1970s the management and sustainability of the Canadian economic union was becoming an important political issue in its own right. As we noted above, economic policy depends on which economy is being considered—regional, national, or global. What is good for one is not always good for the other, and governments in Canada have often competed fiercely to control economic outcomes. The provinces eventually employed the legal, fiscal, and political power at their disposal to resist a movement towards national economic integration that they saw as contrary to their more local interests. In response to their calls for "regional equity," over the decades many policies and programs were put in place by federal and provincial governments to mitigate the free-market effects of the Canadian economic union. By the 1970s, however, the business community, economists, and other observers were expressing concern that, as a result of all these interventions, the fabric of economic union had too many holes and that its benefits could be lost, at a considerable cost to overall economic welfare.

This conflict received particular attention in the work of the Royal Commission on the Economic Union and Development Prospects for Canada (the Macdonald Commission; see Canada, 1985). The Commission found a long list of internal barriers to trade. These included the following:

- agricultural supply management policies restricting the quantities of poultry, eggs, and dairy products that could be shipped from one province to another;
- discriminatory government purchasing policies that favoured local manufacturers or suppliers of goods and services;
- barriers to free movement of labour in the form of occupational qualifications and provincial regulation of professions;
- regionally differentiated federal unemployment policy;
- regulated railway freight rates that discriminated across regions;
- differing provincial labour laws;
- many federal and provincial industrial and primary-sector subsidies that were considered to distort trade.

Tellingly, the Commission found that many of these barriers were as much the fault of the federal government as they were of the provinces (agricultural supply boards, for example, were jointly created).

All these policies had (and some continue to have) important economic and social rationales behind them. The issue is not the merits of such policies but rather their cumulative effect on the economic union. The cost of the barriers to the Canadian economy has been disputed, but the most reliable estimates in the 1980s put it at approximately 1 per cent of annual GDP—not a huge amount, but not an insignificant one either (Trebilcock et al., 1983). The most worrisome factor seemed to be the dynamic effect of increasing recourse to government intervention at cross purposes to the overall growth of the national economy, which gave rise to concern that trade within Canada would become no freer than trade among separate countries (an issue raised again much more recently in the context of the Canada–European Union (EU) Comprehensive Economic and Trade Agreement (CETA)). There were especially serious concerns in the period of freer international trade in the 1970s and 1980s coinciding with a growing movement for an independent Quebec. For the federal government, and increasingly for many of the provinces, tackling internal trade barriers became a strategic necessity with respect to both national unity and national competitiveness in the face of global economic integration.

Identifying the problem is one thing, however; finding a solution that does not upset the balance of power within the federation is another. In the episodic constitutional negotiations from the 1960s to 1992, new rules to strengthen the Canadian economic union were prominent on the agenda. Yet, except for the movement-of-labour provision in section 6 of the Charter of Rights, none of the constitutional rules proposed met with success, largely because the provinces feared they would either increase Ottawa's power over the economy or restrict their ability to intervene in their own economies as they saw fit. It would take the dominance of free trade politics and the pressure of international negotiations (discussed later in this chapter) to make significant headway towards reform.

Macroeconomic Management

Macroeconomic policy concerns the economy as a whole: usually the national economy but sometimes the regional. Its objectives are large-scale: ensuring overall growth and stability with respect to booms and busts, controlling the rate of inflation, and promoting employment. By contrast, microeconomic policy focuses on specific sectors and industries, companies, and households.

Particularly since the Second World War, it has generally been thought that governments have a basic responsibility to stabilize the economy, that is, to even out the booms and busts of the business cycle. Thus, stabilization policy is important, even if the prevailing ideology favours market-driven solutions to problems. The main instruments are fiscal and monetary policies. Fiscal policy involves government expenditure and taxation; monetary policy involves interest rates and the money supply. In the post-war period, fiscal policy was associated with what is known as Keynesianism—using government expenditures as a way of countering the effects of a slowing economy and, conversely, raising taxes, or cutting spending, when the economy shows signs of overheating. Developed by the British economist John Maynard Keynes, Keynesianism was particularly popular during the critical rebuilding phase after 1945, when citizens and policy-makers were anxious to avoid any repetition of the Great Depression. Keynesianism is also associated with the creation of the welfare state: it assumes both a capacity and an appetite for major government intervention in the economic lives of citizens.

For the nearly three decades during which Keynesian thinking held sway, macroeconomic policy gave rise to considerable tension in the federal system. In essence, the federal government—especially the economists in the Department of Finance—became convinced of the need for centrally controlled macroeconomic management along Keynesian lines. This required well-coordinated fiscal and monetary policy but the relative independence of the Bank of Canada, and the fact that fiscal policy (taxation and spending) was shared with the provinces made coordination difficult to achieve. During the war, Ottawa had effectively centralized fiscal control through tax rental agreements with the provinces, but after 1945 it had to gradually relinquish some of that control in the face of politically powerful provincial demands. Still, the perceived need for the strong central control required by Keynesian management strengthened Ottawa's hand.

The relative importance of Keynesian ideas, their effectiveness, and the extent to which Canada actually put them into practice are all open to debate (Campbell, 1987). What can be summarized here is that in the 1970s—an era of rising energy prices and stagflation (inflation combined with low economic growth)—the influence of Keynesianism began to wane and other economic philosophies gained ascendance, particularly those of Milton Friedman and what is variously known as neo-conservatism or supply-side economics. These ideas had significant influence on policy after the election of Margaret Thatcher in the UK in 1979 and Ronald Reagan in the US in 1980. The key component in supply-side economics is monetary policy. Thus a neo-conservative government will respond to a rise in inflation by raising interest rates and/or tightening the money supply, and when economic stimulation is needed it will cut both government expenditures and taxes. The effectiveness of supply-side economics has also been extensively debated. Nevertheless, these ideas took hold in many countries, including Canada, in the 1980s. Thus, Canadian economic policy in the late 1980s and early 1990s relied heavily on high interest rates to tame inflation. Indeed, in the late 1980s, the Bank of Canada pursued what amounted to a "zero inflation" target.

Under section 91 of the Constitution Act, 1867, jurisdiction over money and banking lies with the federal government, which means that Ottawa has effective control over monetary policy. The situation is different with fiscal policy, however, as we have seen in Chapter 6. Both orders of government have the right to impose most types of taxes and they exercise that right extensively. Therefore, both use tax policy to stabilize the economy, although Ottawa's scope in this regard is broader. This is not necessarily the case on the expenditure side. Some of the largest areas of government expenditure are health care, education, social welfare, and infrastructure, all of which are primarily if not entirely under provincial jurisdiction. Consequently, both levels of government have at least some capacity to make macroeconomic policy, although the federal government has the more powerful toolkit.

The issue of which government controls the levers of macroeconomic management is further complicated by the difficulty of developing a single national policy that deals effectively with the needs of all the regions in Canada. One can legitimately ask: is it really possible to have a single, effective macroeconomic policy? With different sectoral strengths, terms of trade, and levels of development across the regions, growth cycles and inflation pressures differ. It is virtually impossible that a *single* monetary policy, for example, with a single national set of inflation targets, a single exchange rate, and a single interest rate, will ever match the optimal requirements for any specific region. Suppose, for instance, that inflation builds up in a high-growth area such as southern Ontario or Alberta, while prices remain flat in low-growth regions: higher interest rates would curb inflation in the hot regions, but would further chill activity in the regions where growth is already low. In another case, as we experienced in the decade of 2004–14, commodity prices for oil were high and production and exports of oil were increasing, mainly from western Canada. This contributed to a "petro dollar" effect driving up the exchange value of the Canadian dollar, in turn making manufacturing exports less competitive (and leading to job losses in those sectors).[2] The job losses in factories occurred mainly in Ontario. Today, international financial markets primarily are pricing the Canadian dollar, and using federal monetary policy to correct the market trend might have unintended consequences or may even be unsuccessful. Using fiscal policy gives the federal government somewhat more leeway for regional flexibility, especially on the spending side, but this can still work against the macroeconomic objectives of one or more regions. For instance, if the federal government cuts its spending to curb inflationary growth, in the process it could dampen sustainable growth in a province or region attempting to catch up.

There is also considerable room for provincial macroeconomic policies to work at cross purposes with those of the federal government. This is precisely what happened in Ontario between 1985 and 1995, when the province's Liberal and NDP governments were increasing their spending in direct contradiction of the federal effort to bring inflation under control. The federal minister of Finance and the governor of the Bank of Canada complained vehemently that Ontario was undermining the effectiveness of their policies. On the provincial side, it naturally helps to be a bigger province with large fiscal resources. A small, poorer province would not have the capacity to launch a counter-cyclical strategy, and the national impact of such activity would be negligible in any event. This notwithstanding, Ottawa's reluctance to turn over additional tax room to the provinces—for financing health care, for example—can be explained at least in part by concern that some provinces might use the tax room for counter-cyclical objectives inconsistent with the objectives that Ottawa has deemed appropriate for the country as a whole.

In brief, federal and provincial governments have clear incentives to work cooperatively, through the mechanisms of executive federalism, when it comes to stabilization and other macroeconomic policies. Ways of bringing the provinces into the deliberations of the Bank of Canada and the federal Department of Finance, and improving coordination over fiscal policy in particular, have been discussed for years. The Continuing Committee of Officials on Fiscal and Economic Matters, which provides for the flow of information between the two orders of government, remains the only body that has attained any kind of quasi-formal standing, and its powers are decidedly limited.

Suggestions that the provinces could play a role in nominating or even appointing members to the Board of Governors of the Bank of Canada have not been followed up.[3] However, the federal government has put in place a more extensive pre-budget consultation process, and the Bank of Canada also consults more widely with the business and other communities, including provincial ministers of Finance, than it did in the past. Ottawa's moves in the direction of greater transparency and wider consultation may not have been intended specifically to increase provincial participation, but they have reduced the pressure to institute more formal federal–provincial mechanisms.

A decade ago the macroeconomic policy area was comparatively calm, largely because economic growth had been strong and relatively balanced across the regions over the previous decade. Unemployment was at a 30-year low and consumer confidence was high (Cross, 2007). The Conservative government had inherited a substantial surplus from its Liberal predecessor, some of which it used to reduce the fiscal gap with the provinces. There were no signs that the Harper government was inclined to adopt a Keynesian-style macro policy or to centralize fiscal policy; but neither was it much inclined to share its governance of monetary policy. Nor were any of the provinces inclined to run deficits to prime their own economies. By mid-2009, however, the worldwide turmoil in financial markets and the global recession forced all governments—federal and provincial—to run deficits, regardless of the ideological position of the party in power or of election promises to balance the budget. Certainly the federal government's inherited surplus had disappeared by late 2008 and would not return until 2015.

An illustration of the regional tensions that have arisen was concern over inflationary pressures fuelled by an overheating resource economy in western Canada and by international oil and food prices, which in turn put upward pressure on interest rates in 2007–8. There was concern as well that provincial governments such as Alberta's were spending too much or encouraging too much investment in the energy sector and not saving their energy revenue windfall. Meanwhile, buoyant resource prices had pushed up the Canadian dollar, creating problems for Canadian exporters. The global economic downturn after 2008 certainly helped to ease inflationary pressures, but the Canadian dollar remained very strong relative to the US dollar, overvalued some would say, because of excessive resource production and exports. In late 2014 the international terms of trade for oil shifted dramatically as the global price fell within weeks by as much as 45 per cent. While this development seems unlikely to reverse entirely Canada's substantial oil and gas production, by mid-2015 the decline in prices was sufficient to result in thousands of lost jobs and major reductions in federal and provincial revenue and to nudge the overall Canadian economy into recession (TD Economics, 2015). The effect of the rapid change illustrates both the importance of the energy sector to Canada and its vulnerability to global market trends, to which governments must respond quickly with changes to their own macroeconomic policies. Also, as discussed in the next chapter on the environment, regional economic tensions between resource-producing provinces and mainly manufacturing provinces contribute to, and are complicated by, differences in environmental policy interests.

In conclusion, when one takes the longer view about managing potential conflict in the federation over macroeconomic policy, one would have to conclude—especially based on how the federation dealt with the global financial crisis—that Canadian governments are learning to avoid the more severe conflict of the past. In any case, the provinces do leave most macroeconomic decisions to the federal government. Where provincial attention is more likely to focus is on regional growth and development—that is, microeconomic concerns.

National versus Regional Economic Development

Canada's economy has always been the product of both natural and human-made forces (Stevenson, 2012). As a political community Canadians have been engaged in economic development activities from the beginning. Even in the current era of relatively free markets and laissez-faire industrial policy, no government in Canada—or anywhere else—can afford to leave economic prosperity entirely to chance or the vagaries of the market. Structural or microeconomic policy is all about shaping the economy in ways that respond to the specific market conditions and needs of individual industries and sectors. To this end governments use various instruments such as regulation, information, taxation, spending, and government ownership to encourage certain kinds of economic activity at the micro level. The fact that the levers of micro policy are shared among the various governments, federal and provincial, means that there is considerable potential for competition both among provinces and between the provinces and the federal government. There has been a long history of both conflict and cooperation in this area.

As we noted in our discussion of the economic union, in the nineteenth century a national economy would not have succeeded without a strategic approach on the part of the new Dominion government. Yet the very efficiency of this new economy—combined, some claim, with a bias in favour of central Canada as the location for more advanced economic activity—ultimately created pressures not only for redistributive justice, which took the form of fiscal transfers such as equalization and Canada-wide social programs, but also for allocative justice. In other words, governments came to recognize that they needed to pay attention to the actual allocation of economic activities across the country.

There are essentially two perspectives on the best way to design an economic allocation policy. One perspective, taken mainly by those in the federal government, the national media, major business and labour organizations, and central provinces such as Ontario, has been to ensure that structural policy is optimal at a national level and then to see what needs to be done for those regions that lag behind. The other perspective, taken by all the provinces and territories with the occasional exception of Ontario, as well as many regionally based industrial and labour interests, is to focus from the outset on the optimal structural policy for a particular provincial or regional economy and assume that the national economy will be strong so long as all the regional economies are strong. Both perspectives can lead to viable economic strategies. However, the region-centred strategy depends more on federal cooperation and provincial economic levers than does the national one. Historically, the nation-centred strategy generated major regional tensions.

Within these two approaches to economic allocation policy, the ideological emphasis on markets versus government intervention has varied over time. Just as macroeconomic policy between 1940 and 1975 was dominated by interventionist thinking along Keynesian lines, so, too, was microeconomic policy. It was considered the state's role to take strategic control over the structure of the economy, favouring one sector over the other and promoting technological sovereignty. Canada's attempts to pursue such a strategy, however, have been affected both by federalism and by our North American setting. In North America, governments have been much less willing than in Europe and Japan (not to mention countries with centrally planned economies, such as the former Soviet Union) to accept centrally directed bureaucratic decision-making about industrial structure. Indeed, the Americans in particular promoted a strong alternative in the form of international liberalism combined with considerable domestic laissez-faire (Dyson, 1980; Hall and Soskice, 2001). This strategy has had adherents in Canada as well. In the brief sketch that follows we outline the interaction of national and regional perspectives in an era when interventionist industrial strategies were assumed to be most effective, that is, up to the mid-1980s. In the following section we deal with the effects of the free trade era on these competing strategies.

Examples of federal programs designed primarily to promote a national economy are not hard to find. They encompass essentially all of federal trade policy in the century between the 1870s and 1970s, military procurement programs during and after the two world wars, public development and ownership of railways and airlines, railway freight rate structures that promoted internal trade in finished goods from central Canada to the West and East, and oil and gas pipeline construction and regulation. Examples of provincial programs designed to promote the regional economy are also legion. They include the development of hydroelectric and other sources for electricity supply, first by Ontario and later by all provinces, including Quebec (where the public takeover of private hydro firms in the 1960s was one of the central events of the Quiet Revolution). All provincial and territorial governments have used their jurisdiction over natural resources, primarily energy, forests, and minerals, to promote specific industries, and many have used Crown corporations to develop the telephone and telecommunications industries.

Somewhat rarer are examples of federal policies that had the effect of promoting the development of only one region or the other, such as the partnership between the federal Atomic Energy Corporation and Ontario Hydro for nuclear power; the 1965 Auto Pact agreement with the US that did so much for the Ontario automobile sector; and various projects to promote the development of petroleum resources off the Atlantic coast. More common are federal subsidy or tax expenditures that are available for economic opportunities in all provinces, but that in practice serve to reinforce existing regional strengths such as the pharmaceutical and aerospace sectors in Quebec, the development of non-conventional oil resources in the West (such as the oil sands), the informatics and computer industry in Ontario, and—in the case of employment insurance—the fisheries sector on the east coast.

The potential for conflict between the various national and regional strategies has been significant. As we outlined in Chapter 1, a certain amount of competition is perceived to be one of the advantages of federalism. And, of course, economic theory points out the value of competition within markets for goods, services, labour—even ideas. Competing provinces can learn from one another about what works best in terms of economic policy. Competition for investment and markets among private-sector actors in regional economies makes the latter more productive. And competition between governments (for votes, one presumes) to attract investment can result in better economic policies all around. Such competition is often benign. But if public spending or tax breaks are designed merely to attract industry away from another jurisdiction without actually increasing net economic activity, this beggar-thy-neighbour or negative-sum approach can be destructive (Brown, 2002).

More fundamentally, sharply competing economic strategies can generate significant political conflict. The energy conflicts of the 1970s and 1980s are a case in point. As David Milne wrote in his 1986 book *Tug of War*, not only did Canada face "incredible gyrations in supply and pricing in the world oil and gas market," but these dynamics "ricocheted back onto the federal structure itself" in a volatile mix of East-versus-West regional politics, centralist versus provincialist constitutional visions, and free-market versus interventionist economic policy (Milne, 1986: ch. 3). In a period of rising international petroleum prices, the oil-producing provinces, especially Alberta, looked to foreign capital to diversify and develop their economies, while the Trudeau government in Ottawa looked to its National Energy Program to restore federal control over a strategic sector, promoting a made-in-Canada oil price and increased Canadian ownership. Seldom have the two perspectives on allocation of economic activity clashed so dramatically.

The current issues over the expansion of interprovincial pipelines in Canada are a contemporary illustration of the continuing tension between national and regional strategies for economic development. They are also about which government gets the upper hand with respect to determining the balance between economic development and environmental issues (for more on the link with environmental issues, see Chapter 9). There have been several proposals in recent years to build new or expanded pipelines, mainly to transport bitumen and related oil sands products from Alberta to markets in North America or overseas. They include the XL Pipeline expansion in the US (which originates in Alberta), the proposed Energy East Pipeline that would have carried product to the Atlantic coast, and two proposals to transmit bitumen from Alberta to the Pacific—the Northern Gateway Project and the expansion of the existing Trans Mountain Pipeline.

These pipelines would clearly be in the economic interests of land-locked petroleum producers, mainly in Alberta and Saskatchewan, but they also have economic benefits for port development, refineries, and pipeline suppliers in other provinces. The competing local or regional interest revolves around environmental impacts and risks and the use of both traditional and municipal lands, thus involving Indigenous governments and treaty groups, municipalities, and the non-producing provinces (Hoberg, 2016). These governments rely on constitutional powers over land management as well as environmental assessment and regulation, although the latter are shared with the federal government. In the case of the Indigenous peoples, specific treaty rights often are involved, as is the right to consultation on developments on traditional lands.

The national interest in pipelines is more complicated than it is for individual regional players such as provincial governments. It includes the overall national economic benefit (which in the case of the expanding oil sands production is substantial), the overall national energy market, and the regulation of interprovincial "works" or infrastructure, as well as considerations of potential transboundary pollutants and, as discussed in Chapter 9, the linkage to national policy on climate change. It is a matter of balancing competing regional interests, economic and environmental issues, and ideological and partisan considerations. The federal government can back its policy decisions with constitutional jurisdiction over trade and commerce, the regulation of interprovincial works, the national interest in the environment, and its fiduciary obligations with respect to Indigenous peoples.

As of late 2018 these contemporary pipeline issues have proven to be difficult intergovernmental and political challenges, with the final outcomes still to come. The Trudeau federal government did reject two major pipeline proposals in early 2017, the Energy East and Northern Gateway projects. The XL Pipeline expansion in the United States is now proceeding, leaving the Trans Mountain Pipeline, proposed by Kinder Morgan, a US-based company, to bear the brunt of controversy and conflict. The British Columbia minority government under the NDP since June 2017 has opposed the project, as have a number of Indigenous groups and municipalities. The Trudeau government has vowed to proceed with the pipeline, with the strong support of Alberta. The federal government's resolve became especially clear in May 2018 when it agreed to purchase the pipeline from Kinder Morgan, thus assuming the risk of continued on-the-ground opposition in British Columbia.

How this conflict will work out remains to be seen, but resolution will likely involve several elements including electoral politics, legal dispute and judicial review, intergovernmental negotiation, and regulatory process. It is not only a federalism issue, of course, but the federalism aspects play a prominent role.

Finally, a more generic form of structural policy area characterized by strong federal–provincial interaction is regional economic development policy: in effect, a set of interventions intended to improve economic conditions in specific areas perceived to be lagging behind other regions. The issue of regional disparities came to the fore in the late 1950s and became a major issue in the 1960s and 1970s. Prime Minister Trudeau recognized the issue as a threat to national unity when he was elected in 1968, and his government established the Department of Regional Economic Expansion (DREE) a year later. More than a decade later, in 1982, the Trudeau government and the provinces agreed to enshrine in the constitution a commitment to the promotion of equal opportunities and the furthering of economic development to reduce disparities in opportunities for all Canadians.[4]

This policy field has been controversial and problematic, however. There is little consensus among policy analysts about what really works or what mix of government policies and programs will genuinely reduce regional disparities and foster economic development. Another concern is the lack of consistency in federal and provincial efforts that results when politicians and bureaucrats become too impatient and insist on changing the programs and agencies delivering regional development before they have a chance to work. Perhaps regional development policy-makers sought to accomplish too much. As the leading student of the field, Donald Savoie, put it, "In trying to be all things to all regions, Canadian regional development has . . . lost its way" (Savoie, 1992: 386). A more cynical view is that regional development policy is whatever a government deems it to be—which means that it can serve a variety of purposes, some of them only tenuously linked to economic development.

One must acknowledge that issues of regional disparity and development funding are not as high on the political agenda as they once were. Part of the reason for the decline of regional development as a federal spending priority has been the uncertainty surrounding its effectiveness, combined with the more neo-conservative, less interventionist approach to economic policy. When governments at all levels have scarcer fiscal resources to apply to the many demands for programs, regional development is not high enough on the list, at least not to merit the levels of spending common in the 1980s. On a more positive note, regional disparities have been shrinking. As measured by GDP per capita, family income per capita, or the unemployment rate, the gap between regions and provinces has been closing (Capeluck, 2014).

For the student of federalism and intergovernmental relations, regional (and local) economic development remains an important field to illustrate the wide varieties of ways in which governments relate to one another. The history of this policy field has seen both intense cooperation and intense competition, large national programs and big dedicated federal bureaucracies, as well as more targeted bilateral arrangements. The funds spent on regional development have sometimes had little or no strings attached, but on other occasions such funding has been the means for Ottawa to intrude extensively and politically in provincial and local matters.[5]

Globalization, Free Trade, and Competitiveness

In Canada, the globalization of business activities accelerated after the recession of 1980–1. Thereafter we see greatly increased international trade and foreign direct investment, the development of a worldwide chain of goods and services providers, and the rise of global capital markets—all facilitated by advances in technology such as personal computers, the Internet, and wireless communications. Economic globalization both fuelled and was fuelled by international liberalization, initially through the auspices of the General Agreement on Tariffs and Trade (GATT), established in 1947, then in Canada's case with the Canada–US Free Trade Agreement (FTA) of 1989 and the North American Free Trade Agreement (NAFTA) of 1994. When the relatively informal GATT transformed into the more institutionalized World Trade Organization (WTO) through the Marrakesh Agreement of 1994, it appeared that economic globalization was here to stay. More recently, the Harper government pursued successfully a number of new bilateral agreements (e.g., Korea, India), signed a major new deal (CETA) with the European Union, and engaged in negotiations with many Asia-Pacific trading partners in the Trans-Pacific Partnership (TPP). The Justin Trudeau Liberal government has essentially maintained this pro-free trade policy, although in more difficult circumstances given the turn in the United States away from some aspects of globalization and trade liberalization with the election of Donald Trump as president. In October 2018, the United States, Mexico and Canada Agreement (USMCA) was concluded, although it had yet to be ratified. The new agreement is intended to replace NAFTA with terms that are more protective of American labour and industry. The initial assessment for Canada was that the USMCA preserves most of the key provisions in NAFTA and thus retains access to the US market, but at some cost to certain sectors in Canada such as dairy producers. In any case, and in the long-term view, the original move towards bilateral free trade with the US was a particularly bold and controversial step that changed fundamentally the context for economic policy-making in Canada.

The decision by the Mulroney government to enter into free trade negotiations with the US marked the end of the road for the old National Policy, with its emphasis on a protected Canadian market and the East–West economic union. In this respect, Quebec's shift in the early 1980s from promoting Canadian protection to embracing freer trade was pivotal. Quebec, at the time under the leadership of Liberal Premier Robert Bourassa, was hoping to develop stronger international trade linkages and at the same time become less dependent on domestic trade. Quebec was joined by Alberta, Saskatchewan, British Columbia,

New Brunswick, and Newfoundland in strong support for liberalization. Ontario and PEI were mainly opposed, while Manitoba and Nova Scotia remained ambivalent (Brown, 1991). Nonetheless, all the provinces, including those on balance opposed to the FTA, had come to the conclusion that the interventionist economic strategies of the Trudeau government, such as the National Energy Program (NEP) and the Foreign Investment Review Agency (FIRA), were not working (Brown, 1993).

In fact, the federal government actively sought the support of the provinces for the bilateral negotiations with the United States. Canada's trade negotiators wanted a comprehensive agreement (a "big deal") and recognized that many of the trade measures on the table were under provincial jurisdiction. Politically, Mulroney was committed to collaborative federalism and believed the controversial policy required broad regional support. This virtually ensured that, even if the provinces would not have a place at the actual bargaining table with US and Canadian negotiators, at least they would be consulted extensively. Mulroney met with the premiers 14 times during the 18-month negotiation period, and provincial ministers and senior officials met with the federal negotiating team once a month or more. The provinces did not have the opportunity to ratify the agreement as such, but the fact that eight of them ultimately supported the FTA gave the federal government considerable political cover.

In constitutional terms, the FTA (and later, the NAFTA and the WTO agreements) had the potential to upset the federal–provincial balance and spark a major court test of the distribution of powers. Some argued that Parliament should be able to implement any trade agreement in its entirety, using a broad interpretation of the "trade and commerce" power in the Constitution Act, 1867 to impose it on the provinces. Others argued that the courts would rule, as they had in 1937 in the *Labour Conventions* case,[6] that the watertight compartments argument still held and that Parliament could not legally enforce the terms of a trade agreement in matters under provincial jurisdiction (Richards, 1991; Whyte, 1990). In the end the actual FTA did not impinge on provincial jurisdiction to the extent that some had feared, because so many of the provisions were prospective (that is, covering only new policy in the future). Still, the full extent of the effect of the FTA, and subsequently of NAFTA and the WTO, remained a subject of controversy for several years (Brown, 2002; Robinson, 2003). Federal legislation implementing the FTA and NAFTA passed without a constitutional challenge, perhaps because it required so few actual changes in provincial measures. It is also likely that provinces such as Ontario preferred not to challenge federal authority in the courts and risk losing a major jurisdictional battle.

Analysts will continue to disagree on the legal consequences of trade liberalization and whether its "neutering" effect is greatest for the federal or the provincial order of government. After all, a free trade agreement like the FTA or NAFTA is, in effect, a form of economic constitution that prohibits the signatory governments from intervening in their economies in a wide swath of policy areas; in other words, such agreements achieve the "negative integration" mentioned earlier in this chapter. Yet political debate did not dwell on this matter, but rather on the general effects of trade liberalization as part of the neo-conservative approach to fiscal and social policy.

In the meantime, free trade became Canada's industrial strategy. Together, the FTA and NAFTA have made it very difficult to impose discriminatory or differential pricing on resources, including oil and gas. They have partly liberalized government procurement markets, some agriculture markets, and some services. In addition, they prohibit direct export subsidies and allow our trading partners to penalize us if we provide subsidies specific to a single industry. However, the WTO does permit generally available government assistance to industry, such as for research and development and for firms in underdeveloped regions.

Some of the same issues involving regional differences over trade policy and provincial jurisdictional concerns arose in the long CETA negotiations from 2008 to 2014, covering an even larger economic space than does NAFTA. All provincial economies are likely to gain from access to the rich and diverse European market. However, provinces were concerned with EU demands for, among other things, access to agricultural markets (especially if it means some dismantling of agricultural marketing regulations in Canada), provincial and municipal procurement, financial services, as well as tougher drug patent regulation (with its potential for increased health-care costs).[7]

Free trade has also affected Canada's internal trade. As noted already, concerns about the fragmentation of the Canadian economic union mounted during the 1970s and early 1980s—concerns that became more urgent with the intensification of integration and liberalization. Since so many aspects of the Canadian economy were being integrated into the continental and global markets, especially its goods-producing sectors, the institutional integration of the FTA and NAFTA set the rules for our national market as well. Neither the federal nor the provincial governments could prevent their new trading partners from identifying policies that were already considered barriers to trade within Canada as barriers to international trade as well. Thus we came to the ironic fact that much of the heavy lifting required to reform the Canadian domestic economic union was achieved not through constitutional amendment or intergovernmental agreement, but through international trade treaties (see Table 8.1).

The process offered a fascinating example of a two-level game in the domestic politics of trade liberalization (cf. Putnam, 1988). Working through international agreements made it easier for the Canadian provinces to agree on the removal of barriers because regional rivalries could be subsumed in a larger pool of potential gains and concessions. The freer the trade became across international borders, the freer it would become within Canada. After all, in political terms it seemed unsustainable that trade could be freer for Ontario with

Table 8.1 International Agreements and Reform of the Canadian Economic Union, 1989–95: Selected Outcomes/Measures Affecting Internal Trade in Canada

Instrument	Selected Measures
FTA (1989)	Freer trade in wine and spirits Non-discrimination in trade by monopolies No performance requirements on investors National treatment for service regulation
NAFTA (1994)	Non-discriminatory government procurement Freer trade in financial services More liberalization of investment Side deals on labour standards, environment
WTO (1995)	"Tariffication" (use of tariffs) in place of agricultural quotas Agreement on subsidies
Agreement on Internal Trade (1995)	Non-discriminatory government procurement Free trade in alcoholic beverages, including beer Non-discriminatory monopoly practices Code of Conduct on Incentives used by federal and provincial governments Access to common carriers (e.g., telecoms) Voluntary mutual recognition of occupational standards

Michigan than with Manitoba. Similar concerns were raised by the Canadian business community in late 2013 when it appeared that the nearly completed CETA would provide provincial trade concessions to member states of the EU that would not be available to other Canadian provinces (McKenna, 2013). However, even with its barriers, the Canadian economic union continues to be much wider and deeper than the North American free trade area, particularly with respect to labour and services. But this had not stopped most Canadian businesses from promoting further opening of markets within Canada as a way of improving their international competitiveness.

Thus the Canadian governments negotiated their own domestic free trade agreement, called the Agreement on Internal Trade (AIT), in 1995 (since replaced by the Canadian Free Trade Agreement, or CFTA, in 2017). The scope and time frame of the AIT were heavily influenced by the international agreements (Doern and MacDonald, 1999). Its 18 chapters were remarkably similar to the 20-odd chapters of the FTA and NAFTA, and many of the general principles and even the jargon and logic of the detailed provisions—and their loopholes—were borrowed from the GATT, the two regional agreements, and the draft WTO agreement. The result was a unique hybrid between an international trade agreement and a domestic intergovernmental agreement.

The AIT had major limitations as a tool for the resolution of intergovernmental disputes, however. It was not constitutionally entrenched, and there were no legal remedies if it was breached. It had a weak administrative structure, and the federal and provincial ministers who form its governing body operated by consensus only. For good or ill, the AIT relied heavily on negative integration, i.e., reducing barriers by imposing new rules applicable to all governments rather than by centralized regulatory power to extend the scope of national integration (Brown, 2002). The limitations of the AIT continue in the CFTA (see below). And to some extent, just as in international trade policy, trade liberalization works best when there is continuous negotiation to remove new barriers to trade and to expand the scope and depth of integration. Over 20 years the parties to the AIT made some progress towards improving the overall rules for internal trade, although many observers found the pace of change too slow (Knox, 1998, 2001; MacDonald, 2002). More progress was made in this period at the regional level; examples of regional commitments include economic integration initiatives in the Atlantic provinces since the early 1990s, the Ontario–Quebec Labour Mobility Agreement of 2006, and the extensive Trade, Investment and Labour Mobility Agreement (TILMA) reached in 2006 between Alberta and British Columbia, later extended to include Saskatchewan under the title of the New West Partnership Trade Agreement.[8]

Finally, the Harper federal government, first elected in January 2006, made strengthening the Canadian economic union a policy priority. The Speech from the Throne of October 2007 referred to "the federal government's rightful leadership" in this context, and Ottawa made it clear to the provinces that it intended to exercise that leadership as a sort of quid pro quo for taking a more decentralized approach to fiscal relations (dealing with the vertical fiscal imbalance) and to social programs (restricting the use of federal spending power) (MacDonald, 2007; Kent, 2007).

The Harper government's specific priorities for reform of the economic union fell into three categories. First was a commitment to work with the provinces on a variety of improvements and extensions to the AIT, including an endorsement and encouragement of the bilateral approach building on the Alberta–BC TILMA. Second was a commitment to extend tax collection and general tax harmonization agreements; an agreement reached with Ontario on corporate income tax in 2006 was a promising first step in this direction. Third was the initiative led by Finance Minister Jim Flaherty to achieve greater integration of regulation of the Canadian securities market; in the spring of 2008 new federal legislation was proposed to create a single new federal regulator.

Progress on these fronts was decidedly mixed, reflecting the fact that internal trade remains a specialized and essentially technical issue on which few politicians place much priority. On improvements to the AIT, the big achievement is an entire new agreement to supersede the AIT. Negotiations began in late 2014 and were completed in the spring of 2017. On 1 July 2017 the Canadian Free Trade

Agreement came into effect, replacing the AIT (Canada, 2017). The new agreement makes some very significant improvements over the AIT:

- more comprehensive coverage of the entire economy, especially services, with no sectors left out;
- a formal, binding process for identifying and eliminating remaining interprovincial barriers to trade (although individual parties can still opt out of proposed liberalization of specific measures);
- improved access to the provincial and territorial government procurement markets, driven by the need to be even more liberal than the provisions in the Canada–European Union Trade Agreement, which also came into provisional force on 1 July 2017.
- an improved dispute resolution system.

The CFTA is an important milestone, even if, like international trade agreements, it continues to build around exemptions and special cases. Some critics would prefer that Parliament had the power to impose economic union rules on the provinces, just as the US Congress can invoke the commerce power of the US Constitution, but of course that type of reform has not been seriously considered since the early 1980s (compare media comments: McGregor, 2017; Coyne, 2017).

On tax harmonization, as noted in Chapter 6, GST and PST harmonization was achieved in Ontario but rejected in British Columbia. Finally, on securities regulation, federal plans were stymied by a major constitutional setback in the Supreme Court's December 2011 rejection of the proposed federal legislation as not falling sufficiently within federal jurisdiction, as discussed in Chapters 4 and 6. The government of Canada went back to the drawing board to propose a cooperative securities regulator with delegated authority from the federal government and all provinces who agree.[9] Finance Minister Jim Flaherty announced in September 2014 an agreement to establish a new "Cooperative Capital Markets Regulatory System" reached with seven provinces and territories (notably excluding Quebec and Alberta), which together compose 65 per cent of the national securities market (Chase, 2013).[10]

To summarize, the dynamics of economic development in the Canadian federal system are significantly different today from what they were 30 years ago. International trade is freer, the Canadian economy is much more dependent on trade, and our governments have taken seriously their obligations under various trade agreements to limit their intervention in the marketplace. The free trade context has forced all governments in Canada to focus on the concept of overall economic competitiveness. Canadian manufacturers of goods—whether fridges, shoes, aircraft, or computer software—must compete directly with firms from around the world in both domestic and international markets. The competition in other sectors is more indirect. Private service sectors, for example, such as banking, retail and consulting, and public services, have less direct competition at home, but still need access to capital and technology, and ultimately cannot survive without the kind of productivity gains made in manufacturing (Porter, 1990). It remains to be seen whether and to what extent a trend to protectionism evident in the US administration and Congress elected in 2016 produces a significantly changed context for Canada's trading economy and for the conditions of economic competition, let alone the institutional and constitutional parameters of Canadian federalism as it affects trade and global integration.

In the meantime, it is certainly the case that governments continue to spend money to promote economic development. The programs are less trade-distorting than they were in the past and more concentrated on building on general advantages by improving training, education, and infrastructure and a establishing a more competitive tax and regulatory framework. Policy is also increasingly focused at the local level and on softer factors such as the environment, social and cultural amenities, community tolerance and cohesion, and overall quality of life. Another dominant idea in economic development circles is the importance of "networks" bringing together private firms (both big and small) with universities and other research establishments and governments to promote denser economic activity. Such networks work best in urban clusters, but with strong strategic support they can also contribute to rural development (Haddow, 2008; Krugman, 1999). The Trudeau federal government's "supercluster" program, announced in early 2018, is a prominent current example of this approach. The intergovernmental challenge is to achieve broad-based horizontal coordination across federal, provincial, and local government agencies, drawing on a wide array of social and economic policies and programs, to overcome obstacles in a specific sub-region or urban area (e.g., northeast New Brunswick or Greater Toronto).

The increasing focus on urban issues reflects a realization that cities are major drivers in the national and global economies. In the game of competitive cities, federalism still matters in Canada and other federations because provincial governments are the most important shapers of urban destiny—see the discussion in Chapter 10 on local government (Sancton, 2008; cf. Courchene, 2005). Provincial spending on economic development declined markedly in the mid-1990s, not because of free trade restrictions but because of fiscal cutbacks. That spending rebounded during the decade of 1998–2008 as federal and provincial budgetary situations improved and, from 2008–11, as part of the economic stimulus program to combat the recession. However, the four richer and larger provinces (Alberta, British Columbia, Ontario, and Quebec) now have a much greater capacity to fund urban and rural development than do the six smaller and generally poorer provinces and the three northern territories. Federal programs alleviate some but clearly not all of this growing disparity (Brown, 2006; Haddow, 2008).

Summary

This chapter has emphasized the fundamental importance of economic issues to the federal system. The creation of a single new economy was one of the original goals of Confederation. The national economy integrates the regional economies but the latter continue to exist, just as Canada's national economy continues to exist despite its increasing integration with the US and global economies. The Canadian economic union is a major achievement, but its relatively weak constitutional status means that it requires continuous attention by the federal and provincial governments. In political terms, the location of economic activity and the level of its development are never neutral issues. The federal and provincial orders of government have considerable powers to shape the national and regional economies with a variety of macroeconomic and microeconomic policy tools. Their often competing goals for economic development can generate sharp conflict.

Certainly the introduction of free trade between Canada and the US presented a major challenge for intergovernmental relations, threatening to upset the constitutional balance in the system and forcing governments to tame many of their development policies. Yet the federal system has proven remarkably adaptable to these new economic conditions, and has done so in a relatively cooperative fashion without provoking a constitutional crisis.

Questions for Critical Thought

1. Are all Canadians better off as a result of the country moving to closer economic union?

2. Should the provinces have a formal veto over international trade agreements?

3. Is the concept of regional equity outdated? Are there other significant issues of economic disparity that should be addressed?

Notes

1. Among these were labour and farmer parties and movements from the 1890s; the Progressive movement and party in the West after 1919; the non-partisan Maritime Rights Movement of the 1920s; the social democratic Co-operative Commonwealth Federation (CCF) formed in 1933; and the more right-wing populist parties of Social Credit (Alberta) and Bloc Populaire (Quebec) formed in the 1930s.

2. For a discussion, see Coulombe (2013).

3. Such suggestions were made by the Macdonald Royal Commission in 1985, and later as part of the "Canada Round" of constitutional negotiations in 1990–1. See Coleman (1991).

4. See section 36(1) Constitution Act, 1982. For a discussion of the history and effects of section 36, see Brown (2007).
5. For a good overview, see Savoie (1992, 2006).
6. *A.G. Canada v A.G. Ontario (Labour Conventions Reference)* (1937) AC 326.
7. The CETA agreement was signed in September 2014, but has not yet been legally ratified. On the federal–provincial issue in Canada, see Saunders (2013).
8. For links to bilateral or regional agreements endorsed by the AIT and CFTA, see the home website for the CFTA (Canadian Free Trade Agreement) at www.cfta-alec.ca (accessed 15 June 2018).
9. For details on the federal plan, see Finance Canada (2015). The reference for the Supreme Court judgement is *Reference re Securities Act*, 2011 SCC 66, [2011] 3 S.C.R. 837.
10. For information, see the agency's website at http://ccmr-ocrmc.ca/ (accessed Aug. 2017).

References

Brown, D.M. 1991. "The Evolving Role of the Provinces in Canadian Trade Policy." In *Canadian Federalism: Meeting Global Economic Challenges?*, edited by D.M. Brown and M. Smith. Kingston, ON: Institute of Intergovernmental Relations, Queen's University and Institute for Research on Public Policy.

———. 1993. "The Evolving Role of the Provinces in Canada–United States Trade Relations." In *States and Provinces in the International Economy*, edited by D.M. Brown and E. Fry. Berkeley: Institute of Governmental Studies Press, University of California.

———. 2002. *Market Rules: Economic Union Reform and Intergovernmental Policy-Making in Australia and Canada*. Montreal and Kingston: McGill–Queen's University Press.

———. 2006. "Still in the Game: Efforts to Tame Economic Development Competition in Canada." In *Racing to the Bottom? Provincial Interdependence in the Canadian Federation*, edited by K. Harrison. Vancouver: University of British Columbia Press.

———. 2007. "Integration, Equity and Section 36." *Supreme Court Law Review* 37 S.C.L.R. (2d).

——— and P.M. Leslie. 1994. "Economic Integration and Equality in Federations." In *Economic Union in Federal Systems*, edited by A. Mullins and C. Saunders. Sydney: The Federation Press.

Campbell, R. 1987. *Grand Illusions: The Politics of the Keynesian Experience in Canada, 1945–75*. Peterborough, ON: Broadview Press.

Canada. 1985. *Report of the Royal Commission on the Economic Union and Development Prospects for Canada*. Ottawa: Ministry of Supply and Services.

———. 2017. *Canadian Free Trade Agreement*. https://www.cfta-alec.ca/canadian-free-trade-agreement-cfta/.

Capeluck, E. 2014. *Convergences across Provincial Economies in Canada: Trends, Drivers, Implications*. Research Report, 2014-03. Ottawa: Centre for the Study of Living Standards.

Chase, S. 2013. "Flaherty Finally Installs Security Oversight Regulator." *Globe and Mail*, 20 Sept.

Coleman, W.D. 1991. "Monetary Policy, Accountability and Legitimacy." *Canadian Journal of Political Science* 24, no. 4: 711–34.

Coulombe, S. 2013. *Terms of Trade Changes, the Dutch Disease and Canadian Provincial Disparity*. Working Paper No. 2013.12. Kingston, ON: Institute of Intergovernmental Relations, Queen's University.

Courchene, T.J. 2005. *Citistates and the State of Cities: Political Economy and Fiscal-Federalism Dimensions*. Montreal: Institute for Research on Public Policy.

Coyne, A. 2017. "No Evidence that Canada Works in New Internal Trade Deal." *National Post*, 7 Apr.

Cross, P. 2007. "Year End Review: Westward Ho!" *Canadian Economic Observer* 20, 4. Catalogue no. 11-010-XIB.

Doern, G.B., and M. MacDonald. 1999. *Free-Trade Federalism: Negotiating the Canadian Agreement on Internal Trade*. Toronto: University of Toronto Press.

Dyson, K. 1980. *The State Tradition in Western Europe*. New York: Oxford University Press.

Economic Council of Canada (ECC). 1991. *A Joint Venture*. Ottawa: Ministry of Supply and Services.

Eden, L., and M.A. Molot. 1993. "Canada's National Policies: Reflections on 125 Years." *Canadian Public Policy* 19, no. 3: 232–51.

Finance Canada. 2015. *The Budget Plan, 2015*. https://www.budget.gc.ca/2015/home-accueil-eng.html.

Haddow, R. 2008. "Federalism and Economic Adjustment: Skills and Economic Development in the Face of Globaliz-ation." In *Canadian Federalism: Perfor-mance, Effectiveness, Legitimacy*, 2nd edn, edited by H. Bakvis and G. Skogstad, 246–65. Toronto: Oxford University Press.

Hall, P., and D. Soskice, eds. 2001. *Varieties of Capitalism*. Oxford: Oxford University Press.

Hoberg, G. 2016. "Pipelines and the Politics of Structure: A Case Study of the Trans Mountain Pipeline." Paper presented to the Canadian Political Science Associ-ation, 31 May–2 June.

Kent, T. 2007. *The Federal Spending Power Is Now Chiefly for People, Not Provinces*. Working Paper. Kingston, ON: Institute of Intergovernmental Relations, Queen's University.

Knox, R. 1998. "Economic Integration in Canada through the Agreement on Internal Trade." In *Canada: The State of the Federation 1997: Non-Constitutional Renewal*, edited by H. Lazar. Kingston, ON: Institute of Intergovernmental Relations, Queen's University.

———. 2001. *Canada's Agreement on Internal Trade: It Can Work If We Want It To*. Toronto: Certified General Accountants Association of Canada.

Krugman, P. 1999. *The Spatial Economy: Cities, Regions and International Trade*. Cambridge, MA: MIT Press.

MacDonald, L.I. 2007. "A Conversation with the Prime Minister." *Policy Options* (Feb. 2007): 5–11.

MacDonald, M. 2002. "The Agreement on Internal Trade: Trade-Offs for Economic Union and Federalism." In *Canadian Federalism: Performance, Effectiveness, and Legitimacy*, edited by H. Bakvis and G. Skogstad. Toronto: Oxford University Press.

McGregor, J. 2017. "'Canada Is Open': Interprovincial Trade Deal a Renewed Push to Drop Barriers." *CBC News*, 7 Apr. https://www.cbc.ca/news/politics/interprovincial-free-trade-friday-toronto-1.4060197.

McKenna, B. 2013. "EU Deal Exposes Weaknesses in Canada's Internal Trade." *Globe and Mail*, 9 Dec.

Mackintosh, W.A. 1939. *The Economic Background of Dominion–Provincial Relations*. Toronto: Macmillan.

Milne, D. 1986. *Tug of War: Ottawa and the Provinces under Trudeau and Mulroney*. Toronto: J. Lorimer.

Porter, M. 1990. *The Competitive Advantage of Nations*. London: Macmillan.

Putnam, R. 1988. "Diplomacy and Domestic Pol-itics: The Logic of Two-Level Games." *In-ternational Organization* 42, no. 3: 427–60.

Richards, R.G. 1991. "The Canadian Consti-tution and International Economic Rela-tions." In *Canadian Federalism: Meeting Global Economic Challenges?*, edited by D.M. Brown and M. Smith. Kingston, ON: Institute of Intergovernmental Relations, Queen's University.

Robinson, I. 2003. "Neoliberal Trade Policy and Canadian Federalism Revisited." In *New Trends in Canadian Federalism*, 2nd edn, edited by F. Rocher and M. Smith, 197–242. Peterborough, ON: Broadview Press.

Sancton, A. 2008. "The Urban Agenda." In *Canadian Federalism: Performance, Effectiveness, and Legitimacy*, 2nd edn, edited by H. Bakvis and G. Skogstad. Toronto: Oxford University Press.

Saunders, Douglas. 2013. "Our Petty Provin-cialism Threatens Free Trade Ambitions." *Globe and Mail*, 25 May.

Savoie, D.J. 1992. *Regional Economic Develop-ment: Canada's Search for Solutions*. 2nd edn. Toronto: University of Toronto Press.

———. 2006. *Visiting Grandchildren: Economic Development in the Maritimes*. Toronto: University of Toronto Press.

Scharpf, F.W. 1996. "Negative and Positive Integration in the Political Economy of European Welfare States." In *Governance in the European Union*, edited by G. Marks. London: Sage.

Shearer, R. 1985. "Regionalism and International Trade Policy." In *Canada–United States Free Trade*, edited by J. Whalley. Toronto: University of Toronto Press.

Simeon, R.E.B., and I. Robinson. 1990. *State, Society, and the Development of Canadian Federalism*. Toronto: University of Toronto Press.

Stevenson, G. 2012. "The Political Economy of Regionalism and Federalism." In *Canadian Federalism: Performance, Effectiveness, and Legitimacy*, 3rd edn, edited by H. Bakvis and G. Skogstad. Toronto: Oxford University Press.

TD Economics. 2015. "Canadian Economy Teeters on the Brink of Technical Recession." June.

Tinbergen, J. 1965. *International Economic Integration*, 2nd edn. Amsterdam: Elsevier.

Trebilcock, M.J. 1987. "Federalism and the Canadian Economic Union." In *Federalism and the Role of the State*, edited by H. Bakvis and W.M. Chandler. Toronto: University of Toronto Press.

———et al., eds. 1983. *Federalism and the Canadian Economic Union*. Toronto: Ontario Economic Council.

Whyte, J. 1990. "The Impact of Internationalization on the Constitutional Setting." Paper presented at Think Globally: Proceedings of the 42nd Annual Conference of the Institute of Public Administration of Canada. Quebec City.

Chapter 9

The Environmental Union

Week 11

Learning Objectives

Learning Objectives

- To understand how different regional interests and values are reflected in positions related to the environment.
- To review the strengths and weaknesses of competition versus cooperation in dealing with overlapping environmental responsibilities.
- To understand the significance of constitutional rules for how environment policy is made.
- To review the many interrelated issues for federalism in the case of climate change/greenhouse gas emissions.

The concept of the environmental union, like its social and economic counterparts, suggests a shared sense of purpose and a Canada-wide approach.[1] At the same time environmental issues pose some of the most difficult, and interesting, challenges facing the Canadian federation, raising questions about constitutional jurisdiction and the effectiveness of our institutions. Climate change—specifically global warming and the international effort to reduce greenhouse gas emissions—is a major political issue, with serious implications for both regional and national interests.

Canada occupies one of the largest land masses on earth. Bordering on three oceans, it encompasses enormous ecological diversity and abundant natural resources. At home and abroad, the image of Canadians as stewards of a vast, untouched northern wilderness has been central to the national identity. The economic value of forests and minerals is obvious, but the basic natural elements—earth, water, air—are priceless, for they underlie all value in any society. Until relatively recently, the quality of these elements was generally taken for granted, but today their economic value is increasingly recognized. Resource allocation and development decisions must take into account the costs of potential environmental degradation, and activities that damage the environment by depleting non-renewable resources, reducing biodiversity, or producing dangerous substances such as greenhouse gases must be restrained. Meanwhile, economic tools and mechanisms (e.g., carbon taxes, emission trading systems) are becoming increasingly important as policy instruments for managing the environment.

The Canadians most affected by major shifts in environmental quality—including climate change, resource depletion, and agricultural or industrial incursion on traditional ways of life—are those living closest to the land: residents of farming, coastal, resource, and remote northern communities. Those who live in more urban settings—64 per cent of Canadians—are even more likely to be exposed to some industrial pollutants. But urban dwellers in general tend to be more removed than their rural counterparts from direct trade-offs between development and environmental protection. Still, among politicians as well as the public, overall awareness of environmental issues has grown tremendously since the 1970s. Perceptions of urgency vary, of course, depending on current events. A major toxic spill, a flood, a health emergency, or a new pipeline proposal will spark a rise in concern, while a sudden economic downturn or a rapid increase in energy prices will easily push environmental issues into the background (Bakvis and Nevitte, 1992). But despite short-term fluctuations, public concern has continued to rise over time (Harrison, 1996).

A significant challenge for policy-makers in this relatively new area of concern is the fact that air, water, and much of the land are public goods from which everyone benefits, and for which no one pays. A policy designed to control the effluents from pulp and paper mills, for example, benefits all Canadians, but the costs must be borne by the pulp and paper industry. Some of these costs can be passed on to the consumers of paper products, but in a highly competitive global market, paper producers see strict pollution control as a disadvantage—especially if their competitors in other provinces or countries are not subject to similar controls. In this way a relatively local problem can become intergovernmental and even international. In the past, Canadian governments have chosen to subsidize the adoption of new, less-polluting technological processes for pulp and paper production. But will that always be the best (or most politically feasible) use of scarce public funds? In any case, what one so often sees in environmental politics is that the interests of those for whom policy costs are concentrated (polluting industries or developers) override the interests of those for whom policy benefits are diffuse (the general public) (Harrison, 1996; cf. Olson, 1971).

In virtually all countries, environmental policy has been a continuing struggle. It pits vested economic and industry interests against local citizens (e.g., those opposed to the development of a new quarry in the neighbourhood) and nationally and internationally organized advocacy groups demanding stronger environmental regulation (e.g., Greenpeace or the World Wildlife Fund). It creates struggles within governments as well as between them as policy-makers weigh real environmental risks against the costs of industrial or social adjustment. Governments must also judge the breadth and depth of public opinion on environmental issues. How much are individuals willing to sacrifice when faced with sharp rises in gas prices, high costs for recycling, or restrictions on their use of land? The challenges multiply for transboundary problems such as greenhouse gases, which involve both domestic and foreign policy interests. Negotiating simultaneously with domestic interests and international players presents a major challenge for the national government, even in a unitary state (see Putnam, 1988). All these complications are magnified in a federation such as Canada.

Federalism and the Environment in Canada

The fact that Canada is constitutionally and politically a federal state has important implications for the way we deal with environmental issues. Federalism is about both sharing power and preserving autonomy—sometimes local and sometimes national. Many federal theorists see federalism as promoting liberal and democratic values by setting up competitive governments capable of satisfying diverse needs and preferences. In this context environmental concerns can be simultaneously local, regional, national, and international in scope. People in different communities may value the environment differently, or may be inclined to make different kinds of economic and social trade-offs to preserve environmental quality. In federations, local and provincial or state governments normally have the power to make decisions on more localized environmental matters such as land use, water treatment, waste disposal, and forest management, while the national or federal government makes decisions about environmental issues that are national in scope or that cross provincial/state boundaries, such as air or water pollutants, or the manufacture, sale, and transportation of toxic substances. In all federations, policies and programs developed by the national (central) government are frequently implemented and delivered by the provincial or state and local governments.

Interactions between governments on environmental matters take three main forms: cooperative, competitive, and concurrent. Cooperation is obviously required for the many environmental issues that cross jurisdictional boundaries. Routine cooperation is for the most part very effective, but has some important limitations.[2] Competition may seem an odd term in this context; it refers to situations in which governments—federal, provincial and territorial, local, Indigenous—operate on their own, following their own inclinations, with or without the approval of other governments. This happens in many environmental policy areas. A particular province may be aggressive or passive, passing tough or lax regulations; the federal government may take strong action on clearly federal matters and impose national policies on provinces, or it may choose to do nothing at all. Analysts distinguish between direct interjurisdictional competition on the one hand (two jurisdictions, each seeking to attract more industry, provide more protection for citizens, or preserve more environment than the other) and policy emulation across jurisdictions on the other (looking at what others have done and trying to do the same, if not better). If the competition offers the most industry-friendly, minimal environmental regime, those jurisdictions are said to be in a "race to the bottom"; if they offer the most stringent environmental protection, they are said to be in a "race to the top" (Harrison, 2006; Olewiler, 2006). Finally, "concurrency" refers to the constitutional principle of an explicitly shared power. In most federations the authority to legislate on environmental issues is considered to be concurrent, although the federal legislation will usually prevail in the event of conflict. This enables federal governments to pass general, framework law on matters such as national standards for emissions or regulatory processes, while leaving considerable scope for provincial or local governments to fill in the details according to their particular regional interests and values.

Canada's unique blend of cooperation, competition, and concurrency is largely a reflection of its size and geographic diversity. Because the federation encompasses several different ecological zones, regional climates, and major watersheds, some environmental problems are confined to one region alone, or have differing effects across regions. And since economic activities and levels of development differ across the country, the issues of concern vary accordingly: environmental problems associated with urban sprawl do not affect all provinces to the same degree, and environmental issues related to oil and gas production are of particular concern in Alberta and the other petroleum-producing provinces. All the provinces and territories are still trying to encourage industrial development, so they will not want environmental policy to impose undue costs on potential investors. On the other hand, environmentally friendly development and a high level of environmental quality are becoming increasingly important for attracting investment and human capital.

Other environmental issues are also regionally concentrated. Depletion of fish stocks, for instance, has severely affected some coastal communities, especially in the Atlantic region. Acid rain was really an issue—though a very serious one—only in eastern Canada, whereas soil salination is a concern confined to the Prairies. A proposed pipeline from the oil sands to the Pacific coast affects most directly only two provinces. Finally, even though the effects of global warming are not confined to the Far North, they are perhaps more pronounced there than anywhere else.

A second factor with significant implications for environmental policy is the constitutional division of powers (Winfield and Macdonald, 2012; Valiante, 2002). Environmental issues, as they came to be defined in the late twentieth century, were not a consideration in the mid-nineteenth century, and so the Constitution Act, 1867 makes no mention of them. Gradually, however, a jurisdictional approach to the environment has emerged through legislation and judicial review. As is common in all federations, aspects of the environment are the concern of all levels of governments. Provincial governments have responsibility for local matters and most issues with respect to the land, its use, and development, as well as the ownership and management of most natural resources (fisheries being a major exception). Therefore the provinces have assumed jurisdiction for most local environmental issues or matters that can be contained within their boundaries. Much of this provincial power is then delegated to the local governments that take responsibility for the water supply, the regulation of land use, and waste disposal. Meanwhile, the federal government has assumed jurisdiction over environmental issues that are more than local in scope, that cross provincial or international boundaries, that are especially costly or technically difficult to handle, or that have major implications for the national economy or national security.

The federal government's constitutional powers are not as strong in Canada as they are in other federations because the provincial powers are explicitly listed rather than being only concurrent, as is common elsewhere. The decision to spell out the provincial powers was deliberate, intended specifically to confine federal power. Nonetheless, the courts have been gradually expanding federal power, and it is possible that one day the federal Parliament will be able to legislate in a broader range of areas. Today, the bulk of Ottawa's legal authority over the environment consists in its jurisdiction over trade and commerce, coastal fisheries, and criminal law, along with the "peace, order, and good government" clause. In fact, environmental protection was at the centre of the 1988 *Crown Zellerbach* case, in which the Supreme Court of Canada ruled that Ottawa could use its POGG power to act in a matter that the provinces concerned were unable to tackle, even though it fell under provincial jurisdiction.[3] As noted in Chapter 4, this reasoning, termed the provincial inability test, was seen as a potential breakthrough, though in fact it has seen little use subsequently. In 1997, the Supreme Court ruled in *R. v. Hydro-Québec* that federal legislation, specifically the Canadian Environmental Protection Act (CEPA), could be upheld using the criminal law power of Parliament.[4]

Legal jurisdiction is especially important in the environmental field because so many of the proposed solutions to environmental problems involve regulation. Governments seek to regulate the way private individuals and companies use the environment because on their own these private actors would not bear the costs of such a public good. But no government holds all the legal resources, and it is often unclear, especially for new and emerging issues, which one has the final authority. In many federations this problem is solved by constitutional concurrency. The federal legislatures of countries such as Germany, the United States, Mexico, Brazil, and Australia pass general regulatory laws, specifying standards, but leave the implementation and enforcement to the provincial and local governments. Although Canada's constitution does not provide for such formal concurrency, de facto concurrency is quite common in environmental matters. Finally, governments may seek to fine-tune the constitutional division of labour, as was done in Switzerland (Watts, 2008: ch. 5). In most federations, however, problems of ambiguity and overlap are still most commonly addressed by way of intergovernmental negotiation.

Intergovernmental Cooperation and Competition

Intergovernmental cooperation is no more the rule in the environmental union than it is in any other aspect of the Canadian federation. Governments often act unilaterally when the matter in question is sufficiently clear-cut or localized—a cleanup of a specific site, for example, or an environmental impact assessment of a minor project. In other cases, however, they act unilaterally because other governments will not cooperate with them, or because they need to take action that fully meets the needs of their electorate and that is not compromised by the interests of other governments. Competitive policy-making can amount to an incredibly rich experiment in what works and what does not, especially in a federation with multiple jurisdictions making decisions that affect millions of people. In the US, where 50 individual states have been making their own environmental policy choices, the overall effect has been a moderate "race to the top" led by California, which has tended to set the standard for vehicle emissions, for example (Rabe, 2004: ch. 1; also Rabe, 2007). This kind of interjurisdictional competition occurs on the international scale as well—between the US and Canada, for instance, or among the member countries of the European Union.

Canada, too, has seen interjurisdictional competition on the environmental front in recent years. Later in this chapter we detail how individual provinces took the lead in the past decade on implementing taxes and other approaches to control greenhouse gas emissions, largely in the absence of effective federal regulation. A study of environmental policies and indicators in six provinces found that intergovernmental competition on the environment has not amounted to the "race to the bottom" that some might have feared. Governments have not been competing to reduce pollution controls, for instance, in order to attract industry. The general trend has been more positive: in the late 1980s, for example, some provinces set out on their own to raise the standards for dioxin emissions in the pulp and paper industry. These standards were superseded in 1992 by new, less stringent, national standards for dioxin emissions (Olewiler, 2006: 138–40). However, steps taken during the past decade by provinces including Quebec, Ontario, British Columbia, and most recently Alberta have suggested that a new "race to the top" may be getting underway with respect to carbon emissions. This, of course, is subject to change as governments change hands.

Responding to environmental problems of national, international, or even global scope would logically seem to be the business of the federal government alone. Unilateral federal action is called for when an environmental problem requires a single, unambiguous, and consistent regulatory regime of a kind that would be very difficult for the provinces to agree on. The federal Parliament already has partial jurisdiction over large areas of the environmental policy field, including fish habitat and transboundary air pollutants. And the Supreme Court's rulings in the *Crown Zellerbach* and *Hydro-Québec* cases suggest that the POGG and criminal law powers in the Constitution Act, 1867 could justify new federal regulatory powers in certain circumstances. Environmental advocacy groups have been calling for strong unilateral action ever since the 1960s (Boardman, 1992). But even key milestones of federal environmental legislation—the Canada Water Act, 1970; amendments to the Fisheries Act, 1970; the Clean Air Act, 1971; the Canadian Environmental Protection Act, 1992; and the Canadian Environmental Assessment Act, 1992—were usually the product of extensive intergovernmental consultations.

The alternative to competition or unilateral action is cooperation of some kind. Two or more neighbouring governments will cooperate to deal with a specific regional issue or to take a particularly regional approach to a national or international issue. In the long lead-up to the Canada–US Air Quality Agreement of 1991, for example, governments on both sides of the border cooperated extensively, especially in the "downstream" region represented by the Conference of New England Governors and Eastern Canadian Premiers. Similarly, in 2007 Quebec, British Columbia, Manitoba, Ontario, and Quebec began collaborating with seven US states on a project called the Western Climate Initiative, aimed at setting regional goals for reducing greenhouse gas (GHG) emissions and establishing a regional cap-and-trade system.[5] The federal government and one or more provinces will occasionally come together in a bilateral or regional forum to hold a joint environmental assessment (e.g., the Great Whale hydro project in Quebec; the Hibernia oilfield project off the Newfoundland coast). For larger, more complex efforts, however, the most important forums are still the multilateral federal–provincial–territorial conferences of ministers and the subsidiary meetings of senior officials and experts.

Kathryn Harrison, a leading scholar in the field, has suggested that one reason the federal government is willing "to relinquish the lead role to the provinces" and embrace intergovernmental cooperation is in order "to avoid electoral blame"—in effect, to pass the buck (Harrison, 1996: 20). In any case, Ottawa is averse to trampling on provincial jurisdiction lest it provoke regional discontent, and to pick a fight with Quebec could be damaging to national unity. Unilateral action would also require strong public support, and Canadians' record on that score has not been consistent. Finally, leadership is costly: for Ottawa to develop and enforce a new set of environmental standards would entail major bureaucratic and technical investment, potentially duplicating provincial efforts. With a few exceptions, such investments have been considered more than Ottawa could afford, especially in the fiscal crisis years of the 1990s. More recently, environmentalists who seek a stronger federal role were dismayed with the Harper government's decisions in 2012 to reduce its regulatory role altogether, as seen in the omnibus bills passed in Parliament to streamline or eliminate environmental processes in order to promote energy and other resource projects.

For all these reasons, the more common approach has been for the federal government to work with the provinces and territories on environmental problems.

If a regulatory standard or process is required, it is not "federal" but "national"—jointly created either by all the governments or by a few of them through bilateral or regional arrangements. This collaborative approach has produced a long series of agreements, and the intergovernmental machinery devoted to it is well established. The problem—by no means confined to environmental policy—is that Canadian intergovernmental institutions do not deal well with issues requiring uniform, consistent regulatory results (see Chapter 5). The main intergovernmental body, the Canadian Council of Ministers of the Environment (CCME), brings together hundreds of officials in committees and task forces, and conducts extensive consultations with the environmental NGO community. When the product of all those efforts goes to the ministers for final approval, however, the decision is made on the basis of consensus bargaining alone. Typically, no votes are taken; governments can refuse to take part; and agreements cannot be enforced in law. Thus the CCME and similar processes tend to produce lowest-common-denominator outcomes (Fafard, 2000).

Intergovernmental processes can take years to complete, and even then the results are often weak and unsubstantial. The Canadian Environmental Protection Act—broad federal legislation first introduced in 1988—underwent four years of negotiations before Ottawa felt it had sufficient consensus to pass through Parliament. The "Big Four" provinces—British Columbia, Alberta, Ontario, and Quebec—opposed the original bill vigorously and relented only after the legislation was changed to allow for the recognition of "equivalent" provincial measures to stand for potential new federal regulations in some cases. Negotiations over the Canada-Wide Agreement on Environmental Harmonization took five years, from 1993 to 1998; and—as discussed further below—it took three years, from 1997 to 2000, to produce an anodyne and ultimately ineffective agreement on a "national action plan" to deal with greenhouse gas emissions.

One way of dealing with the limitations of the cooperative machinery is by reducing the need for cooperation in the first place. Thus, federal and provincial governments try to fine-tune their respective responsibilities to avoid overlap. In this approach, termed "rationalization" (Harrison, 2002: 125–7), the governments involved negotiate new national standards for environmental regulation and then decide definitively which level of government will be responsible for implementing and enforcing the regulations. This approach offers the same certainty as unified federal action, but allows the governments to choose the style of implementation they prefer: more decentralized and flexible, or more uniform and centralized. Rationalization has always been an option in Canadian intergovernmental relations. It has been used much more extensively in the environmental field, and in other areas, since the 1995 federal budget cuts forced Ottawa to abandon a strong federal implementation and enforcement presence.[6] The best example is the Environmental Harmonization agreement of 1998, which set in train a variety of processes, overseen by the CCME, to review environmental problems. The key outcome has been a series of new Canada-wide standards negotiated in separate sub-agreements. Although most of them call for flexible provincial implementation, they can be amended only with the unanimous consent of the parties, any one of which can withdraw on six months' notice. These sub-agreements place "a strong emphasis on 'one-window' delivery of environmental protection services by a single order of government" (Winfield and Macdonald, 2008). Examples include sub-agreements on environmental assessment, for specific sets of pollutants such as mercury, dioxins, and furans, and the cleanup of contaminated sites. In some cases the federal Department of the Environment takes the lead in implementation (e.g., monitoring major air pollutants).

Nevertheless, the harmonization accords have been likened to a series of "joint decision traps," relying too much on consensus and producing lowest-common-denominator results (Fafard, 2000). Standards are being set and enforced, but according to observers—in particular environmental NGOs—they tend to be weaker than might be expected if only one jurisdiction were involved. Provincial governments with strong economic interests in resisting higher standards have generally been successful in doing so (Winfield and Macdonald, 2008: 281–4). On the other hand, the threat of unilateral federal action seems to have produced a more stringent Canada-wide standard in some cases (Harrison, 2002: 134–9).

Individual federal administrations (e.g., Chrétien, Martin, Harper) will favour different modes of interaction, some choosing mostly cooperation, some mostly competition.[7] However, in recent decades most federal governments have shown little determination to take strong centralized action on the environment. The Harper government, with its apparently decentralist, classical approach to federalism, certainly did not break with this pattern. Yet discontent over the Harper Conservatives' approach to environmental issues, including climate change, played a factor in the 2015 federal election campaign. The two principal opposition parties, the NDP and Liberals, promised a more concerted approach that included working closely with federal, provincial, local, and Indigenous governments, but also bolder central government action as well. As outlined below, the Trudeau government has worked to restore some of the federal programs cut by its predecessor and to develop a stronger domestic and international position on climate change. However, the Trudeau government also addresses the difficult oil and gas pipeline issues, trying to maintain a balance between regional, environmental, and economic interests.

The Case of Climate Change Policy

Many of the issues addressed so far in this chapter—the difficulties of accepting environmental costs; the interaction between the economy and the environment; regional and jurisdictional differences over environment policy; and the mechanisms and dynamics of intergovernmental and international relations—come together in the climate change file. Although other environmental issues also have international dimensions, climate change is likely to become the classic example of the challenges posed by multi-level governance. For Canada the issue has two external dimensions: as a major foreign policy matter with significant multilateral implications that must be handled through the United Nations, and as a major bilateral and continental issue with the United States. Domestically, addressing the issue means negotiating a variety of difficult federal–provincial issues and adjusting to a carbon-reduced economy, in addition to the challenges of reaching intergovernmental consensus where required.

The issue of climate change is in fact a cluster of issues: it is about greenhouse gas emissions (carbon dioxide, methane, and others) that create a heat-trapping greenhouse effect in the earth's atmosphere. It is about whether or not one accepts the scientific evidence that the emissions are contributing to global warming, in turn creating relatively rapid, human-made, and destructive climate change. And it is about the task of reducing or stabilizing GHG emissions—an enormous collective action problem. No one country can solve it. Canada has a high "carbon footprint"—we have one of the world's highest per capita rates of carbon production and consumption. On the consumption side this is due to our northern climate, advanced economy, and reliance on fossil fuels as a primary source of energy in industry, transportation, and heating. The main sources of GHG emissions in Canada as of 2012 were, in order of magnitude: oil and gas production, transportation, electricity generation using fossil fuels, residential and commercial fuel consumption, industrial production, and agriculture. Whereas fossil fuels are used for transportation across Canada, oil and gas production, along with electricity generation from carbon sources (oil, coal, natural gas), are regionally concentrated. By 2004 Alberta's oil and gas industry, including the oil sands projects, had made the province the largest producer of GHG emissions in Canada. Ontario, with the largest population, greatest urban density, and significant industrial production, was the second largest emitter overall while Saskatchewan, also a significant oil and gas producer, with a big agricultural sector, had the highest per capita emissions. Provinces that rely on hydroelectric power for most of their electricity and industrial production, such as Quebec, British Columbia, and Manitoba, are much less emissions-intensive (Simpson, Jaccard, and Rivers, 2007: 23–6; Hardy, 2012) (see Table 9.1). In sum, a regional political geography of GHG emissions creates interprovincial conflict and poses complex issues for the federal government related to coordination and national unity.

The need to reduce greenhouse gas production has been on the international agenda since at least 1992, when the Rio de Janeiro Earth Summit produced the United Nations Framework Convention on Climate Change. The commitments made at that time to stabilize greenhouse gas emissions were largely voluntary. Five years later, the international consensus had strengthened to the point that an international meeting in Kyoto, Japan, set binding targets for GHG reductions,

Table 9.1 Greenhouse Gas Emissions in Canada by Province and Territory, 1990 and 2015

	GGEs (megatonnes) 1990	GGEs (megatonnes) 2015
Canada	603	722
Newfoundland and Labrador	9	10
Nova Scotia	20	16
Prince Edward Island	2	2
New Brunswick	16	14
Quebec	87	80
Ontario	179	166
Manitoba	18	21
Saskatchewan	45	75
Alberta	174	274
British Columbia	51	61
Yukon	<1	<1
Northwest	n.a.	1
Nunavut	n.a	<1

Source: Environment Canada, 2017; Environment and Climate Change Canada, 2018. Figures have been rounded to the nearest full megatonne.

applicable to all industrialized countries. When Canada signed the Kyoto Protocol, it agreed that by 2010 it would reduce its GHG emissions to a level 6 per cent below its output in 1990. Most recently, in December 2015, the Paris Agreement superseded Kyoto in a more geographically comprehensive international agreement, encompassing all the major contributing producers of GHGs, including Canada, and setting out more stringent targets in an aim to limit actual global warming. The agreement is now ratified by over 150 countries, including Canada.

On-the-ground implementation of international commitments on GHG reductions requires the participation of all levels of government. Every government is responsible for a certain amount of carbon and other emissions through its own administrative operations. The provinces and territories have control over almost all natural resources and their management, as well as practically all major electricity producers, while local governments can influence land use and urban development, transportation use, and other consumer behaviour. All governments also have at their disposal important fiscal and regulatory instruments they can use to induce emission reductions in the society and economy at large. The provinces clearly have the right to regulate GHG emissions in the industry sectors within their jurisdiction; but could the federal Parliament pass a Canada-wide scheme? A major court decision in the 1930s established that Ottawa has clear jurisdiction over the negotiation and ratification of international treaties, but that it cannot implement them in areas of provincial jurisdiction.[8] Some refer to recent Supreme Court decisions in support of their view that federal legislation such as the Canadian Environmental Protection Act could be used to regulate GHG emissions.[9] It seems that the Martin, Harper, and Justin Trudeau governments have all contemplated this option (Marshall, 2007). Yet for all the reasons noted above (national unity constraints, regional differences, and a commitment to act collaboratively rather than unilaterally)—and also, perhaps, because it remains unclear how far federal legislation could go before it provoked a constitutional challenge—Ottawa has chosen thus far not to pursue the route of unilateral legislation. In any event, the jurisdictional problem has been secondary to the economic and political challenges of deciding what to do, how far to go, and how fast. The answers to those questions have been partly ideological, pitting the green movement against business, and in Canada have revealed some significant differences between the Conservative Party and its centre-left opponents—the Liberals, NDP, Bloc Québécois, and Green Party.

The prospects for Canada meeting its commitments under the Paris Agreement are discussed below, but first it is important to outline briefly the difficult history of Canada's attempts to meet its Kyoto obligations and the implications of this experience for federalism. There are two parts to this story. The first part is about attempts to achieve Canada-wide federal–provincial–territorial consensus; the second is about the more decentralized and competitive approach of each province and territorial government doing their own thing.

The Chrétien government signed onto the Kyoto Accord in 1997 and ratified it in 2002. But shortly after its election in January 2006, the Harper Conservative government announced that the Kyoto targets were not realistic and that Canada would not be able to honour its commitments after all. In December 2011 the Harper government (by then with a majority in Parliament) took the further step of actually withdrawing from the treaty (Environment and Climate Change Canada, 2011).

Since the Rio Summit, climate change issues have been a major agenda issue in Canadian domestic intergovernmental relations. Under the joint auspices of the CCME and the Council of Ministers of Energy, intergovernmental coordinating committees worked on a national action plan, released in 1995. According to Winfield and Macdonald (2008), this plan amounted to little more than seeking voluntary reductions of emissions and promising a variety of incentive programs to conserve energy. Meetings intensified in the lead-up to the international meetings in Kyoto, and the provinces agreed with the Chrétien government on the modest target of reducing emissions to the 1990 level by 2010. However, the prime minister unilaterally deepened Canada's commitment not once but twice, breaking ranks with the provinces (although Quebec did support tougher targets), first to 3 per cent below the 1990 level, then to 6 per cent below it (Harrison, 2007). While Chrétien was apparently moving to maximize Canada's influence in bridging the gap at Kyoto between the EU and other industrialized countries, his actions soured the intergovernmental mood in Canada. Back home, meeting privately with the other first ministers in January 1998, he was forced to admit that he had no plan for achieving the Kyoto targets and agreed that he would consult with them further before ratifying the protocol, if indeed Canada were to ratify it at all (Simpson et al., 2007: 61).

Nonetheless, the Chrétien government was committed to a joint implementation strategy. Over a period of three years, it negotiated with the provinces and territories to produce a National Implementation Strategy and Business Plan, signed by all the parties except Ontario and released in October 2000. The plan laid out broad principles, spending commitments, and voluntary undertakings, but it set no specific provincial or sectoral targets for achieving the Kyoto commitments, nor did it establish any binding regulatory process for reducing emissions. In the words of one prominent account, it was "a roadmap to nowhere" (Simpson et al., 2007: 63).

Once the Harper government took power in 2006, and in the context of rising GHG emissions in Canada in part because of increased oil and gas production, the federal government's approach was to ignore the Kyoto Accord and instead to seek a new international consensus on what it saw as a more realistic approach, with binding commitments not only from all industrialized countries but also from the developing world. The government also moved to regulate emissions by Canadian industry on a sectoral basis, implementing these if possible through equivalency agreements with the provinces (Environment Canada, 2007a, 2007b). In 2009 Ottawa declared a new target of reductions—this time to reduce emissions to 607 megatonnes by 2020, which would be 17 per cent below 2005 emissions (and, according to one analysis, the equivalent of a 3 per cent reduction from the 1990 base) (Bramley, 2009). The 2009 federal target was not accompanied by a detailed plan on exactly how it was to be achieved, and for some time the federal government declared that it was waiting until the details of a national GHG emission reduction regime in the US became clearer (McCarthy, 2009).

When it became clear that the Obama administration could get nowhere with the US Congress with national legislation for a carbon pricing regime, the Canadian government sought where it could to harmonize its sectoral regulations with those in the US, such as standards for emissions from renewable fuels, for automobiles, and for the electricity sector (the latter aimed at phasing out coal production), as well as proposed regulation of the oil and gas production sector. Finally, the 2015 federal election brought to power a government more committed to a tougher approach on climate change and determined to assume more aggressive international leadership and to implement, with the provinces if possible, a national carbon pricing regime (discussed below).

Now to the second part of the story about how Canada dealt with the Kyoto Accord. This is where several provinces have taken the lead with their own, in some cases more stringent, emission reduction targets and related measures. Indeed, a recent Suzuki Foundation report describes them as "all over the map," reflecting various combinations of regional interests and ideological values. The provincial governments' positions on climate change in general have reflected the intensity of their emissions (Marshall, 2006) (see Table 9.1 for basic data comparing Canadian provinces and territories). Alberta, Ontario, and Saskatchewan were slow to get on board and indeed resisted the initial Kyoto bandwagon, while Manitoba and Quebec had less to lose and embraced the Kyoto agenda early on. British Columbia, initially hostile, has since 2006 become one of the leading provinces in terms of climate change policy (Harrison, 2012). Provinces that are major hydrocarbon producers—chiefly Alberta but also Saskatchewan and Newfoundland and Labrador—have been anxious lest emission reductions put a halt to the burgeoning petroleum-based growth of their economies. In May 2015, Albertans elected an NDP provincial government that has taken a significantly different approach to oil and gas regulation and taxation than its predecessor Progressive Conservative governments, and has adopted a more aggressive stance towards reducing GHG emissions. Alberta has played an important role since 2015 in seeking broader intergovernmental cooperation to achieve more ambitious reductions, in this respect becoming an important ally of the Trudeau government. At the same time, Alberta continues its strong advocacy of the Trans Mountain Pipeline to transport bitumen to the Pacific, relying on the federal government for its support for the project, but this stance has resulted in major friction with the neighbouring province of BC, where most of the pipeline is located. Meanwhile, Saskatchewan, governed by the centre-right Saskatchewan Party for more than a decade, has assumed Alberta's former role in resisting federal regulatory encroachment and defending the energy sector from aggressive GHG reduction targets.

In Ontario, where stricter emission controls would have serious implications for the auto industry and the costs of reducing coal-fired electricity production were seen as too high, the neo-conservative Mike Harris government (1995–2002) was skeptical about global warming in general and hostile to the Kyoto process. More recently, the Liberal governments of Dalton McGuinty and Kathleen Wynn succeeded in totally eliminating coal-fired energy generation by 2014 and supported a North American cap-and-trade proposal (discussed below). However, the June 2018 election of the Progressive Conservatives led by Doug Ford has led to a return to the Ontario government's hostile position to national carbon-pricing measures. Premier Ford has announced the intention to scrap the cap-and-trade regime as well as to legally oppose the Trudeau government's carbon-pricing framework. Premier Ford has announced that Ontario will pursue sectoral regulatory approaches instead. Other provinces such as Nova Scotia and Prince Edward Island depend heavily on fossil fuels for electricity generation, and both have concentrated on developing renewable energy sources. And all provinces worry about their general economic competitiveness if the regulation of carbon and other emissions in Canada is substantially more stringent than it is in the United States.

In terms of actual policy initiatives some provinces took the lead in the 2000s to fill what they perceived as a policy vacuum in Ottawa. In 2007 Quebec introduced a narrowly based tax on carbon fuels, and a month later British Columbia became the first jurisdiction in North America to implement a broad-based carbon tax—despite opposition from Ottawa. In addition, British Columbia, Manitoba, Ontario, and Quebec joined with seven US states on a project called the Western Climate Initiative, aimed at setting regional goals for reducing GHG emissions and agreeing in principle to establish a regional cap-and-trade system. Unfortunately, in 2011 all of the US states except California withdrew from the scheme. Nonetheless, Ontario and Quebec recommitted to a joint cap-and-trade system with California in April 2015, moving towards actual implementation by 2017. Many observers believe that carbon taxes and cap-and-trade regimes are the most effective policy instruments for deep and long-term reductions in carbon emissions (Simpson et al., 2007). And even the provinces with the most to lose from carbon tax or regulatory regimes are putting major efforts into alternative approaches based on new technologies, such as Saskatchewan's ambitious plan to use carbon capture and storage to substantially reduce their emissions.

These varied provincial initiatives pointed the way ahead for their own jurisdictions when national consensus was lacking or perceived as too weak. This is appropriate, since policy responses to climate change must be tailored to local and regional conditions. This much competitive federalism can deliver. However, it is not enough—nationally or globally—if the sum of provincial efforts does not add up to a national response at least as significant as Canada's share of the global problem. By 2012, according to research undertaken for the National Roundtable on Environment and the Economy, carbon reduction initiatives proposed or underway across the provinces would not, unless significantly upgraded, enable the provinces to meet their various targets and thus, by extension, would not sufficiently contribute to meeting the Harper government's 2020 targets. Indeed, counting initiatives underway or planned against the national target, all public policy actions at that time would take Canada to only approximately 54 per cent of its 2020 goal (Navius Research, 2012). Moreover, observers worried that a piecemeal, province-by-province approach would not be consistent or comprehensive. And there would be a risk that the patchwork of schemes would fracture the Canadian marketplace in ways that would make it significantly more difficult to operate competitively.

Thus we come to the most recent developments of the Paris Agreement of December 2015 and the Canadian intergovernmental response detailed in the December 2016 document *Pan-Canadian Framework on Clean Growth and Climate Change* (Government of Canada, 2016a). The Paris Agreement, which the newly elected Trudeau government readily endorsed, significantly ratchets up the commitment to reduce GHG emissions. Canada's commitment is to reduce emissions from 742 megatonnes in 2016 to 523 by 2030, in other words, a 30 per cent reduction in just 14 years—in the context of emissions in Canada having been reduced by only 2 per cent in the past 10 years (Government of Canada, 2016b). However, with the election of new governments in Ottawa and Alberta with more aggressive positions on reducing GHGs, the prospects for a more substantive intergovernmental consensus, especially in comparison with weak results on the Kyoto Accord, seemed possible.

This has indeed been the result with the new *Pan-Canadian Framework*. The outcome of an intensive year of intergovernmental negotiations, involving three federal–provincial–territorial ministerial councils (Environment, Energy and Innovation, and Finance) and two formal first ministers' meetings, the document makes a clear commitment to meeting or exceeding the Paris target. It signals a collaborative approach among all governments and Indigenous peoples. It declares that "pricing carbon pollution" is central to the Framework, and obtained the agreement of the provinces and territories to enact a carbon pricing regime by 2018 in the form of either a tax or cap-and trade regulation. Any revenues generated by such schemes would remain with the provinces. The document also claims to promote flexibility to enable each province and territory to adopt its own regime, building on major efforts already underway such as the carbon taxes in Quebec and BC, the new carbon levy introduced by Alberta in 2015, and the phasing out of coal for electricity production in Ontario and Alberta, among other initiatives. The Framework also makes various commitments regarding climate change adaptation and clean growth innovation, including the promise of significant federal funding for provinces that comply.

A few cautions should be noted, however. First, the Framework agreement is not unanimous. Saskatchewan explicitly refused to sign and Manitoba held out for a year (McCarthy, 2017). As noted above, the new Progressive Conservative government in Ontario has withdrawn its cap-and-trade program, as well as a provision of subsidies for electric vehicles. At the Council of the Federation meeting in July 2018, the premiers of Ontario and Saskatchewan reiterated their intention to oppose in the courts the federal framework plan. Second, the document remains vague as to how the 2030 target is to be reached without a clear estimate of what proportion of reductions a carbon pricing regime will achieve. Third, the notion of the federal government stepping in and imposing a carbon pricing regime on any province that does not enact one in time is detailed only briefly, in an annex to the Framework agreement. It remains to be seen how and when federal legislation would be introduced. And finally, while the Framework promised an effectiveness review, it would only be after six years. One may conclude that the Framework is the most substantive Canadian intergovernmental agreement in the 25-year history of the climate change issue, but that the goals are ambitious and there are many potential roadblocks on the way to successful implementation.

Summary

This chapter has offered a brief sketch of the issues and dynamics involved in an important, relatively new area for intergovernmental relations in Canada. As with so much of public policy, the truth is in the details, and those are beyond the scope of this book. The environment is of increasing concern to Canadians and is an important part of our identity. It is not yet clear, however, that Canadians agree on either the standards of environmental quality they want to see enforced or the social and economic trade-offs they are willing to make to deal with major environmental problems.

Federalism only adds to the difficulty of addressing environmental concerns, since different regional interests must be accommodated and multiple levels of government share responsibility for dealing with various types of environmental issues. The environment is, de facto, a concurrent, overlapping responsibility among our governments. The challenge, therefore, is for those governments to get their act together. However, underlying the constitutional and regional factors are the same competing values of federalism that we have seen elsewhere in this book. Our institutions privilege local and provincial autonomy and decentralized responses to many issues. In many cases this is appropriate. At the same time, Canadians expect fairness, equality, and consistency on matters that are Canada-wide in scope. Intergovernmental mechanisms for addressing environmental issues are well established, but—as is usual with executive federalism—their effectiveness is limited by the length of time it takes to reach agreement and by the fact that outcomes are frequently diluted and compromised. A fascinating by-product of the difficulty of developing an adequate national policy is what we have been calling competitive federalism, in which the federal, provincial, and territorial governments simply go ahead with their own solutions. This can have the effect of encouraging—or shaming—other jurisdictions into following suit. But competitive, piecemeal policy is no substitute for comprehensive, binding, and consistent policy, perhaps especially in the environmental realm. Canadian federalism makes the latter very difficult to achieve.

Noteworthy as well is the importance of elections, and in particular the timing of elections. The election of the Justin Trudeau government in 2015 clearly brought about a change in Ottawa's position on climate change. So, too, did the election of an NDP government in Alberta earlier that year, which resulted in that province agreeing to impose its own carbon tax, though with the understanding that Ottawa would continue to support the Trans Mountain Pipeline. But then 2017 saw the defeat of a BC Liberal government sympathetic to this arrangement by an NDP minority government supported by the Green Party that was adamantly opposed to the expansion of the pipeline. The election of the Ford government in Ontario in 2018, with its leanings towards market solutions, and the possibility of a change in government in Alberta's forthcoming 2019 election raise further doubts about the longer-term viability of the *Pan-Canadian Framework* and illustrate how electoral cycles, federally and provincially, need to be factored into major intergovernmental agreements.

The climate change file illustrates all these points. It offers many examples of the challenges posed by multi-level governance: from the rules hammered out in the United Nations International Convention on Climate Change and the Kyoto Protocol right down to the policies adopted by the local municipality to cut back on greenhouse gas emissions. In the context of foreign policy, it tests the federal government's authority to enter into and ratify treaties, and underlines its apparent inability to implement such treaties in areas of provincial responsibility. It is often difficult to avoid the conclusion that Canadian governments collectively have been hiding behind their ineffective intergovernmental machinery and blaming each other for their failure to act. Even so, it would be unfair to lay all the blame at the feet of federalism. Climate change has been a deeply contested issue in Canada, as it is in most parts of the world. Very substantial economic, social, and political interests and values are at stake. Even if a broad national consensus on what to do in this area seems to have been achieved at last, there will be many delays and obstacles on the road to implementation of a national climate change plan. In the meantime, governments are responding to their own needs with a mixture of partly coordinated and partly competing efforts.

Questions for Critical Thought

1. Why has strong federal leadership on the environment been so absent?

2. What should each province's contribution be to reducing greenhouse gas emissions?

3. Is it fair to expect the province that produces the most to reduce the most?

4. Both the federal and the provincial governments find power in the constitution to back their positions on the environment. Should there also be entrenched environmental rights?

Notes

1. See the contributions to Fafard and Harrison (2000).

2. We are using the terms "cooperation" and "competition" rather than "collaboration" in this context because the latter term has come to imply involvement of government and non-government actors, whereas the former terms are more inclusive of governments alone.

3. The case citation is *R. v. Crown Zellerbach*, [1988] 1 S.C.R. 401. For comment, see Lucas (1989: 174–7).

4. *R. v. Hydro-Québec*, [1997] 3 S.C.R. 213. For discussion, see Baier (2002: 26–7).
5. Under a cap-and-trade system, government sets an overall limit, or cap, on total emissions, but allows polluters to trade emission credits among themselves.
6. Rationalization is often discussed as an example of New Public Management. See Aucoin (1995) and, specifically on the environment, Doern and Prince (2012); Harrison (2002); and Winfield and MacDonald (2008).
7. For a concise review of various governments' approaches to the environment from 1972 to 1995, see Harrison (1996). For the Chrétien era, see VanNijnatten and MacDonald (2003). On the climate change file in particular, see Simpson et al. (2007).
8. See the discussion of the *Labour Conventions* case in Chapter 8.
9. See the case citations in notes 3 and 4 above.

References

Aucoin, P. 1995. *The New Public Management: Canada in Comparative Perspective*. Montreal: Institute for Research on Public Policy.

Baier, G. 2002. "Judicial Review and Canadian Federalism." In *Canadian Federalism: Performance, Effectiveness, and Legitimacy*, edited by H. Bakvis and G. Skogstad. Toronto: Oxford University Press.

Bakvis, H., and N. Nevitte. 1992. "The Greening of the Canadian Electorate: Environmentalism, Ideology, and Partisanship." In *Canadian Environmental Policy: Ecosystems, Politics, and Process*, edited by R. Boardman. Toronto: Oxford University Press.

Boardman, R., ed. 1992. *Canadian Environmental Policy: Ecosystems, Politics, and Process*. Toronto: Oxford University Press.

Bramley, M. 2009. *Climate Leadership, Economic Prosperity: Final Report on an Economic Study of Greenhouse Gas Targets and Policies for Canada*. Vancouver: Pembina Institute and David Susuki Foundation.

Doern, G.B., and M. Prince. 2012. *Three Bio-Realms: Biotechnology and the Governance of Food, Health and Life in Canada*. Toronto: University of Toronto Press.

Environment Canada. 2007a. "Turning the Corner: An Action Plan to Reduce Greenhouse Gases and Air Pollution." News release. Ottawa: Environment Canada.

———. 2007b. "Prime Minister Stephen Harper Calls for International Consensus on Climate Change." News release, 4 June. Accessed July 2007. http://ecoaction.gc.ca/speeches-discours/20070604- eng.cfm.

Environment and Climate Change Canada. 2011. "Canada's Withdrawal from the Kyoto Accord." Accessed Oct. 2018. http://www.ec.gc.ca/Publications/.

———. 2018. "Greenhouse Gas Emissions by Province and Territory." From *National Inventory Report 1990–2015: Greenhouse Gas Sources and Sinks in Canada*. https://www.ec.gc.ca/indicateurs-indicators/default.asp?lang=en&n=18F3BB9C-1&wbdisable=true.

Fafard, P. 2000. "Groups, Governments and the Environment: Some Evidence from the Harmonization Initiative." In Fafard and Harrison (2000).

——— and K. Harrison, eds. 2000. *Managing the Environmental Union: Intergovernmental Relations and Environmental Policy in Canada*. Kingston, ON: Institute of Intergovernmental Relations, Queen's University.

Government of Canada. 2016a. *Pan-Canadian Framework on Clean Growth and Climate Change*. Ottawa: Government of Canada. https://www.canada.ca/content/dam/themes/environment/documents/weather1/20170125-en.pdf.

———. 2016b. "The Paris Agreement." https://www.canada.ca/en/environment-climate-change/services/climate-change/paris-agreement.html.

Hardy, B. 2012. "Provincial and Territorial Climate Change Policies: Emissions." Paper presented to The National Roundtable on Environment and the Economy, Mar. Kingston, ON.

Harrison, K. 1996. *Passing the Buck: Federalism and Canadian Environmental Policy*.

Vancouver: University of British Columbia Press.

——. 2002. "Federal–Provincial Relations and the Environment: Unilateralism, Collaboration and Rationalization." In *Canadian Environmental Policy: Context and Cases*, 2nd edn, edited by D. VanNijnatten and R. Boardman. Toronto: Oxford University Press.

——. 2006. "Provincial Interdependence: Concepts and Theories." In *Racing to the Bottom? Provincial Interdependence in the Canadian Federation*, edited by K. Harrison. Vancouver: University of British Columbia Press.

——. 2007. "The Road Not Taken: Climate Change Policy in Canada and the United States." *Global Environmental Politics* 7, no. 4: 92–117.

——. 2012. "A Tale of Two Taxes: The Fate of Environmental Tax Reform in Canada." *Review of Policy Research* 29, no. 3.

Lucas, A. 1989. "The New Environmental Law." In *Canada: The State of the Federation, 1989*, edited by R.L. Watts and D.M. Brown. Kingston, ON: Institute of Intergovernmental Relations, Queen's University.

Marshall, D. 2006. *All Over the Map 2006: Status Report on Provincial Climate Change Plans*. Vancouver: David Suzuki Foundation.

——. 2007. *Briefing Note: Picking up the Slack: The Provinces' Potential to Act on Climate Change*. Vancouver: David Suzuki Foundation.

McCarthy, S. 2009. "Canada's Strategy: Promise Now, Implement Later." *Globe and Mail*, 10 Dec.

——. 2017. "Manitoba and Saskatchewan Could Be Cut out of Federal Low-Carbon Program." *Globe and Mail*, 15 June.

Navius Research. 2012. "Provincial and Territorial Climate Change Policies: Economic Modelling." Paper presented to The National Roundtable on Environment and the Economy, Mar. Kingston, ON.

Olewiler, N. 2006. 'Environmental Policy in Canada: Harmonized at the Bottom?' In

Racing to the Bottom? Provincial Interdependence in the Canadian Federation, edited by K. Harrison. Vancouver: University of British Columbia Press.

Olson, M. 1971. *The Logic of Collective Action: Public Goods and the Theory of Groups*. Cambridge, MA: Harvard University Press.

Putnam, R. 1988. "Diplomacy and Domestic Politics: The Logic of Two-Level Games." *International Organization* 42, no. 3: 427–60.

Rabe, B.G. 2004. *Statehouse and Greenhouse: The Merging Politics of American Climate Change Policy*. Washington, DC: Brookings Institution Press.

——. 2007. "Environmental Policy and the Bush Era: The Collision between the Administrative Presidency and State Experimentation." *Publius: The Journal of Federalism* 37 (Summer): 413–31.

Simpson, J., M. Jaccard, and N. Rivers. 2007. *Hot Air: Meeting Canada's Climate Change Challenge*. Toronto: McClelland and Stewart.

Valiante, M. 2002. "Legal Foundations of Canadian Environmental Policy: Underlying Values in a Shifting Landscape." In *Canadian Environmental Policy: Context and Cases*, 2nd edn, edited by D. VanNijnatten and R. Boardman. Toronto: Oxford University Press.

VanNijnatten, D., and D MacDonald. 2003. "Reconciling Energy and Climate Change Policies: How Ottawa Blends." In *How Ottawa Spends: 2003–04*, edited by G.B. Doern. Toronto: Oxford University Press.

Watts, R.L. 2008. *Comparing Federal Systems*, 3rd edn. Kingston, ON: Institute of Intergovernmental Relations, Queen's University.

Winfield, M., and D. Macdonald. 2012. "Federalism and Canadian Climate Change Policy." In *Canadian Federalism: Performance, Effectiveness, and Legitimacy*, 3rd edn, edited by H. Bakvis and G. Skogstad, 241–60. Toronto: Oxford University Press.

Chapter 10

Local Government and Federalism

Week 13

Learning Objectives

- To understand what local government is and what it does.
- To explore the growing importance of cities and the challenge they present to intergovernmental relations.
- To compare provincial–local and federal–local relations.

Much of our discussion so far has concentrated on the relationship between the two orders of government that formed the original Confederation compact: the provinces and what was then called the Dominion, now known as the federal government of Canada. From time to time we also have made reference to the territorial governments. For many purposes, however, the territories can be considered equivalent to the provinces, particularly since the Charlottetown process of 1992, when they became full participants in first ministers' meetings and annual premiers' conferences. Two very different types that we have not yet discussed are the subjects of this chapter and the next: local and Indigenous governments.

"Local government" is a broad category, including not just municipalities of all types—from villages and rural districts to towns, cities, counties, and (sub-provincial) regions—but a wide variety of local and regional agencies responsible for services such as education (school boards), policing (regional police services), health care, and regional planning. Municipal governments in Canada are directly elected. So are many of the special-purpose agencies. The latter cover defined territories that are sometimes the same as the municipalities with which they are associated, and sometimes these agencies encompass a number of municipal units.

Local governments exercise an impressive array of executive and legislative powers, including the powers to levy taxes, regulate businesses, and determine land use for construction and development purposes. It could even be argued that their impact on the daily lives of Canadians is at least as great as that of the provincial governments. Yet local government is not constitutionally recognized as an order of government. Nor do local governments have anything like the legal and financial autonomy that the federal and provincial governments enjoy. In fact, any or all of a local government's powers can be taken away by the provincial government, which has constitutional jurisdiction over it. In this era of increasing "glocalization"—simultaneous emphasis on the global and the local, and the links between them—interdependence, and multi-level governance, it is especially important to look at the place of local government in Canadian federalism.

Cities and Local Government

Canada is a heavily urbanized country, with over 59 per cent of the population living in population centres of 100,000 persons or more.[1] The government closest to those people, the one in charge of the infrastructure of everyday life, is the city government, and local government remains one of the primary sites for participation in democratic self-government. Economically, too, cities play an increasingly important role. In the past the focus was usually on the overall performance of the national economy, and the crucial factor determining a country's success was thought to be the policy of the national government. Today, however, it is recognized that national competitiveness is also a reflection of the success of local economies—which themselves depend on responsive, efficient local governments to provide the public goods and services they need. Finally, a common expression in the social justice and environmental movements—"Think globally, act locally"—points to the recognition that local, decentralized action can often be more effective than standardized policy developed at the centre. In any case, policy interdependence places a greater burden on all governments in a federal system to act more harmoniously, to manage conflict better, and to cooperate more effectively when required.

Yet Canada's federal system consists of two entirely separate intergovernmental relationships that only rarely intersect. The relationship between our federal and provincial orders of government is one of equals, in principle if not always in practice. But there is no such equality in the relationship between the province and the local level. In fact, Canada's provinces are essentially unitary systems. Under the Constitution Act, 1867, local governments are created by provincial governments, they exist at their pleasure, and the provinces have the power to intervene in local affairs as they wish. A province could even decide to dissolve a local government—though to do so would be to risk voters' wrath. In Germany local government is recognized as a third order of government and concurrent legislative powers give the federal government the authority to act in local matters. While not constitutionally entrenched as such, in the United States local government is generally recognized as a third order. In Canada, by contrast, exclusive provincial jurisdiction means that the only way for Ottawa to play an active role in local affairs is by using the federal spending power to allocate funds to individuals and organizations at the local level. Moreover, in Canada the network of intergovernmental relations does not normally extend to local government as it does in some federations. Canada as a whole may be one of the most decentralized federal systems in the world, but within each province the formal centralization of power is almost complete.

Still, local government is a vital part of the democratic system. Local government came to Canada, as it did to the United States, from the English municipal tradition of counties and towns. Under the French regime and in the early days of British rule, local governments were essentially instruments of the colonial authorities (Graham, Phillips, and Maslove, 1998). Local democracy took hold only in the nineteenth century with the gradual emergence of local elected councils. The settled agricultural lands of the eastern colonies (except Newfoundland) were divided into administrative units called counties, within which were rural municipalities and towns. Cities—beginning with Saint John, New Brunswick, which was granted a royal charter in 1785—became corporate entities with a measure of decision-making autonomy, provided their bylaws did not conflict with colonial law. In 1867 the BNA Act (now called the Constitution Act, 1867) assigned municipal government and local special-purpose bodies (school and hospital authorities, etc.) to the jurisdiction of the provincial legislatures, but otherwise made no reference to local government.

To repeat, when it comes to local government, the provinces are essentially unitary states. Provincial legislatures do occasionally reform the functions, fiscal relations, and boundaries of municipalities, though they would rarely abolish them altogether (Corry, 1947). Has the time come to change this arrangement? Questions along these lines have been raised repeatedly since the 1960s, and in recent years a number of specific reforms have been proposed. For example, under the rubric of a "new deal" for cities in the 2000s, it was suggested that provinces could grant cities greater legislative autonomy through "city charters": "separate provincial acts [establishing] asymmetrical and more empowering relationships between cities and provinces" (Good, 2007: 4). One example is the Greater Toronto Area Charter proposed in 2001, under which the greater Toronto area would become a full partner with the federal and provincial governments, would be fully entitled to participate in intergovernmental discussions over matters such as transfer payments, and would assume responsibility for matters including housing, health care, and immigrant and refugee settlement (Good, 2007: 7).[2]

Both the Toronto City Charter proposal and the concept of city charters generally were endorsed and promoted by the Federation of Canadian Municipalities. Interest in these ideas has grown significantly since the 1990s, when provinces such as Ontario, Quebec, and Nova Scotia undertook large-scale municipal amalgamation projects and what were euphemistically called "service exchanges," in which municipalities were relieved of some responsibilities but then assigned new ones. Among the consequences of these changes was the mobilization of citizens as well as civic leaders in protest against them. As Kristin Good notes, "the amalgamation of Toronto . . . created a powerful new political unit that could serve as a platform for local leaders and more effectively challenge provincial power" (Good, 2007: 6). Interest in these ideas continues, especially as the need for infrastructure renewal becomes increasingly urgent.

What Local Government Does, and How

What local governments actually do differs somewhat across the provinces. The core functions are the same everywhere: garbage, roads, water, sewers, land-use planning and control. But in other areas there are significant differences. In British Columbia, for instance, the province is directly responsible for public transit, while in Ontario the province ceased all contributions to the operating budgets of public transit systems in 1998, only to start a long process of restoring some of that funding in 2001 and to re-establish a provincial Crown corporation for inter-city transit. Most recently, all three levels of government in the greater Toronto area have been announcing multi-billion dollar investments in public transit.

In large cities in western and central Canada, policing is provided directly by the municipality, while across much of rural Canada it is provided either by the Royal Canadian Mounted Police or by other police forces under direct contract from the province. In Manitoba and Ontario, municipalities deliver social assistance and other social services directly and pay for a portion of those services. Elsewhere this is a direct provincial responsibility. School boards have greater or lesser autonomy in one province or the other, and are funded to varying degrees by municipal property tax revenues. Overall, though, the breadth and scope of municipal governments and special-purpose local bodies of all kinds (police commissions, planning councils, watershed boards, school boards, health authorities, etc.) are similar. Provincial differences are somewhat greater with respect to rural municipalities. In Ontario, for instance, governance arrangements vary depending on community size and history; and in most cases services for several small lower-tier municipalities are provided by a larger upper-tier entity called a county, region, or district. British Columbia has no counties and instead is divided into roughly 30 regional districts, each of which encompasses multiple city, town, or village governments, while Manitoba has chosen a single-tier approach.

Canada has gone through two waves of municipal mergers, amalgamations, and "rationalization" of functions. The first wave, in the 1950s and 1960s, resulted in the annexation by the core city municipalities of large stretches of suburban and rural land for anticipated development and the creation of new regional, multi-purpose municipalities, such as the Urban Community of Montreal, Metropolitan Toronto, Ottawa–Carleton, and the "unicity" of Winnipeg. The second wave, which hit eastern Canada in the late 1990s, saw the creation of more rationalized, single-tier city structures through amalgamation of the sort imposed on Halifax, Montreal, and Toronto. The second wave proved to be highly contro-versial. In Quebec, for example, the PQ government forced the amalgamation of the Montreal, Quebec City, and Hull–Gatineau urban regions, shortly after it released a White Paper on the topic (Hamel and Rousseau, 2006). The Quebec Liberal Party took advantage of popular discontent with this top-down move in the 2003 election, promising the affected municipalities that, if elected, it would give them the opportunity to retrieve a good part of their lost autonomy through a local referendum process. The Liberals won and kept their word. On the Island of Montreal, former suburban municipalities held de-merger referenda and 15 of them successfully regained much—but not all—of the autonomy they had lost, leaving citizens, as well as the municipalities, uncertain about which government was responsible for what (Hamel and Rousseau, 2006: 155). As a consequence, the provincial government was forced to create a new level of government for the Island of Montreal to coordinate the activities of the two types of local govern-ment. More than a decade later a study used the Montreal case as an example of the pitfalls of de-amalgamation (Miljan and Spicer, 2015).

Amalgamation in Ontario was more permanent but no less controversial. A number of municipalities that stood to be swallowed up resisted, launching cam-paigns for the hearts and minds of local citizens. Among the rationales put forward by the Ontario and Nova Scotia governments to justify amalgamation were direct cost savings from economies of scale and consolidated services and the need to create a single administrative and political platform in order for an urban entity "to be able to compete in the world marketplace" (quoted in Sancton, 2002: 269).[3] At the time, critics questioned the promise of cost savings, noting that the integra-tion of different collective agreements and service standards under conditions of amalgamation generally led to increases in wages and service expectations, thereby pushing up costs. It has indeed been found that costs have gone up rather than down.[4] Of the risk that urban areas would be unable to compete in the global econ-omy without amalgamation, Andrew Sancton, citing findings from the American literature, has argued that

> municipalities are *not* critical to launching explosive cycles of regional growth, but they are crucial in managing growth. . . . If municipalities are able to do well the things that municipalities have traditionally done, their cities will be more competitive over a longer period of time. (Sancton, 2002: 267–8)

Generally, Canadian local government has enjoyed a worldwide reputation for effective and efficient local infrastructure and services. In a period when many American cities were experiencing urban decay and unplanned sprawl, Canadian cities were recognized as being better run and more livable—"cities that work." The quality of both the infrastructure and the services—and, therefore, their value in terms of economic competitiveness—has been put in question in the past 20 years, however, as a result of painful adjustments to the entire Canadian public sector. Local governments are now increasingly preoccupied with economic development issues. Yet few of them have the policy levers they need to renew their economies, let alone rebuild their infrastructure—certainly not without the cooperation, and financial support, of the provincial and federal governments. Justified or not, a perception has arisen in Montreal, Vancouver, and especially Toronto that the provincial governments ignore them politically and are too pre-occupied with the problems of smaller cities, towns, and rural areas to attend to their needs (Berridge, 2002; FCM, 2005; Broadbent, 2008; Sancton, 2012).

Provincial–Local Relations

The basic structure of the relationship between provincial and municipal gov-ernments has changed little in more than 150 years. The legal relationship in all provinces is modelled on legislation adopted by the United Province of Canada in 1849. Under the Baldwin Act (and its successor, the Municipal Act, as well as the corresponding legislation in other provinces), all local government powers were specifically delegated. The legislation typically assigns more power and respons-ibility for services and infrastructure to the larger cities (Graham et al., 1998), but it is not a general grant of power and it constrains municipalities as much as it empowers them in legislative and fiscal terms.

In recent years four provinces—Alberta, British Columbia, Newfoundland and Labrador, and Ontario—have reformed their basic legal relationship with local governments, creating more room for local decision-making. Alberta's Municipal Government Act of 1994 provided the most comprehensive reform (Graham et al., 1998; FCM, 2001): it defined local functions more broadly; granted municipalities powers as "natural persons" (i.e., enjoying full status under corporate law); stream-lined the number of additional statutes that govern local government; provided for inter-municipal dispute resolution; permitted municipalities to carry a deficit, within defined limits; allowed for some expanded tax room in areas such as enter-tainment, retail sales, and gasoline taxes; and in general restricted provincial inter-vention to matters of declared "provincial interest." Similarly in British Columbia, a provincial law called the Community Charter, passed in 2003, established a set of principles for municipal–provincial relations, an accountability regime, and a number of broadly defined powers, including provisions for concurrency. Signifi-cantly, provisions in the BC Charter require extensive public consultation and local referenda in the event of any proposed amalgamation or merger of munici-palities. It also provides for a dispute settlement mechanism should conflicts arise between municipalities or between municipalities and the provincial government. BC and Alberta are the only two provinces where municipal–provincial relations are referred to as "intergovernmental."

Recent legislation in Newfoundland and Labrador goes a step further, recognizing each of the province's eight cities as an autonomous order of government. It provides a general grant of power covering 15 spheres, subject only to general provincial standards covering environment, protection of persons and property, and building codes, and undertakes not to amend the legislation without consulting the city or cities affected.

It may be only a matter of time before most of the other Canadian provinces adopt legislation similar to that described above. In the meantime, day-to-day relations between provincial and local governments are defined largely by the political environment in the province and by the provincial fiscal and expenditure decision-making process. Local government powers, even where they are expanding, remain limited and must be exercised with sensitivity to the overall provincial regulatory stance, whether it is pro-development, pro-environment, devoted to comprehensive planning, or open to local flexibility and manipulation. By the same token, local expenditures and revenue patterns are highly dependent on provincially determined policy, including transfer payments.

Apart from the formal legislated relations between provinces and municipalities, direct political relations are also important. Every province has a federation or association of municipalities. These bodies provide formal avenues for representation and lobbying, principally to the Department of Municipal Affairs and its minister, but often also to the premier, Finance minister, or cabinet as a whole. The Federation of Canadian Municipalities plays a similar role at the federal level. Both the federal and the provincial organizations play important roles in providing policy advice and technical support to individual municipalities, especially the smaller ones.

Less structured political connections are formed through the direct relationships that develop between individual mayors or councils and provincial ministers and officials. All the larger cities rely as much or more on their own lobbying efforts as they do on their membership in provincial associations. Partisan connections are also important for some local politicians, even though at the local level political parties are weak or non-existent. Political coalitions thrive in some cities (e.g., Montreal's Civic Party), but in most places there is no party structure at all, let alone any formal linkage with federal or provincial parties. For the most part, then, local politicians and bureaucrats are free to pursue non-partisan relations with all governments and parties. On the other hand, the virtual absence of political mobilization at the municipal level may mean that local and urban issues are insufficiently debated or considered in a systematic way in the political community at large (for discussion, see Graham et al., 1998).

Finances are central to the provincial–local relationship. Local government finances in relation to overall public financial arrangements in Canada are noteworthy. In 2017, Canadian expenditures on local government (broadly defined) totalled 6.5 per cent of GDP and were almost half as large as total provincial spending.

The per capita spending varied enormously, from $320 in Prince Edward Island to $1,650 in Ontario. These differences reflect varying urban size, service costs, and the fact that municipalities deliver a narrower range of services in some provinces, especially the Atlantic provinces (Kitchen, 2000). What local government spends its money on changes only marginally from year to year: the three largest categories are transportation, protection of persons and property, and environment. Two important trends in the past two decades have been an overall reduction in debt charges and increased spending on social services. In the latter case, however, the increase is due not to any absolute growth in spending on social services but rather to the shifting of some responsibilities from the province to the local level.

On the revenue side, local government increasingly relies on "own-source" revenues (as opposed to transfer payments from the province), particularly for the general government services provided by municipalities. Own-source municipal revenues increased from 77.1 per cent of total municipal revenues in 1988 to 84.6 per cent in 1998 and 82.8 per cent in 2005; these increases were reflected in significant increases in property taxes (both rates and yields) and user fees. Transfer payments to municipal governments accounted for only 15.4 per cent of their revenues in 1998, principally in the form of conditional grants from the provincial governments (although there is also a trend to "block" grants with fewer conditions attached). However, transfer payments to the local government sector as a whole—i.e., municipalities and other local governments combined—take up a larger share of total revenues, at 38.8 per cent, and underscore the increasing dependence on provincial transfers of school boards in particular.[5]

Fiscal federalism economists tend to advocate that municipalities and other local governments will enjoy greater fiscal health if they secure more own-source revenue rather than rely on transfers from other governments.[6] Two recent developments in this direction have been, first, the general trend for increased revenue from user fees, and second, the agreements to enable municipalities to share in the revenues from the GST and the federal gasoline excise tax. In keeping with the trend to greater reliance on own-source revenues, municipal governments have also seen modest increases in their ability to levy taxes. Examples of municipal taxes (some in place for many years now) include hotel occupancy taxes (Vancouver), business occupancy taxes (Winnipeg), and gasoline and other fuel taxes (Vancouver, Victoria, Montreal, and Calgary). In addition, Manitoba practises a form of revenue-sharing, transferring a fixed share of provincial personal income tax (2 percentage points) and corporate income tax (1 percentage point) to municipalities in the form of unconditional grants (FCM, 2001).

Two significant long-term funding arrangements from the federal government have been put in place. First, in 2004 Ottawa began rebating to municipalities all of the funds the latter paid on the GST for purchases of goods and services, at an estimated cost of $7 billion over 10 years. Second, in 2005 the federal government began sharing with the municipalities, through agreement with the provinces, a portion of the federal excise tax on gasoline (five cents per litre, or one-half of the federal tax). Money from this Gas Tax Fund is paid to municipalities through the provinces on a per capita basis, and is to be used for environmentally sustainable infrastructure.

Throughout the 1990s the trend in provincial–municipal finance across Canada had been towards a clearer allocation of expenditure responsibilities in line with local revenue bases, with a reduced reliance on provincial transfers. To manage the increased responsibilities resulting from what they see as provincial "offloading," local governments have been—and still are—forced to reduce costs (either by improving delivery efficiency or by cutting service levels), and in some cases to raise local property tax rates. Where the fiscal problems were most severe, in eastern Canada, they contributed to the wave of municipal mergers set in motion by provincial governments convinced that "rationalization" would lead to long-term cost savings. Still, chronic fiscal problems at the local level in Canada have in turn led to important policy trends. First is the trend towards public–private partnerships as a means of delivering services both more economically and more effectively (Graham et al., 1998). Second is a preoccupation with expanding the local tax base through a variety of economic development efforts. Third is a tendency to neglect longer-term investment and maintenance in infrastructure, both provincial and local, until problems—economic, social, environmental—become critical. The important contributions from the federal government aside, the overall fiscal situation of municipal government has not changed. Municipalities remain heavily dependent on property taxes. It remains to be seen whether a new age of carbon taxes and other environment-oriented levies is about to begin; if it does, these policy instruments may require a rethinking of the fiscal tools at the disposal of the city governments in particular.

The Federal Role

By now it should be clear that the primary relationship for local governments is with the provincial governments that have created them and often dominate them in fiscal and regulatory terms. Yet local governments welcome a larger role for the federal government, both as a counterbalance to provincial dominance and to provide a national focus for urban and local government issues with more than local impact. Over the years the question has been whether the federal government has sufficient political interest to sustain such a policy focus. Over the years, Ottawa has at times shown strong interest in the urban agenda, only to backtrack when the provinces have resisted. The most notable example was the short-lived Ministry of State for Urban Affairs (MSUA), which Ottawa created in 1971 and disbanded in 1978 in the face of provincial opposition and criticism from federal line departments that resented the MSUA's efforts to persuade them to take a more active interest in urban matters. As explained below, in recent years the intensity of federal-local relations has varied, according to the party in office in Ottawa.

The constitutional division of powers ensures that the federal government has no direct influence on local government. But federal operations such as airports, railways, and defence establishments have a real effect on local communities. So do federal spending programs in areas such as health, post-secondary education, support for Indigenous people in urban areas, job training, housing, and community, regional, and industrial development. Yet in most cases the federal government treads softly where municipal and other local government authorities are involved, and it has more than once been warned off by provincial governments. Quebec even has special legislation that prevents municipalities from accepting money directly from the federal government.

Nonetheless, members of the federal Parliament take a keen interest in local issues. Individual MPs are often frustrated by the constitutional constraints on their activity with respect to their constituencies, and in a competitive political environment they may seek to outflank provincial governments (especially those of different political ideology) in appealing directly to voters on matters of local interest. For MPs in particular, the political interest in local issues—urban or rural—is all about their own democratic legitimacy and relevance. MPs gain visibility and credit in their constituencies when they are able to persuade the federal government to invest in local infrastructure projects, especially when the MPs themselves announce and help to shape the program.

Furthermore, the federal government has historically played an important role in local and urban issues.[7] With strong direct advocacy from Canadian municipalities during the Great Depression, Ottawa provided direct funding to local governments for public works. And after the Second World War it provided support for local initiatives such as agricultural and regional development, sewage treatment works, and make-work projects. The most important and sustained effort, extending from the 1940s to the late 1970s, was the Central Mortgage and Housing Corporation (CMHC), which played a crucial role in developing housing standards, funding public housing, and promoting community planning (Stoney and Graham, 2008). Many of these programs were delivered through intergovernmental agreements with the provinces, allowing funds to pass through to local authorities. In addition, from 1971 to 1978 the Ministry of State for Urban Affairs had a mandate to coordinate various federal economic and social programs important to urban development.

In general, Canadian federal governments have been less closely connected to local governments since the 1970s. Since 1980 federal involvement in local government programs has declined in terms of both money and intensity. Its direct involvement is now confined to a few significant issues and programs: economic development through the federal regional agencies, as targeted to specific urban areas, often in partnership with provincial/territorial and local governments; the national tri-level infrastructure programs; funding for certain social housing programs (but much reduced from the more general federal housing programs of the past); an increasing federal role in contributing funds to public transit projects; and the recent GST rebate and Gas Tax Fund (Sancton, 2012; Bradford and Wolfe, 2012; Hilton and Stoney, 2009).

Paul Martin's brief term as prime minister, from December 2003 to February 2006, represented the high-water mark in terms of recent federal interest and involvement in urban and local affairs (Sancton, 2008: 321–5). Martin himself shared the growing intellectual interest in what Neil Bradford (2004) has called the "new localism." Emphasizing the importance of local, place-specific factors in both economic prosperity and social health, advocates of the new localism call for collaborative governance (by the public and private sectors) at the local level, and argue that upper-level governments should enable local solutions, not impose them. They also stress the need to scale down or even redesign regional or province-wide social policies with neighbourhood dynamics in mind. The policy focus on urban dynamics drew attention to the inadequacy of infrastructure investment, the need to address urban-specific social issues such as immigrant settlement, and the extent to which the fiscal system has starved city governments. Politically, however, the Martin government could not ignore rural and small-town municipalities. Thus, it was always careful to present its policy agenda as one for both cities *and* other communities. Its most significant contributions were a renewed commitment to the infrastructure program (a further $7 billion in 2004) and the new fiscal arrangements noted above, such as the Gas Tax Fund. All of these arrangements benefit small municipalities as much as they do the large cities.

As outlined elsewhere in this book, the Harper government's approach to federalism can be summarized as respectful of traditional jurisdictional divisions ("classical federalism"); decentralist in social policy matters; and avoiding entanglement with provincial/territorial and local government in program implementation. In so doing, however, one must note the essentially pragmatic application of their ideological approach, thus creating two main exceptions to the general rule. First was the Harper government's early decisions to extend and then to make permanent the GST rebate and the gas tax transfer begun by the Martin government. This initiative may be seen as a principled extension of the broader efforts to fix the vertical fiscal imbalance (see Chapter 6), i.e., to redistribute federal resources to local governments, thereby allowing them to meet their jurisdictional responsibilities (Steinberg, 2013: 226–7). Second was a set of federal–local interventions linked to major national goals such as economic management and competitiveness. These included: the continued contribution to social housing—$4.4 billion over 10 years, 2009–19; the $5 billion in federal funds to leverage a total of $13 billion spending on public transit, in partnership with provincial and local governments; and, of course, the continuation of the Chrétien-Martin policy of a tri-level national infrastructure program, in which the federal government plays an active role in project selection as well as funding.

The latter program was an especially important policy instrument to combat the financial crisis of 2008–9.

The Harper government's legacy was also, however, one of retrenchment from tripartite, comprehensive direct spending on other urban issues. A notable case is the federal government's decision to allow the expiry of a set of Urban Development Agreements in place for several western Canadian cities. These agreements tackled complex sets of economic and social issues in core city populations. In the federal view these agreements did not match its priorities for a more disengaged relationship with provinces and local government, or its search for more direct accountability. Nor did they match with the government's general set of spending priorities (Doberstein, 2011).

Another subtle shift in emphasis of the federal approach under the Conservatives from 2006 to 2015 reflected the fact that their base of electoral support had been suburban rather than urban (Sancton, 2008). For example, the Conservatives were more willing than the Liberals were to allow federal funds to be spent on roads—a more pressing issue for suburban and rural voters than for city dwellers, but notably not at the expense of their substantial multi-year contribution to public transit. The Harper government also pursued its (sub)urban agenda on a more political level, approaching directly the mayors of big cities, for example, rather than working through bureaucratic channels. Under the previous Liberal government a fairly close network of links and interactions had developed between city bureaucrats and their colleagues in federal departments such as Transport Canada, Infrastructure Canada, and Human Resources and Development Canada, as well as through the urban policy group established in 2002 in the Privy Council Office. According to Loleen Berdahl (2006), the federal government's main regional development agency in the West, Western Economic Diversification, was particularly important as a point of contact for municipal officials under the Chrétien and Martin governments. The Harper government, with its penchant for centralizing policy initiatives, put more emphasis on direct contact at the political level within municipalities, particularly in areas such as Vancouver and the Lower Mainland of BC, possibly because urban and suburban areas in Ontario and BC offered attractive opportunities to make electoral gains.

Justin Trudeau's Liberal government has taken a somewhat different approach. During their successful 2015 election campaign, the Liberals made significant funding promises to cities, focusing more on urban issues than did the Conservatives. They promised more funding for affordable housing, facilities for seniors, and cultural and recreational facilities, and further pledged that affordable child-care capacity would be expanded to cover all families in need of the service. Altogether, the Liberals promised $20 billion in extra funding for Canada's social infrastructure.

In government, the Liberals have followed through on some of their plans to invest in urban infrastructure. For example, in March 2017 the federal government announced an additional $1.8 billion in funding for the GO Transit Regional Express Rail being built to connect Toronto with surrounding communities such as Etobicoke, Hamilton, and Oshawa. This project is designed to allow workers to commute more easily and to prevent overcrowding of roads. In the 2017 budget, the federal government also allocated $11.2 billion over 11 years for affordable housing. About 40 per cent of this funding will be used to create a new National Housing Fund, which will lend money to help finance new rental housing construction, while also providing extra funding to social housing providers. The funds provided by the National Housing Fund are slated to ramp up slowly, from $141 million in the 2018–19 fiscal year to $707 million in 2024–5.

One of the most important links between the federal government and municipalities is the Federation of Canadian Municipalities (FCM). Although it describes itself as a lobby group working on behalf of more than 3,700 municipalities, in many ways this organization serves as a bridge between municipalities and the federal government. With its headquarters in Ottawa and a staff of more than 120, it actually has a much more substantial presence than the Council of the Federation. It also has a solid connection with the federal government, largely because it manages and delivers a good deal of international development work for the latter, much of it involving urban development and local government issues. In fact, the FCM is Canada's primary source of expertise in this field. Even though it is not clear exactly how this international development expertise helps the FCM in promoting its domestic agenda, the organization has been remarkably successful in highlighting the infrastructure needs of Canadian municipalities. In 2006, for example, when the ongoing debate on the fiscal imbalance was at its peak, the FCM released its own statement on the issue in a document entitled *Building Prosperity from the Ground Up: Restoring Municipal Fiscal Balance* (FCM, 2006), which stressed the fact that inadequate funding was starving the municipalities more than it was the provinces. It seems likely that the FCM's efforts in Ottawa had something to do with the federal government's increased commitment to infrastructure programs and the launch of the Gas Tax Fund.

According to Stevenson and Gilbert (2005: 541), the FCM's success can be credited to effective leadership and to a strategy of avoiding the "high politics" of constitutional issues—an area that the FCM emphasized in the 1970s and 1980s—in favour of the "low politics" of practical issues important to citizens, such as improved infrastructure. The Big Cities Mayors Caucus within the FCM has been particularly effective in helping the organization cater to its diverse members and manage tensions between them. As tri-level relations among municipalities, provinces, and the federal government have become more of a reality, the FCM can take a good portion of the credit; it has also become an integral part of this tri-cornered relationship.

Assessing the Intergovernmental System: Is There a Need for Tri-level Relations?

Over the past 20 years in Canada, intergovernmental issues related to municipalities can be classified in three groups. Some have been primarily *local*: the widespread movement to regional coordinating bodies and multi-purpose bodies; the increasing recourse to public–private partnerships; and, especially in eastern Canada, boundary and governance issues in the context of municipal amalgamation. Others have been primarily *provincial–local*. These include reductions in provincial transfer payments and the offloading of program responsibilities; and the movement in some provinces to reform municipal legislation to reduce the regulatory burden, increase fiscal flexibility, and provide for a broader definition of municipal spheres of jurisdiction. Finally, some issues have been truly tri-level: *federal–provincial–local*. Three issues in particular are worth noting: the renewal of local infrastructure through cooperative cost-shared, tri-level agreements such as the Building Canada program; the federal government's involvement in housing programs, most recently affordable housing under the Trudeau government; the resettlement of Syrian refugees; and the federal government's responsibility for Indigenous peoples, which—as we shall see in the next chapter—involves it in complex Indigenous–municipal–provincial negotiations.

The intergovernmental system through which the above issues and others are debated, managed, and resolved (or not) is divided into two subsystems that only rarely intersect. One is the federal–provincial system, which thrives on informality and a competitive ethos that encourages each government to pursue its own interests. This subsystem offers the governments concerned a broad range of choice as to when, how, and under what conditions they will pursue cooperative solutions.

The other subsystem is the provincial–local one. In this system the municipalities have less formal status than even the smallest province in the first subsystem, because their position is not entrenched in the federal constitution. The provinces and territories are the units that together make up the federation, but municipalities have no such constituent role in relation to the provinces. In principle, then, a province might feel no more obliged to negotiate with its municipalities than it would with any given interest group. If formal processes for joint decision-making are inadequate in the federal–provincial system, they are non-existent in the provincial–local one. This is not to say, however, that negotiations do not take place: they do, especially when major reforms are proposed. And, as we have noted, some provinces have moved to grant local governments more autonomy. In the meantime, the fact that Ontario, Nova Scotia, and Quebec were able to force municipalities to amalgamate illustrates the fundamental inequality of the relationship. The competitive ethos we have described in the context of federal–provincial and interprovincial relations is alive and well in inter-municipal relations, too. Cooperation through joint bodies, agreements, and various communication mechanisms does resolve many overlapping issues. Unlike the federal government in its relations with the provinces, however, most provincial governments have both the legal power and the political will to impose "take-it-or leave-it" cooperation on municipalities when inter-municipal devices fail.

We have noted that the federal–provincial and provincial–municipal rarely intersect. If all three levels of government are to be involved, the negotiations typically take place in two stages—first, federal–provincial; then, provincial–municipal. Even in the Canada Infrastructure Program, the nature and extent of municipal involvement in the identification and management of projects varied by province. Each provincial government essentially determined the municipal role in their province (Andrew and Morrison, 1995). The chief exceptions to this pattern have come in specific urban settings involving one province only, such as the Winnipeg Core Initiative or the Halifax gateway transportation planning initiative (Bakvis, 1991; Graham et al., 1998). These tri-level arrangements often use innovative mechanisms such as jointly owned and controlled Crown corporations to manage the projects in question.

Despite the grand schemes of some in the municipal sector, especially those in the big-city governments, major reform in this area seems unlikely. To integrate federal–provincial with provincial–municipal relations in a sort of super tri-level relationship is likely more than the system could bear. A formal and comprehensive tri-level relationship could be unwieldy at best and might only magnify the existing weaknesses of executive federalism, such as its dependence on consensus decision-making.

Regional diversity is another reason for avoiding multilateral tri-level relations: local problems need local solutions tailored to fit the regional context. On the other hand, limiting the federal role in local matters is not conducive to the national definition and mobilization of consent for broader public policy objectives. For Ottawa to deal with individual cities on a one-by-one basis could lead to regional antagonisms and injustices.

In conclusion, the need for Canadian governments to pursue tri-level coordination is likely to increase. A fully integrated tri-level system will not be required, but our governments will have to find new ways to achieve that coordination. Plenty of room exists for Ottawa to develop a renewed federal vision on urban issues, if it is prepared to work sensitively with the provinces and flexibly in each urban area with the relevant local governments.

Summary

Constitutionally, municipalities are creatures of the provinces. Yet many analysts have argued that multi-level governance—from global to local, as well as at every level in between—is where the future lies. Is there an argument to be made that, regardless of their legal status, local governments have a role to play in the inter-governmental scheme of things?

Certainly there have been tri-level arrangements in which local governments have collaborated with the provincial and federal orders of government on joint initiatives or on arrangements that cross international boundaries. However, these projects have tended to be one-of-a-kind, involving a single province or cross-border relationship, and focusing on a particular place or issue, such as Vancouver's Downtown Eastside or border security between BC and Washington State. The provinces usually determine the extent to which municipalities participate, and the centralized, top-down nature of our Westminster parliamentary system means that they tend to keep municipalities on a relatively short leash. So far, then, it is not possible to say that local governments have proven their ability to function as equals with the senior orders of government.

This is not to say that the municipal governments should not be given more autonomy, however, including autonomy in raising revenues. Large urban conglomerates are essential for fostering national well-being and economic growth, and municipal governments can play an important role in creating the conditions that will favour such growth. Those conditions include not only good-quality infrastructure but also a general policy climate made up of less tangible factors related to culture and diversity. It remains with the provinces, however, to decide whether to give municipalities more room for manoeuvre—as BC, Alberta, and Newfoundland and Labrador have done. Constitutionally, the federal government can exercise only indirect influence; it is not in a position either to grant additional tax sources to cities or to change their constitutional status unilaterally. In examining the argument that municipalities should be seen as major players in the intergovernmental game, we noted the basic logistical problem of trying to integrate federal–provincial with provincial–municipal relations into a sort of super tri-level relationship. Such a move is likely more than the system can bear, we argue. On the other hand, organizations such as the Federation of Canadian Municipalities have been effective in giving voice to municipalities on critical issues such as the need for rebuilding infrastructure and linking municipalities to Ottawa. And one consequence of the spate of municipal amalgamations—unintended, to be sure—was the development of larger platforms for the political leaders of Canada's largest cities. Use of those platforms in mobilizing public opinion can be seen as another element in the dynamic interplay among municipalities, provinces, and the federal government.

Finally, the rush of federal–provincial–municipal programs introduced late in the Chrétien period and pushed to the forefront during Paul Martin's brief tenure as prime minister has left a legacy in the form of a few important ongoing initiatives. The allocation of funding from Ottawa to the municipalities under the Municipal Rural Infrastructure Fund and the Gas Tax Fund is managed by oversight committees, one for each province. In the case of the Gas Tax Fund, the oversight committees are currently composed of the federal minister of Infrastructure and Communities and his counterpart at the provincial level, the senior officials at the federal and provincial level, and, critically, the provincial municipal association in each province. According to Michael Buda (2008: 37), these committees "provided provincial and territorial municipal associations with, in most cases, their first entry into federal–provincial relations, . . . [allowing] them to build capacity and a network in this area." Although the Conservative government was more cautious than its Liberal predecessors and successor in pursuing the urban and communities agenda, it nonetheless continued to work with the oversight committees in implementing and managing the Gas Tax Fund. Those committees may well serve a template for federal–provincial–municipal activities and interactions in the future.

Questions for Critical Thought

1. Should local government be enshrined in the constitution as a protected and independent third order of government?

2. What are the most pressing multi-level issues involving *all* levels of government in Canada?

3. Should some of our biggest cities, such as Toronto, Montreal, and Vancouver, have a seat at the national intergovernmental tables?

4. Is it important that MPs in the federal Parliament have a direct role in local affairs in their constituencies?

Notes

1. See http://www.statcan.gc.ca/eng/subjects/standard/sgc/notice/sgc-06 (accessed 2 Sept. 2015).

2. For a more general set of proposals for greater city autonomy within the federal system, see Broadbent (2008).

3. The governments held these views despite skepticism in academic and other circles about the claim that amalgamation saves costs. See Downing and Williams (1998); Lightbody (1998); Vojnovic (1998); Sancton (2002).

4. For example, James McDavid (2002: 538), in his study of police services following amalgamation in the new Halifax Regional Municipality, found that the process resulted in "higher costs (in real dollar terms), lower number of sworn officers, lower service levels, no real change in crime rates, and higher workloads for sworn officers." For further views, see the sources listed in note 3.

5. See McMillan (2006).

6. See, for example, Bird (1986); Kitchen and Slack (2003).

7. For a useful study on federal–local mechanisms of cooperation, see Stoney and Graham (2008). This study is part of a comprehensive research program undertaken in 2006–13 and led by Robert A. Young on public policy in Canadian municipalities, focusing in part on the federal role (Young, 2013).

References

Andrew, C., and J. Morrison. 1995. "Canada Infrastructure Works: Between Picks and Shovels and the Information Highway." In *How Ottawa Spends 1995–96: Mid-Life Crises*, edited by S.D. Phillips. Ottawa: Carleton University Press.

Bakvis, H. 1991. *Regional Ministers: Power and Influence in the Canadian Cabinet*. Toronto: University of Toronto Press.

Berdahl, L. 2006. *Political Identities in Western Canada*. Calgary: Canada West Foundation.

Berridge, J. 2002. "Cities in the New Canada." Toronto: TD Forum on Canada's Standard of Living.

Bird, R.M. 1986. *Federal Finance in Comparative Perspective*. Toronto: Canadian Tax Foundation.

Bradford, N. 2004. "How Ottawa Spends: Managing the Minority." In *How Ottawa Spends: Managing the Minority*, edited by G.B. Doern. Montreal and Kingston: McGill-Queen's University Press.

——— and D. Wolfe. 2012. "Playing against Type? Regional Economic Development Policy in the Harper Era?" In *How Ottawa Spends, 2012–13: The Harper Majority, Budget Cuts and the New Opposition*, edited by B. Doern and C. Stoney, 71–88. Montreal and Kingston: McGill-Queen's University Press.

Broadbent, A. 2008. *Urban Nation: Why We Need to Give Power Back to the Cities to Keep Canada Strong*. Toronto: HarperCollins.

Buda, M. 2008. "Understanding the New Federal–Municipal Landscape: Mapping and Optimizing the Role of the Federation of Canadian Municipalities in Canada's Emerging Multi-level Governance Environment." Master's Project, School of Public Administration, University of Victoria.

Corry, J.A. 1947. *Democratic Government and Politics*. Toronto: University of Toronto Press.

Doberstein, Carey, 2011. "Institutional Creation and Death: Urban Development Agreements in Canada." *Journal of Urban Affairs* 33, no. 5: 529–48.

Downing, T.J., and R.J. Williams. 1998. "Provincial Agendas, Local Responses: The 'Common Sense' Restructuring of Ontario's Municipal Governments." *Canadian Public Administration* 41, no. 2: 210–38.

Federation of Canadian Municipalities (FCM). 2001. *Early Warning: Will Canadian Cities Compete? A Comparative Overview of Municipal Government in Canada, the United States and Europe*. Ottawa: FCM.

———. 2005. *Cities: Partners in National Prosperity*. Ottawa: FCM, Big Cities Mayors Caucus.

———. 2006. *Building Prosperity from the Ground Up: Restoring Municipal Fiscal Balance*. Ottawa: FCM.

Good, K. 2007. "Urban Regime-Building as a Strategy of Intergovernmental Reform: The Case of Toronto's Role in Immigrant Settlement." Paper presented at the Canadian Political Science Annual Meeting, Saskatoon.

Graham, K., S. Phillips, and A. Maslove. 1998. *Urban Governance in Canada*. Toronto: Harcourt.

Hamel, P., and J. Rousseau. 2006. "Revisiting Municipal Reforms in Quebec and the New Responsibilities of Local Actors in a Globalizing World." In *Canada: The State of the Federation, 2004: Municipal–Federal–Provincial Relations in Canada*, edited by R. Young and C. Leuprecht. Kingston, ON: Institute of Intergovernmental Relations, Queen's University.

Hilton, R., and C. Stoney. 2009. "Federal Gas Tax Transfers: Politics and Perverse Policy." In *How Ottawa Spends 2009–2010: Economic Upheaval and Political Dysfunction*, edited by A. Maslove, 175–93. Montreal and Kingston: McGill-Queen's University Press.

Kitchen, H. 2000. "Provinces, Municipalities, Universities, Schools and Hospitals: Recent Trends and Funding Issues." In *Canada: The State of the Federation 1999–2000: Toward a New Mission Statement for Canadian Fiscal Federalism*, edited by H. Lazar. Kingston, ON: Institute of Intergovernmental Relations, Queen's University.

——— and E. Slack. 2016. *New Tax Sources for Canada's Largest Cities: What Are the Options?* Toronto: Institute on Municipal Finance and Governance.

Lightbody, J. 1998. "Council Multiplicity and the Cost of Governance in Canadian Metropolitan Areas." *Canadian Journal of Urban Research* 7, no. 1: 27–46.

McDavid, J.C. 2002. "The Impacts of Amalgamation on Police Services in the Halifax Regional Municipality." *Canadian Public Administration* 45, no. 4: 538–65.

McMillan, M.L. 2006. "Municipal Relations with the Federal and Provincial Governments: A Fiscal Perspective." In *Canada: The State of the Federation, 2004: Municipal–Federal–Provincial Relations in Canada*, edited by R. Young and C. Leuprecht. Kingston, ON: Institute of Intergovernmental Relations, Queen's University.

Miljan, L., and Z. Spicer. 2015. *De-amalgamation in Canada: Breaking Up Is Hard to Do.* Vancouver: Fraser Institute.

Sancton, A. 2002. "Municipalities, Cities and Globalization: Implications for Canadian Federalism." In *Canadian Federalism: Performance, Effectiveness, and Legitimacy*, edited by H. Bakvis and G. Skogstad, 261–77. Toronto: Oxford University Press.

——. 2008. "The Urban Agenda." In *Canadian Federalism: Performance, Effectiveness, and Legitimacy*, 2nd edn, edited by H. Bakvis and G. Skogstad, 314–33. Toronto: Oxford University Press.

——. 2012. "The Urban Agenda." In *Canadian Federalism: Performance, Effectiveness, and Legitimacy*, 3rd edn, edited by H. Bakvis and G. Skogstad, 302–19. Toronto: Oxford University Press.

Steinberg, J. 2013 "The Policies and Politics of Federal Public Transit Infrastructure Spending." In *How Ottawa Spends 2013–14. The Harper Government: Mid-term Blues and Long-term Plans*, edited by C. Stoney and B. Doern, 223–35. Montreal and Kingston: McGill-Queen's University Press.

Stevenson, D., and R. Gilbert. 2005. "Coping with Canadian Federalism: The Case of the Federation of Canadian Municipalities." *Canadian Public Administration* 48, no. 4: 528–51.

Stoney, C., and K. Graham. 2008. "Creatures of the Provinces? The Impact of the Federal Government on Municipalities and Urban Affairs." Paper presented at the Canadian Political Science Association Annual Meeting, Vancouver.

Vojnovic, I. 1998. "Municipal Consolidation in the 1990s: An Analysis of British Columbia, New Brunswick and Nova Scotia." *Canadian Public Administration* 41, no. 2: 239–83.

Young, R.A. 2013. "Multilevel Governance and Public Policy in Canadian Municipalities: Reflections on Research Results." Paper presented to the Canadian Political Science Association Annual Meeting, 6 June, Victoria, B.C.

Chapter 11

Indigenous Peoples and Federalism

Week 14

Learning Objectives

- To examine the role played by Indigenous peoples and their governments in the Canadian federal system.
- To understand how the Indigenous nationalism movement, with its emphasis on Indigenous rights, Aboriginal title, and self-determination, is transforming Canadian politics and government.
- To explore the differing perspectives on emerging models of Indigenous governance and the challenge for intergovernmental relations.

Indigenous governance is a challenging topic for a book on Canadian federalism. The subject matter is complex and perceptions of the issues are fundamentally contested among political actors and scholars alike. Yet Indigenous governments, policy, and politics are increasingly salient issues for Canadians. Here we confine ourselves to an overview of the most significant trends affecting the federal system as a whole, the emerging and diverse characteristics of Indigenous government, and the nature of multi-level governance involving Indigenous peoples.

Since the early 1970s, Indigenous nationalism has joined Quebec nationalism as a significant challenge to the Canadian federation. The existence in Canada of political communities with separate or coexisting national identities has led many Canadians to think of their country as not merely a bilingual, multicultural union of provinces, but as a special kind of entity that Kymlicka (2003) calls "multi-national."[1] Indeed, some Indigenous people reject Canadian sovereignty and seek something amounting to independent status. Many Indigenous nations and communities claim collective ownership over land and other natural resources as an unsurrendered Aboriginal right, challenging the control and ownership of the Canadian state, both federal and provincial. Many Indigenous organizations have condemned the failure of Canadian political institutions to provide for Indigenous representation within them. Meanwhile, Indigenous people continue to face racism—some would say neo-colonialism—in the broader Canadian society.

In response to these challenges many different solutions have been proposed. These include restoration of Indigenous nations as sovereign states, recognition of "Aboriginal government" as a third order within the federation, development of what has been called treaty federalism or confederalism, an "Aboriginal house of Parliament," separate "Aboriginal" electoral districts, and a Royal Proclamation on Reconciliation. Meanwhile, the structures and practices of contemporary Canadian federalism present some significant obstacles to Indigenous aspirations of self-determination and decolonization.

Indigenous peoples did not take part in the negotiation of the Confederation deal and were not consulted on its terms. Rather, the Canadian state took over the role of the British Crown without any explicit Indigenous consent, including the fiduciary obligations towards Indigenous peoples first set out in the Royal Proclamation of 1763 (RCAP, 1992: 10–19; Russell, 2017). The only reference to Indigenous matters in the entire Constitution Act, 1867 came in section 91(24), which awarded jurisdiction over "Indians, and lands reserved for Indians" to the federal Parliament.[2] Accordingly, Ottawa continued the effort, begun under the government of the United Province of Canada (1840–67), to settle the Indigenous population on reserves under the terms of the Indian Lands Act of 1860 and its successor statutes.

A further obstacle to Indigenous aspirations is the fact that the Constitution Act, 1867 distributed all law-making powers between the two orders of government, federal and provincial. Thus, part of the problem today is to create a space for Indigenous governments and governance within the dual monopoly of power established by the federal constitution.

Just as the provincial legislatures continue to hold authority over the local governments under their constitutional jurisdiction, so the federal Parliament continues to have jurisdiction over the band governments established under the Indian Act of 1876. For many years the band-and-council governance of reserves was almost completely hollow; administrators with the Department of Indian Affairs made all the key decisions. In the 1960s, Indian Affairs withdrew from day-to-day administration on reserves and encouraged bands to assume local management functions, but the strictures of the Indian Act, along with the broader bureaucratic and accountability procedures of the federal government, continue to constrain band leaders. The governance power that band councils exercise is not fully theirs, but is delegated to them by the Act. And rather than being general in scope it is limited to local matters. The federal minister of Crown–Indigenous Relations and Northern Affairs has wide powers under the Indian Act to disallow or override band actions, set aside elections, and suspend financial management. Although band governments have a range of options for the specifics of their financial relationship with the federal government (involving more or less autonomy), they have no options with respect to the basic legal status of the band council established in the Act. The band members hold band property—both land and most housing—communally, are exempt from many federal and provincial taxes, and pay no municipal property tax. Bands' own-source revenues come from the sale of natural resources, leasing of land and buildings, and direct profits from band enterprises. Still, for most bands these sources provide no more than 10 per cent of the total annual budget; the rest of their funding comes from annual transfers negotiated with the Department of Crown–Indigenous Relations and Northern Affairs (RCAP, 1996: vol. 1, ch. 9; Abele, Lapointe, and Prince, 2005). There are more than 600 bands currently registered under the Indian Act, with a median size of fewer than 1,000 persons. The relatively small size of each band limits its financial and administrative capacity; thus there is concern that First Nations governments, as they now generally prefer to be called, are simply too small to serve as the basis for broader innovation in Aboriginal self-government.

Because Indigenous peoples were not considered partners in the creation of the federation, no provision was made for them, either formally or by convention, to have specific representation in its central intrastate institutions—in Parliament, in cabinet, or in any other government post. Indeed, the treatment of most Indigenous persons assumed one of two positions: a separate existence as registered "status Indians" on reserves and outside Canadian citizenship (until the Citizenship Act of 1960), or as "non-status Indians" living off-reserve and undistinguished from other Canadians. Therefore, there is a historic legacy of division between the status and non-status Indian populations.

The two other groups that, with Indians, are named in the Constitution Act, 1982 as "aboriginal peoples" are the Inuit and the Métis. Formerly known to outsiders as Eskimos, the Inuit—Inuktitut for "the people"—are indigenous to the territory north of the tree line, in the Northwest Territories, Nunavut, northern Quebec, and Labrador. Their language and culture differ significantly from those of the First Nations and Métis. The Métis are descendants of the intermarriage of Indigenous people and Europeans, beginning in the fur trade era. Although there are Métis people in eastern Canada, the Métis Nation is centred in the West, where a unique Métis society, culture, and economy were well established by the time of Confederation. Today the Métis Nation is pursuing a number of Indigenous rights, mainly relating to traditional resource use. Neither the Inuit nor the Métis have ever been explicitly part of the Indian Act regime, but in April 2016 the Supreme Court of Canada, in the *Daniels* case, broke major new ground in declaring that the definition of "Indians" under the Indian Act (and therefore federal jurisdiction) extends to Métis and non-status Aboriginal persons, a development that will likely take some time to be sorted out on the ground (Roman, 2016).

Since Indigenous governments were recognized by the Canadian state only in the form of band councils, they did not have the standing or the political clout to be included in the evolving executive federalism of the twentieth century. Worse,

Indigenous peoples became "victims of the competitive nature of Canadian federalism" (Papillon, 2012: 288). The federal and provincial governments have alternately claimed jurisdiction over Aboriginal persons or rejected responsibility for them as it suited their interests. This has been especially true for the growing numbers of Indigenous people living in cities, who in 2011 made up 56 per cent of Canada's Indigenous population, and for the Métis, who have often fallen between the jurisdictional cracks, ignored by both established orders of government.

For these reasons Indigenous peoples have been largely alienated from federalism and the Canadian state in general. From the late 1970s onward, the question of whether and under what terms Indigenous peoples should fit into the federal system has been a significant constitutional and political issue. The importance of this issue is much greater than mere numbers might suggest (Murphy, 2005: 22). According to the 2016 census, the 1.7 million Indigenous Canadians make up 4.9 per cent of the total Canadian population. However, the Indigenous population is growing four times faster than the Canadian population as a whole and is much younger than the Canadian average, with 48 per cent under the age of 24, compared with just 31 per cent for the non-Indigenous population (Statistics Canada, 2008). Also, the social and economic conditions in which many Indigenous people live—both in their own communities and in cities—are far below Canadian norms. Incomes and employment rates are far below average, while rates of financial dependence are far above. Infant mortality rates, life expectancy, and disease prevalence (including addictions) are also much worse in Indigenous communities. These are the bare facts that give Indigenous issues their moral and political urgency.

From Colonialism to Indigenous Nationalism

Political relations between the European settlers and Indigenous peoples under the French and British empires, though troubled, were on a more equitable footing than they would be after 1867, and at various times, such as during the War of 1812, Indigenous nations and individuals acted and were treated as allies and equals by the European colonial powers. According to contemporary observers and current scholars alike, the early French and British treaties (those before 1763) described essentially confederal arrangements in which Indigenous peoples retained a large degree of autonomy and continued to govern themselves (RCAP, 1992: 11–19). The Royal Proclamation of 1763, covering most of what is now eastern Canada, confirmed the right of Indigenous people to their traditional lands, which by law could be ceded only through formal treaties with the Crown.

Even so, by Confederation, the room for nation-to-nation relationships had shrunk considerably as a result of European settlement, the division of British North America into provinces and territories under settler control, and the much reduced importance of the military and economic partnership that had been the basis of the more equitable early relationship. Eleven new treaties (the "numbered" treaties) were signed between 1871 and 1921 with Indigenous nations west of the Great Lakes, but the Indigenous–state relationship became increasingly colonial. Under the Indian Act regime in particular, lands for exclusive Indigenous use were reduced to small, often isolated reserves, and policies were specifically designed to hasten assimilation by suppressing Indigenous languages, cultures, and traditional forms of governance.

Canadian citizenship was extended to all Indigenous persons in 1960, and in 1969 the Trudeau government issued a White Paper proposing an end to the special relationship of Indigenous peoples with the Canadian state. The White Paper outlined plans for the abolition of the Indian Act regime, an equitable end to the historic treaties entered into with Indigenous nations, and the final extinguishment of all special rights. Arguing that "the road of different status has led to a blind alley of deprivation and frustration," it sought full equality and undifferentiated citizenship for persons of Indigenous descent, so that Indigenous people would be treated constitutionally no differently from any other Canadians (Cairns, 2000: 51–2). Ironically, but in hindsight not surprisingly, this plan sparked a powerful movement for Aboriginal rights. Led by treaty-based First Nations in the West, Indigenous political organizations successfully resisted the proposed changes. These First Nations galvanized other Indigenous peoples and organizations around national and local strategies to restore their cultures, their rights to Aboriginal title, and their rights under the various, near-dormant treaties, with the aim of replacing the Indian Act regime with constitutionally protected self-government. In the process they found allies in progressive political parties and other movements, in the media and academic community, and in an international movement of post-colonial Indigenous peoples.

Major victories came with the Supreme Court's judgements in the *Calder* (1973) and *Baker Lake* (1980) cases,[3] which established the legal grounds for recognition of Aboriginal title and claims to compensation for lands seized without consent. An even more important milestone was the recognition and affirmation of "existing aboriginal and treaty rights" in section 35 of the Constitution Act, 1982. Just as the Charter of Rights and Freedoms has empowered rights-oriented citizens and interest groups in Canada as a whole to litigate their interests with the state, so section 35, along with section 25 of the Charter, has empowered Indigenous people to use the courts to define and defend their rights in the constitution. As Martin Papillon has put it, the Supreme Court has "effectively created a legal space, albeit a limited one, for Aboriginal peoples to assert their presence in the political landscape of the Canadian federation" (Papillon, 2012: 290). Major cases such as *Guerin, Sioui, Sparrow, Delgamuukw, Marshall,* and *Tsilhqot'in*[4] have established rights to land, resource-sharing, the nature of consent for development on traditional lands, and aspects of governance and Indigenous culture. On the other hand, the Supreme Court in particular has been criticized for its generally expansive interpretation of Aboriginal rights; the controversy in this area is clearly reminiscent of the one surrounding judicial activism and the role of the courts in connection with the Charter.[5]

Other consequences flowing from the 1982 Constitution Act include the prospect in section 35(3) that new treaties based on land claim agreements also gain constitutional protection—a vitally important provision given that huge expanses of traditional Indigenous territory, including Labrador, most of the Yukon and Northwest Territories, and practically all of British Columbia, had never been subject to treaties and title to the land had not been formally ceded to the Crown. This has set in train a series of negotiations, many concluded but others still ongoing, for new land settlements and treaties.

A second consequence of the Constitution Act, 1982 was a series of conferences held in 1983–7 in which the federal and provincial governments met with Indigenous representatives to discuss constitutional matters affecting them, in particular to clarify their rights under section 35. Those discussions resulted in constitutional amendments to section 35, establishing that treaty rights would include existing and future land claim agreements, that "aboriginal and treaty rights" were guaranteed equally to "male and female persons," and that the federal and provincial governments would consult with Aboriginal representatives before amending sections 25 and 35 of the Constitution Act (dealing with Aboriginal rights).[6] Although the process was disappointing to Indigenous groups in that significant differences remained on the meaning and implementation of a right to self-government (Hawkes, 1989), it did give Indigenous leaders a national forum, as well as valuable experience in finding consensus among their very diverse communities.

The limitations of Indigenous political and legal power became painfully clear in 1987, when—a few weeks after rejecting Indigenous demands for extensive definition and clarification of their self-government rights—the same federal and provincial governments, meeting at Meech Lake, unanimously agreed to Quebec's conditions for re-entering the constitutional fold. In the long march between Meech Lake in 1987 and the Charlottetown Accord of 1992, which included the famous Mohawk stand-off at Oka, Quebec, in the summer of 1990, Indigenous people played a prominent role. First they helped to block the ratification of Meech; then they played a central role in the negotiation of the Charlottetown agreement, which would have formally established the inherent right of self-government and recognized "Aboriginal governments" as one of three orders of government in Canada (CICS, 1992). The Charlottetown Accord was rejected by voters, including many Indigenous people, in the national referendum of October 1992 (Turpel, 1993: 141–4). Nevertheless, the experience made it abundantly clear that most Indigenous people consider themselves constituent parts of the Canadian federation, and that fundamental change to the constitution cannot take place without their participation.

The RCAP Model and Its Critics

The opening for major reform of the federal constitution to accommodate and embrace Indigenous peoples closed in 1992 with no prospect of a return in the foreseeable future. The "post-constitutional" era has been marked by continuing contestation over the meaning of Indigenous self-determination and the appropriate model for Indigenous governance and relations within the federal and intergovernmental system. Even so, we have witnessed a series of political developments that would have seemed impossible two decades ago, which amount to substantial, if at times frustratingly slow, progress towards Indigenous self-determination and national renewal.

An important part of that progress was the 1996 report of the Royal Commission on Aboriginal Peoples (RCAP). The Commission produced the most comprehensive review in Canadian history of the constitutional, legal, political, economic, social, and cultural issues affecting Indigenous Canadians. The final report and recommendations addressed matters at the heart of the federal system, and are still considered an important set of benchmarks against which subsequent government actions and policy options have been measured.

The RCAP focused primarily on restoration of Indigenous nationhood and self-determination, finding that only by returning to some approximation of the original 60 to 80 tribal groups ("nations" in the RCAP terminology) in what is now Canada, based on traditional territories and cultures, could the artificial legal divisions and inequalities among Indigenous peoples be overcome. A nation-to-nation relationship would encompass existing and new treaties, but would require a transition from the 600-plus small, independent band governments to larger, more administratively feasible units. Such a relationship, in the RCAP view, would also provide for Indigenous people outside the Indian Act system, especially those living in cities, to exercise Aboriginal rights, including the right to self-government. It envisaged a third order of government negotiating new agreements with the federal, provincial, and territorial governments to deal with jurisdictional powers, financial transfers, and access to land and other resources (RCAP, 1996: vol. 2).

In addition to the nation-based territorial model, the report noted two other governance models: the public government model now operating in Nunavut, where Inuit make up such a large proportion of the population as to be guaranteed significant power; and a "community of interest" model, a non-territorial form of government for Indigenous persons living in cities or in a single province, but not governing the traditional land base.

Taken as a whole, the RCAP vision built on the rights entrenched in the Constitution Act, 1982, and it is close to what was proposed in the Charlottetown Accord: a model of Indigenous self-determination and self-government embedded in the federal system. Among its other key recommendations were a new treaty process, a lands and treaties tribunal, new principles-based financial arrangements, and a royal proclamation to signal the beginning of a new relationship.

Not all Indigenous people have accepted the basic RCAP paradigm, however. Existing band chiefs and councils, with all their vested interests in reserve communities, have been wary of any plan to eliminate their power base, even if a new model might ultimately provide their communities with more political power and government services. Even more critical have been those who argue for greater separation from the Canadian state than the RCAP recommended, in what would essentially be internationally sovereign enclaves surrounded by Canadian territory (see Alfred, 1999; Borrows, 2010; Ladner, 2003). Other critics have called for a more unambiguous emphasis on treaties: under "treaty federalism," each nation would have its own treaty with the federal government and exist outside the federation as such (see Henderson, 1994; Ladner, 2003; Tully, 2000). For most Indigenous critics, what counts is not so much the model of Indigenous government that is adopted, but that Indigenous rights, particularly over lands and resources, be recognized and protected.

Concern over the RCAP and other models of Indigenous self-determination has also been expressed outside the Indigenous community. Thomas Flanagan, a Calgary political scientist with close ties to the Harper Conservatives, staked out a comprehensive, essentially neo-liberal critique of Indigenous rights and self-government aspirations in *First Nations, Second Thoughts* (Flanagan, 2000). He argues there is widespread unease with the notions of Indigenous nationality and a multinational Canada. He also outlines concerns about the political, economic, and administrative feasibility of constitutionally protected Indigenous governments with extensive powers akin to those of provinces, though he would support such government on a municipal scale. In his view, the best way for Indigenous societies to make progress would be by emphasizing individual rights—for example, individual ownership of property on reserves that is now held communally. One can see many similarities with Flanagan's arguments and the general approach to these issues adopted by the Conservative governments led by Stephen Harper in 2006–15 (discussed below).

Another prominent non-Indigenous academic analysis of the RCAP report is Alan Cairns's book, *Citizens Plus*. He is more sympathetic to the Indigenous cause but concerned about how far Indigenous national self-determination should be pursued; he argues that the RCAP model would create a kind of parallel citizenship, and that the emphasis would be better placed on Indigenous people's participation in a common, shared Canadian citizenship. He also worries that Indigenous communities that are set too far apart from the Canadian polity would lose their claim to the financial and other resources their people need to improve their lives (Cairns, 2000).

Responses to the RCAP from the federal, provincial, and territorial governments were piecemeal. Policies on cultural reconciliation, symbolic recognition, and urban issues have been taken up by various federal and provincial governments. The federal government under Jean Chrétien shied away from large-scale constitutional solutions, however, preferring to focus on more modest reforms, although these included formal recognition of the inherent right of self-government as one of the "existing" Aboriginal rights affirmed in section 35 of the Constitution Act, 1982.[7]

Emerging Models of Indigenous Governance and Intergovernmental Relations

More than 20 years after the release of the Royal Commission report, some key governance structures remain unchanged while some new ones are emerging. The Indian Act and the 600 small band councils are still in place. Neither non-status Indians nor registered Indians living off-reserve benefit from self-government. And Métis claims to land, resources, and self-government to date have been only minimally realized, proceeding for the most part through the courts. In 2013, the Supreme Court ruled in *Manitoba Metis Federation v. Canada (Attorney General)* that the Canadian government had failed to provide land grants that had been promised the Métis. Negotiations for compensation and self-government between the Métis and Ottawa are ongoing, with a compensation payment of more than $150 million established in September 2018 (MacLean, 2018).

As Michael Murphy concludes, the literature on Indigenous issues has tended to focus on abstract legal and normative theories rather than on what actually works on the ground (Murphy, 2005: 8). Yet what is happening on the ground is in fact impressive. Four key developments are worth noting here.

First, significant progress has been made in settling comprehensive land claims and establishing self-governing arrangements in the northern territories, as well as in Labrador (see Alcantara, 2013). In none of these areas has the Indian Act applied. Land claim agreements have been concluded with the Inuit and Innu of Labrador, the Council of Yukon Indians (CYI), and the Tlicho in the western part of the Northwest Territories. In the Inuit-dominated eastern part of the Northwest Territories, a claims settlement reached in 1993 with the Inuit led to the division of the territory and the creation of the Nunavut public government in 1999. Covering a quarter of Canada's land mass, the new territory stands as a major milestone in self-determination for the Inuit, who constitute roughly 85 per cent of its population.

In Yukon, where Indigenous peoples make up about 20 per cent of the population, the federal and territorial governments reached a comprehensive Umbrella Agreement with the CYI on a framework for self-government in 1993. Negotiations with the 16 individual First Nations on community self-government agreements are underway, of which several have now been completed. In the Northwest Territories, where Inuvialuit, First Nations, and Métis constitute about 50 per cent of the population, negotiations are proceeding on two tracks: one to settle land

and resource claims (essentially a new treaty process) and self-government agreements with the specific Indigenous peoples and the other to devolve powers from the federal government to the territory, as well as further devolution within the territory. The negotiations are complex and seem frustratingly slow, but the stakes could not be higher for the Indigenous peoples concerned, given their growing populations, the growing resource and development pressures in the North, and the impacts of climate change on Indigenous communities.

Second is the British Columbia treaty process, established for a province where, except for its northeast corner and small parts of Vancouver Island, no historic treaties had been made. This process involves a tripartite negotiation with the provincial and federal governments on treaties specifying land use, resource-sharing, and governmental jurisdiction. As of 2018, 65 BC First Nations were participating in or had completed treaty negotiations, and of these, seven (eight including the Nisga'a) had achieved and were implementing treaties (BC Treaty Commission, 2018). To date, the landmark achievement here is the Nisga'a Final Agreement, which became law through the federal Nisga'a Final Agreement Act in 2000 and established local and regional government by the Nisga'a people over a defined territory in northern British Columbia, with participation by members of the community resident in urban locations in the province. The agreement is truly federal in that it specifies in significant detail the sharing of jurisdictional authority between the federal Parliament, the province of British Columbia, and the Nisga'a government. In cases of conflict, the federal or provincial law is to prevail in most instances, but there are some circumstances in which the Nisga'a law takes precedence (Russell, 2004: 260–1). The Nisga'a deal has been criticized by non-Indigenous people as overly cumbersome and ceding too much jurisdiction to the Nisga'a, and by Indigenous people as conceding too many rights (and too much land). However, the agreement is now entrenched and protected under the constitution.

Third, a host of innovative arrangements have been negotiated by First Nations, either individually or in groups, with federal, provincial, and local governments to assume control over various aspects of community life. This is a ground-up approach focusing on regional and local solutions. Examples include the 1997 agreement under which the Mi'kmaq in Nova Scotia have gained what amounts to shared jurisdiction over primary and secondary education in the province (a model now being extended to other provinces); resource co-management agreements and ongoing negotiations in most provinces and territories, covering wildlife and fisheries as well as forest and mineral resources; and partnership contracts between governments (federal, provincial, and municipal) and dozens of urban Indigenous organizations for the conception, planning, and provision of public services to meet the specific needs of Indigenous people living in cities and also in many small towns and rural locations (Alcantara and Nelles, 2016). In addition, it is worth noting that, despite the restrictions of the Indian Act, considerable progress has been made towards devolution of program and financial responsibilities to Indigenous people.[8] Examples include options for levying property taxes, multi-year financial arrangements to provide flexibility in program funding, and the establishment of urban reserves.

Fourth is the continuing effort to develop national-level responses to Indigenous demands through negotiation with national organizations such as the Assembly of First Nations (AFN) and the Congress of Aboriginal Peoples. The primary variable here is the overall policy approach of the federal government in power, but the nature of Indigenous leadership is also important. Until recently the government with the most ambitious agenda for reforming the federal–Indigenous relationship has been that of Paul Martin in 2003–6 (Abele et al., 2005). The Martin government focused on symbolic acts of recognition and respect for Indigenous peoples, while improving basic programs to cover essential services such as health, water, and housing in Indigenous communities. The culmination of this effort came in November 2005 with the signing of the Kelowna Accord, in which national Indigenous organizations, the provinces and territories, and the federal government reached agreement on a plan to increase program funding to Indigenous communities by $5 billion over 10 years (CICS, 2005). Martin's key ally in this more pragmatic effort was AFN National Chief Phil Fontaine.

The Conservative government of Prime Minister Stephen Harper, first elected in 2006, chose not to proceed with the Kelowna Accord and pursued instead its own approaches, largely in keeping with neo-liberal themes of constraining public spending, greater accountability for public funds, and promoting market-based options for economic and social development. And, in general, the Harper government took a more cautious approach than its predecessors on Aboriginal rights, including self-government. Still, the Conservatives did not abandon the ongoing negotiations for new treaties and self-government agreements outlined above, and they retained their legal and constitutional obligations, clearly outlined by the courts, to uphold and respect Aboriginal and treaty rights.

One of the more significant achievements of the Harper era was to compensate former students of the residential school system and to present a formal apology in the House of Commons. Part of that process was to establish a Truth and Reconciliation Commission, whose final report, released in 2015, has helped to set the ongoing agenda for Indigenous–state relations. The Harper government also worked with the AFN to draft new legislation, passed by Parliament in 2008, to expedite the settlement of specific land claims. These are claims made by specific First Nations against the government of Canada related to correcting past injustices or shortcomings with respect to the federal administration of First Nation lands or other assets, or in the fulfillment of treaties and other agreements. Hundreds of specific claims have been settled in recent years, with many more to come involving land, compensation, and related matters. As such, this process remains an important federal–Indigenous intergovernmental process (Crown–Indigenous Relations and Northern Affairs Canada, 2018).

Over the past 10 to 15 years, including throughout the Harper era, Indigenous governments and organizations have continued their diverse and often innovative efforts to establish partnerships with the federal, provincial, and territorial governments and also with municipalities and a wide variety of business, labour, and other civil-society organizations. These arrangements cross a wide range of policy fields, including education, policing, health care, social services, economic development, and land and other resource management. Indigenous organizations are on the ground across the country delivering essential services to their people. The resulting multi-level governance is a major contribution to the ongoing evolution of the federal system (Papillon, 2014). And though some aspects of Indigenous governance are still highly dependent on the "senior levels" of government, especially in financial terms, the cohesiveness and collective values of Indigenous communities provide advantages in intergovernmental relations that even the largest Canadian city governments are unlikely ever to possess.

Despite this progress on multi-level governance, one must note that the federal–Indigenous relationship deteriorated in the latter years of the Conservative government. Both the formal leadership and grassroots organizations—the Idle No More movement a prominent example—became increasingly dissatisfied with the lack of progress on treaty and other rights, with cutbacks in social and environmental programs, and with the federal government's promotion of major projects such as pipelines, which the Indigenous community opposed. This discontent fed into the federal opposition parties, Liberal and NDP, promising a different approach.

The Liberal Party platform promised to renew a "nation-to-nation" relationship, to implement the recommendations of the Truth and Reconciliation Commission, and to make progress, including increased funding, on the "most important issues" for Indigenous communities, which it listed as "housing, infrastructure, health and mental health care, community safety and policing, child welfare, and education" (Liberal Party of Canada, 2015: 46). Elected with a majority in October 2015, the new Liberal government under Prime Minister Trudeau has a strong mandate to pursue its renewed approach to Indigenous issues, yet much is on its plate. This includes the many "Calls to Action" of the Truth and Reconciliation Commission. While not necessarily reopening the constitutional file, these 94 recommendations point to a number of potentially contentious legal and intergovernmental issues, including full support without qualification of the United Nations Declaration on the Rights of Indigenous Peoples, which the Trudeau government formally announced in May 2016. From the specific perspective of executive federalism, it is important to note the re-establishment of annual multilateral ministers' meetings. On 10 June 2016 the newly established Federal, Provincial, Territorial and Indigenous Forum held its first meeting, consisting of the federal minister of Indigenous and Northern Affairs,[9] Carolyn Bennett, her provincial and territorial counterparts, and the leaders of five national Indigenous organizations.

Summary

In conclusion, the Aboriginal/Indigenous governance revolution—if that is not too bold a word—has forced us to change our perceptions of the Canadian federation. We are living with a new reality of diverse self-rule and shared-rule arrangements that reflect an increasingly broad, if still contested, recognition and accommodation of Indigenous nationalism. Indigenous governance and intergovernmental relations remain as works in progress. There is as yet no overarching constitutional framework into which every Indigenous people and all aspects of Aboriginal rights can be placed. Yet major legal, political, and administrative changes are underway, along with a slow but steady process of cultural, social, and economic renewal in Indigenous communities. In the meantime, social and economic challenges continue to mount. The persistence of poverty, underdevelopment, and abuse in many Indigenous communities is unacceptable in a society as wealthy and developed as Canada as a whole. Progress in bridging the gap between these two realities is painfully slow, but much has been achieved since 1969. The hope and expectation of the Indigenous peoples, and of many other Canadians, are that achieving greater self-determination will play an even bigger role in closing the gap in the years to come.

Questions for Critical Thought

1. Can Canadian sovereignty and Indigenous sovereignty coexist? What does federalism as a set of ideas suggest about this issue?

2. What would be the best way to achieve longer-term financial security and autonomy for Indigenous governments?

3. Should First Nations have a veto over large development projects, such as pipelines, that are proposed for their traditional territories?

Notes

1. Compare Gagnon and Tully (2001); Gagnon, Rocher, and Guibernau (2003); and Norman (2006).

2. In legal terms, "Indian" refers to a specific category of Indigenous people defined by the Indian Act. "Status Indians" are registered with the federal government and are entitled to a number of rights and benefits not available to "non-status Indians." Other than Indians, two other peoples are named in section 35(2) of the Constitution Act, 1982: Inuit and Métis. Most of those covered under the "Indian" category now use their specific national names (e.g., Cree, Nisga'a, Mi'kmaq, etc.) or use the more generic term "First Nations."

3. *Calder et al. v. Attorney-General of British Columbia*, [1973] S.C.R. 313 (S.C.C.);

Hamlet of Baker Lake et al. v. Minister of Indian Affairs and Northern Development (1980) 107 D.L.R. (3d) 513 (F.C.T.D.).

4.   *Guerin v. the Queen* (1985) 13 D.L.R. (4th) 321 (S.C.C.); *Sioui v. Attorney General for Quebec* (1987) C.N.L.R. (4th) 118 (Q.C.A.); *Regina v. Sparrow* (1987) 36 D.L.R. (4th) 246 (B.C.C.A.); *Delgamuukw v. The Queen*, [1997] 3 S.C.R. 1010; *Regina v. Marshall*, [1999] 3 S.C.R. 456 (S.C.C.); *Tsilhqot'in Nation v. British Columbia*, [2014] 2 S.C.R. 244

5.   For various views on the role of the courts, see Macklem (2001); Cairns (2000); Flanagan (2000); and Murphy (2001).

6.   Subsections 35(3), 35(4), and 35.1 were added to the Constitution Act, 1982 by the Constitutional Amendment Proclamation, 1983.

7.   See Indian and Northern Affairs Canada (1995, 1997).

8.   For a critical analysis of the various funding arrangements for Indigenous governments in Canada and comparison with mainstream fiscal federalism, see Prince and Abele (2005).

9.   The Trudeau government initially renamed this department the Ministry of Indigenous and Northern Affairs, but following a cabinet reshuffle in August 2017 the government divided the department into two separate ministries: Crown–Indigenous Relations and Northern Affairs, and Indigenous Services.

References

Abele, F., R. Lapointe, and M. Prince. 2005. "Symbolism, Surfacing, Succession and Substance: Martin's Aboriginal Policy Style." In *How Ottawa Spends, 2005–06: Managing the Minority*, edited by G.B. Doern. Montreal and Kingston: McGill-Queen's University Press.

Alcantara, C. 2013. *Negotiating the Deal: Comprehensive Land Claims Agreements in Canada*. Toronto: University of Toronto Press.

——— and J. Nelles. 2016. *A Quiet Evolution: The Emergence of Indigenous–Local Intergovernmental Partnerships in Canada*. Toronto: IPAC/University of Toronto Press.

Alfred, T. 1999. *Peace, Power, and Righteousness: An Indigenous Manifesto*. Toronto: Oxford University Press.

BC Treaty Commission. 2018. "Frequently Asked Questions." http://www.bctreaty.ca/faq.

Borrows, J. 2010. *Canada's Indigenous Constitution*. Toronto: University of Toronto Press.

Cairns, A. 2000. *Citizens Plus: Aboriginal Peoples and the Canadian State*. Vancouver: University of British Columbia Press.

Canadian Intergovernmental Conference Secretariat (CICS). 1992. *First Ministers Meeting on the Constitution, Consensus Report on the Constitution, Final Text, Charlottetown, 28 August 1992*. Ottawa: CICS.

———. 2005. *Strengthening Relationships and Closing the Gap, November 24–25, Kelowna, B.C.* Ottawa: CICS.

Crown–Indigenous Relations and Northern Affairs Canada 2018. "Specific Claims." Accessed October 2018. www.rcaanc-cirnac.gc.ca.

Flanagan, T. 2000. *First Nations? Second Thoughts*. Montreal and Kingston: McGill-Queen's University Press.

Gagnon, A.-G., M. Guibernau, and F. Rocher. 2003. "The Conditions of Diversity in Multinational Democracies." In *The Conditions of Diversity in Multinational Democracies*, edited by A.-G. Gagnon, M. Guibernau, and F. Rocher. Montreal: Institut de recherche en politiques publiques.

——— and J. Tully, eds. 2001. *Multinational Democracies*. Cambridge: Cambridge University Press.

Hawkes, D.C. 1989. *Aboriginal Peoples and Constitutional Reform: What Have We Learned? Aboriginal Peoples and Constitutional Reform*. Kingston, ON: Institute of Intergovernmental Relations, Queen's University.

Henderson, J.Y. 1994. "Empowering Treaty Federalism." *Saskatchewan Law Review* 58: 241–329.

Indian and Northern Affairs Canada. 1995. *Aboriginal Self-Government: The Government of Canada's Approach to the Implementation of the Inherent Right and the Negotiation of Aboriginal Self-Government*. Ottawa: INAC, Public Works and Government Services.

———. 1997. *Gathering Strength: Canada's Aboriginal Action Plan*. Ottawa: INAC, Public Works and Government Services.

Kymlicka, W. 2003. "Citizenship, Communities and Identity in Canada." In *Canadian Politics*, 3rd edn, edited by J. Bickerton and A. Gagnon. Peterborough, ON: Broadview Press.

Ladner, K. 2003. "Treaty Federalism: An Indigenous Vision of Canadian Federalism." In *New Trends in Canadian Federalism*, 2nd edn, edited by F. Rocher and M. Smith. Peterborough, ON: Broadview Press.

Liberal Party of Canada. 2015. *A New Plan for a Strong Middle Class*. https://www.liberal.ca/wp-content/uploads/2015/10/New-plan-for-a-strong-middle-class.pdf. Accessed 16 July 2018.

Macklem, P. 2001. *Indigenous Difference and the Constitution of Canada*. Toronto: University of Toronto Press.

MacLean. C. 2018. "$154M Plan with Federal Government Step toward Self-Government for Métis: Manitoba Metis Federation." *CBC News*, 22 Sept. https://www.cbc.ca/news/canada/manitoba/metis-self-government-plan-1.4834608.

Murphy, M. 2001. "Culture and the Courts: A New Direction for Canada's Jurisprudence on Aboriginal Rights?" *Canadian Journal of Political Science* 34, no. 1: 109–29.

———. 2005. "Relational Self-Determination and Federal Reform." In *Canada: The State of the Federation 2003: Reconfiguring Aboriginal–State Relations*, edited by M. Murphy. Kingston, ON: Institute of Intergovernmental Relations, Queen's University.

Norman, W. 2006. *Negotiating Nationalism: Nation-building, Federalism, and Secession in the Multinational State*. Oxford: Oxford University Press.

Papillon, M. 2012. "Canadian Federalism and the Emerging Mosaic of Aboriginal Multilevel Governance." In *Canadian Federalism: Performance, Effectiveness, and Legitimacy*, 3rd edn, edited by H. Bakvis and G. Skogstad, 284–301. Toronto: Oxford University Press.

———. 2014. "Framing Self-Determination: The Politics of Indigenous Rights in Canada and the United States." In *Comparing Canada: Methods and Perspectives in Canadian Politics*, edited by L. Turgeon et al., 27–49. Vancouver: University of British Columbia Press.

Prince, M., and F. Abele. 2005. "Paying for Self-Determination: Aboriginal Peoples, Self-Government and Fiscal Relations in Canada." In *Canada: The State of the Federation, 2003: Reconfiguring Aboriginal–State Relations*, edited by M. Murphy, 237–63. Montreal and Kingston: McGill-Queen's University Press.

Roman, K. 2016. "Métis Infighting Follows Historic Daniels Ruling by Supreme Court." *CBC News*, 12 July.

Royal Commission on Aboriginal Peoples. 1992. *Partners in Confederation: Aboriginal Peoples, Self-Government and the Constitution*. Ottawa: Department of Supply and Services.

———. 1996. *Final Report*. 6 vols. Ottawa: Public Works and Government Services Canada.

Russell, P. 2004. *Constitutional Odyssey: Can Canadians Become a Sovereign People?* 3rd edn. Toronto: University of Toronto Press.

———. 2017. *Canada's Odyssey: A Country Based on Incomplete Conquests*. Toronto: University of Toronto Press.

Statistics Canada. 2008. *Aboriginal Peoples in Canada in 2006: Inuit, Metis and First Nations, 2006 Census*. Ottawa: Public Works and Government Services.

Tully, J. 2000. "A Just Relationship between Aboriginal and Non-Aboriginal Peoples of Canada'. In *Aboriginal Rights and Self-Government: The Canadian and Mexican Experience in North American Perspective*, edited by C. Cook and J. Lindua. Montreal and Kingston: McGill-Queen's University Press.

Turpel, M.E. 1993. "The Charlottetown Discord and Aboriginal Peoples' Struggle for Fundamental Political Change." In *The Charlottetown Accord, the Referendum, and the Future of Canada*, edited by K. McRoberts and P. Monahan. Toronto: University of Toronto Press.

Chapter 12

Quebec and the Future of Canadian Federalism

Learning Objectives

- To learn about Quebec's role in Confederation and how it has evolved over time.
- To understand how Quebec's unique identity and position are shaped as part of the Canadian federation.
- To appreciate how the federation has been shaped by Quebec's presence.
- To understand the legacy of Harper's "open federalism" on Canada–Quebec relations.

Introduction

In several of the previous chapters we have referred to Quebec's unique position in the Canadian federation—the special challenges it faces in maintaining its identity as the most significant French-speaking community in North America and in pursuing the important role it has played in shaping the nature of Canadian federalism. It has often been said that in the absence of Quebec, Canada would be a much less decentralized federation; and, we would add, it would also be much less interesting as a subject of study. In this chapter we examine some of the factors that have shaped, fostered, and hindered Quebec's development as a "nation" within Canada over the years and how both the constitutional framework and the dynamics of Canadian federalism have been shaped by Quebec's presence. Our focus will be on the developments since 2005. While lacking the drama of the constitutional debates of the eighties and nineties and the referendum of 1995, there were nonetheless significant court challenges triggered by the Harper government regarding the roles of the Senate and the Supreme Court, and some critical and continuing demographic changes stand to affect the balance of power between Quebec and the rest of Canada.

In Chapter 2 we noted that political communities can have their origins in a variety of sources, including linguistic and cultural differences or as the consequence of boundaries and institutions defined by government. One of the most significant influences on both the creation and the functioning of the Canadian federation has been a linguistic and cultural one—the French factor in North America. The persistence of two separate socio-political communities during the period of the United Province of Canada (1841–67), despite the best efforts of Lord Durham to fuse them together, demanded a new federal arrangement in which Quebec (Canada East) would be recognized as a separate entity. And the particular needs of Quebec—to protect its religion and civil code and to secure control of education, health care, and related matters—directly shaped the distribution of powers in the 1867 Constitution Act.

Over the years, and particularly since the transformation of Quebec society in the 1960s under the rubric of the Quiet Revolution, the Canadian federation has been profoundly affected by developments in Quebec. Many Quebecers, even among those who do not support the movement for sovereignty, consider their society to be more akin to a nation than a province like the others. In this context, "nation" means a body of people closely connected by heritage and language, who form a relatively complete society without necessarily having (or even demanding) the status of a separate sovereign state. It was in this sense that the word "nation" was used in the 2006 House of Commons resolution affirming that "the Québécois form a nation within a united Canada" (Bakvis and Tanguay, 2012: 96).

As we saw in Chapter 1, the "two-nations" conception of the Canadian constitution has been a staple in political and juridical thinking in Quebec since Confederation (Black, 1975). But it is also worth noting that nationalist sentiment in Quebec has changed over the past 150 years. That sentiment originally had a firmly religious basis, with the Roman Catholic Church and Quebec political elites feeling that Quebec (and indeed French Canada as a whole) had a very special mission, effectively since 1789 representing the last bastion of French Catholicism in the world. Furthermore, Britain, through the Quebec Act of 1774, among other pieces of legislation, was willing to afford the Church and associated institutions, such as schools and hospitals, a measure of protection in Quebec to a degree not available elsewhere and certainly not in Britain itself.

In addition, well into the twentieth century, many notable French-Canadian nationalists—Henri Bourassa is one who comes to mind—saw nothing contradictory in claiming to be at once a strong Quebec nationalist and a loyal Canadian (Cook, 1972). They believed that Confederation was essentially a partnership between two peoples, French and English, and that Quebec, as the homeland of the French-speaking population, had a special responsibility for safeguarding that community's values. The French language was important, of course, but in a sense it was seen as secondary, a necessary protection for a set of values that centred on faith and the Church. This perspective manifested itself in a kind of institutional self-segregation in areas such as schooling and health care; people were encouraged to enter professions such as law and medicine and to avoid occupations that would expose them to secular, materialist values.

On the other hand, the influence of the Church has in some respects been exaggerated. The Church itself was far from monolithic. In the 1890s, for instance, many parish priests openly supported Laurier and the Liberals, even though the Catholic hierarchy was still firmly committed to the Conservative Party. And although it was true that the Church-dominated educational system neglected subjects such as commerce and engineering, it was also the case that English-speaking elites were predominant in most important sectors of Quebec's economy, especially at the higher levels, making it difficult for francophones to pursue careers in those areas without abandoning their language and culture.

The Quiet Revolution

What changed with the Quiet Revolution, with the election of the Jean Lesage government in 1960, was that Quebec nationalism became much more outward-looking. As well, certain strands of Quebec nationalism took a decidedly sovereignist or separatist turn. Among the most important factors contributing to the Quiet Revolution were the dramatic changes taking place in the Church itself under Pope John XXIII, including a new emphasis on ecumenicalism and movement towards more liberal attitudes on social and moral issues. A decline in recruitment into the religious orders had already been evident in the 1950s, and in the next decade increasing numbers of priests and nuns began leaving the Church, with the result that many Church-run institutions no longer had the human resources to keep operating. Thus Quebecers increasingly looked to the rapidly expanding state for services and career opportunities that until then had been provided mainly by the Church. Meanwhile, the classical colleges, most of them run by religious orders, were gradually replaced by a modern secondary and post-secondary educational system.

Another key development in the Quiet Revolution was Quebec's nationalization of privately owned power companies, which led to the creation of Hydro-Québec, for the first time providing significant opportunities for young Quebec engineers to practise their profession in a largely francophone setting. Hydro-Québec was to become the largest single element in Quebec's economic development, culminating in the completion of the first phase of the huge James Bay Project by the 1980s.

Developments on the political front were equally dramatic. The election of the Lesage Liberals in 1960 spelled the end of the Union Nationale era (in power for most of the years since 1936). Long-time Union Nationale Premier Maurice Duplessis upheld a traditional, classical concept of federalism (i.e., watertight compartments) in order to keep federal government intrusions at a minimum. And in response to the federal government's Royal Commission on National Development in the Arts, Letters and Sciences (the Massey Commission) in the early 1950s, Duplessis struck his own Royal Commission to Inquire into Constitutional Problems, known as the Tremblay Commission after its chair (Kwavnick, 1973).

Though ostensibly focused primarily on fiscal issues, the Tremblay Commission provided nothing less than a thorough restatement of the raison d'être for the Quebec state, emphasizing time-honoured Catholic values and the need for a highly defensive posture to protect them.

The Lesage government, by contrast, went on the offensive, demanding that Ottawa not only withdraw from Quebec jurisdictions but provide compensation for the funds that would have been spent in Quebec through joint programs in which Quebec had sometimes refused to participate. More generally, Lesage argued that the challenge facing Quebecers was not survival but self-assertion as a people. Quebec intellectuals became much less inclined to think of Confederation as a compact between either provinces or "founding nations." Rather, they referred increasingly to the inherent right of nations to self-determination. This led to demands for Quebec independence or to significant reform of the federal system. Such advocacy became a prominent part of Quebec party politics from the 1960s onward. In the meantime, the government of Quebec expanded and modernized its administrative capacity, and brought under the public-sector umbrella matters that had formerly been the preserve of the Church, such as health care and education. In addition, Quebec deliberately increased its capacity to manage federal–provincial relations. The case of the Canada Pension Plan and Quebec's alternative proposal, cited in earlier chapters, was one such example.

No less important than these developments inside Quebec were the responses from elsewhere in Canada. First, on a practical level, most of the other governments, federal and provincial, were surprised not only by the scale and type of the new Quebec's demands, but also by the sophistication with which Quebec was pursuing its external agenda. The capacity of the Quebec government to provide detailed analysis of various proposals, supported by a large team of experts in various fields, made a profound impression. Soon provinces such as Ontario, along with the federal government, were creating dedicated central agencies for the management of intergovernmental relations. In other words, simple emulation of Quebec's approach to intergovernmental relations in and of itself altered the basic dynamics of federalism. No longer were political executives content to leave intergovernmental relations to unelected officials in line departments. Furthermore, even smaller provinces recognized the need for greater in-house expertise if they were going to negotiate effectively.

For their part, Quebec's partners in the federal system, the federal government and the other provinces, were initially prepared to be accommodating. Ontario in particular under premiers such as John Robarts and William Davis played the role of conciliator, stressing the importance of flexibility and understanding in response to Quebec's aspirations. The acceptance of the Quebec Pension Plan in the 1960s symbolized a tacit if not active recognition that Quebec was, in some important respects, different from other provinces. This tacit acceptance of asymmetrical federalism began to fade by the late 1960s. Nonetheless, Ottawa's initial responses to Quebec's demands during the period of the Quiet Revolution are worth noting (Smiley, 1987: 134–41):

- Opting-out arrangements: Quebec could opt out of cost-shared programs and, at the same time, receive funding or more tax room for comparable programs without being required either to provide matching funds or to meet other conditions. The opting-out arrangements were in theory available to all provinces, but—consistent with the tacit acceptance of asymmetrical federalism where Quebec was concerned—in practice it was understood that only Quebec would take advantage of those arrangements.
- Constitutional review and reform: This began in earnest in 1967, continued throughout the 1970s, and culminated with the patriation of the constitution and the introduction of the Charter in 1982.
- Reform of the public service: Launched in 1963, the Royal Commission on Bilingualism and Biculturalism was tasked with examining how to ensure that federal public servants could communicate effectively within the federal government in either of Canada's two official languages, that citizens could do the same in their dealings with the federal government, and that the linguistic and cultural values of both language groups would be reflected in public-service recruitment and training.
- Enhancement of the francophone presence at the highest political level in Ottawa: Specifically applicable to the federal cabinet, governments in Ottawa sought to better reflect the country's linguistic duality by placing more francophone parliamentarians and public servants in positions of authority.

With respect to constitutional reform, efforts to find a suitable formula for amending the constitution had been underway for a number of years, but they took on a greater urgency during the 1960s. These discussions of constitutional reform were extended to include the possibility of introducing a charter of rights and giving explicit recognition to Quebec's unique position in Confederation. Constitutional reform would be the major federal–provincial issue from the late 1960s to the early 1990s (Russell, 2004). Over that time it came to be a matter of considerable importance to all governments and a host of citizen groups, as well as Indigenous peoples, but the initial impetus for it came out of direct concern for Quebec and its place in Confederation.

The "French Fact" and Federal Politics

With respect to reform of the federal public service, the recommendations of the federal government's Bilingualism and Bicultural (B&B) Commission had wide-ranging effects, most specifically in the form of the Official Languages Act of 1969. This Act expanded the conditions under which citizens could expect service in either of Canada's two official languages and set requirements for competence in both languages for senior public servants. Among other things, the Commission pointed out that francophones were under-represented in the federal public service at all levels but particularly at the highest levels; that the instruments and approaches used in public-service recruitment favoured the use of the English language; and that at the political level francophones tended to be allocated portfolios such as Justice and Public Works rather than Finance or Industry. Even before the Commission reported in 1967, the Liberal government of Lester B. Pearson had begun taking steps to change the face of the federal government, especially vis-à-vis francophone citizens. Initiatives ranged from re-naming federal bodies (Trans-Canada Airlines became Air Canada) to recruiting notable Quebecers directly into the federal cabinet (among them Pierre Trudeau). Perhaps most significant, in 1965 Parliament adopted the maple leaf design as the national flag. The B&B Commission also legitimized the idea that Canada had two founding cultures, French and English, and that the differences be-tween them extended beyond language. It was at this point, however, that the federal government stopped short. Whereas the Pearson government had been sympathetic to the notion of two cultures and supportive of special treatment for Quebec, the Pierre Trudeau government rejected both.

Pierre Trudeau drew a sharp distinction between language and culture, ac-cepting the importance of the former but rejecting the legitimacy of the latter, at least the notion that culture was linked directly to language. Trudeau's vision continues to shape the federal government's policy with respect both to Quebec and to Canadian federalism in general, although the Progressive Conservative government under Brian Mulroney (1984–93) and more recently the Conservative government under Stephen Harper have been more amenable to special status for Quebec. Essentially, Pierre Trudeau argued that all governments, federal and provincial, were responsible for promoting linguistic duality throughout the coun-try, and rejected the notion that Quebec, home to the majority of francophones in Canada, should have special powers and status. Furthermore, according to Pierre Trudeau, "the term biculturalism does not accurately depict our society; the word multiculturalism is more precise in this respect" (quoted in McRoberts, 2003).

Trudeau's emphasis on multiculturalism served to downplay Quebec's unique-ness, but it also reflected and recognized a very real change in the demographic composition of Canada as a whole. Since 1945 Canada's immigration policy had been gradually liberalized, with the result that the population outside Quebec was becoming increasingly heterogeneous (Quebec also experienced significant immi-gration into the Montreal area, with the majority of its new arrivals coming from Southern Europe and later Africa and the Caribbean). Arguing that bilingualism was the responsibility of all governments across the country and that Quebec's unique culture was just one of several unique cultures in Canada, the federal government challenged the rationale behind the dualist vision. Thus Ottawa actively worked to promote bilingualism throughout the nation and equal treatment for all provinces, regardless of language. Inside Quebec, meanwhile—and as part of the broader nationalist movement—the emphasis shifted from French–English dualism to French primacy, with legislation restricting access to English education, requiring French-only commercial signs, and promoting the use of French as the language of work (McRoberts, 2003). Legislative initiatives by the Quebec government on language matters began in the 1960s but reached their peak with the comprehensive Charter of the French Language of 1977 (also known as "Bill 101"). Ottawa in its turn became equally hard-nosed about rejecting Quebec's claims to special status—especially when the Liberals were in power.

The Sovereignist Movement and Constitutional Politics

As discussed in Chapter 3, differing conceptions and interpretation of the Canadian federal union date back to the original debates of Confederation in the 1860s. The more intensified debate launched by Quebec's Quiet Revolution reached a new stage, however, with the election of the first Parti Québécois (PQ) government in 1976 under the leadership of René Lévesque, who had been the architect of the nationalization of Hydro-Québec as a Liberal cabinet minister under Jean Lesage. The election of Lévesque and the PQ was soon followed by negotiations that led to constitutional patriation despite the Quebec government's opposition, and two referenda in Quebec conducted by PQ governments, the most recent of which, in 1995, saw the prospect of sovereignty rejected by only the slimmest of margins. Efforts by the Conservative government of Brian Mulroney to bring Quebec into the constitutional fold ended in failure, with the collapse of the Meech Lake Accord in 1990 and the rejection of the Charlottetown Accord in a nationwide referendum in 1992.

Over the past 25 years support for sovereignty among Quebec voters has fluctuated between 32 and 55 per cent (Leger Marketing, 2008, 2012). On the twentieth anniversary of the 1995 referendum, the Quebec-based research firm CROP presented the findings of a large-scale survey showing that only 34 per cent of respondents said "yes" to the question of whether Quebec should become an independent country, 60 per cent said "no," and 6 per cent indicated "don't know." It has also been pointed out by various analysts that hard-core sovereignists likely represent only about 20 to 25 per cent of the Quebec population at most (Aubin, 2005; Fournier et al., 2013). The referendum questions themselves have been ambiguous.[1] In 1980, the 106-word question was tied to the idea of sovereignty-association, a concept suggesting that an independent Quebec would continue in an economic union with the rest of Canada, with free movement of goods and services and use the Canadian dollar as its currency. The 1995 question was shorter and deleted the reference to sovereignty-association but indicated that sovereignty would be declared only after the failure of negotiations over a new constitutional relationship with the rest of Canada. At times when more than 50 per cent of Quebec voters have indicated in surveys a willingness to vote "yes," they have typically included a number of federalists who—unhappy with the constitutional status quo or in response to specific events—have done so in order to send a message to Ottawa and the rest of the country.

As just noted, there has been a gradual decline in support for sovereignty since its peak in the 1990s, especially among the youngest generation. In the 2015 CROP survey, 26 per cent of those between 18 and 34 said "yes" to sovereignty versus 38 per cent of those 55 years or older (CROP, 2015). Even among francophones, support for the "yes" side of the question was only 40 per cent. For non-francophones in Quebec it was much lower, at 12 per cent, which at the same time also illustrates that there is still sharp polarization on the sovereignty question between the francophone and non-francophone communities in that province. In September 2012 the Parti Québécois regained power as a minority government, lasting less than two years until April 2014, but there is little evidence that its limited electoral success indicated fresh support for sovereignty. Two weeks after the election of the PQ only 32 per cent of Quebec respondents to an Angus Reid poll stated that they would vote "yes" in a referendum on whether Quebec should secede from Canada (Angus Reid, 2012). The 2018 election in Quebec that brought the Coalition Avenir Québec (CAQ) to power and reduced the PQ to third-party status is seen as further evidence of a desire by Quebecers to move on from the sovereignty debate. At the same time, the CAQ, led by François Legault, a former PQ cabinet minister, ran on a distinctly autonomist and nationalist platform. Coupled with its right-of-centre orientation, in some ways the CAQ represents a throwback to the days of the old Union Nationale.

Still, even if outright sovereignty would likely be unacceptable to the majority of Quebec voters, there are relatively few who find the status quo acceptable. In a 2012 Ipsos poll, 44.5 per cent of Quebec respondents said they would support secession from Canada "if the constitution could not be changed enough to satisfy the majority of the province" (cited in Blatchford, 2012). Only among anglophones and some allophones in Quebec would there be any significant support for the current arrangement. Worth noting is that in the 2018 election the Quebec Liberal Party suffered one of its worst setbacks in its 150-year history, with all but two of its 31 elected members concentrated in non-francophone ridings (Yakabuski, 2018).

The status quo is essentially determined by the current constitutional order, which makes no explicit or formal provisions for Quebec's unique status within Confederation. Gagnon and Iacovino (2007: 159), in drawing a distinction between de facto and de jure special status for Quebec, note that at the de facto level Quebec has made several important gains and obtained concessions, including many achieved during the era of Pierre Trudeau. The frustration lies in the fact that those gains have failed to receive appropriate legal or symbolic recognition—most notably within the constitution. This strategy of working to make incremental gains, referred to as *étapisme*, continues. For example, as discussed in Chapter 7, Quebec refused to sign the Social Union Framework Agreement (SUFA) in 1999 and still considers the Constitution Act of 1982 to lack legitimacy. But it was able nevertheless to reach an understanding with Ottawa that would allow it to receive the additional funding for health care that Ottawa made available through SUFA, for example. What emerged during the 1990s was a pattern Roger Gibbins (1999) described as "9-1-1 federalism": Ottawa reaching agreement with the nine provinces and then coming to a separate understanding with Quebec. This separate understanding often takes the form of agreeing to disagree. Even though 9-1-1 federalism has been largely overshadowed by sequential bilateralism, it is still the case that Quebec expects special recognition for its unique position in particular fields, as happened in the case of the Canada Job Grant program. Overall, the extent to which the two sides have been able to reach quiet, informal consensus on major issues is often quite surprising. For example, Quebec appears willing to accept money from federal infrastructure programs and funding for research chairs at Quebec universities—arrangements that would likely have been unacceptable to the Duplessis government in the 1950s (Bakvis, 2008). As well, despite Quebec's refusal to sign SUFA back in 1999, Ottawa and Quebec have at times shared remarkably similar perspectives on medicare and social policy, particularly when the Liberals held power in Ottawa from 1993 to 2005.

While profound discontent over intergovernmental issues in Canada and demands for special treatment for special circumstances have not been confined to Quebec, the particular gap in Quebec between de jure and de facto asymmetrical federalism remains. And since the salience of that gap depends as much on nationalist sentiment as anything else, events that might be seen outside Quebec as relatively benign could still be enough to trigger a surge of support for the sovereignty option among Quebecers. Thus the evidence of kickbacks to the federal Liberal Party revealed at the Gomery Inquiry into federal sponsorship programs in Quebec set off a wave of revulsion in Quebec that in the spring of 2005 temporarily pushed support for the sovereignty option to well over 50 per cent (Leger Marketing, 2008).

Overall, it was the Quebec agenda that drove the constitutional reform process throughout the 1970s and 1980s. By the early 1990s, however, the failure of the Meech Lake and Charlottetown accords made it clear that constitutional reform was no longer primarily an issue in the country as a whole, or even in Quebec. Especially in Ontario, BC, and Alberta, population growth, fuelled in good part by immigration, made issues associated with multiculturalism and the needs of large urban areas much more salient. These issues, which continue to grow in importance, have much less to do with territory than with groups and communities dispersed across the country, and they have made the local level of government much more relevant (Gibbins, 1999). At the same time, both Meech Lake and Charlottetown drove home the point that significant constitutional change is unlikely to occur unless due consideration is given to Canada's "first" founding people (the Indigenous peoples), whose presence was rarely even acknowledged until a little over three decades ago.

Much more recently, the controversies over the niqab and putative alien cultural practices associated mainly with Islam that have roiled public opinion across the Western world, including Canada, has had much greater resonance in Quebec than in the rest of the country. In a 2015 poll commissioned by the Privy Council Office, a clear majority of Canadians, 82 per cent, were opposed to the wearing of face coverings during citizenship ceremonies and Quebec respondents were most opposed, at 93 per cent (Levitz, 2015). For the past decade in Quebec the issue of cultural accommodation for immigrant minorities has been prominent in political discourse. Responding to the 2008 declaration of cultural standards issued by the small municipality of Hérouxville, the Liberal government of Jean Charest established a consultative commission (the Bouchard-Taylor Commission) to review the issue province-wide. That report (Quebec, 2008) and the reaction to it underscores the differences between Quebec and the rest of Canada with respect to tolerance and accommodation of cultural practices (mainly Muslim) practised by immigrant minorities. The Bouchard-Taylor Commission took a position, which they termed "interculturalism," advocating broad accommodation similar to multicultural practice in Canada generally. A majority among French speakers in Quebec were opposed to the report. Rather, they supported a position on integration/accommodation more akin to that of France and other European countries (Sharify-Funk, 2010). As an example, both the PQ and Liberal governments of the past decade have proposed or passed legislation banning the wearing of religious symbols by those in positions of public employment (Peritz, 2017), and the CAQ appears set to follow this pattern given that its stance on this issue in the 2018 election was distinctly more hard-line than that of the Liberals. Tensions between the general Canadian population and newer immigrant communities over controversial cultural practices are not confined to Quebec. However, these issues do have the potential to expose other Quebec–Canada fault lines. Three such divisions stand out: the Quebec Charter of Rights versus the Canadian Charter of Rights; the overall Canadian attachment to multiculturalism versus Quebec's antipathy to that policy and the nuances of its own forms of cultural accommodation; and the realities of Quebec having more practical autonomy over immigration than the other provinces. These are a set of federalism issues to be managed but to date they have not contributed to a critical division.

Harper's "Open Federalism" and Quebec

When Stephen Harper became Conservative Party leader he began articulating his vision of federalism, including a number of elements that on the face of it should have had a strong appeal to Quebec. As Roger Gibbins (2006) noted, in its initial phase "open federalism" was in large part a Conservative electoral strategy designed to make gains in the province of Quebec. In his December 2005 speech in Quebec City during the 2005–6 federal election campaign, Conservative leader Stephen Harper sought to ensure Quebecers that a Conservative government would resolve Quebec's long-standing concern over the fiscal imbalance between Ottawa and Quebec, as well as the other provinces, provide Quebec with greater opportunities for direct representation in international forums, and usher in an era of "open federalism" to replace the paternalistic model of the Liberals. These ideas were fleshed out further in the 2006 Speech from the Throne in which the Harper government referred to "the unique place of a strong and vibrant Quebec in a united Canada" (quoted in Gibbins, 2006: 67). This sentiment then served as the basis for the subsequent joint parliamentary resolution that "the Québécois form a nation within a united Canada" (*Hansard*, 22 Nov. 2006).

The Harper government's approach to federalism, whether called "open federalism" or simply a variant of classical federalism, has been described by David Cameron as a "highly significant shift in Ottawa's traditional conception of its role in the federation" (Cameron, 2015: 286). In previous chapters we have discussed the details of the Harper approach and its consequences for intergovernmental relations in fiscal, economic, social, and environmental policies, and we shall return to this briefly in the Conclusion.

Harper's classical federalism was also illustrated by the federal government's approach to executive federalism, in particular the tendency to avoid multilateral negotiations with the premiers. Referring to federal–provincial relations in general and especially Quebec, John Ibbitson (2016) has described the Harper years as a "pax Harperana"—a period in which the very disengagement from provincial affairs reduced overall conflicts and tensions in the federation as such. Quebec's continuing place in the federation during the Harper era can be further illustrated by two sets of dynamics. First is federal electoral politics in Quebec featuring the Conservatives' attempts to regain a foothold in the province. Second (and more indirectly related to electoral politics) were developments involving the Supreme Court, which have a special bearing on Quebec.

After 2006 it appeared that the Conservatives might be pursuing the same electoral strategy used by John Diefenbaker after he won a minority government in 1957 with very little support in Quebec. Subsequently, Diefenbaker made strong efforts (with the help of the Union Nationale in Quebec) to woo Quebec voters, culminating in the warning to Quebecers during the 1958 election campaign that they risked being left out of what was very likely to be a majority

Progressive Conservative government.[2] In the case of the Harper Conservatives, they appeared keen on expanding their representation from Quebec in the House of Commons, but nonetheless introduced a number of ill-timed policies just prior to the 2008 fall election. None of these policies were necessarily significant on their own, but cumulatively they strongly suggested that the Harper and the Conservatives had a tin ear as far as Quebec was concerned. For example, just before that election the Conservative government, as a way of reinforcing its core electoral base, trumpeted its cuts of $64 million to cultural organizations across the country. According to Paul Wells (2012), "just about every arts organization in Quebec rose up to campaign against the Conservatives in the 2008 elections." As it turned out, the Conservatives failed to make gains in Quebec and remained at 10 MPs from the province. In the 2011 election the Conservatives were reduced to five, an election that also saw the defeat of Lawrence Cannon, the minister of Foreign Affairs who had come closest to playing the role of Quebec lieutenant, a role that Harper never really acknowledged.

The controversy over the culture support grant cuts in 2008, which played out mainly in Quebec, also contributed to the wider gulf between the Harper government and Quebec on issues ranging from criminal justice to social policy. The heated debate over the abolition of the long-gun registry also concerned primarily Quebec, with the Quebec government going to court to try and retain the records for Quebec. On social policy, Quebec's daycare program, which offers subsidized daycare spaces to all for between $7.30 and $20 per day and which is unique in Canada, was clearly at odds with the Harper government's universal child-care benefit where money was transferred directly to parents and where no effort was made to support or deliver actual daycare spaces. On health-care transfers from Ottawa to the provinces there was actually much less of a gulf between Ottawa and Quebec. While Quebec did not appreciate the fact that the federal government was planning on a reduction in the growth of transfers to the provinces effective 2016, on the other hand it quietly welcomed the fact that Ottawa was also planning to be much less intrusive in enforcing provisions of the Canada Health Act.

In the area of labour market training, again the Conservative federal government appeared to ignore Quebec sensitivities and the understanding reached in the post-1995 referendum period where Ottawa effectively turned over jurisdiction in this field to the provinces, finally acceding to a strongly held and long-standing demand by consecutive Quebec governments that this field properly belonged under the heading of education, which is under provincial jurisdiction (section 93 of the Constitution). In seeking to launch its new labour market initiative (the Canada Job Grant) to provide direct grants to those willing to upgrade their skills, the Conservatives were in effect not only bypassing those Quebec agencies responsible for labour market training but also seeking to take back those powers that had been given to the provinces several years earlier.

While the federal Conservative Party had its limitations in appealing to Quebec, the necessity for doing so in order to achieve power has been declining. Despite electing only five MPs from Quebec in the 2011 election, the Conservatives still succeeded in winning a majority government for the first time since coming to power in 2006. In fact, the seats won by the Conservatives outside of Quebec were sufficient to constitute a parliamentary majority, a first in Canadian electoral history that marked the end of one of the truisms in Canadian politics: that any party wishing to achieve a majority government needs, if not a solid base in Quebec, at least a significant number of that province's seats (78 Quebec seats in the House of Commons as of the 2015 federal election). For decades, this need for an electoral coalition between Quebec and the rest of Canada gave Quebec leverage in Ottawa, forcing Ottawa to take Quebec into account in national policy-making (Bakvis and Macpherson, 1995). Combined with Quebec representation in cabinet it has probably constituted the single most important form of intrastate federalism—representation of the regions directly in the centre (see Chapter 1)—in what is generally an interstate federation.

The electoral outcome in 2011 reflected in part the Conservative Party's success in Canada outside of Quebec but also pointed to a gradual but important demographic shift. In 1951 Quebec constituted 28.9 per cent of the Canadian population; by 1993 it was down to 25 per cent; and by 2013 that had shrunk to 23.1 per cent (Statistics Canada, 2015). Given relatively stronger population growth in Ontario and the West, that percentage will continue to shrink. So, too, will the instances of Quebec being able to use its electoral weight to decide the difference between a minority or majority government—the 2015 election result notwithstanding—as well opportunities to use that clout in cabinet and the governing party caucus.

To be sure, this sort of informal intrastate federalism is no longer as important as it was 25 to 30 years ago. Beginning with the Chrétien government in 1993, in which close to two-thirds of Liberal MPs came from Ontario, there was less opportunity for ministers and caucus members from other provinces to exercise influence. The Harper government, even as a minority, was actually more balanced in terms of representation, and Conservatives did elect 10 MPs in Quebec in 2008, five in 2011, and 12 in 2015. However, the tight control exercised by Harper and the Prime Minister's Office, over ministers specifically and the government apparatus as a whole, has been unprecedented, even by Canadian standards, with the result that there was little scope for ministers to function in either a sectoral or regional capacity.

The 2011 federal election was significant for Quebec in other ways. The Bloc Québécois (BQ), essentially Quebec's voice and face in Parliament for close to two decades, saw its electoral support collapse, reducing it from 49 seats to four. Equally surprising, the NDP moved from one Quebec seat, held by party leader Jack Layton, to 59 seats, effectively displacing the BQ as Quebec's primary federal party. While the result clearly demonstrated Quebec's disenchantment with the BQ, at the time it was not yet clear, and indeed it is still not entirely clear, whether Quebec voters were simply using the NDP as a temporary parking lot as they pondered their future or whether the result portended a major shift in how they see themselves playing a role in federal politics and protecting their interests (Bakvis and Tanguay, 2012). One analysis of the 2011 election by Fournier et al. (2013) makes the intriguing, and persuasive, argument that in addition to the charisma of Jack Layton the gap between the Quebec electorate and the NDP on a number of issues was much narrower than that between the electorate and the Bloc. And one of the major factors serving to widen the gap in the case of the Bloc, and leading to its subsequent electoral setback, was its ill-advised decision to focus in the last few weeks of the campaign on the importance of working towards sovereignty as distinct from its more traditional stance of representing Quebec in Ottawa.

The 2015 election results suggest a scenario that is much more back to the future, with the Liberals becoming the largest single party in that province with 40 seats, followed by the NDP, down to 16 seats, the Conservatives with 12 seats, and a mild revival for the BQ with 10 seats. In the run-up to the 2019 federal election the Conservatives under Andrew Scheer actively recruited conservative nationalists as candidates in the Quebec City area and succeeded in winning in 2018 a crucial by-election, taking a seat from the Liberals, as a way of re-establishing a foothold in Quebec. It may well be that the province's voters have collectively decided they would like to revert to a more traditional pre-1993 role where the Quebec wing of the governing party carries lots of clout in cabinet and caucus, especially when the Quebec contingent represents a sizable number of seats. In the Mulroney era, for example, the Quebec caucus at times represented up to one-third of total government seats. And in the 1980 majority government of Pierre Trudeau the Quebec contingent constituted slightly over half the government bench.

As noted in earlier chapters, the Supreme Court of Canada (SCC) is one of the few formal intrastate bodies in the Canadian federation and easily outranks that other formal intrastate state body, the Senate, in terms of significance. This significance became evident in the latter half of the Harper period and it involved the SCC itself. Of the cases discussed in Chapter 4 only one directly affected Quebec, namely the appointment in 2013 of Justice Marc Nadon of the Federal Court of Appeal, at one time a member of the Quebec bar, to the Supreme Court as one of the three justices from Quebec. The appointment, and the subsequent changes made to the Supreme Court Act, was challenged by a private citizen and the government of Quebec. In March of 2014 the SCC ruled that the appointment ran contrary to the Quebec-related provisions in the Act and, further, that changes to the composition of the SCC require a constitutional amendment based on the approval of Parliament and all 10 provinces. In stating that it was important to ensure "that the court has civil law expertise and that Quebec's legal traditions and social values are represented on the Court and that Quebec's confidence in the Court be maintained," the Court's affirmation of the constitutional legitimacy of Quebec's representation on the SCC went much further than what many were anticipating (*Reference re Supreme Court Act ss. 5 and 6*, 1 S.C.R. 433 [2014]).

Two other decisions affected all provinces but involved issues of particular interest to Quebec. As noted in Chapter 8, in 2010 the Conservative government introduced legislation for a single national securities regulator, legislation that was promptly challenged by the provinces of Alberta and Quebec, arguing that it was ultra vires federal jurisdiction. Both provinces referred the legislation as reference questions to their appeal courts. The Alberta court rejected the proposed legislation in its entirety while the Quebec court found valid some components that bore on criminal law matters. Ottawa then had little choice but to refer the proposed Act to the Supreme Court for its opinion, asking whether it was within the legislative authority of the Parliament of Canada. The SCC in turn ruled that the legislation could not be justified under the federal power over trade and commerce, that it effectively overreached by seeking to regulate all aspects of contracts for securities, which clearly intruded on provincial jurisdiction over property and civil rights. At the same time, there were clearly some matters related to systemic risk where federal intervention could be justified. The Court stated that, while it was not its role to say what alternative scheme or schemes might gain the approval of the Court, "we may appropriately note the growing practice of resolving the complex governance problems that arise in federations, not by the bare logic of either/or, but by seeking cooperative solutions that meet the needs of the country as a whole as well as its constituent parts" (*Reference re Securities Act*, 3 S.C.R. 837 [2011]). (For more discussion on the Supreme Court's recent views promoting "cooperative federalism" solutions to jurisdictional disputes, see Chapter 4.)

Quebec's interests in the issues of this case are unique among Canadian provinces. Aside from its civil code, which means contracts and other private law are handled differently in Quebec, it is also the case that the provincially regulated financial sector as whole is structured differently and is more sizable than elsewhere (Coleman, 2002). Caisse populaires (roughly the equivalent of credit unions) handle far more financial transactions than banks. The Desjardins Group, for example, constitutes the country's sixth largest financial institution. Quebec, and specifically Montreal, has a financial services sector that is only second to Toronto's in size. As a result, over the years the province developed a far more extensive regulatory apparatus and a capacity to deal with its variegated financial sector than the other provinces, including Ontario. The proposed national regulator would thus have far more impact on Quebec (*CBC News*, 2011).

At the same time, while Quebec saw the ruling as a positive one for the province, it was likely discomfited by the ruling's reference to cooperative federalism. What the Supreme Court had in mind was not, in the words of one writer, "your grandfather's cooperative federalism" (Carrière, 2018), seeing instead more in the way of joint solutions rather than the top-down, cost-shared federalism of the 1950s. Nonetheless, Quebec no doubt saw echoes of the latter, a fear at least partially realized when, subsequent to the ruling, the Conservative government launched its Cooperative Capital Markets Regulator initiative. Quebec referred this new federal legislation to its own court of appeal, which ruled the legislation invalid mainly on the grounds that "It subjects the province's power to legislate in this matter to the approval of an external entity (the council of ministers), which is not permitted" (quoted in Van Praet, 2017). The Quebec minister of Finance indicated that "the current passport system works well" (quoted in Van Praet, 2017), but one suspects what was truly at stake was the fact that Quebec could see no recognition at all of its unique position in this field in the new federal legislation.

The other key decision was the Senate reference case. The Senate, a body that many provinces would like to see abolished, became a source of major frustration for Prime Minister Harper and became fodder for another key reference case. In his first parliamentary session in 2006 the Conservative government introduced legislation to limit future senatorial terms to eight years and to provide for consultative elections. The proposed legislation did not address the issue of the need to rebalance representation from the provinces. Close to seven years and two further pieces of legislation later, the issues were submitted to the Supreme Court in the form of a reference question, with the hope, if not the expectation, that limiting senatorial terms and the use of consultative elections would at least be found to be within the jurisdiction of Parliament.

The SCC decision (*Reference re Senate Reform*, 1 S.C.R. 704 [2014]), when it arrived in April 2014, like the decision on Supreme Court appointments, went much further that many anticipated. It stated that even changes such as term limits or consultative elections required the 7/50 rule outlined in section 37 of the Constitution Act, 1982, that is, seven provinces representing 50 per cent of the population concurring. Senate abolishment would require the consent of all the provinces and Parliament. The reaction to the Court judgement among provinces was mixed. Some, like Saskatchewan, whose premier, Brad Wall, had strongly argued for abolition, expressed clear disappointment with the decision. Others were more lukewarm or non-committal. Premier Kathleen Wynne of Ontario, for example, stated that Senate reform was not a priority but would be willing to participate in "pan-Canadian discussions about Senate reform" under the leadership of the federal government. For Manitoba, Senate reform was also not a priority, but the NDP-led government indicated its preference for abolition if push came to shove. The only province that was clearly pleased with the decision was Quebec, hailing the unanimous decision as "historic." The Quebec justice minister said it indicated that "it's not up to the federal government to dictate reform" (quoted in MacCharles, 2014). For Quebec, the decision was clearly an affirmation that it had the capacity to say no to substantial changes, even for an institution that it held in low esteem and to which it attached little importance.

Of the three SCC cases noted above, the Nadon case involving appointments to the highest court from Quebec is the one that most clearly protected Quebec's interests. While the case arose out of the concern by private citizens about both Nadon's capacity and qualifications to be a Supreme Court justice, it was his rather tenuous connection to the Quebec bar and the province as whole and the fact that the federal government was willing to stretch the rules that gave Quebec pause. To the extent that this concern was prevalent not just within Quebec government circles but also in the Quebec bar, the Quebec judiciary, and the legal community more broadly—and evidence suggests that this was indeed the case—the Nadon decision provided solid reassurance that the SCC would go to some lengths to protect the unique nature of appointments from that province.

With respect to the Senate reform decision, Quebec had the most to lose from Harper's reforms because as the only province with a majority French language and culture, let alone other aspects of distinctiveness, Quebec fears being outnumbered by the federal government and the other provinces. Therefore, it appreciates more than most the actual and potential value of the Senate itself, as well as being attached to the federal principle that such intrastate institutions should only be reformed with the strong consent of the provinces, including Quebec. And the national securities regulator case also protected Quebec's interests. One analyst reviewing these decisions and drawing comparisons with other institutions concluded that "At this stage in Canada's political history it [the Supreme Court of Canada] is now the ultimate protector and guarantor of Quebec's position in confederation and the overall federal–provincial balance" (Bakvis, 2014: 74). It is a somewhat bold statement, but only mildly so.

Summary

Most current discussions of Canada–Quebec relations focus on how much less turbulent they are now than even 10 years ago, a perception reinforced by the fact that support for outright sovereignty has been at the lowest level for several years. However, the same survey data also show respondents in Quebec find the status quo still unacceptable. While Quebec–Canada relations are perhaps calmer than in previous decades, we would argue this also has had something to do with developments such as Supreme Court decisions and the internal divisions within the PQ and the Bloc. We also noted the high level of uncertainty among Quebec voters, particularly when it comes to federal elections. In a little more than three decades the Quebec electorate has moved from supporting the Liberals as their primary federal party, to the Progressive Conservatives, to the Bloc Québécois, and then, in rapid succession, to the NDP before reverting back to the Liberals. In many ways these voter shifts are a metaphor for how Quebec relates to the rest of the country.

In the past, particularly at the times of the constitutional negotiations and the two referenda, it was commonplace to speak of Quebec, and Canada, as being at a crossroads. Now it looks much less like a crossroads and more like a round-about with a sizable number of voters veering off in new directions, as happened in the 1 October 2018 general election. Two relatively new parties increased their seats: the CAQ from 21 to 74 seats in the National Assembly, enough to form a secure majority government; and Québec Solidaire from 3 seats to 10. These results broke the dominance of the Liberals and PQ in Quebec politics, with the Liberals falling from 68 seats to 31, and the PQ from 28 to 10. And, as noted, only two of the Liberals' 31 seats are from francophone ridings. This shift in party support at both federal and provincial levels represents genuine efforts on the part of voters and elites in the province to find effective means to pursue their interests and to find a workable arrangement with the rest of Canada. At times, the Quebec electorate has sought to work within and through the governing party in Ottawa, as was the case under the governments of Pierre Trudeau and Brian Mulroney, or outside the governing party as it did when it supported the Bloc and, more recently, the NDP. The role played by political parties and party systems and their importance in the functioning of the Canadian federation has not received as much attention by political scientists as it should. The case of Quebec provides good evidence as to why more attention is warranted to this important dimension of Canadian federalism.

The arrival of the Liberal government in Ottawa in October of 2015 with a new "sunny ways" approach to federalism and to governance more generally sug-gested that there would be a different approach to Quebec compared to that of the Harper Conservatives, if only because there was now a significantly larger contingent of MPs from Quebec (40) on the government side. However, the pres-ence of Quebecers in cabinet proved to be only slightly higher than it was in the Harper cabinet. As well, like Stephen Harper, Justin Trudeau declined to designate anyone in his cabinet as his Quebec lieutenant (nor, for that matter, were regional ministers more generally identified), and there were no plans to resurrect this role. At the same time, the Trudeau government appears sensitive to Quebec issues, carefully avoiding the legal controversies over the niqab ban and cancelling the Energy East pipeline project, which local Quebec politicians and citizens fought against because of serious environmental concerns. The test may well come in the subsequent federal election where Liberal "new" politics will be pitted against what appears to be a more traditional Conservative electoral strategy.

When it comes to the constitutional question, "sunny ways" notwithstanding, it is highly unlikely that Trudeau is willing to reopen this Pandora's box. Indeed, it is unlikely that Justin Trudeau and the Liberals possess knowledge of a magical pathway allowing Quebec to become part of the constitutional family, a pathway that has so far escaped all previous governments. It is also a real challenge to think of what the Liberals can do to persuade Quebec to become more accepting of present arrangements. In the meantime, continuing issues are bound to strain Quebec–Canada and Quebec–federal relations. Such issues as Indigenous affairs, environmental management, fiscal arrangements, and international trade relations all have the potential to flare. However, none seems likely to lead to a return to a regime-threatening crisis over Quebec's place in Canada. The period of intense and prolonged crisis is over; the ongoing mutual challenge of making Quebec at home in the federation remains.

Questions for Critical Thought

1. What will be the impact and legacy of Stephen Harper's "open federalism" and his approach to policy and governance on the future of Canada–Quebec relations?

2. What effect will Justin Trudeau's "sunny ways" approach to federalism have on Canada–Quebec relations?

3. In what ways does the Quebec case illustrate the importance of elections and party politics in the functioning of Canadian federalism?

Notes

1. On the impact of question wording on support for sovereignty, see Yale and Durand (2011).
2. Diefenbaker did indeed win a landslide majority; but while a number of Quebecers were recruited into cabinet, none were placed in key portfolios, none of them played the long-standing role of Quebec lieutenant, and they were largely ignored.

References

Angus Reid. 2012. "Appetite for Sovereignty Remains Lukewarm in Quebec." Press release, 21 Nov.

Aubin, B. 2005. "Polls May Show Separatism Rising." *Maclean's*, 9 May.

Bakvis, H. 2008. "The Knowledge Economy and Post-Secondary Education." In *Canadian Federalism: Performance, Effectiveness, and Legitimacy*, 2nd edn, edited by H. Bakvis and G. Skogstad. Toronto: Oxford University Press.

———. 2014. "Canada: A Crisis in Regional Representation?" *The Tocqueville Review* 35, no. 2: 51–77.

———and L.G. Macpherson. 1995. "Quebec Bloc Voting and the Canadian Electoral System." *Canadian Journal of Political Science* 28, no. 4: 659–92.

———and A.B. Tanguay. 2012. "Federalism, Political Parties, and the Burden of National Unity: Still Making Federalism Do the Heavy Lifting." In *Canadian Federalism: Performance, Effectiveness, and Legitimacy*, 3rd edn, edited by H. Bakvis and G. Skogstad. Toronto: Oxford University Press.

Black, E.R. 1975. *Divided Loyalties: Canadian Concepts of Federalism*. Montreal and Kingston: McGill-Queen's University Press.

Blatchford, A. 2012. "Sovereignty far from a Dead Issue in Quebec, Poll Finds." Canadian Press, 26 Mar.

Cameron, D. 2015. "Canada's Constitutional Legitimacy Deficit: Learning to Live with It." In *Thinking Outside the Box: Innovation in Policy Ideas*, edited by K. Banting et al., 277–94. Montreal and Kingston: McGill-Queen's University Press.

Carrière, S. 2018. "Not Your Grandfather's Cooperative Federalism: Constitutional Themes at the Supreme Court Hearing of Redwater." Faculty of Law, University of Calgary, 2 Apr. Accessed 16 July 2018. https://ablawg.ca/2018/04/02/not-your-grandfathers-cooperative-federalism-constitutional-themes-at-the-supreme-court-hearing-of-redwater/.

CBC News. 2010. "Single Securities Regulator Bad for Quebec: Group." 10 May. Accessed 24 June 2016. http://www.cbc.ca/news/canada/montreal/single-securities-regulator-bad-for-quebec-group-1.873190.

Coleman, W. 2002. "Federalism and Financial Services." In *Canadian Federalism: Performance, Effectiveness, and Legitimacy*, edited by H. Bakvis and G. Skogstad. Toronto: Oxford University Press.

Cook, R. 1972. *French-Canadian Nationalism*. Toronto: Macmillan of Canada.

CROP. 2015. *Les 20 Ans du Référendum de 1995*. Montreal: CROP, Oct.

Fournier, P., F. Cutler, S. Sorokka, D. Stolle, and E. Bélanger. 2013. "Riding the Orange Wave: Leadership, Values, Issues, and the 2011 Canadian Election." *Canadian Journal of Political Science* 46, no. 4: 1–35.

Gagnon, A.-G., and R. Iacovino. 2007. *Federalism, Citizenship, and Quebec*. Toronto: University of Toronto Press.

Gibbins, R. 1999. "Taking Stock: Canadian Federalism and Its Constitutional Framework." In *How Ottawa Spends, 1999–2000*, edited by L. Pal. Toronto: Oxford University Press.

———. 2006. "Open Federalism: Thoughts from Alberta." In *Open Federalism: Interpretations, Significance*, edited by K. Banting et al. Kingston, ON: Institute of Intergovernmental Relations.

Ibbitson, J. 2016. "Stephen Harper, Canada's True Father of Federation." *Globe and Mail*, 27 May.

Kwavnick, D., ed. 1973. *The Tremblay Report: Report of the Royal Commission of Inquiry on Constitutional Problems*. Toronto: McClelland and Stewart.

Leger Marketing. 2008. "Quebec Political Survey." 11 Nov.

———. 2012. "Quebec Political Survey." 24 Nov.

Levitz, S. 2015. "Polling Data on Niqabs Shows Quebecers Overwhelmingly Support a Government Ban." *Globe and Mail*, 24 Sept.

MacCharles, T. 2014. "Supreme Court Rejects Harper Government Proposals for Senate Reform." *Toronto Star*, 25 Apr.

McRoberts, K. 2003. "Conceiving Diversity: Dualism, Multiculturalism, and Multi-nationalism." In *New Trends in Canadian Federalism*, 2nd edn, edited by F. Rocher and M. Smith. Peterborough, ON: Broadview Press.

Peritz, I. 2017. "Quebec Bans Face Covering in Public Services, Raising Worries among Muslims." *Globe and Mail*, 18 Oct.

Quebec. 2008. *Building the Future: A Time for Reconciliation* (Bouchard-Taylor Report). Quebec: Government of Quebec.

Russell, P. 2004. *Constitutional Odyssey: Can Canadians Become a Sovereign People?* 3rd edn. Toronto: University of Toronto Press.

Sharify-Funk, M. 2010. "Muslims and the Politics of 'Reasonable Accommodation': Analyzing the Bouchard-Taylor Report and Its Impact on the Canadian Province of Québec." *Journal of Muslim Minority Affairs* 30, no. 4: 535–53.

Smiley, D.V. 1987. *The Federal Condition in Canada*. Toronto: McGraw-Hill Ryerson.

Statistics Canada. 2015. The Canadian Population in 2011: Population Counts and Growth, Figure 4, Population Share of Canada's Regions, 1951 to 2011. Accessed 17 June 2016. https://www12.statcan.gc.ca/census-recensement/2011/as-sa/98-310-x/2011001/fig/fig4-eng.cfm.

Van Praet, N. 2017. "Quebec Court Rules National Regulator Plan Is Unconstitutional." *Globe and Mail*, 10 May.

Wells, P. 2012. "Stephen Harper's Secret Weapon in Quebec." *Maclean's*, 14 May.

Yakabuski, K. 2018. "Quebec's Liberals Contemplate a Future on the Fringes." *Globe and Mail*, 18 Oct.

Yale, F., and C. Durand. 2011. "What Did Quebeckers Want? Impact of Question Wording, Constitutional Proposal and Context on Support for Sovereignty 1976–2008." *American Review of Canadian Studies* 41, no. 3: 242–58.

Conclusion

Ambivalent Federalism

> **Learning Objectives**
> - To be able to summarize the key structural (social and institutional) constraints on the ongoing development of the Canadian federal system.
> - To summarize the major intergovernmental issues of the past 50 years.
> - To look forward to challenges in the twenty-first century for Canadian federalism.

The Deep Pathways of Canadian Federalism

Many years ago the constitutional scholar J.A. Corry is said to have advised a student that "A neat and tidy mind is a crippling disability when studying federalism" (quoted in Burgess, 2011: 191). The complexity and nuance of Canadian federalism are certainly daunting. Yet mastering the often messy details is essential for a deeper understanding. As in any complex political and social system, the full truth is in the minutiae. But understanding is also to be found in looking at big pictures and identifying the broad forces driving the federation and its evolution. Thus far we have focused on the specifics of the Canadian federal system and the relations between its constituent governments. Now, in our concluding chapter, we turn to a summary of the key characteristics of Canadian federalism, a portrait that can emerge more clearly now that the detail has been laid out.

Our grasp of why the federal system operates the way it does and what drives its structures and dynamics is based on three foundational concepts in the political science of complex government systems: federal society, its ideology and values, and the nature of the specific regime, including its institutions and operating norms. While the overall system can be seen as the product of interaction between state and society, we believe that institutions are embedded in a specific society and nurtured by a specific political culture (ideology and values), both of which are also federal (cf. Cairns, 1986). Canadian federalism is ambiguous in both its goals and its character, and its foundational premises remain contested, primarily because the federal components of the society and political culture are often at odds with the existing institutions and their operating norms. And as much as these institutions reflect their contemporary social and cultural context, they occupy deeply grooved pathways—reinforced after 140 years of operation.

For prominent scholars of federalism, such as W.S. Livingston, a federal society both gives rise to and sustains a federal system of government (Livingston, 1952; cf. Smith, 2004). The underlying society is "federal," in his view, where diversity is more than just territorial and where that diversity in itself leads to federal governance. Federalism is thus a political theory of power-sharing for diverse or multiple societies, adopted historically by numerous separate societies that have come together to form a single new political community. The process of union, and the ongoing process of integration that follows, may create a less federal society over time; this has arguably been the case in Australia and Germany. In Canada the original federal society of French and English linguistic communities, Catholic and Protestant religious communities, and pre-existing colonial units guaranteed that a federal form of union would be adopted in the 1860s for the British North American colonies, rather than the unitary state on the British model that some preferred. Here, however, despite the development of strong integrative forces, we have not seen a lessening of the federal aspect of our society. In English-speaking Canada, including the poly-ethnic immigrant communities that have been integrated into it, economic and social mobility and the development of common values and symbols, including the Charter of Rights, have created a vibrant pan-Canadian nationalism. On the other hand, we have an equally vibrant Quebec nationalism, well established in the Canadian psyche since the 1960s, which for much of the past 50 years has posed a serious threat to the sustainability of the federal regime. Deliberately left out of the original federal bargain, Indigenous peoples also have nationalist, in some cases separatist, attachments—and remain significantly alienated from the Canadian state, including the federal system.

Regional Identities in the Canadian Federation

The territorial diversity of the original provinces and the ecological, economic, and cultural differences are inevitable in a country as vast as Canada. These *regional identities* remain highly potent, as anyone who has lived in or even visited Calgary, Halifax, or Iqaluit can attest. Still, the regional landscape is changing with intensifying urban development and the westward movement of population and economic clout. The globalized economy integrated in a North American context also complicates the picture. North–south integration with the United States may have weakened one of the original rationales for the union—a point not lost on Quebec sovereignists. As of October 2018, it still remains to be seen how significant the current US trend to retreat from global and continental integration will be. The recently concluded United States, Mexico and Canada Agreement (USMCA) is designed to replace NAFTA and is somewhat more protectionist of US interests but leaves much of NAFTA intact. However, if continued, these trends could lead to a renewed emphasis in Canada on our own economic union. In any case, there is no discernible lessening of the desire for a separate political community (or communities) north of the US: quite the contrary. As in 1867, the underlying society in Canada remains resolutely federal in the Livingston sense; the only difference is that the cleavages have changed to some degree.

Political Values and Ideology

A second component of Canadian federalism is *federal ideology* and its underlying basis in the specific political values of the federal society. In the original Confederation bargain, several competing federal ideologies were at work, and these differing ideologies continue to be reflected in the constitutional regime. Each has its own ideas about the nature of the federal union and the purposes to which it should be put. Many of the founders of Confederation sought a strong central government that would have a more or less imperial relationship with the provinces, and emphasized the components' common British allegiance and heritage. They assumed that the new union would integrate the diverse colonies over time, reducing regional differences and transcending linguistic and religious differences. Another view of the union, centred in Quebec, envisioned a pact of two nations, in which federal government was not simply a way station to national unity but a permanent form of power-sharing that preserved minority rights and sectional self-government. A variant of this perspective is that the federation is a pact among regions or provinces, without the connotation of a special role for Quebec that the two-nations theory entails. The advocates of each of these three ideological perspectives would find comfort in various provisions of the existing constitution and the ways in which they have been interpreted by judicial review. On many issues, however, the constitution remains ambiguous or silent (Simeon and Robinson, 1990: ch. 3; Whyte, 1987; Gibbins, 1999).

The very act of compromise—a common feature in the founding and sustaining of all federations—reflects another value in federal ideology (Riker, 1964). Federal bargains among competing interests, and the striving for an equitable balance in the institutional design and operation of a federation, are expressions of this spirit. The emphasis on balance between linguistic interests, between federal and provincial powers, and between richer and poorer regions has been present from the beginning. It is seen in the rhetoric of George-Étienne Cartier's "new political nationality," in the legal theory of the Judicial Committee of the Privy Council (and later the Supreme Court of Canada), and in the work of more contemporary federal theorists and scholars.[1] One can recognize and witness the existing federal bargain in practice, even if many would reflect that it is not suffi-ciently balanced towards the national aspirations of Quebec, or of the Indigenous peoples.

Nonetheless, in general political discourse in Canada, federalism is often restrained rather than bold, and implied rather than explicit. Of course, in the original political debates and election campaigns over union in the 1860s, pol-itical factions identified themselves as either for union or against it, and later, when Newfoundland was considering union with Canada in 1947–8, Joseph Smallwood's "confederates" successfully combined a social brand of liberalism with federal values. In recent years, however, it is mainly in Quebec and in the context of significant support for a post-federal future for Quebec (variously known as sovereignty, sovereignty-association, confederalism, or separation) that "federalists"—defined as those who support a continued federal union with Canada—become a major defining force in politics. Few people in Alberta, Ontario, or Nova Scotia would feel any need to call themselves federalists. In that sense, almost all Canadians outside Quebec would be federalist, but they would give their federal ideology meaning through greater or lesser support for regional or provincial autonomy, for regional equity, for federal balance between the federal and provincial governments, and for pan-Canadian values, among other concepts.

Federal ideology in Canada gets blended with and subordinated to other ideological movements affecting broad or narrow segments of the society. These include conservatism, liberalism, socialism, and variants of nationalism. Social democrats and social liberals tend to promote a view of federalism that empha-sizes pan-Canadian standards and social entitlements, as well as strong support of individual and collective rights, particularly as expressed in broad interpretations of the 1982 Charter of Rights and Freedoms. At the same time they recognize the value of federalism in providing multiple sites for progressive politics; a common example is the pioneering of medicare in Saskatchewan in the 1960s. Economic liberals and conservatives would tend to support a more decentralized vision of fed-eralism and its operation, emphasizing the "classical" interpretation based on the division of powers and provincial autonomy over social programs, with somewhat less emphasis on regional sharing. As liberals they would also support the Charter, but not perhaps in its broadest interpretations. Neo-conservatives and others have been inspired as well by economic theorists of the public choice school who stress the importance of federalism for preserving liberty and enhancing democratic par-ticipation. Their emphasis is on competitive federalism: reduced overlap among jurisdictions, less collusive cooperation (that is, fewer deals behind closed doors among governments), and more diverse policy outcomes. Finally, nationalists, too, find federal ideology useful, as long as it serves national goals. In Quebec even fed-eralist parties must put Québécois nationalist perspectives first. Indigenous nation-alists will similarly embrace federalism where it suits their interests—for instance, in the concept of treaty federalism. Canadian nationalists are more conflicted. Few would want a non-federal future for Canada, and all are realistic enough to recognize that Canada is not governable in the absence of federalism. There is a simple, patriotic support for the federal union, but often without a deep understanding of what the actual operation of the federation means for national goals (for example, according to a *Globe and Mail* poll, few Canadians know that the provinces own their natural resources, let alone support the idea) (Walton, 2008).

One more characteristic of Canada's political culture is important to underscore. This is the changing nature of democratic norms and political beliefs in citizens' rights and capacity to judge for themselves about political matters. In recent decades we have witnessed a significant decline in deference to authority among Canadians, a trend that is consistent with decreasing trust in government and a general decline in citizens' sense of their ability to change government policies (Nevitte, 1996, 2002). This has had major consequences for the practice of elite accommodation that has made possible so many of both the initial and the sustaining compromises in the history of the federation. Most analysts would cite this change in the political culture as a major factor in the failure of the Meech Lake and Charlottetown accords, placing significant limits on what political leaders can achieve without mass support. These limits, though not unique to Canada, certainly present a challenge to the politics of federal integration in a diverse and divided society. They make it especially important that federal ideology be articulated in such a way that ordinary citizens can understand and act on it.

The Federal Regime

The actual *federal regime* is the third element in our summary sketch of Canadian federalism. Students of Canadian politics have had drilled into them the three main features of the overall Canadian regime: Parliament, federalism, and the Charter. In terms of the daily operation of our federation, the combination of a federal constitution with Westminster parliamentary traditions is by far the most prominent institutional feature, not only in the actual rules but also in the conventional norms that drive the regime. Canada was the first parliamentary federation in history, and one characteristic it shares with all the others that followed (Australia, Germany, India, and Malaysia, among others) is the dominance of the executive in intergovernmental relationships—a dominance exemplified by "executive federalism," which has been discussed at some length in this book. Arising from the fusion of the executive and legislative branches in the form of government cabinets drawn from and responsible to the legislature, executive dominance remains a fact of life for government in Canada at both the federal and the provincial levels. Executive federalism is a by-product of that fact.

A second major regime feature is the distribution of powers. Canada is unique in that its constitution—in the Constitution Act, 1867—sets out two long lists of exclusive federal and provincial legislative powers. Most federations rely much more on concurrent or shared powers. Over time, depending on the public mood and policy necessity, Canadian governments have cooperated extensively in ways that suggest a more concurrent spirit (for example, in the creation of national social programs, in the negotiation and implementation of free trade agreements, and in joint environmental review processes). But the presence in our federal society of strong social forces working against integration—Quebec nationalism, various movements for greater regional autonomy—acts as a natural brake on cooperation and collaboration to a degree unknown in federations such as Germany, Australia, or even the United States. These social forces have been supported by the courts' interpretation of the division of powers, especially in the first 75 years after Confederation. Time and again the courts, and especially the Judicial Committee of Privy Council in London, emphasized the "water-tight compartments" of legislative jurisdiction, or at the least the need to retain federal–provincial balance in awarding jurisdiction in case of disputes. The result has been a federal system that continues to put a much greater emphasis on the autonomy of constituent units than do most other federations, where concurrent or federal framework legislation serves as a significant constraint on the actions of states or provinces.

Third, the relatively decentralized nature of fiscal federalism in Canada—for instance, the provinces' ownership of their natural resources, and the fact that federal–provincial transfers are largely unconditional—reinforces the legal capacity of the provinces to act on their own, often in competition with one an-other. Although the enormous differences in fiscal capacity between the smaller provinces and a powerhouse such as Alberta or Ontario mean that horizontal im-balance is significant, the vertical fiscal gap between the federal government and the provinces as a whole is nonetheless the smallest among the federations. The Equalization Program not only illustrates the federation's explicit commitment to horizontal equity but also sustains provincial autonomy.

Finally, our electoral and party institutions also play a role in maintaining the federal system. The single-member plurality electoral system has a tendency to produce majority governments,[2] especially at the provincial level, reinforcing the separate political bases of the federal and provincial party systems. Moreover, the party system in Canada is only weakly integrated (Bakvis and Tanguay, 2012). A Conservative premier such as Danny Williams in Newfoundland and Labrador did not need the help of the federal Conservative Party to get elected. And a federal Conservative government cannot always rely on the support of provincial conservative parties either, as the 2008 federal election showed.[3] Each first minis-ter must rely on his or her own electorate. These features reinforce the Canadian tendency towards competitive federalism.

The mantra of provincial autonomy is especially strong in Quebec, which alone resisted the development of the federal welfare state back in the 1950s. The ideology of provincial autonomy is of course rooted in the fact that only Quebec has a French-speaking majority, with a mission to promote and protect its unique society in the North American context. But there also is a strong minority instinct that leads Quebecers to fear that their preferences will be overshadowed by those of "English Canada"—although the latter has never been as monolithic as many Quebecers assume. Together, Quebec's insistence on autonomy and its fear of persecution as a minority in the Canadian whole have had profound consequences for the federal regime. Not only does Quebec review especially carefully any cooperation proposal coming from Ottawa and the other provinces, and often that province seeks some form of asymmetry in policy or administration, but also it resists any changes to the rules of the federation that might put it in a position to be outnumbered or to lose the autonomy achieved in the original Confederation settlement. The effect of Quebec's continuing ideological position is to reinforce the general tendency to competitive and decentralized outcomes. There is no clearer example of this regime feature than the case of the Council of the Federation. As we saw in Chapter 5, the Quebec Liberal government of Jean Charest strongly promoted the creation of this new body (achieved in 2003) as a way of increasing the provinces' capacity to reach agreement among themselves. Yet the operating rules of the Council as agreed to in 2003 only reinforced the essential autonomy of each member, and did nothing to facilitate substantive outcomes. None of the provinces at the table in 2003 objected.

The consequences of Quebec's attachment to autonomy for Canada's ability to deal with future challenges are taken up later in this conclusion. First, however, it is worth noting that the current disinclination of the federal partners, and Canadians more generally, to commit to a more cooperative federation, one less wedded to the autonomy of federal and provincial governments, is unlikely to change any time soon. Peter Russell, in *Constitutional Odyssey* (2004), probably puts it best. He observes that even in the heyday of efforts at formal constitutional change, from the 1960s to 1992, Canadians failed to express popular support for a new constitutional regime in either a national referendum or a federal election. As significant as the achievements in the 1982 Constitution Act are, Russell contends that since 1867 constitutional change in Canada has generally been much more organic than revolutionary. Moreover, Russell suggests that the window of opportunity for significant formal constitutional change effectively closed with the failure of the referendum on the Charlottetown Accord. In his view, Canadians became tired of repeated attempts to amend the constitution and are wary of the instability engendered by constitutional politics.

If Russell's assessment is correct, one would have to be pessimistic about our future ability to provide for meaningful provincial or regional representation in the Senate, for instance, or to permit constitutional recognition of local government, or to achieve reconciliation with the Indigenous peoples in a constitutional form, or to improve the capacity for intergovernmental decision-making, or, for that matter, to give more formal recognition to Quebec's national identity. On the other hand, the relatively successful record of organic adaptation through the institutions of executive federalism, judicial review, and fiscal federalism provide grounds for a more optimistic assessment. These processes have contributed significantly to the staying power of the federal regime and remain full of potential.

Continuity and Change: Intergovernmental Outcomes since 1970

We now move from the pathways of federalism to the traffic that has flowed along them. Here we deal with the specific policy outcomes and operations of intergovernmental relations, variables that are dependent on the society, ideology, and institutions of federalism. In several chapters of this book we have examined the interactions and relationships between governments and society. We focused on what can be considered its primary features: the institutional and constitutional frameworks that make up the intergovernmental system; the political leaders and government officials who work the system and animate it; the main economic, social, and political issues that provide grist for the intergovernmental mill; and the major challenges facing the system now and in the future.

What have we learned? At a macro level it appears that the system has changed little since the early 1970s. This was the time when Richard Simeon, in his landmark *Federal–Provincial Diplomacy*, first highlighted the federal–provincial arena as the main crucible for Canadian policy-making. Arguing that federal–provincial diplomacy constituted the modus operandi of Canadian federalism, at least with respect to major policy issues, Simeon drew attention to the people representing the federal and provincial governments, the relations and relationships between them, and the arenas in which they operated. Forty-five years later, the basic institutional framework, the actors, and the strategies that these actors have used in pursuing their interests have remained largely the same. The first ministers' conference remains, in potential, at the pinnacle of the intergovernmental system, even if it is used much less today than it once was. Certainly the first ministers themselves are still Canada's primary political actors, using the many levers available to them to ensure that they control their governments' agendas. Ministers and ministerial councils also remain important, as do the officials of both orders of government as they race from one meeting or teleconference to another, laying the groundwork for another meeting of elected officials, patching up tattered relations after a failed meeting, or, better yet, working out the details of implementation or preparing for a new intergovernmental agreement. As was the case in the 1960s and early 1970s—essentially the era described by Simeon—non-governmental actors continue to try and gain entry to intergovernmental sessions, with varying degrees of success.

To a lesser extent the same can be said of the public policy issues driving the system. In the 1960s and early 1970s fiscal federalism and social policy were among the main items on the intergovernmental agenda, along with the constitution. The last issue is currently much less prominent. Since the failure of Charlottetown, five prime ministers have declined to reopen the constitutional file, though elements of the constitutional debate still surface occasionally—at the time of the debate around the Clarity Act, for instance, or in proposals to reform or abolish the Senate. But the other two issue domains—social policy, centred on health care, and fiscal federalism—continue to dominate intergovernmental discussion.

Key developments challenging the federation in the past 50 years include: two referenda over Quebec sovereignty, the second of which in 1995 failed by only the slimmest of margins; two bitter battles over energy policy in the 1970s and early 1980s between Ottawa and the West (more specifically Alberta); constitutional patriation and the adoption of a Charter of Rights and Freedoms; and two major efforts at constitutional amendment aimed primarily at securing Quebec's position but also secondarily the position of Aboriginal peoples in the constitution, including a nationwide referendum that went down to defeat. The same period saw a dramatic transformation of the party system, with the Progressive Conservatives dropping from a governing majority party to just two seats, the rise of the Bloc Québécois in Quebec and Reform in the West, and the Liberals governing with a majority that was anchored almost exclusively in Ontario. This highly regionalized party system, coupled with the Quebec referendum in 1995, suggested that the Canadian federation in the 1990s was on the cusp of the perfect storm; only a "no" vote in the Quebec referendum prevented the federation from sliding into what could well have been the final end-game.

Another major set of developments centred on a retrenching role of the state, with large impacts on the federal system. The federal government's Program Review in the mid-1990s and the election of a distinctly right-of-centre government in Ontario, followed by provincially initiated discussions on the state of the Canadian social union, appeared to herald a dramatic transformation of the social safety net that had been brokered and put in place in the 1960s (Banting, 2012). Ottawa, in creating the Canada Health and Social Transfer, at the same time cut overall transfers to the provinces. In return, the provinces were tacitly given more leeway in areas such as social assistance (previously funded under the Canada Assistance Plan) and the environment, but not in health care, where Ottawa retained a keen interest in maintaining its self-proclaimed role as the guardian of medicare. The Social Union Framework Agreement of 1999 promised a new era of collaborative federalism, progress in areas such as mobility rights, transparency, and limits on the federal spending power, despite the fact that Quebec was not a signatory to the agreement. Twenty years later, SUFA is but a historical memory with no practical effect, but the federal role in social program transfers remains significant.

The Free Trade Agreement with the US of 1989, followed by the North American Free Trade Agreement of 1994, appeared to both proponents and critics to signal a new era of north–south trade flows (Courchene and Telmer, 1998; Hale, 2004). At the same time, this more institutionalized trade regime suggested the erosion of Ottawa's sovereignty, the rise of new political and economic linkages in the form of alliances between cities, provinces, and states in various combinations, and new forms of multi-level governance. Yet, while municipalities have become more active and cohesive, and Ottawa has been paying more attention to cities and local communities, the primary focus remains on the federal–provincial relationship. Battles between the federal and provincial governments still dominate the intergovernmental agenda. Canadian municipalities, in part working though the Federation of Canadian Municipalities, were successful in raising the profile of municipalities and drawing attention to their enormous infrastructure needs. However, both Ottawa and the provinces have been very careful in managing the fledging federal–local relationship. Indeed, the Harper government, under the rubric of "open federalism," signalled that it preferred working through the provinces and respecting provincial jurisdiction.

The 1990s also saw what has been perhaps the single most important challenge to executive federalism so far. Throughout the 1970s and 1980s, executive federalism had been under attack by citizen groups and academics, foremost among them Donald Smiley (1979). This may reflect the general decline in deference to political authority mentioned earlier. In brief, even though the Charlottetown Accord went down to defeat in 1992, the process used to craft it arguably marked a definitive change in the broad political culture. That process involved extensive public consultations, inclusion of Indigenous leaders directly in high-level negotiations, and, of course, the use of a referendum. "The End of Executive Federalism?" (Brock, 1995) is the title of an often cited article suggesting that the executives of the federal, provincial, and territorial governments could not go back to their old pattern of negotiating behind closed doors and excluding legitimate actors such as First Nations. Yet this is exactly what happened with the AIT and SUFA negotiations in the 1990s. Indigenous leaders were excluded, and the many public interest groups that had played an active role in Charlottetown were kept at a safe distance. The spirit of Charlottetown appeared to revive briefly in 2005, when Indigenous organizations, the provinces, and the federal government reached agreement on the Kelowna Accord. But that agreement was quickly rejected by the incoming Harper government. To be sure, the frequency of first ministers' meetings has been reduced, particularly under Prime Ministers Chrétien and Harper (less so under Martin and Justin Trudeau), and a full-fledged first ministers' conference has become a rare event. However, ministerial councils and meetings of senior and middle-ranking officials are as frequent as ever, likely even more so. Indeed, new technologies have promoted increasingly easy communication by e-mail and teleconferencing among the officials laying the groundwork for sessions between elected officials.

This summary of the traffic in the pathways of federalism shows that, despite considerable societal and economic changes over the past half-century, both the basic nineteenth-century constitutional framework and the mechanics and practices of twentieth-century executive federalism remain intact. Despite all the tumult and drama, the Canadian federal system appears to be remarkably stable. How well equipped is it to deal with twenty-first century challenges?

Challenges Ahead

What are the challenges likely to be in the coming years and decades? Many would cite the future of globalization and, in particular, north–south trade with the United States. The lack of a single securities regulator, the continuing presence of interprovincial barriers to trade, the absence of a coherent labour market strategy, and our lagging productivity growth rate all appear to suggest that Canada could be performing much better. Yet for more than a decade Canada has been near the top of OECD and G8 countries with respect to unemployment, deficit reduction, and overall economic performance. Canada, especially under the FTA and NAFTA, developed what some have seen as an unhealthy dependence on US markets. In the wake of US demands for reform and towards protectionism, thus far manifest in the USMCA, Canadian policy will likely seek to diversify our international trade markets. The prospect of reduced access to US markets and turmoil in international trade regimes certainly brings its own set of challenges.

Thus the international economic environment will continue to be challenging, but there is no evidence that federalism will be an impediment to the management of the Canadian economy or that Canada's performance will decline in relation to that of other countries. On the contrary, Chapter 8 outlined how the federation managed to achieve a reasonable degree of intergovernmental consensus on major changes in Canada's international trade regime without upsetting the federal balance. Similarly, there is no evidence that regional blocs of provinces or cities, with or without allies south of the border, are problematic (Canada, 2006). The cap-and-trade agreement on carbon emissions announced by several Canadian provinces and US states in 2008 and similar arrangements updated in 2016–17 suggest that cross-border alliances can serve to encourage innovation and action, even if they do not always provide an adequate substitute for strong national (central) government action.

Responding to the needs and demands of Indigenous peoples will be another continuing challenge. We have seen clear progress on these issues, both in Indigenous societies and institutions and in their relations with the Canadian state, including the intergovernmental system. However, problems will continue to grow with the Indigenous population, adding greater urgency to deal with such matters as health, economic development and employment, housing, and criminal justice, among other issues. The greater visibility of the problems is already leading governments to address these and other issues in more substantial ways, including through comprehensive institutional reform. For example, in 2018 the federal government moved forward with its new Department of Indigenous Services and set out the parameters for 10-year largely unconditional funding for some First Nation governments.

Yet it is difficult to foresee a resolution of Indigenous constitutional concerns, especially if Quebec's ambivalent position in the federation is not addressed. Quebecers' support for major regime change in the form of secession (or sovereignty) has reached new lows in recent years and its major proponent, the Parti Québécois, does not favour another referendum, at least for now. But support for some sort of change in the relationship between Quebec and Canada remains strong. Only a small minority of Quebecers support the status quo. At the same time, however, to address Quebec's constitutional issues without also addressing those of Indigenous peoples would seem to take us back to Meech Lake, while addressing both sets of issues simultaneously would take us back to Charlottetown. No one wants to return to either the Meech Lake or Charlottetown processes anytime soon. How, and under what political circumstances, one could foresee a return to comprehensive constitutional negotiations remains as unclear now as it was in 1992—underscoring Peter Russell's observation that since 1992 the federation has essentially reverted to its more standard pattern of organic, incremental evolution.

Over the past decade the Supreme Court has delivered some key rulings that served to protect in various ways the interests of both Indigenous people and Quebec. In the case of Quebec, for example, as discussed in Chapter 12, there were three decisions during the time of the Harper's majority government (2011–15) where Quebec interests were protected, with one of them bearing directly on the status of appointees to the three positions on the Supreme Court allocated to Quebec. Also during the last few years of the Harper government, Supreme Court judgements continued to refine the legal definition of Indigenous rights, such as in the *Tsilhqot'in Nation v British Columbia* case, which provided further obligation about the duty to consult Indigenous peoples on developments in their traditional lands. Thus the Supreme Court has played a critical role in preserving the federal balance. However, in recent years, as noted in Chapter 4, the balance has been tilting in the direction of the provinces—and in affirming the importance of clear rules, as with its ruling on the secession case (*Reference Re Secession of Quebec*, 1998), the Court cannot be expected to resolve the more fundamental issues in changing the Canadian constitution.

The ambivalent and paradoxical position of Quebec brings us to the final item on our list of the fundamental challenges facing the Canadian federation. This is the absence of effective mechanisms, institutions, and decision rules governing the resolution of even relatively mundane matters. The years since the failure of Charlottetown have seen the creation of the Agreement on Internal Trade and the Council of the Federation, both designed to deal with major issues affecting relations between governments: internal trade in the case of the AIT and national as well as interprovincial issues in the case of the COF. Both of these structures stopped short of adopting meaningful rules for achieving co-decision on substantive issues, and the AIT's dispute resolution mechanism (essentially retained in the new Canadian Free Trade Agreement) has been criticized as weak-hearted (Brown, 2006). Papillon and Simeon (2004) have suggested that one of the main reasons the first ministers' conference constitutes the "weakest link" in the intergovernmental system is its lack of meaningful decision rules.

The working rules of our intergovernmental system reflect the strong political culture of competition and arm's-length autonomy among governments. With few exceptions—notably the constitutional amending formula (section 38, Constitution Act, 1982) and the rules governing changes to the Canada Pension Plan—agreement in Canadian intergovernmental relations is achieved by consensus alone. Typically, decisions that will produce substantial and binding outcomes require unanimity. Thus, even the smallest participant has veto power. Otherwise, reaching a consensus means accepting the kind of watered-down general principles and anodyne language typical of international diplomacy. Three reforms already adopted in other federations or quasi-federations might be helpful in Canada. First, intergovernmental bodies could increase their decision-making capacity by adopting a "qualified majority" rule.[4] Second, intergovernmental councils could increase the institutional support available to them by establishing more bodies (secretariats, for instance) capable of undertaking independent research. Third, greater frequency and regularity in scheduling, and clearer provisions for agenda-setting, would not only permit all governments involved to agree in advance on what is to be discussed at what would become annual or semi-annual conferences, but would allow for more thorough preparation. All these features are found in the Council of Ministers of the European Union and in the intergovernmental system in Australia (Brown, 2002; Scharpf, 1999; Painter, 1998).

The problems associated with having consensus as the default decision rule in Canada are compounded by the presence of the electoral cycle at both the federal and the provincial levels. As illustrated in Chapter 10 on the environmental union, for example, the accord carefully worked out by the Justin Trudeau government on carbon pricing quickly ran into difficulty by changes in government at the provincial level. And one need only reflect back on the failure of the Meech Lake Accord. There, during the three-year ratification period, provincial elections resulted in three governments changing hands with two of those, Manitoba and Newfoundland, ultimately rejecting the accord.

On the other hand, ambiguity remains an important element in governing the Canadian federation. In the past, the cloaking of intergovernmental agreements in ambiguity has allowed the various actors to read into such agreements their particular objectives and understandings and to reach a consensus of sorts. In a diverse and binational federation such as Canada, "institutionalized ambivalence" (Tuohy, 1992) can go a long way towards preserving harmony and stability. To repeat Harvey Lazar's observation, ambiguity "was the mid-wife of Canada's birth [and] remains central to the Canadian politics of today" (Lazar, 2004: 4). Many of the intergovernmental success stories noted above involved the judicious application of ambiguity. Similarly, Gagnon and Erk (2002: 324) note that "when important differences between the constituent nations of a federal partnership exist, ambiguity can be a potential source of longevity for the federal arrangements." But they also stress that ambiguity must be supported by an underlying trust among the federal partners.

The benefits of ambiguity notwithstanding, greater precision and transparency in some of the ground rules governing the operation of the federation may still be beneficial in an era where citizens are more sophisticated and less deferential. Ground rules might also help to forestall increasing centralization of the system, if only because in the face of stalemate the federal government is often the only government that can fill the resulting power vacuum. The Clarity Act of 2000 showed how helpful it can be to establish some basic rules and understandings. In recognizing the legitimacy of a province's attempt to secede from the federation—following the expression of the people's consent through a referendum on a clear question—and by specifying the mutual obligations of both parties, the Clarity Act largely succeeded in lowering the temperature of the sovereignty debate. It has also allowed the debate to shift focus to the question of clearer recognition of Quebec's position within the Canadian federation.

The most powerful actors in the federal system—the federal government and the largest provinces—have the most to gain from continued ambiguity and loose working rules in intergovernmental relations, since these give them the flexibility they need to either take a strong public stance or fudge the issues, as it suits them. According to the theory of competitive federalism, power in a federal system is best kept divided and at arm's length, and governments should not be encouraged to rely too much on cooperation. Certainly, formal requirements for joint decision-making can lead to political gridlock, as has been the case in the past in Germany and the European Union (Scharpf, 1988, 2006). Yet in light of our own regionalized political culture and strong provincial autonomy, we would argue that Canada may suffer from too much competition rather than too little. There are cases where jurisdiction cannot easily be divided, and governments must cooperate. In fact, some of the most difficult challenges facing our system in the future are likely to come in situations where multi-level governance is unavoidable. In such cases—when public health services must be coordinated to deal with an epidemic, for instance, or the need for ever more ambitious measures to reduce our carbon footprint, or a strategy for negotiating new trade relations with the US—failure to achieve timely and substantive multi-level governance will be costly.

If political consensus across the country is sufficiently strong, intergovernmental agreement usually follows, as happened with respect to health-care funding between 1998 and 2004. But the weak record of agreement on climate change and greenhouse gas emissions from 1992 to 2015 underscores the consequences of a lack of consensus. In such cases, ambivalence leads in the short run to mutual veto and in the longer run to a vacuum that can be filled only by the federal government, which could well argue that the courts should award it permanent jurisdiction in that area. More effective rules for genuine federal–provincial and interprovincial co-decision could limit institutional ambiguity and the freedom of movement of each government, while forestalling central dominance of the system. Changing the rules to allow more effective joint decision-making would be difficult, but the changes could be incremental and need not involve constitutional amendment. Reaching basic agreement on such rules is likely the most critical challenge facing the Canadian federation over the coming decades.

Meeting that challenge will not be easy, but there is a lot to be optimistic about. As hard as it may be to make the federal system work, and however strongly its underlying values and premises may be contested, it is nonetheless the political system that makes Canadian unity possible. It is the platform from which millions of Canadians get on with their productive lives, building one of the world's largest and most dynamic economies and achieving a level of societal well-being that ranks regularly in the top 10 of the United Nations Human Development Index. Most Canadians take for granted or ignore the complexities of federalism and the continuing negotiations that are necessary to maintain our union. Their support for federalism, where it exists at all, is often shot through with ambivalence. But few would deny the ultimate success of Canada as a whole. In our view, this success is due in no small measure to our federal arrangement.

Questions for Critical Thought

1. What policy challenges in the future might draw out a federal system response of much greater centralization (or, alternatively, decentralization)?

2. Does it matter that there appears to be more support for Canada as a country than for Canada as a federation?

Notes

1. See, for example, Trudeau (1968); Lederman (1975); and LaSelva (1996).
2. The tendency is not ironclad. In the 2000s three federal elections produced minority governments (2004, 2006, and 2008), and in recent years at least five Canadian provinces have elected minorities as well, but majority government is still the rule.
3. During the 2008 election Williams ran what he called an "ABC" ("Anyone But Conservative") campaign, urging voters throughout the Atlantic provinces to reject Conservative candidates. No Conservatives were elected in Newfoundland and Labrador. See *Globe and Mail* (2008).
4. The term "qualified majority" refers to a decision rule in which consent requires a majority that is qualified, such as by granting a veto to some but not all parties, or by requiring a level of consent higher than 50 per cent, for example, a two-thirds vote in favour. The qualified majority procedure can be used in intergovernmental relations to avoid the need for unanimous consent. Its use by European countries enabled rapid progress in the late 1980s to create the European Union. See Leslie (1996); Brown (2003).

References

Bakvis, H., and B. Tanguay. 2012. "Federalism, Political Parties and the Burden of National Unity: Still Making Federalism Do the Heavy Lifting?" In *Canadian Federalism: Performance, Effectiveness, and Legitimacy*, 3rd edn, edited by H. Bakvis and G. Skogstad. Toronto: Oxford University Press.

Banting, K. 2012. "The Three Federalisms: Social Policy and Intergovernmental Decision-Making." In *Canadian Federalism: Performance, Effectiveness, and Legitimacy*, 3rd edn, edited by H. Bakvis and G. Skogstad. Toronto: Oxford University Press.

Brock, K. 1995. "The End of Executive Federalism?" In *New Trends in Canadian Federalism*, edited by F. Rocher and M. Smith. Peterborough, ON: Broadview Press.

Brown, D. 2002. *Market Rules: Economic Union Reform and Intergovernmental Policy-Making in Australia and Canada*. Montreal and Kingston: McGill-Queen's University Press.

———. 2003. "Getting Things Done in the Federation: Do We Need New Rules for an Old Game?" *Constructive and Co-operative Federalism? A Series of Commentaries on the Council of the Federation*. Kingston and Montreal: IIGR and IRPP.

———. 2006. "Still in the Game: Efforts to Tame Economic Development Competition in Canada." In *Racing to the Bottom? Provincial Interdependence in the Canadian Federation*, edited by K. Harrison. Vancouver: University of British Columbia Press.

Burgess, M. 2011. "Success and Failure in Federation: Comparative Perspectives." In *The Federal Idea: Essays in Honour of Ronald L. Watts*, edited by T.J. Courchene, J.R. Allan, C. Leuprecht, and N. Verrelli, 189–206. Montreal and Kingston: McGill-Queen's University Press.

Cairns, A. 1986. "The Embedded State: State–Society Relations in Canada." In *State and Society: Canada in Comparative Perspective*, edited by K. Banting. Toronto: University of Toronto Press.

Canada. 2006. *The Emergence of Cross-Border Regions between Canada and the United States, Roundtable Synthesis Report*. Ottawa: Policy Research Initiative.

Courchene, T.J., and C. Telmer. 1998. *From Heartland to North American Region State: The Social, Fiscal and Federal Evolution of Ontario*. Toronto: Centre for Public Management, University of Toronto.

Gagnon, A.-G., and J. Erk. 2002. "Legitimacy, Effectiveness, and Federalism: On the

Benefits of Ambiguity." In *Canadian Federalism: Performance, Effectiveness, and Legitimacy*, edited by H. Bakvis and G. Skogstad. Toronto: Oxford University Press.

Gibbins, R. 1999. "Taking Stock: Canadian Federalism and Its Constitutional Framework." In *How Ottawa Spends, 1999–2000*, edited by L. Pal. Toronto: Oxford University Press.

Globe and Mail. 2008. "PM Dismissive of Nfld., Premier Says." 15 Jan., A4.

Hale, G.H. 2004. "Canadian Federalism and the Challenge of North American Integration." *Canadian Public Administration* 47, no. 4: 497–524.

LaSelva, S.V. 1996. *The Moral Foundations of Canadian Federalism: Paradoxes, Achievements and Tragedies of Nationhood*. Montreal and Kingston: McGill-Queen's University Press.

Lazar, H. 2004. *Canadian Social Union: Reality and Myth*. Kingston, ON: Institute of Intergovernmental Relations, Queen's University.

Lederman, W.R. 1975. "Unity and Diversity in Canadian Federalism: Ideas and Methods of Moderation." *Canadian Bar Review* 53: 597–620.

Leslie, P.M. 1996. *The Maastricht Model: A Canadian Perspective on the European Union*. Kingston, ON: Institute of Intergovernmental Relations, Queen's University.

Livingston, W.S. 1952. "A Note on the Nature of Federalism." *Political Science Quarterly* 67, no. 1: 81–95.

Nevitte, N. 1996. *The Decline of Deference: Canadian Value Change in Cross-National Perspective*. Peterborough, ON: Broadview Press.

———, ed. 2002. *Value Change and Governance in Canada*. Toronto: University of Toronto Press.

Painter, M. 1998. *Collaborative Federalism: Economic Reform in Australia in the 1990s*. Cambridge: Cambridge University Press.

Papillon, M., and R. Simeon. 2004. "The Weakest Link? First Ministers' Conferences in Canadian Intergovernmental Relations." In *Canada: The State of the Federation, 2002: Reconsidering the Institutions of Canadian Federalism*, edited by J.P. Meekison, H. Telford, and H. Lazar.

Kingston, ON: Institute of Intergovernmental Relations, Queen's University.

Riker, W.H. 1964. *Federalism: Origin, Operation, Significance*. Boston: Little, Brown.

Russell, P. 2004. *Constitutional Odyssey: Can Canadians Become a Sovereign People?* 3rd edn. Toronto: University of Toronto Press.

Scharpf, F.W. 1988. "The Joint-Decision-Making Trap: Lessons from German Federalism." *Public Administration* 66: 239–78.

———. 1999. *Governing in Europe: Effective and Democratic?* Oxford: Oxford University Press.

———. 2006. "The Joint-Decision Trap Revisited." *Journal of Common Market Studies* 44, no. 4: 845–64.

Simeon, R. 2006 [1972]. *Federal–Provincial Diplomacy: The Making of Recent Policy in Canada*. Toronto: University of Toronto Press.

———and I. Robinson. 1990. *State, Society, and the Development of Canadian Federalism*. Toronto: University of Toronto Press.

Smiley, D.V. 1979. "An Outsider's Observations of Federal–Provincial Relations among Consenting Adults." In *Confrontation and Collaboration: Intergovernmental Relations in Canada Today*, edited by R. Simeon. Toronto: Institute of Public Administration of Canada.

Smith, J. 2004. *Federalism: Canadian Democratic Audit*. Vancouver: University of British Columbia Press.

Supreme Court of Canada. 1998. *Reference Re: The Secession of Quebec*, 161 D.L.R. (4th) 385 (1998).

———. 2014. *Tsilhqot'in Nation v. British Columbia*, [2014] 2 S.C.R.244.

Trudeau, P. 1968. *Federalism and the French Canadians*. Toronto: Macmillan of Canada.

Tuohy, C. 1992. *Policy and Politics in Canada: Institutionalized Ambivalence*. Philadelphia: Temple University Press.

Walton, D. 2008. "Albertans Reticent in Sharing Revenues, Poll." *Globe and Mail*, 26 Jan.

Whyte, J. 1987. "Federal Powers over the Economy: Finding New Jurisdictional Room." *Canadian Business Law Journal* 13: 257–302.

Index

among, 77–8, 83; justice system and, 11–12; Kyoto Accord and, 209–11; labour market training and, 262; Liberal health transfers and, 134; local government and, 5, 217–19, 222–5, 230; macroeconomic policy and, 179; microeconomic policy and, 181; *Pan-Canadian Framework* and, 212; powers of, 50, 52–3, 54, 56–7; recession in, 139–40; regional economies and, 182; revenue raising and, 59–60, 121–3; rights of, 36, 90; social program delivery and, 147–8; status of, 53; urban and rural development and, 192; US trade and, 187; *see also* Canadian West; specific provinces
provincial-compact theory, 19
"provincial inability test," 77
Provincial Sales Tax (PST), 191
public opinion: face coverings and, 260; health care and, 148; sovereignty and, 257–8
public–private partnerships, 225
public service: executive federalism and, 15; language and, 255, 256; reform of, 255
public works, 226

"qualified majority rule," 283
Quebec: autonomy in, 276–7; child care and, 156; constitution and, 16–19, 54–5, 57–8; Council of the Federation and, 94, 96; debt and, 139; environment and, 211; federal funding and, 37, 38; federalism and, 2, 251–70, 273, 282; federalists in, 274; financial sector in, 265; free trade and, 186; Harper and, 63, 256, 261–7; health care and, 163; influence of, 39–40; intergovernmental agency and, 102; joint social policy and, 133–4; local government in, 221, 226; as nation, 63; Ontario and, 106, 254; referenda in, 279; secession of, 61–3; Senate reform and, 266; separatism in, 253; social policy and, 39; social programs and, 147–8, 150; social union and, 151–2; status of, *xii*, 42–3; SUFA and, 92, 60; Supreme Court and, 251, 261, 264–7; transfers and, 162; *see also* asymmetrical federalism
Quebec Act, 49, 252
Quebec Charter of Rights, 260
Quebec City, 220
Quebec Liberal Party, 253, 254, 258, 260; Council of the Federation and, 95–6
Quebec Pension Plan (QPP), 16, 157–60; *see also* Canada/Quebec Pension Plan
"Quebec round," 58
Québec Solidaire, 268
"Quiet Revolution," 40, 252, 253–5; response to, 254

race: "to the bottom," 16, 200, 202; "to the top," 200, 202
racism: Indigenous peoples and, 237
Rae, Bob, 149

railways, 31–2, 35, 36, 174; local government and, 226
"rationalization": federal–provincial, 204; local government and, 220–1, 225
Reagan, Ronald, 178
recession, 180; impact of, 139; response to, 138–41
Reference Re: Anti-Inflation Act, 76
Reference Re: Canada Assistance Plan, 80
Reference Re: Firearms Act, 70, 77, 84
Reference Re: Hydro Quebec, 84
Reference Re: Secession of Quebec, 62, 69, 282
referendum: Charlottetown, 61–2; Quebec secession and, 61, 62, 257–8, 279; sovereignty, 58
refugees: local government and, 230
regional bodies, 106–8, 217
"regional equity," 175
regional identities, 272–3
regional interests, 12
regions, 62; CETA and, 188; economic, 175; inflation and, 180; monetary policy and, 178–9
regulations: environmental, 201, 204; free trade and, 188; sectoral environmental, 209; Supreme Court and, 69
religion: Quebec and, 252–3, 260
representation: Indigenous, 238; Quebec and, 263; of subunits, 3, 4–5
Re: Regulation and Control of Aeronautics in Canada, 73
Re: Regulation and Control of Radio Communication in Canada, 73
residential school system: compensation for, 246
resource revenues, 121; equalization program and, 136, 137, 138
responsible government, 48; Durham and, 49–50
revenue: balance with expenditure and, 119; Indigenous own-source, 238; local government and, 224–5; own-source, 224–5; provincial, 59–60, 121–3; recession and, 139; resource, 121, 136, 137, 138; sources of, 121–3
revenue dependency: provinces and, 29–30
rights: civil, 71, 72, 74–5; Indigenous, 79, 240–1; natural resources and, 56; property, 71, 72, 74–5; provincial, 36, 90
Riker, William, *xiv*, 22–3, 28
Robarts, John, 254
Roman Catholic Church, 252–3
Romanow Report, 163
Rowell-Sirois Royal Commission on Dominion–Provincial Relations, 36
royal assent, 52
Royal Canadian Mounted Police (RCMP), 220
Royal Commission on Aboriginal Peoples (RCAP), 242–4
Royal Commission on Bilingualism and Biculturalism, 255–6
Royal Commission on National Development in the Arts, Letters and Sciences (Massey Commission), 37, 253